TRACKING AMERICA'S ECONOMY

TRACKING AMERICA'S ECONOMY

FOURTH EDITION

NORMAN FRUMKIN

M.E.Sharpe
Armonk, New York
London, England

Copyright © 2004 by Norman Frumkin

All rights reserved. No part of this book may be reproduced in any form
without written permission from the publisher, M.E. Sharpe, Inc.,
80 Business Park Drive, Armonk, New York 10504.

Library of Congress Cataloging-in-Publication Data

Frumkin, Norman.
  Tracking America's economy / Norman Frumkin.—4th ed.
    p. cm.
  Includes bibliographical references and index.
  ISBN 0-7656-1240-2 (alk. paper) ; ISBN 0-7656-1241-0 (pbk.)
    1. Economic forecasting—United States. 2. Economic indicators—United States.
  3. United States—Economic policy—1981-1993. 4. United States—Economic policy—
  1993-2001. 5. United States—Economic policy—2001- I. Title.

  HC 106.8F78 2004
  338.5′44′0973—dc22   2003065847

Printed in the United States of America

The paper used in this publication meets the minimum requirements of
American National Standard for Information Sciences
Permanence of Paper for Printed Library Materials,
ANSI Z 39.48-1984.

⊗

| BM (c) | 10 | 9 | 8 | 7 | 6 | 5 | 4 | 3 | 2 | 1 |
| BM (p) | 10 | 9 | 8 | 7 | 6 | 5 | 4 | 3 | 2 | 1 |

To
Sarah, Jacob, Samuel, Susan, Isaac, and Ann

In memory of
Anne Frances Feldman Frumkin and Joseph Harry Frumkin

Contents

2 • Framework for Macroeconomic Analysis and Policies 45

3 • Economic Growth 76

8 · Employment, Worker Income, and Employer Costs

9 · Unemployment

10 • Productivity

11 • Inflation and Deflation

12 • Finance   299

Tables and Figures

TABLES

FIGURES

Preface

The question of how best to revive the weak American economy was in the forefront of the nation's domestic agenda as the manuscript for this book was completed in the summer of 2003. This is a complete turnaround from the sustained economic growth, new job creation and lower unemployment, improved income growth of workers, increased business profits and investment for equipment and structures, decline in the poverty population, and the growing general optimism about the future during most of the 1990s through 2000. In addition, the federal government budget deficits of a half century became growing budget surpluses beginning in the late 1990s. It is also noteworthy that inflation remained modest in this expansionary environment.

This is not to say that all workers and all businesses participated in the prosperity of the 1990s and 2000. Also, the income distribution of households became more unequal, with high-income households accounting for a larger share of total income. But while the prosperity did not reach all Americans, and there were growing income disparities, the thrust for the majority of the population was upward.

The changing economic climate evolved initially while the nation experienced a recession, a reduction in federal individual upper income tax rates, and the September 11 terrorist attacks—all occurring in that order in 2001. The recession of 2001 and the weak recovery in 2002 and 2003 are characterized by the contraction and demise of many "new economy" telecommunications companies that spread to other directly- and indirectly-related industries, substantial net job losses with new job creation not compensating for job losses, high unemployment, slower income growth for most workers and in some cases wage cuts, an increase in the poverty population, low business profits and investment for equipment and structures, volatile price movements in the stock market and the exposure of large stock market frauds, shrunken retirement funds invested in the stock market, growing federal government budget deficits in the years ahead, and shortfalls in state and local governments budgets. Overlaid on this are the domestic war on terrorism, the wars in Afghanistan and Iraq and their aftermath, and the impasse with North Korea on its development of nuclear weapons. The extent and depth of the recession were moderated by low interest rates, growth in household spending for consumer goods and services, high levels of housing sales and construction, rising values of existing housing, low inflation, and increased federal government outlays for defense.

I hope the book is helpful in assessing the various prescriptions for reviving the economy and keeping it on a sound footing in the mid- to late-2000s. Short spurts of seeming economic prosperity that revert to long-term weak economic growth and continued high unemployment are unsatisfactory.

The book aims to make complex ideas and the statistical data related to them accessible to persons without special training in economics. It also provides a framework for questioning the varying interpretations given by economists of the flow of often conflicting economic data coming out daily. In turn, interpretations of the data are the rationales given by economists, elected officials, journalists, political pundits, and talk show hosts for policies to reinvigorate the economy or whatever macroeconomic policies they favor. In short, the book focuses on giving a better understanding of the performance of the economy and for evaluating proposals intended to influence its future course.

Statistical measures of the economy are referred to as economic indicators, and various economic indicators are the underpinning of the book. Trends in the indicators are analyzed both for their movements over time and to explore the causes and consequences of the movements.

The book has two broad audiences: (a) college undergraduate and graduate students in macroeconomics, public policy, and business administration, and (b) economists, executives, union leaders, journalists, elected officials, investors, and the general public who are interested in the overall economy. As in each new edition of *Tracking America's Economy*, this fourth edition sharpens and expands the content of the previous one. It has these new features:

- Reclaiming American manufacturing
- Differential patterns of the expansions of the 1980s and the 1990s to 2000
- Wealth effect of stock market and housing prices
- Significance of consumer confidence surveys
- Age of nonresidential structures and equipment and future investment
- Housing affordability
- Government spending and tax components
- Frequency of tax changes
- Taxation and work effort
- Sustainability of balance of payments deficits and foreign indebtedness
- Jobless recoveries in 1991–92 and 2002–03
- Interstate variations in income and unionization

- Interstate variations in unemployment insurance
- Job openings and unemployment
- Terrorism impacts on economic growth and productivity
- Spread of oil price changes to the non-energy sectors
- Deflation and the economy
- Federal budget and debt shifts versus interest rates
- Interaction of fiscal and monetary policies
- Company buybacks and dividend yields
- Improving real time in the leading indicator system
- Noneconomic intangibles that affect the economy
- Delay in designating end of the 2001 recession

Two guiding principles continue to be followed in this edition. First, because it is important that the content and meaning of the economic indicators be understood, the text includes the data methodology used in preparing the indicators. Understanding the methodology helps one interpret the indicators. Second, every effort is made to write the book clearly.

Underlying the methodology is the assumption that the data are obtained using high statistical standards that are not subsequently compromised by actual or even a hint of political tampering to promote a political agenda. It is essential for a democracy that the credibility of the data is beyond reproach. This is discussed in chapter 1 in the section on Data Integrity.

Several analytic sections include graphic plots of the data. When these are done with an independent variable (X horizontal axis) and a dependent variable (Y vertical axis), they give an overall picture of the movements of one variable, such as the gross domestic product, in relation to the other variable, such as employment. Because they are intended only to give a visual notion of the relationship, no estimates of statistical reliability or of regression coefficients for use such as in forecasting are given or implied. The selection of which item is the independent variable that drives the response of the dependent variable is based on a judgment by the analyst of what makes economic sense. If the designation of independent and dependent variables is reversed, a similar but not identical visual depiction occurs. More generally, cause-and-effect relationships are difficult to establish categorically because there are a host of factors affecting the outcomes that are specified inadequately or not at all, as well as a complex set of interactions among all of the factors.

These quantitative analyses are based on the available economic data. But for several noneconomic topics that intuitively seem to affect the economy, it has not been feasible to assess their impact on the economy. This gap is discussed in chapter 14, "Noneconomic Intangibles."

Tracking America's Economy concentrates on the macro economy, although it is built up from the microeconomic "real world" transactions. The micro economy represents the myriad transactions occurring every moment among individual buyers and sellers, employers and employees, lenders and borrowers, private parties and governments, and U.S. individuals and businesses and those of other countries. Thus, the macro economy is in some sense an abstraction in that it summarizes the myriad micro transactions into aggregate statistical measures. Stated differently, the micro economy contains the building blocks of the macro economy. But notwithstanding this characteristic of the "real" micro preceding the "abstract" macro, there are feedback effects of the macro economy on the micro economy. For example, changes in interest rates stemming in part from the monetary actions of the Federal Reserve, and legislative changes by the U.S. Congress and the state and local legislatures as well as the spending actions of the president, governors, and mayors affect the sum total of all federal, state, and local governments' tax and spending programs, which in turn influence the economic environment in which the subsequent micro transactions of individual household, business, government, and international parties are made.

Chapter 1 discusses general attributes of economic indicators, an important but often neglected topic in economic analysis. Chapter 2 provides a framework for analyzing and forecasting the economy; it also places the individual topics in chapters 3 through 13 in an overall perspective. Chapter 3 covers the aggregate dimensions of economic growth. Chapters 4 through 7 cover the household, business, government, and international sectors of the economy. Chapters 8 through 10 cover the labor indicators of employment, unemployment, and productivity. Chapter 11 discusses inflation and deflation. Chapter 12 focuses on finance. Chapter 13 covers the leading indicator system. Chapter 14 addresses noneconomic intangibles that affect the economy.

The chapters include short statements in italics capsulizing the discussions of what the analyst should focus on in evaluating recent movements of the indicators. Review questions at the end of each chapter aid in solidifying an understanding of main topics in the chapter. Reference in one chapter to the same topic in other chapters indicates the extensive interrelationships in analyzing the economy.

The bulk of the data is produced by U.S. government agencies: Bureau of the Census and Bureau of Economic Analysis in the Department of Commerce, Bureau of Labor Statistics in the Department of Labor, Federal Reserve Board, Department of the Treasury, and the Office of Management and Budget. Selected data series are produced by private organizations such as The Conference Board and international organizations such as the United Nations. The specific data sources are noted in the chapters where they are used, including how to obtain the data on the Internet. Much of the data used in the book is compiled monthly in *Economic Indicators*, a secondary source publication prepared by the U.S. Council of Economic Advisers for the Joint Economic Committee of Congress. The appendix tables to the annual *Economic Report of the President*, also prepared by the Council of Economic Advisers, are the most convenient source for historical data.

I thank Lynn Taylor, executive editor for economics of M.E. Sharpe, for supporting this edition. And I thank Myron Sharpe for including my work in his publishing house since the late 1980s.

Edward Steinberg, on the economics faculties of New York University and Quinnipiac University, reviewed the entire manuscript. He insightfully and uniquely enhanced the content and clarity of the book, imprinting the book throughout. Gerald Donahoe, formerly associate director for national economic accounts with the Bureau of Economic Analysis in the U.S. Department of Commerce, sharpened the methodology section of the gross domestic product in the chapter on economic growth. Charles Anderson, Joel Darmstadter, Gerhard Fries, Jacob Frumkin, Samuel Frumkin, Sarah Frumkin, William Lang, Robert Parker, Howard Rosen, and Kenneth Stewart gave acute comments on selected sections. I had helpful discussions with Robert Arnold, Wallace Babbitt, Martin N. Baily, Jared Bernstein, Sue Betka, Mary Bowler, Gerald Bracey, Steven Braun, Angie Clinton, Shelly Dreiman, Stanley Duobinis, Kimberly Elliot, Arturo Estrella, David Findley, Anthony Freeman, Richard Freeman, Sheldon Friedman, William Gale, Daniel Ginsburg, Michael Glenn, Lisa Goldstein, Jon Hiatt, Chih-Chin Ho, Henry Holzer, Bruce Hunter, Randy Ilg, Patrick Jackman, Jeff Lee, Thea Lee, Jeffrey Lowe, Clinton McCully, Robert McGuckin, Catherine Mann, Jaime Marquez, Raymond Mataloni, Benjamin Mintz, Daniel J. B. Mitchell, Thomas Nardone, Jane Oates, Peter Orszag, Ataman Ozyildirim, Michael Palumbo, Kenneth Petrick, Edward Potter, Lee Price, Brooks Robinson, Harry Rosenberg, Larry Rosenblum, Andrew Samet, Stuart Scott, Eugene Seskin, Robert Shepard, Stu Smith, Gerald Sroufe, Stephen Wandner, George Werking, Henry Wulf, and Victor Zarnowitz. Lorin Evans gave exceptional help with the computer hardware and software. Sarah Frumkin assisted in preparing the figures. Daisy Rosenberg provided ideas for the cover design. Sylvia Elan assisted in proofreading the prepublication printed pages. The editorial staff of M.E. Sharpe, assisted by Westchester Book Services, did a fine job of turning the manuscript into a book. Esther Clark prepared the manuscript for production; Angela Piliouras was the production editor; Andrew Hudak coordinated the production; Martha Mesiti was the copyeditor; Binghamton Valley Composition was the typesetter; Wanda Dietrich prepared the index.

I thank all of the above for their help, which was substantial. But they may not agree with particular aspects or the overall approach of the book. I am responsible for everything in the book.

I worked on the manuscript from the fall of 2002 to the summer of 2003 at home in Washington, D.C., in the enjoyment of each day with my wife, Sarah.

1

Attributes of Economic Indicators

The statistics central to evaluating and forecasting the macro economy of the United States are often referred to as economic indicators. This chapter discusses several conceptual and statistical topics that underlie the indicators: business cycles, determining cyclical turning points, seasonality, index numbers, data accuracy, calculating and presenting growth rates, price-adjusted dollars, the underground economy, distinctions among "goods," "services," and "structures," the production of economic statistics, and data integrity.

BUSINESS CYCLES

Business cycles are the recurring rises and falls in the overall economy as reflected in production, income, employment, sales, profits, and prices. They are associated with capitalistic societies in which production, employment, prices, wages, and interest rates are largely determined in the marketplace. They are primarily associated with industrially advanced nations that have highly developed business and financial structures, in contrast to developing nations that have a large agricultural component that is subject to the vagaries of weather and the consequent abundant or poor harvests. Business cycles reflect the inability of the marketplace to accommodate smoothly such factors as shifting markets for new and substitute products, new technologies, uncertainties and risks in business investments, stock market speculation, global competition and currency volatility, terrorism, and shortages and gluts created by wars (including their buildups and aftermaths), weather-dependent harvests, and the manipulation of supplies and prices by cartels.

Economists have offered various theories to explain the causes of business cycles in the past, and they continue to provide varying explanations today.[1] The theories are tested empirically against the movements of the relevant economic indicators to determine how well the theories conform to the data. This is a continuing task of the economics profession in its pursuit of better insights into the workings of the economy. A basic purpose of the profession is to provide ever-better guides for government policies to foster maximum and stable economic growth, contain price inflation, and raise living conditions among all income groups, and in general to provide better guides for households and businesses to consider their spending, saving, and investment decisions in light of prospects for the overall economy.

While business cycles do not recur on a regular basis, and each cycle has unique characteristics, there are discernible regularities in the behavior of business cycles over time, as Victor Zarnowitz, the foremost student of business cycles, points out.[2] Examples of regularities are that business cycles are national and even international in scope, they last several years, and they often show repetitive patterns from cycle to cycle in the statistical movements of production, employment, various industries, household expenditures, business investment, prices, and interest rates.

The overall thrust of the American economy fits the competitive model even though the federal, state, and local governments provide public services and intervene in the economy in other ways, and though there are monopolistic aspects in the private sector that are insulated from fully competitive markets. While the American economy has changed considerably over the past two centuries because of new technologies and the growing population, business cycles are not new. They occurred repeatedly in the nineteenth and twentieth centuries.

The rising phase of a business cycle is typically referred to as expansion and the falling phase as recession. Although business cycle analysis focuses on the overall economy, it recognizes that particular sectors may be moving against the overall trend—a stagnant or declining industry may not participate in the prosperity of a general expansion, and a growth industry may be insulated from a general recession.

Determining Business Cycle Phases

What is a recession? Generally speaking, we know there is a recession when we see slack business activity and high unemployment. But there is also an observable measure of a recession period. The Business Cycle Dating Committee of the National Bureau of Economic Research, Inc. (NBER), a private nonprofit organization in Cambridge, Massachusetts, designates such periods. These recession periods are considered "official," although they are not designated by a U.S. government agency.

Under the auspices of the NBER, the Business Cycle Dating Committee, which is composed of seven economists, is convened specifically to determine the beginning and ending points of expansions and recessions by assessing the preponderant direction of a wide range of economic indicators. The NBER Business Cycle Dating Committee has established a reputation for objectivity, and its designations are accepted by liberal and conservative economists and politicians alike.[3]

The advantage of having a nongovernmental body such as the NBER Dating Committee designate expansions and recessions is clear. It reduces the possibility that the administration in office will politicize the designations to put its own policies in the most favorable light, or even revise designations for previous periods to make the opposition party look worse, as the executive branch of the federal government runs the government's statistical programs.

The NBER Business Cycle Dating Committee designates a recession as beginning in the month in which the overall direction of a broad spectrum of economic indicators turns downward; similarly, an expansion is designated as beginning in the month in which the overall direction turns upward.[4] While various numerical tests are applied to the indicators to assess their direction, ultimately the decision is based on the judgment of the NBER Dating Committee. For example, a recession is popularly defined as occurring when the real gross domestic product (i.e., the price-adjusted GDP) declines for two consecutive quarters, but this definition is often not determinate, as some periods have been designated as recessions even though they did not include two consecutive quarters in which real GDP declined. The NBER Dating Committee considers a variety of monthly and quarterly data before making a determination, including but not limited to business sales, bank debits outside New York City, industrial production, unemployment rate, nonfarm employment and hours worked, personal income, and the less cyclically sensitive GDP in current and price-adjusted dollars. Because the cyclical turning point centers on a particular month, quarterly data such as the GDP cannot be strictly applied to the specific turning point. Nevertheless, movements in the quarterly data, even if showing an acceleration or deceleration rather than a change in direction, give more credibility for gauging the approximate time of the directional change.

An inherent limitation in determining the precise cyclical turning points is that the NBER Business Cycle Dating Committee functions close to when an economic downturn and recovery are occurring. Thus, of necessity it relies on the contemporaneous data available at the time. But subsequent revisions to the preliminary data sometimes alter the earlier picture of the economy given in the contemporaneous data. For example, when the Business Cycle Dating committee announced in November 2001 that a recession began in March 2001, the data then available to the Committee showed the decline in real GDP during 2001 first occurring in the third quarter of the year. Yet in July 2002, revised real GDP data showed a decline in each of the first three quarters of 2001.

A notable exception to the typical designations occurred after World War II. There was a short recession in 1945 from February to October (the war ended in August). It turned out to be a surprisingly modest transition to a peacetime economy. Unemployment rose substantially in the postwar period from 670 thousand workers in 1944 to 1.04 million in 1945, and to 2.27 million in 1946. However, forecasts for unemployment increases of about 8 million did not materialize.[5] In 1946 and 1947, real GDP declined by 11 percent and 1 percent, respectively. The sharp drop was due entirely to the demobilization and concomitant plunge in defense outlays. In contrast, the private sector and civilian government components of the GDP rose during the demobilization. Because the "recession" in 1946 was *sui generis* due to the conversion from war to a peacetime economy, it was not considered a recession period by the NBER Business Cycle Dating Committee.

While "expansion" is the general term for the upward phase of the cycle, the upturn immediately following a recession, until the economy regains its previous peak level of activity, is often referred to as "recovery." The period that starts when economic activity begins to exceed the highest levels attained in the previous expansion is traditionally called "expansion." An analogous designation that the author makes with respect to the downward phase is the transition from recession to contraction. The immediate downturn is called "recession"; and if overall activity falls below the lowest level of the previous recession, the depressed period is called "contraction." However, such a contraction has not occurred since the depression of the early 1930s, when economic activity at the low point of the depression in March 1933 was below that at the low point of the previous recession in November 1927, and so "recession" and "contraction" are used interchangeably in current terminology.

The high point of an expansion before it turns downward to recession is called the "peak," and the low point of a recession before it turns upward to recovery is the "trough." A complete cycle is composed of both the expansion and recession phases and is typically viewed from the peak of one expansion to the peak of the following expansion. This way of looking at the cycle emphasizes the long-term growth of the economy independent of short-term cyclical movements, although for some analyses it may be useful to measure the cycle from the trough of one recession to the trough of the next recession, which is also a complete cycle.

The last term used in this categorization is "depression." A depression is a collapse of the economy such as last occurred in the 1930s. It involves a general breakdown of economic life affecting people in all social and economic strata, including mass unemployment, widespread loss of assets such as homes and life savings, the disappearance of established businesses through bankruptcy, and an overall undermining of the financial system through failures of the banking, securities, and insurance industries. A depression is far more devastating than a recession. For example, unemployment reached a high of about 25 percent in the 1930s, compared with peaks of 9 percent and 11 percent during the severe recessions of 1973–75 and 1981–82, respectively.

Figure 1.1 shows business cycle recessions, recoveries, and expansions from

Figure 1.1 **Business Cycle Phases: 1958–2003**

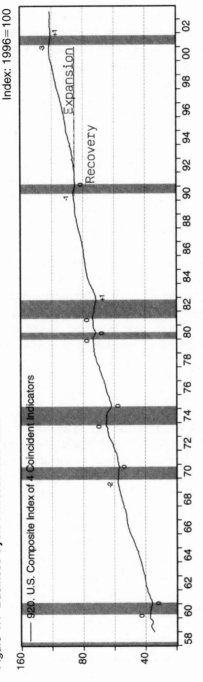

Index: 1996=100

Source: The Conference Board, *Business Cycle Indicators*, September 2003.

Note: The figure is the coincident index of the leading, coincident, and lagging indicator system (chapter 14). The bars represent recession periods. The expansion begins when the recovery from the recession exceeds the previous expansion peak. Numbers are leads (−) and lags (+) in months from business cycle turning points.

1958 to June 2003. The recession periods are those designated by the NBER Business Cycle Dating Committee. The coincident index of the leading indicator system represents actual production (chapter 14 details the system). The cyclical turning points of the coincident index approximate, and often are the same as, the NBER Dating Committee turning points. As noted above, the committee bases its designation of cyclical turning points on a judgment of the movements of a variety of economic indicators, not on any single indicator such as the coincident index.

Since the end of World War II, the closest a recovery has come to falling below the peak of the previous expansion was the 1980–81 upturn. The July 1981 peak barely exceeded the peak of the previous expansion in January 1980. Had the NBER Business Cycle Dating Committee determined that the January 1980 high point exceeded the July 1981 peak—however slightly—the committee probably would not have identified the 1980–81 episode as a separate recession.[6] This absence of recoveries turning into recessions reflects the twentieth-century pattern, but particularly that since the end of World War II, in which recovery and expansion are typical of the United States' long-term growing economy, with periods of rising economic activity being much longer than declining periods. The closest a recession has come to worsening into a contraction since World War II was the 1981–82 recession, when the coincident index in November 1982 was minimally below the trough of the previous recession in July 1980. But that did not have the properties of a contraction, which is characterized by an unambiguously lower level of output than the low point of the previous recession.

All told, as indicated in Table 1.1, the average length of the ten completed expansions since the end of World War II was 57 months. For the eight peacetime expansions (excluding the Korean and Vietnam wars), the average was 52 months. In contrast, the average recession was 11 months for all cycles and for peacetime cycles. Thus, since World War II, the average expansion lasted five times as long as the average recession. These durations are an improvement over the experience of the 1919–45 period and even more so over the previous century, when the length of expansions was only slightly longer than the length of recessions. This improvement is most telling for peacetime cycles, which do not have the stimulus of wartime production (detailed below in Changing Characteristics of Business Cycles Since the Nineteenth Century).

Delays in Designating Cyclical Turning Points

Turning points in business cycles are identified only with a lag, and often a considerable lag. For example, the recession that ultimately was determined to have started in August 1990 was first announced by the NBER Business Cycle Dating Committee eight months later, in April 1991, and the subsequent recov-

Table 1.1

Average Duration of U.S. Business Cycles (in months)

	Expansion	Recession
All cycles		
1854–1919 (16 cycles)	27	22
1919–45 (6 cycles)	35	18
1945–91 (9 cycles)	50	11
1945–2001 (10 cycles)	57	11
Peacetime cycles		
1854–1919 (14 cycles)	24	22
1919–45 (5 cycles)	26	20
1945–91 (7 cycles)	43	11
1945–2001 (8 cycles)	52	11

Source: For 1854–1991, *Survey of Current Business,* October 1994, p. C-1.

Note: For 1945–2001, the author weighted the 1991–2001 expansion of 119 months into the 1945–90 expansions. For the 1945–2001 recessions, the author weighted the 2001 recession of eight months into the 1945–91 recessions.

ery that began in April 1991 was first announced by the committee twenty-one months later, in December 1992.[7] These delays reflect the fact that movements in the various economic indicators around the cyclical turning points often give ambiguous and contradictory signs of the direction of the economy. This uncertainty in the contemporaneous data is heightened by revisions to the preliminary indicators that come out every month. Thus, before reaching agreement on the timing of a turning point, the committee waits for clear confirmation of the change in direction of the business cycle. This delay has its tradeoffs: economic analysts and the public are deprived of timely intelligence on the business cycle, but once the designations are announced they are unlikely to be revised. Indeed, the Business Cycle Dating Committee, which was formed in 1978, has never revised its designation of a cyclical turning point.

The onset of the recession that began in April 2001 was identified in November 2001, seven months later. And the subsequent recovery from the end of the recession, which began in December 2001, was first announced by the Dating Committee in July 2003, twenty months later.

The composite coincident index of the leading indicator system (chapter 14) tracks current economic activity on a monthly basis in determining the peaks and troughs of business cycles, and historically has approximated or been the same as the Dating Committee designation of cyclical turning points. The committee assesses a variety of economic indicators in determining cyclical turning points, as noted previously. And because the cyclical turning points are identified with a specific month rather than a specific quarter, monthly indicators determine the actual turning point.

Viewing the recovery from the end of the recession in November 2001 to July 2003, the composite coincident index increased by 0.7 percent over the twenty-month period. Among the four component indicators of the composite coincident index over the same recovery period, workers on nonfarm payrolls fell by 0.8 percent, personal income less transfer payments adjusted for price change increased by 1.6 percent, manufacturing and trade sales adjusted for price change increased by 2.8 percent (data for May 2003 because of the one-month lag in the their availability), and the industrial production index increased by 0.8 percent. And from the March 2001 peak of the previous expansion to June 2003, the composite coincident index *decreased* by 0.7 percent. Thus, based on the composite coincident index, the level of economic activity in mid-2003 was below that at the peak of the previous expansion in 2001. But based on the price-adjusted GDP, economic growth rose by 4 percent from the end of the recession in the fourth quarter of 2001 to the second quarter of 2003. And the level of the GDP in the second quarter of 2003 was 4 percent above that at the peak of the previous expansion in the first quarter of 2001. The Dating Committee noted that the "divergent behavior of output and employment was a key reason" for delaying the identification of the end of the recession until July 2003.[8]

In this review of the designation of cyclical turning points of the 1990–91 recession and the 2001 recession, the Business Cycle Dating Committee has designated the onset of a recession much more quickly than the onset of a recovery. This probably reflects the weakness and ambiguity of the data on the recoveries from both recessions.

Business Cycles and Economic Growth

A question is often raised about the relationship between cyclical stability and economic growth. Specifically, does the economy grow faster during periods of cyclical stability, that is when there are relatively few recessions, or when there is more instability and more frequent recessions? The short answer is that the evidence is inconclusive in the close to sixty years since the end of World War II, and for a 100-year period ending in 1980 there is at best a hint of a direct relationship between economic growth and cyclical stability.

Table 1.2 shows the annual economic growth rates approximately by decade from the late 1940s to the early 2000s and the number of recessions in each period. Following the acceleration in economic growth from 3.7 percent in the 1950s to 4.4 percent in the 1960s, the growth rate ranged from 3.0 to 3.2 percent

Table 1.2

Economic Growth and Cyclical Stability

	Annual growth rate (compounded)	Number of recessions
1948–59	3.7%	3
1959–69	4.4	1
1969–79	3.2	2
1979–89	3.0	2
1989–2000	3.1	1

Note: Growth rates from expansion peak to expansion peak are based on the gross domestic product in 1996 dollars (see under Calculating and Presenting Growth Rates: Long-Term Growth Rates). Recessions are based on the designations of the Business Cycle Dating Committee of the National Bureau of Economic Research.

from the 1970s to the early 2000s. But there is little relationship between this pattern of growth rates and the number of recessions in each period. Thus, the 1960s had the highest growth rate and one recession; the 1950s had the next highest growth rate and three recessions, the largest number of all the periods; and the 1970s and 1980s with two recessions, and the 1990s to early 2000s with two recessions, had the lowest growth rates.

In a sophisticated analysis of this question for the period from 1882 to 1980, Victor Zarnowitz finds that while there is a suggestion that economic growth is faster during periods of greater stability, this is far from conclusive.[9] He has reservations on statistical grounds and also because equally competing arguments can be made for faster growth being related to more stable and less stable cyclical environments. But he does conclude that economic growth is impeded by periods of severe economic depression.

Changing Characteristics of Business Cycles Since the Nineteenth Century

In an assessment of how the durations of expansions and recessions change over time, peacetime cycles are the best indicator, since peacetime economic activity excludes the temporary but significant stimulus of military wartime production. Table 1.1 shows that on average peacetime expansions became progressively longer and peacetime recessions progressively shorter over the 147-year period from 1854 to early 2001. But most of this improvement occurred after World War II. During 1854–1919, expansions and recessions were almost equally long (24 months for expansions and 22 months for recessions); during 1919–45, expansions were 6 months longer than recessions (26 months and 20 months, respectively); and during 1945–2001, expansions were 41 months longer than recessions (52 and 11 months, respectively). The 1945–2001 estimate assumes that the recession that began in 2001 will last about one year when the NBER Business Cycle Dating Committee ultimately designates the end of the recession.

In my view, there are three broad categories of reasons why the economy has performed better since World War II. First, Keynesian economics fostered a greater understanding of the economy as well as more widespread recognition of the importance of federal government budgets. The government's more active role in influencing the economy resulted from this triumph of Keynesianism over the classical belief that full employment would occur automatically. The Keynesian perspective was in turn critiqued and modified by several developments: the greater recognition of interest rates as a key factor affecting economic activity; the importance given by monetarists to the money supply; the Phillips Curve analysis of the tradeoff between unemployment and inflation; the integration of potential output and inflation with unemployment in Okun's Law; the rational expectations theory that the market adjusts to and frustrates government intervention in the economy; and the NAIRU concept of the nonaccelerating inflation rate of unemployment.

The second reason the economy has done better is that this greater understanding is applied to economic policies. Thus, the federal government actively stabilizes the economy through tax and spending fiscal policies. The active role of the government was encouraged by the Employment Act of 1946, which enunciated the pursuit of national goals for maximum employment and purchasing power. This was heightened by the monetary policy change of 1951 (i.e., the Treasury Department-Federal Reserve accord), which allowed the Federal Reserve to pursue interest policies to benefit the economy independent of their effect on interest rates of government securities used in financing the federal debt. Subsequently, the Full Employment and Balanced Growth Act of 1978 (Humphrey-Hawkins Act) set the first numerical goals for unemployment and inflation (see chapter 2).

Third, there is a general category of institutional factors contributing to the economy's improved performance. These include the cushioning effect of unemployment insurance and other income maintenance programs that provide an income floor during recessions; bank deposit insurance and actions taken by the federal government and the Federal Reserve to prevent a widespread financial collapse of failing banks; and the increasing sophistication of companies using greater amounts of economic information to balance sales and production. This last factor may also result in better inventory control and thus moderate production fluctuations.

The long-term shift to services and the increasing role of foreign trade are among other factors that affected the long-term performance of the economy.

Services producing industries have been less cyclically volatile than goods producing industries, but growth in the technology-based services may increase the volatility of services in the twenty-first century. The growing globalization of the U.S. economy also makes it more vulnerable to international cyclical fluctuations in the twenty-first century.

Christina Romer has challenged the data in Table 1.2 suggesting that the economy has become more stable since World War II, while David Weir, Stanley Lebergott, and Victor Zarnowitz have objected to her thesis.[10] Romer maintains that statistics on unemployment, the gross national product (GNP), and industrial production are misleading because the underlying data on which they are based changed considerably after World War II. The prewar statistics used far more fragmentary and less reliable underlying data than the postwar statistics. When historical statistics are reconstructed to simulate a consistent methodology over the prewar and postwar periods, Romer's argument continues, the prewar economy appears to be similar to the postwar economy in terms of both the severity of economic declines and the volatility of output and unemployment as measured by yearly deviations from long-term trends. Weir, Lebergott, and Zarnowitz maintain that Romer's methodology of superimposing post-1948 data characteristics on the pre-1930 period, but without providing fresh underlying data, is based on the faulty assumption that sectoral output-employment relationships, cyclicality of labor force participation rates, sectoral composition of employment, and GNP-commodity output relationships have not changed over the entire time period. In short, this rebuttal states that Romer's methodology is based on a synthetic estimation procedure that prejudges the question and thus insures the outcome.

Whatever the merits of Romer's argument, her reconstructed measures do not refute the data showing that the relative durations of expansions and recessions have improved. Because the methodology does not alter the dates for the turning points of business cycles, the reconstructed statistics do not contradict the traditional measures that indicate an improvement over time toward longer expansions and shorter recessions.

SEASONALITY

Economic activity is bumpy not only on a daily, weekly, monthly, and quarterly basis, but also minute-by-minute as reflected in price quotations in commodity and financial markets. Even when cyclical movements continue in the same direction over several periods (rising during an expansion and declining during a recession), there are continuing deviations from the general upward or downward movement as households, businesses, and governments speed up or slow down their rate of spending. These short-term fits and starts have many causes: the intrinsic tempo of economic life with its bursts and lulls in activity followed by a return to the routine pace; quick response to changes or perceived changes in the economic environment; surprise shocks of nature such as hurricanes, severe snowstorms, floods, droughts, and earthquakes; surprise shocks of human origins such as oil spills, strikes, lockouts, government shutdowns, and terrorist attacks; and expected repetitive seasonal variations within every twelve-month period resulting from such factors as farm crop planting and harvesting seasons, school vacations, holidays, Christmas shopping, less outside construction during winter months, automobile plant shutdowns for model year changes during the summer, the payment and reimbursement of annual individual income taxes in the first four calendar months of the year, and federal, state, and local government fiscal year budgets that affect their year-end spending patterns.

Such inherent bumpiness in the real world presents problems for analyzing short-term movements in economic indicators, because the gyrations may give misleading appearances of sharp changes in the direction of economic activity when in fact they are only temporary. For example, in construction the normal pattern is that much of the drop in work on buildings and roads in the winter months stems from the cold weather, but this is reversed in the spring when construction activity increases greatly. Thus, unless it is recognized that when the weather becomes warmer, construction will likely pick up, someone just observing the winter decline may conclude that construction is in a longer-term doldrum. Because of the intense interest in short-term economic movements, many economic data obtained from weekly, monthly, and quarterly surveys of households and businesses are routinely adjusted by statistical methods to approximate what their movements would be if there were no repetitive changes within every twelve-month period due to such factors as the weather, vacations, holidays, model changeovers, government fiscal year budgets, and tax payment dates.

Estimates of seasonal adjustment are based on the economic experience of previous years. When consistent seasonal patterns for particular months (or quarters, in the case of quarterly data) show on average that the indicator is a certain amount higher or lower, or is the same as the monthly (quarterly) average based on the entire year, then the indicator is adjusted accordingly that month. For example, if sales of women's shoes typically are 5 percent below the monthly average for the year in January and 7 percent above the monthly average for the year in April, actual January sales are increased by 5 percent and actual April sales are reduced 7 percent. And if sales in June typically are the same as the monthly average for the year, no change is made to the actual June data.

In a broader perspective, seasonal variations are generally periodic and predictable, and work themselves out within the year. Thus, seasonal ups and downs do not cause the personal and social distress of recessions, because businesses and workers have considerable experience in accommodating to them, as Victor Zarnowitz points out.[11]

Extraordinary Events

The economic effects of extraordinary events such as strikes, lockouts, floods, hurricanes, earthquakes, government shutdowns, and terrorist attacks are not included in the development of seasonal factors. For example, sharp declines in sales and employment in months when the extraordinary events occur show up as "outliers" in the computer programs, and these sharp declines are excluded from the calculation of the seasonal factors for that year. This is done because the purpose of seasonal adjustment is to capture the repetitive seasonal changes from year to year. For that reason, cold and hot weather extremes in a particular year that have atypical seasonal effects on business activity may also appear as outliers that are excluded from the calculation of seasonal factors. The outliers arising from the computer programs are not used mechanically, but are reviewed by analysts to ensure that they reflect extraordinary or extreme events. To include the effect of the extraordinary events and extreme weather changes in the calculation of the seasonal factors would distort the meaning of seasonally adjusted data.

However, the actual economic activity levels of the various monthly and quarterly economic indicators include the effects of the extraordinary or extreme events in the periods when they occur, and thus are included in the seasonally adjusted data. The only effect of excluding outliers in the seasonal adjustment process is that the outliers are not used in developing the seasonal factors, which in turn are used to modify the actual activity levels to obtain seasonally adjusted levels.

Figures 1.2a, 1.2b, and 1.2c show total retail sales of all products in 2000, 2001, and 2002 both "seasonally adjusted" and "not seasonally adjusted." Data for the three years illustrate the effects of the terrorist attack of September 11, 2001. The seasonally adjusted sales are far less volatile than the actual, not seasonally adjusted sales in all three years. Thus, given the normal buying patterns before and after Christmas, actual sales are much higher in December and much lower in January and February than the seasonally adjusted sales data. The main difference is in the seasonally adjusted data in the three years, in which the sharp increase in the October 2001 sales (Figure 1.2b) following the September 11 terrorist attacks, did not occur in the 2000 and 2002 data for October (Figures 1.2a and 1.2c).

Sophisticated techniques are used to seasonally adjust economic data. The procedures are too technical to detail here, but the following usages illustrate the general method.

• At least five years of historical experience are usually used to develop seasonal factors.

Figure 1.2a **Seasonal Patterns of Retail Sales: 2000**

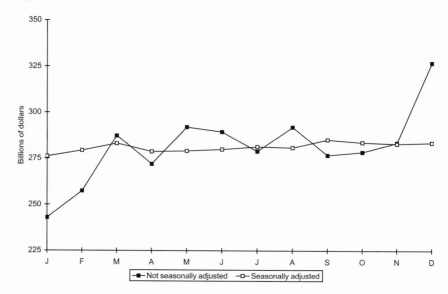

Note: Based on U.S. Bureau of the Census data.

Figure 1.2b **Seasonal Patterns of Retail Sales: 2001**

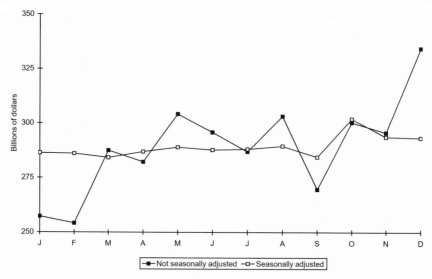

Note: Based on U.S. Bureau of the Census data.

Figure 1.2c **Seasonal Patterns of Retail Sales: 2002**

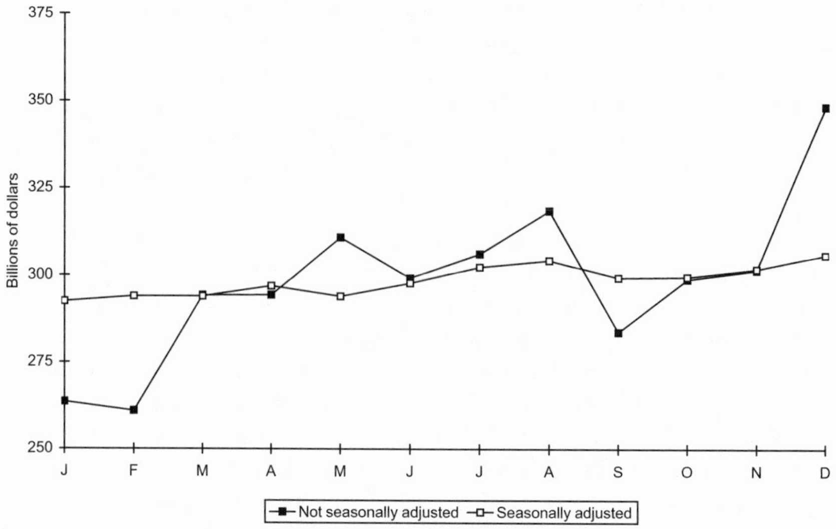

Note: Based on U.S. Bureau of the Census data.

• Seasonal patterns of recent years receive greater weight than those in earlier years.

• Revisions of the last few years' seasonal factors are made every year. The time span of years used to compute the seasonal factors is usually updated each year by adding the data for the most recent year and dropping the data for the earliest year used in the previous year's computations. That is, a rolling fixed period of years is used. For example, in a series for which six years of data from 1997 to 2002 were used to compute seasonal factors for adjusting 2003 data, 1998 to 2003 seasonal factors would be used for adjusting 2004 data.

• Extreme values of the indicator in particular months or quarters, such as those due to an earthquake or government shutdown, are downweighted or excluded as an aberration.

• An increasing number of data series are based on a "concurrent adjustment" method which uses actual data from the most recent period to develop seasonal factors for the latest month. The concurrent adjustment method reduces revision errors in the monthly level and the monthly movement of the seasonally adjusted data.

• In some cases, the trend of seasonal factors in previous years is projected one year ahead for use in the current year. For example, during 2004 seasonal factors were available only through 2003. In order to apply seasonal factors to current data in 2004 that are considered appropriate for 2004, a forecast is made of the expected 2004 seasonal factors. As in the case of the above concurrent adjustment method, the projected seasonal factors lower revision errors, but not as much as the concurrent method.

While it is desirable to prepare seasonally adjusted data for use in economic analysis, they come with caveats. Regardless of the technique used, seasonally adjusted economic indicators are a statistical artifact. Thus, seasonally adjusted data reflect a type of measurement that, while usually adequate for its intended purpose, is inevitably less than perfect. Although seasonally adjusted data are based on the average experience of past years, seasonal variations may be atypical in any particular year. For example, the winter may be colder or warmer than normal, or automobile model year changeovers may be more or less extensive than average. On the other hand, movements that appear to be merely seasonal, such as a decline in business from December to January, may in fact reflect an actual deterioration in the health of the economy that will become apparent only when the data for subsequent months appear. Also, seasonally adjusted data contain an unknown amount of random movements that reflect the complexity of the economy and that ideally should be eliminated but cannot be quantified; this has been a long-standing limitation in the methodology of seasonal adjustment.

The majority of economic data are seasonally adjusted. But some are not. The reasons for no seasonal adjustment vary: the monthly or quarterly data may be too erratic to establish a seasonal pattern; in the case of new data series, there may be insufficient historical experience; or the organization providing the data may not think a seasonal pattern is relevant, as in the case of interest rates and stock market price indexes. When an indicator is not seasonally adjusted, one indirect means of understanding the seasonally adjusted movement is to compare percent changes between the current period (month or quarter) and the same period (month or quarter) of a year earlier for several consecutive periods. While this indirect approach provides a broad magnitude of the current seasonally adjusted movement, it cannot indicate cyclical turning points. The result also may be misleading if differences in the calendar are significant from year to year. For example, in one year, March could have more weekends than in the next year; this fact could affect the amount of business activity in the month.

INDEX NUMBERS

Economic data represent the myriad of transactions between buyers and sellers in consumer, industrial, labor, and financial markets involving both private parties and governments. In order to analyze this vast amount of detail, the individual transactions are combined and summarized into subgroupings and overall totals. One method of summarizing is through index numbers, which are a convenient way of quickly assessing the direction and amount of change in economic activity. Index numbers are used for various types of economic activity, such as production, prices, wages, productivity, and leading and lagging indexes.

An index number starts with a base period, usually a single year or the average of a few consecutive years. The base period is typically, but not always, defined as equivalent to 100, and all movements of the indicator before and after the base period are represented as percentage differences from the base. For example, using the base of 100, an index of 95 means that the indicator for that period (month, quarter, or year) is 5 percent below the base period, and an index of 128 means the indicator is 28 percent above the base period. The formula for calculating the percent change between two periods is:

$$\frac{\text{Period 2}}{\text{Period 1}} - 1.0 \times 100$$

Thus, in the text example of the index numbers for periods 1 and 2,

$$\frac{128}{95} = 1.347$$

$$[1.347 - 1.0] \times 100 = 34.7\%$$

Assuming 95 is the period 1 index and 128 is the period 2 index, the change between the two periods is 34.7 percent.

Indexes are calculated by multiplying each item's relative importance in the base period, referred to as the items's weight, by the percent change in the item's value since the base period; the sum of these calculations for all items is the index for the current period. The combination of several items into an overall index also causes a problem, however, because the relative importance of the various items in the index will have changed since the base period.

Table 1.3 illustrates this in a hypothetical price index which compares two different price movements that are due simply to differences in weights from a previous period to a more recent one. This example calculates two price changes from 1995 to 2003 for a price index composed of bananas, airline flights, and computers, one using 1995 weights and one using 2000 weights. The actual price changes for the three individual product items are the same in both weighting structures. The index with 1995 weights *increases* 9 percent over the 1995–2000 period, while the index with 2000 weights *decreases* 2 percent over the same period. The difference is due to the greater weight for computers (whose prices fell from 1995 to 2003) based on 2000 expenditures than that based on 1995 expenditures.

Table 1.3

Index Number Weights and Price Change (illustrative only)

	1995 Expenditure Weights		
	1 1995 expenditures (% distribution)	2 Ratio of 2003 price to 1995 price	3 2003 price index (1 × 2)
Bananas	50%	1.10	55
Airline flights	40	1.20	48
Computers	10	0.60	6
	100%		109
	2000 Expenditure Weights		
	1 2000 expenditures (% distribution)	2 Ratio of 2003 price to 1995 price	3 2003 price index (1 × 2)
Bananas	40%	1.10	44
Airline flights	30	1.20	36
Computers	30	0.60	18
	100%		98

Some index numbers are based on the same fixed weights that add up to 100 percent in the base period for several years. Other index numbers allow these proportions to change more frequently, such as every year, to reflect more current production or consumption patterns. The weights change because on a relative basis some items increase in use and others become less important due to changing buyer preferences, competition from substitute products, and differential price movements. Because the relative importance of individual items in the index changes over time—for example, housing may rise faster than food prices, or a new product with rapidly growing sales often has a high price when first introduced and the price subsequently declines as output expands—the overall index will show a differential rate of change depending on whether earlier or later proportionate weights are used.

This "product mix" problem is a continuing issue in the construction of index numbers. Use of a weighting scheme that incorporates the geometric mean of the weights between two periods gives a still different view of price change (see chapter 11 under Differential Averaging of Weights).

For example, in the case of price indexes, one that maintains the same relative *quantities* of the various items purchased as in the base period is likely to show a higher rate of price increase (or lower rate of decline) than when the index represents the actual items bought in each period. This occurs because on average buyers tend to switch to substitutes that have more slowly rising prices,

and to new products after the new product price declines. Analogously, a production index that holds the relative *prices* of the various items produced constant at their base-period relationship tends to show a higher rate of production
growth (or lower rate of decline) than when the index represents the actual prices
paid in each period, because the introductory high price of a new product usually
declines with the growth in production.

There is no right or wrong way to construct index numbers. Usually the
choice of which period weights to use is based on a judgment concerning the
use of the index. For example, when the goal is to measure price change for
the same items over time, the base-period weights of the items purchased are
held constant for several years. But when interest is in measuring price change
to reflect the continuing change in the types of items purchased, the proportions
of items purchased are changed in every period to reflect actual buying patterns.
Even including an index number method based on the geometric mean of the
weights between two periods as noted above, it remains a case where one size
does not fit all.

The base period of an indicator may represent a single year, such as the
industrial production index where 1997 = 100, or a few consecutive years, such
as the consumer price index (CPI) where 1982–84 = 100. The base period of
index numbers can be in any time frame, and can differ noticeably from the
time frame used to develop the weights. Thus, the base period of the CPI of
1982–84 = 100 compares with the weights of the CPI that represent household
expenditure patterns in 1993–95. The process of changing the base period results
in slight numerical changes over a historical period that affect the historical
continuity of the index, which is why there are no plans at the time of this
writing to update the base period of the CPI (discussed further in chapter 11 on
inflation and deflation). A reason for having the base period in a similar time
frame as the weights is that it gives the user an immediate understanding of the
underpinnings of the index.

DATA ACCURACY

Several types of questions can be raised about the accuracy of economic indicators. Conceptual issues, such as whether the indicators measure what they
purport—for example, if the unemployment rate truly represents the proportion
of people out of work or if the consumer price index truly represents inflation
to the consumer—are beyond the scope of this book. More practical considerations, such as how closely the underlying data represent the definition of the
indicator, are also incapable of being measured. Thus, data based on income tax
returns that were originally developed for assessing the economic effects of
income tax laws and of proposed changes in tax laws are also used for estimating
certain components of the gross domestic product and for obtaining information

on small firms for the economic censuses. Even though some data sources may not exactly correspond to the definitional concepts of certain indicators, secondary sources are used in preparing economic indicators to hold down the costs of data collection and to limit the reporting burden on the public.

Beyond the above issues of how closely the data conform to the meaning and definition of the indicator, there are two fairly simple ways to evaluate the accuracy of economic indicators, however. One reflects the extent of revisions to preliminary data. And in the case of indicators based on information from surveys obtained from probability samples of household, business, and government respondents, the accuracy is based on the sampling reliability of the surveys.

Error due to revision reflects changes in the indicators from when they are initially provided to the later, more accurate information. The size of revision error is based on the past experience of these changes. For example, in the case of the real gross domestic product from 1978 to 1998, two-thirds of the revisions between the advance estimates published twenty-five days after the quarter and the latest estimates based on the most recent annual and five-year benchmark revisions were within a range of −1.1 to 2.0 percentage points. Thus, at a 67 percent confidence, it is likely that an advance quarterly estimate of real GDP growth at an annual rate of 3.0 percent will be revised within a range of 1.9 to 5.0 percent. Raising the confidence level to 90 percent increases the likely revision to a range of −1.6 to 3.4 percentage points.

Error due to sampling results from the likelihood that data obtained from a sample of a population differ from what they would be if the entire population were surveyed. Estimates of sampling error are developed from mathematical formulas of probability, and there is a predetermined direct relationship between error size and its chances of occurring. For example, the sampling error for housing starts based on a 67 percent confidence is plus or minus 3 percent. Thus at a confidence of 67 percent, it is likely that a monthly figure of housing starts at an annual rate of 1.5 million units would range within 1.455 and 1.545 million if all starts were surveyed. Raising the confidence level to 95 percent approximately doubles the sampling error to a range of 1.41 to 1.59 million.

When such estimates are available, it is important to take them into account. However, whether error estimates are available or not, it is clear in all cases that any single number provided by an indicator cannot always exactly represent reality. Because of the various sources of error inherent in economic data, in general an indicator should be considered as representing a range rather than a single number. Analysis of the actual or related data, as well as estimates of the size of revisions or sampling errors available, can sometimes suggest whether actual measurements fall closer to upper or lower bounds of that range.

Revisions

Economic indicators are developed from data obtained in surveys of households, businesses, and governments, and from tax and regulatory reports submitted to the federal and state governments. The indicators are available weekly, monthly, quarterly, or annually, depending on the data series on which they are based. Because policymakers in the presidential administration, Congress, and the Federal Reserve System want the indicators as soon as possible following the month or quarter to which they refer, the data are initially provided on a preliminary basis and are subsequently revised as more complete and accurate survey information is received. The use of preliminary and revised information results from the tension between the need for both timely and accurate data. Revisions are sometimes substantial, and therefore it is important that preliminary information be treated as tentative.

Contemporaneous Revisions

Economic activity over short spells of three to six months moves in fits and starts with varying rates of growth, and sometimes temporarily reverses the dominant upward or downward direction before resuming the dominant pattern (see Seasonality above for causes of these short-term interruptions). At the time these movements are occurring, however, it is not clear if they signal a basic change in the tempo of economic life or a limited interruption of the underlying momentum. Because of frequent fits and starts in marketplace activity and because data revisions become available shortly after the preliminary numbers are published, it is important not to be swayed by the most recent blip in the indicators. A changed movement of at least six months should be identified before determining that the overall pace or direction of the economy is strengthening or weakening.

Nevertheless, data revisions within a somewhat longer, twelve-month period have occasionally shown that the earlier information gave a different emphasis, or even misleading movements, of the contemporaneous economic activity. For example, the growth rates of the initial real gross domestic product estimates for the first two quarters of 2001 were revised significantly downward from increases to decreases in the annual GDP revisions published in July 2002. In contrast, the revised data showed less of a decline in the third quarter and a greater increase in the fourth quarter growth rates than previously published. For all of 2001, the real GDP growth rate was revised downward from 1.2 to 0.3 percent. These revisions did not change the perception of a weak economy, although they indicate that the decline in economic growth was more serious than previously thought.

Revisions play a fundamental role in the system of leading, coincident, and lagging indexes that are used to forecast economic activity (chapter 13). With the exception of the 1980 recession, the contemporaneous data of these indexes have not given clear advance signs that the economy was heading for a recession (see chapter 13 under Limitation for Forecasting and Table 13.1). Clear signals of an impending recession become apparent only long after the fact, when the much later revised data were incorporated in the indexes in subsequent years. This is an inherent weakness in the forecasting record of the leading indicator system.

Benchmark Revisions

In addition to revisions that are made on a current basis, there are revisions called "benchmarks" that are based on a comprehensive set of data that typically undergoes no further improvements. They are made at annual, five-year, ten-year, or other long-term intervals depending on the economic indicator. Benchmark numbers include survey data from the most representative samples, including, in some cases, the universe of survey respondents, better methodologies for statistical estimating, and new definitions for components of the indicator. These more accurate and detailed data also improve the quality of the preliminary indicators in later periods.

For particular indicators, benchmarks result in a revision of all historical data as in the case of the gross domestic product; in other cases, application of the new definitions and data estimating methodologies is limited to future estimates of the indicator, as for the consumer price index. The decision about whether to revise historical data is based on a consideration of several factors—the need to have a consistent series over time balanced against the lack or weakness of comparable data for earlier time periods, the theoretical question of whether to "rewrite history" by including factors that previously were not considered in economic analysis and policymaking, and the additional costs for statistical programs to make the more extensive revisions. When the historical data are not revised, there is a break in the series where the previous data are not fully consistent with the new data.

The analyst should recognize these data inconsistencies when analyzing long-term trends.

Revised vs. Contemporaneous Data

The use of revised data in economic analysis and forecasting gives the analyst the best information for seeing what happened in past periods. Thus, revised data result in more explanatory power than the contemporaneous data had for understanding how the economy functioned. And the relationships developed from the revised data are applied for analyzing current contemporaneous data in future periods.

Yet data in those future periods themselves will be subject to revision, as unending revisions are a fact of economic measurement. The importance of revisions is that they occasionally show that the contemporaneous analysis was clouded.

Sampling Reliability

A survey is typically based on a sample of respondents from the universe of the entire population. Many indicators are derived from data collected from a probability sample survey, which represents all groups of the universe in proportion to the size of each group. However, it is unlikely that any single sample corresponds precisely to the distribution of the groups in the universe. Therefore, a sampling error is calculated to indicate the possible range of error in the survey data. Sampling errors can be calculated only for surveys based on probability samples. The unemployment rate and housing starts are examples of economic indicators for which a sampling error is provided.

Some indicators are published with numerical ranges of confidence and error due to sampling of survey respondents. For example, assuming a sampling error of 3 percent and a confidence of 95 percent, the chances are nineteen out of twenty that the estimate is off by 3 percent in either direction. In such instances, one should allow for a lower and upper range of the number in assessing movements over time. When the error range is larger than the movement in the current indicator (say, the error is plus or minus 3 percent and the monthly movement in the indicator is only 1 percent), the single-period movement is highly tentative. But if such small movements cumulate in one direction over several periods, the trend is more significant. For example, an unemployment rate change of 0.1 percentage point in one month is not statistically significant in two of three cases because it is within the likely sampling error of 0.13 percentage point. However, if the unemployment rate rises or falls by 0.1 percentage point in the same direction for two or more months, the cumulative change is significant.

If a sample does not fully represent the components of the universe in accordance with the relative importance of each component, the survey is not based on a probability sample. For an indicator based on a nonprobability sample, only a revision error can be calculated. The survey of manufacturers' shipments, orders, and inventories, and the surveys of foreign direct investment in the United States and of U.S. direct investment abroad are examples of economic indicators based on nonprobability sample surveys for which revisions are provided, but a revision error rate is provided only for the manufacturers' shipments, etc., survey.

Even for probability samples, the present state of statistical methodology does not allow an estimate of the accuracy with which respondents answer survey questions. Error attributable to inaccurate answers is known as nonsampling or reporting error, and all survey data, including those obtained from the universe as well as from a sample of respondents, contain an unknown amount of such inaccuracy.

Also, with the present state of statistical methodology, sampling errors for probability samples of surveys on different topics cannot be added to arrive at an overall sampling error for all of the surveys combined. For example, the gross domestic product is prepared from a variegated database of many different topics for its household, business, government, and international components that include both probability and nonprobability sample surveys. Even if all of the surveys were based on probability samples, the various sampling errors could not be added to get an overall sampling error for the GDP. Because of this methodological limitation, the GDP includes a revision error but not a sampling error (see Revisions above).

CALCULATING AND PRESENTING GROWTH RATES

The public's perception of economic growth rates is affected by how the trends of economic indicators are calculated and how the data are presented. This section highlights three aspects of preparing and presenting growth rates: annualized and annual movements, long-term growth rates, and charting data graphically.

Annualized and Annual Movements

Three measures are used in gauging various types of annual movements of economic indicators: the seasonally adjusted annual rate, annual change, and year-over-year change.

Seasonally Adjusted Annual Rate (SAAR)

The SAAR reflects what the yearly movement of the indicator would be if the same rate of change (adjusted for seasonal variation) were to continue for the next eleven months (monthly indicator) or for the next three quarters (quarterly indicator). This number extends the same rate of change for the current month or quarter compounded to the rest of the year. The SAAR provides a quick view of how a subannual movement looks over a twelve-month (or four-quarter) period. It also facilitates comparisons of growth rates for periods of different lengths. However, it is important to recognize that the SAAR number assumes a constant rate of change for comparative purposes only—it is not a forecast of what is expected to happen.

Year-Over-Year Change

This compares the average level of the indicator in one year with the average level of the previous year. The annual averages are computed for the twelve months or four quarters of the indicator. The yearly averages smooth out the effects of unusually high or low levels in particular months or quarters. Before the year is over, one way to anticipate the annual average level for the entire year is to average the data for the second and third quarters of the year—April to September for the monthly data, and April–June and July–September for the quarterly data.

December to December or Fourth-quarter-to-Fourth-quarter Change

These focus on the movement of the indicator from the end of one calendar year to the end of the next calendar year. This kind of change is often used in economic reports at the beginning of the calendar year to provide a more current assessment of the most recent twelve-month or four-quarter period than the annual change numbers mentioned above. The caveat is that any single period within the year may have abnormally high or low rates of economic growth or inflation. Because these data are not averaged over an annual period, they can distort the view of annual change.

Long-Term Growth Rates

Long-term growth rates span short-term cyclical expansions and recessions. Therefore, long-term rates are influenced by the economic conditions at the beginning and ending dates of the period independently of the cyclical movements within the period. In calculating long-term growth rates, it is necessary to use the appropriate initial and terminal dates to avoid distorting the growth rate, as average rates of growth for approximately the same period differ somewhat if the end points are changed slightly.

Table 1.4 illustrates this in the case of the real gross domestic product during 1990–2001. It shows four annual growth rates with varying initial and terminal years and quarters (GDP peaks and troughs may differ by one quarter from the official cyclical turning points). Alternate initial years and quarters are the 1990 second quarter and 1991 first quarter, and terminal years are the 2000 fourth quarter and 2001 third quarter. There are two correct measures: from the expansion high point to expansion high point (1990 fourth quarter to 2000 fourth quarter), or from the recession low point to recession low point (1991 first quarter to 2001 third quarter). These correct measures vary slightly, from expansion to expansion of 3.1 percent, and from recession to recession of 3.2

Table 1.4

Real Gross Domestic Product, Alternative Growth Rates:
1990–2001 (billions of 1996 dollars, seasonally adjusted annual rate)

1990:2	6,731.7 (expansion high)
1991:1	6,631.4 (recession low)
2000:4	9,243.8 (expansion high)
2001:3	9,186.4 (recession low)

Average annual growth (compounded)

1990:2–2000:4	3.1% (expansion high to expansion high)
1991:1–2001:3	3.2% (recession low to recession low)
1990:2–2001:3	2.8% (expansion high to recession low)
1991:1–2000:4	3.5% (recession low to expansion high)

Note: Number after colon is quarter of year.

---

percent. The other variants from the expansion high point to the recession low point understate the growth rate at 2.8 percent, and from the recession low point to the expansion high point overstate the growth rate at 3.5 percent.

Charting Data Graphically

Data are depicted visually on charts to convey the main points of the statistics, while requiring a minimum effort by the reader. Use of such graphics is related to the adage that "a picture is worth a thousand words." Different types of scales are used on the axes of charts to highlight absolute or relative (percentage) changes in the data: arithmetic scales are used to illustrate absolute changes, and ratio scales are used to illustrate relative changes. These are different measures, and the viewer of graphic data should know which type of scale is used on the chart.

Arithmetic scales have the same distance (for example, as measured in inches) between points when the absolute difference between one set of numeric values is the same as the difference between another set of numeric values, regardless of the size of the numbers. Thus, on an arithmetic scale, the distance between 10 and 100 is the same as the distance between 100 and 190. The absolute difference in both cases is 90. On an arithmetic scale, if the absolute differences from point to point are the same all along the line (for example, each point is ten units higher than the previous point), then the slope of the line is the same between all points. When the absolute differences between two sets of two points are not the same, the slope of the line changes accordingly by becoming more or less steep.

By contrast, ratio (or logarithmic) scales have equal distances when the ratio between one set of two numbers is the same as the ratio between another set of two numbers, regardless of the size of the numbers. In this case, the relative comparison, not the absolute, governs. For example, on a ratio scale, the distance between 10 and 100 is the same as the distance between 100 and 1,000, since the ratio is ten to one in both cases. Thus, on a ratio scale, the slope of the line between 10 and 100 is the same as the slope between 100 and 1,000. When the ratios between two sets of two points are not the same, the slope of the line also changes by becoming more or less steep.

Conventionally, time is shown on the horizontal (x) axis and data values are shown on the vertical (y) axis of the chart. Time—weeks, months, years and so on—is always on an arithmetic scale because there is no reason to vary distances for periods of the same time segments. On the other hand, data values are shown on an arithmetic scale when the analysis emphasizes absolute change, but on a ratio scale when relative change is the primary interest. Because a ratio scale is based on logarithms of the data, a chart in which the horizontal axis of time is an arithmetic scale and the vertical axis of data values is a ratio scale is also called a semilogarithmic (or semilog) chart.

Figures 1.3a and 1.3b illustrate the difference between arithmetic and ratio

Figure 1.3a **Exports of Goods, Arithmetic Scale: 1990–2002**

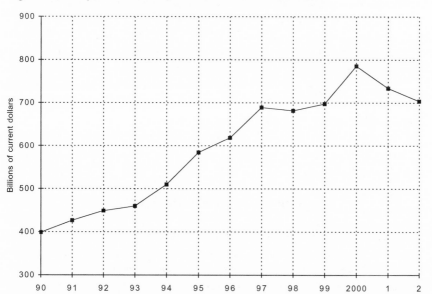

Note: Vertical distance of line indicates yearly absolute change. Periods with the same distance have the same dollar change.

Figure 1.3b **Exports of Goods, Ratio Scale: 1990–2002**

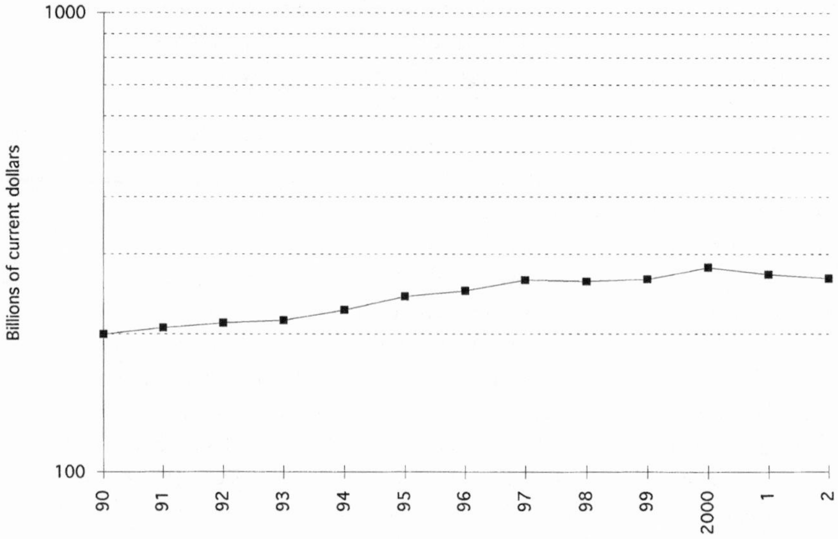

Note: Slope of line indicates yearly relative change. Periods with the same slope have the same percentage change.

scales. They both use goods (as distinct from services) exports data from 1990 to 2001: exports rose from $398.5 billion in 1990 to $733.5 billion in 2001. Although they use the same data, the two graphs are not comparable. The year-to-year changes in Figure 1.3a represent the absolute change, while the year-to-year changes in Figure 1.3b represent the percentage change.

Differences in the two graphs are highlighted by the slopes of the lines. The arithmetic scale would show the same upward slope if the year-to-year *absolute* increase is the same. The ratio scale would show the same upward slope if the year-to-year *relative* (percentage) increase is the same. Both scales show a long-term rising rate of increase, but the relative increase is much steadier in the ratio scale than the absolute increase is in the arithmetic scale.

PRICE-ADJUSTED DOLLARS

Many economic indicators are measured in current and price-adjusted dollars, which refers to the effect of price changes over time. Current dollars represent the actual prices in each period, which over time include the combined effect of changes in quantity and price, and thus represent the *dollar value* of economic activity. For example, the value of retail sales of shoes includes the number of pairs of shoes sold multiplied by their unit prices. By contrast, price-adjusted dollars abstract from price movements from one period to the next, and thus include only the effect of changes in quantity over time, which is the *physical volume* of economic activity. Price-adjusted dollar measures, sometimes referred to as constant dollars, are stated in prices of a particular base period such as 1996 dollars.

In the above example, retail shoe sales in 2004 constant dollars for all years are calculated by dividing the dollar value for each year by the ratio change in prices between 1996 and the actual year. To illustrate, in estimating shoe sales in 2004 in 1996 dollars, if shoe prices rose by 15 percent between 1996 and 2004, the actual dollar value of sales in 1996 is divided by 1.15 to arrive at sales in 1996 dollars. But if shoe prices declined by 5 percent from 1996 to 2004, the dollar value of sales in 2004 is divided by 0.95 for the price-adjusted dollar number. Of course, the current and price-adjusted dollar numbers for 1996 are the same. In practice, these calculations are done separately for various categories of shoe sales such as distinguishing among women's, men's, and children's shoes.

Price-adjusted dollar numbers are difficult to relate to in everyday terms because of price changes since the base period. Thus, in the early 2000s, it is difficult to think of wages or prices in 1996 dollars. But price-adjusted dollars are highly relevant for gauging relative movements over time. In such analyses as rates of economic growth or changes in workers' purchasing power, a measure of quantity (in price-adjusted dollars) rather than a measure of value (in current dollars) is the relevant number. It is far more meaningful to evaluate the percentage change in weekly wages in price-adjusted dollars than in current dollars because of the effect of inflation on purchasing power. While wages may have risen in current dollars from one period to the next, wages may have declined in price-adjusted dollars because the prices of goods and services that workers buy rose more than wages, and consequently workers' purchasing power (i.e., real income) declined.

THE UNDERGROUND ECONOMY

The "underground economy" (UE) refers to income derived from both legal and illegal activities that is not reported or is understated on tax returns and in economic surveys. In addition to raising the federal government budget deficit, the UE raises questions about the accuracy of various economic indicators. Thus, while UE activity is not directly included in economic indicators, it is indirectly included when the derived UE incomes are respent in the measured economy.

Legal sources of income include employment, investments, and income-support programs that are consistent with national and state laws. Illegal income is associated with street drugs, unauthorized gambling and prostitution, theft, fraud, illegal firearms sales, loan-sharking, and many other activities. Economic indicators typically do not reflect illegal activity, either because it is excluded from the definitions used or because, as a matter of reality, it is unlikely to be reported on tax returns and surveys. The exclusion of illegal activity should be remembered when making economic comparisons with other countries in which certain activities banned in the United States are not banned abroad.

Two different methodologies are used to estimate the size of the UE. One uses "direct" measurements—for example, studies of compliance with the income tax laws—in reporting business incomes. The "indirect" approach uses information that suggests attempts to hide income such as the tendency to use cash rather than checks in business transactions. The direct approach is more appealing, although it involves considerable estimating. Estimates of the UE based on the direct method tend to be lower than those based on the indirect technique.

There was a spate of studies on the effect of the UE on economic indicators in the late 1970s and the 1980s.[12] The studies' estimates of how much the UE causes the overall economy to be understated ranged from 1 to 33 percent of the gross national product in these studies. Some observers also concluded that the UE grew faster than what is shown in the published indicators. They raise the point that if the economy was in fact substantially stronger than was apparent in the indicators, fiscal and monetary policies adopted to guide the economy on a path of low unemployment and low inflation were more expansionary than they would have been otherwise, and possibly inflationary.

A basic question is whether the UE has risen over time as a proportion of the measured economy. The above scenario of overstimulating the economy would be more likely if the relative size of the UE increases. But if it hasn't, there is less of a chance of overstimulating the economy because period-to-period movements of economic indicators, which are the basis for formulating economic policies, would at most be only minimally affected by the UE.

The gross domestic product is the only economic indicator that includes at least partial statistical adjustments for UE activity. The adjustments are based on Internal Revenue Service estimates of noncompliance with federal income tax laws by nonfilers of income tax returns and misreporting on income tax returns.[13]

The unemployment rate is another major indicator impacted by the UE, but the effect of the UE is not known. Respondents to household surveys on employment and unemployment may report they are not working, when in fact they do have jobs, either in legal or illegal activities. The effect of this misreporting, which is probably most serious among those whose sole job is in the underground economy and among undocumented foreign workers, is to lower employment and raise the unemployment measures.

A review of the literature on the problem in 1984 concluded that there are no sound estimates of the effect of the underground economy on the unemployment rate.[14] The review did not estimate the effect of misreporting on the official employment and unemployment numbers, but it questioned the validity of other analysts' estimates, such as that the 1978 official unemployment rate was overstated by 1.5 percentage points. The review of the household survey data on employment and unemployment did not substantiate the claims of a significant effect on the unemployment rate.

Incorporating the effects of the UE on economic indicators is difficult. The UE is a disturbing problem that refuses to go away and adds one more uncertainty to interpreting the movements of economic indicators.

In addition, the effects of the UE on the federal government budget deficit are substantial. As of this writing, the latest available estimates of unpaid federal individual income taxes is for 1992. The Internal Revenue Service estimated for 1992 that unpaid individual income taxes associated with legal activities (due to unreported and underreported income, overstated deductions and exemptions, calculation errors, and other factors) was $80 billion, compared with the federal budget deficit of $290 billion.[15] The $80 billion is a net number that represents the gross unpaid taxes of $95 billion minus $15 billion for IRS enforcement costs. The net unpaid taxes for 1985 and 1988 were $58 billion and $64 billion, respectively.

The next IRS estimates of unpaid federal individual income taxes, referred to as the "tax gap," will cover 2001, for which preliminary estimates are planned for early 2004. If the tax gap increased at the same rate from 1992 to 2001 as it did from 1985 to 1992, the 2001 tax gap would be in the neighborhood of $140 billion.

I believe the absence of tax gap estimates between 1992 and 2001 reflects the opposition of some in Congress toward the progressive income tax, and in some instances, to the income tax *per se*. This spills over to opposition to the IRS in its role of collecting income taxes through enforcement of the income tax laws. It resulted in the Congress not funding the taxpayer compliance measurement program (TCMP) for much of the 1990s. The TCMP is the linchpin for the tax gap estimates. The TCMP was funded for the 2001 estimates only. Future funding depends on the Congress and the president.

Beneath the tax gap numbers are the systematic fraudulent schemes by high-income individuals not to pay taxes; reduced resources of the IRS to pursue tax cheaters; and the IRS focus on auditing income tax returns of modest- and low-income individuals that have relatively small amounts of tax cheating and underpayments, to the neglect of auditing and pursuing the vast tax frauds by some wealthy individuals. These weaknesses and attempts to remedy them were noted in a report in 2002 by Charles Rossotti, Commissioner of the Internal Revenue Service. And they were illuminated in 2002 and 2003 in several articles by David Johnston. But there was also a backtracking in 2003 when the IRS focused on making it more difficult for the working poor to apply for the earned-income tax credit in order to prevent errors and cheating.[16]

In addition, the vastness of the tax cheating makes it difficult to fully account for the loss in tax collections, so that the IRS estimates based on the above TCMP data themselves are understated. This reflects the fact that the TCMP data are derived from a random sampling of tax returns for audit, and thus the audits are not specifically targeted at known or suspected problems with taxpayers or nontax payers.

The general problem of tax cheating has been worsened by the political drive to "reign in" the IRS by limiting its funding and enforcement power beginning in the 1980s. Cases of abuse by the IRS in searching out possible tax cheats are not acceptable, and action should be taken to prevent such abuses in the future. But neither should abuses be used as an excuse to deny the IRS sufficient resources and enforcement power to do its job.

It will take many more staff resources and therefore funding for the IRS, plus the political will and direction of the Congress and the president to enforce the tax laws in pursuing wealthy tax cheats, if progress is to be made in closing the tax gap of unpaid taxes.

DISTINCTIONS AMONG "GOODS," "SERVICES," AND "STRUCTURES"

Economic output produced in various industries is classified as goods or services. In some cases the definition is obvious, although the distinctions are sometimes ambiguous. The various industries are coded by number in the North American Industry Classification System.[17]

Goods are three-dimensional products as well as liquid and gas products that may be transported from one location to another. All goods are materials that have a mass. Gases are invisible but they may be stored in a container. Goods are commodities that are produced in the agricultural, mining, and manufacturing industries.

Services are outputs produced in all of the nongoods industries except construction. They are summarized in this negative manner because their heterogeneous nature makes it difficult to describe them with uniform characteristics. While service industries interact with goods industries, services are characterized by something other than goods. Personal, business, finance, insurance, real estate, and professional services industries may facilitate, enhance, or otherwise affect goods production, but they do not directly produce goods. Communication, electric and gas utilities, transportation, and wholesale and retail trade industries are more closely associated with goods products. They are not defined as goods industries, however, for the following reasons: communication and utilities industries are dependent on invisible forms of energy such as radio waves and kilowatts of electric power, and so the output of these industries is not a good; truck, rail, air, ship, and pipeline transportation industries move goods that are produced in agricultural, mining, and manufacturing industries; and wholesale and retail trade industries distribute and market goods that are produced in agricultural, mining, and manufacturing industries.

Structures are residential, commercial, school, hospital, and other buildings, as well as nonbuilding facilities such as roads, bridges, dams, and power plants. Structures are produced in the construction industries. While structures are three-dimensional products, they are not classified as goods because they are built as an integral part of the land and consequently are not moved from place to place.

The three-way classification is governed by the primary activity of the enterprise producing the item or the primary mode of production, rather than by the ultimate use of the item. For example, a bakery that makes bread and sells it to stores for sale to the public is classified as a manufacturing industry, while a bakery that makes bread on the same premises as the store that sells it to the public is classified as a retail trade industry. To take another example, mobile homes are made in factories and thus are classified as manufacturing industry products; although a mobile home is subsequently attached to the ground when it is bought for housing, it nevertheless is defined as a manufactured product rather than as a structure.

THE PRODUCTION OF ECONOMIC STATISTICS

This book describes how macroeconomic indicators are used to analyze movements in the U.S. economy and formulate fiscal and monetary policies to foster economic growth and lower unemployment and inflation. The lifeblood of such analyses is the weekly, monthly, quarterly, annual, and less frequently provided statistical data such as the five-year economic census and the ten-year population census. Most of these statistics are produced by a small group of federal government agencies: Bureau of Labor Statistics in the U.S. Department of Labor, Bureau of the Census and the Bureau of Economic Analysis in the U.S. Department of Commerce, National Agricultural Statistics Service and the Economic Research Service in the U.S. Department of Agriculture, Internal Revenue Service in the U.S. Department of the Treasury, and the Federal Reserve. Spending for the statistical programs of these agencies (excluding the year 2000 population census and the Federal Reserve programs) is estimated at $1.2 billion in fiscal year 2003.[18]

Many private organizations also provide macroeconomic indicators. Examples are: The Conference Board, Stock and Watson Indicator Report, and selected financial firms and trade associations.

The $1.2 billion total for the federal government's statistical programs may seem costly, but the expense cannot be evaluated without considering the importance of quality economic data to successful economic analysis. The most sophisticated analytic techniques are only as good as the data they rely on. Economic data are central in formulating fiscal and monetary policies that affect trillions of dollars of economic output and the lives of hundreds of millions of people. Relevant, credible, and timely economic data that are readily available to the public are essential to the well-being of a democratic nation.

Obtaining increased funding to vitalize statistical data programs is difficult. This reflects the fact that elected officials are generally reluctant to spend money for intangibles that are not readily perceived as making a difference in people's lives. Unlike spending for income maintenance, housing, education, health, environmental, and defense programs, the payback from increased spending for better economic data is not visible. Even though the costs of statistical programs are relatively small, and even though quality statistical data are necessary for effective implementation of civilian and defense programs, neither the public nor elected officials are generally convinced of the need to spend money to maintain, let alone improve, economic statistics. Such resistance is heightened by objections to the reporting and paperwork burden imposed by surveys, and also by the increasing tendency among households and businesses not to respond to surveys.

Making the case for strengthening economic statistics is not easy.[19] The difficulty is intensified by a complaint of economic policymakers that when a new issue arises, relevant data to address it are not readily available. Thus, despite the existing stock of mountains of data, unique problems come up that find the stockpile wanting. This may result from the surprise nature of the problem that was not anticipated, or from a previous awareness of the possibility of the "surprise" event but which was not considered likely to happen.

One way to make the case for needed economic data is for statistical agencies and economic policymakers to convey the needs in concert at the presidential and congressional hearings that plan the budget for the upcoming fiscal year. These budget hearings are instrumental in making decisions on which programs to fund and at what dollar level.

DATA INTEGRITY

Economic indicators are more than "statistics." They are the factual base for public policies and actions that affect the economic well-being of all Americans. It is essential for the vitality of a democracy that these data be impeccably objective, that they be prepared with the highest professional standards, and that they have no hint of political interference. Only with such integrity will the people have confidence in the data. Both the executive branch of government (the president) and the Congress provide economic data that must be protected from political tampering.

Executive Branch

Economic indicators are produced mainly by statistical agencies in the executive branch of the U.S. government that are organized to be insulated from political interference by the presidential administration. The statistical agencies include, but are not limited to, the Bureau of the Census and the Bureau of Economic Analysis in the U.S. Department of Commerce, Bureau of Labor Statistics in the U.S. Department of Labor, National Agricultural Statistics Service in the U.S. Department of Agriculture, Energy Information Administration in the U.S. Department of Energy, Bureau of Justice Statistics in the U.S. Department of Justice, Center for Education Statistics in the U.S. Department of Education, and the Internal Revenue Service in the U.S. Department of the Treasury.

From the 1970s to the early 2000s, there were occasional allegations that the indicators were politicized by "cooking" the preparation of the statistics to make the president who was in office at the time look better. On further examination, these allegations of tampering with the data were shown to be unfounded. Although this is comforting, it still leaves the possibility of future tainting, which must be guarded against. Some data appear to be more vulnerable to "cooking" than others—for example, the estimation of the gross domestic product is based on many different sources of underlying data that involve several statistical judgments that, because the judgments substitute for the absence of concrete data, conceivably could provide opportunities for political officials to pressure the statistical agency to lean in a particular direction. The unemployment rate, in contrast, is based on household survey information that seems less vulnerable to political tampering, but the possibility of tampering exists with all data.

One institutional device for insulating statistical agencies from political pressure is for the head of the agency to be appointed by the president subject to confirmation by the Senate, as is done for the Director of the Census, Commissioner of Labor Statistics, Commissioner of the Internal Revenue Service, Administrator of the Energy Information Administration, and the Commissioner for Education Statistics. This may give the agency heads the appearance, if not the reality, of heightened stature for resisting pressures from their political superiors, which in these cases are the Secretary of Commerce, Secretary of Labor, Secretary of the Treasury, Secretary of Energy, and Secretary of Education, respectively, who in turn take their direction from the president. Senate confirmation probably has greater weight when it is specified for a period of time that does not coincide with the presidential term. At the same time, a career civil service employee probably has more independence than a political official. Thus, to the extent that an agency head who is confirmed by the Senate is a political official, the "independence effect" of the confirmation is diminished. There obviously are no tidy answers.

A second institutional device that may lessen political interference with the data is the practice of statistical agencies of the federal government to limit access to their facilities where the data for major economic indicators are being prepared preceding the day when they are released to the public. During this period, which may last several days, only certain employees of the statistical agency have access to the data. This limited access extends to the day the data are released to the public, when the press and government officials are confined to a room in the agency where the data are stored so they cannot comment on the data before they are released. This practice was originally instituted to prevent leaks of unpublished data that give recipients of leaks an unfair advantage in financial markets, but it could have a secondary benefit of fending off attempts of political officials to interfere with the data preparation. On the other hand, the argument can be made that if many people know a number ahead of time, a political appointee could not have the number changed without causing a scandal; but if only a few people know the number, the political appointee could conceivably use some leverage (for example, the threat of funding cuts) to get them to change the number. Again, there are no tidy answers.

There is one exception to this restriction on preventing the disclosure of economic indicators before they are released to the public. This is the authorized disclosure of economic indicators by the heads of the statistical agencies to the president through the Council of Economic Advisers when the data are ready but before they are publicly released.[20] The council is then permitted to distribute the data to other parties. In practice, this pre-release of the data to the Council of Economic Advisers occurs in the late afternoon of the day before the indicators are released, and the council then distributes the data to the chair of the Federal Reserve Board and to the Secretary of the Treasury, as well as to the president and the vice president. This is a possible fissure in preventing the politicization of the data, although to my knowledge, no instances of such tampering have come to light.

Another prong for protecting the integrity of the data is the publicity offered by an active press.

Credibility of Economic Data and Economic-Related Data Questioned

To illustrate the sensitivity of economic data and economic-related data, five examples are noted here of questions raised concerning the politicization of the data: (a) employment statistics prepared by the U.S. Department of Labor, (b) gross domestic product statistics prepared by the U.S. Department of Commerce, (c) crime statistics prepared by the U.S. Department of Justice, (d) education statistics prepared by the U.S. Department of Education, and (e) federal budget forecasts prepared by the Congressional Budget Office.

Employment Statistics

In February and March 1971, with the release of the monthly employment and unemployment numbers by the Bureau of Labor Statistics (BLS), the BLS spokesperson at the monthly press briefings was less positive about the significance of changes in the employment and unemployment data than the Secretary of Labor was in press releases. Shortly thereafter, the secretary terminated press briefings by the BLS, which resulted in allegations of politicizing the statistics. With the termination of the press briefings, the Joint Economic Committee of Congress began holding monthly hearings with the Commissioner of Labor Statistics on the day the employment and unemployment numbers are released. These hearings have continued as a permanent routine with the release of the monthly data on employment and unemployment.

Subsequent reviews of the termination by two congressional committees, the House Committee on Government Operations and the Committee on the Post Office and Civil Service, concluded in reports that there was no evidence of tampering with the data, but warned of the need to maintain the objectivity of the data and the public confidence and credibility in the statistics. The Committee on Government Operations also concluded that the reasons given for terminating the BLS press briefings were unpersuasive and recommended that the briefings be immediately reinstituted.[21] But the briefings were not reinstituted, and the Joint Economic Committee has continued its monthly hearings with the BLS Commissioner to the present time.

Gross Domestic Product Statistics

In the fall of 1992, in the context of the presidential election of that year, it was alleged that the estimates of the economic growth rate of the real GDP for the third quarter of the year that were released on October 27, the week before Election Day, were overstated.[22] According to the press report in note 22, officials of the Bureau of Economic Analysis of the U.S. Department of Commerce, which prepares the GDP estimates, met with reporters from the *New York Times* and the *Wall Street Journal* two weeks after the election to detail the preparation of the GDP estimates. The government officials denied tampering with the data, and also described the system for examining and cross-checking suspicious data for consistency.

The allegations of "cooking" the data, which were reported in the press before and after the election, were based on forecasts by some private forecasters that the GDP growth rate for the third quarter of 1992 (which comprises July, August, and September) would be lower than the official estimate that was subsequently published. But there was no consensus among private forecasters, as others had predicted a higher growth rate than the official estimates.

The following elaborates the context and aftermaths of the incident based on my June 2003 discussion with Robert Parker, who was the associate director for national economic accounts in the U.S. Bureau of Economic Analysis (BEA) in 1992, and in later years its chief statistician. The allegations arose because the assumptions that BEA used in preparing the GDP estimates were released to the public one day after the estimates were published. The allegation of over-statement was made on the day the data were released, and was based on sup-positions regarding certain assumptions. When the assumptions were released the following day, there was no specific criticism of the assumptions. While the assumptions were not normally released until the following day (sometimes with a two-day delay), they were available the previous day with the GDP release, if requested. As a result of the problem caused by the one-day delay, BEA changed its practice to release the assumptions on the day the GDP estimates were released.[23]

The subsequent revisions of the third quarter 1992 GDP estimates over the years gave changing patterns of which political party gained an advantage from the pre-election estimates. The initial allegation was that the growth rate had been overstated, favoring the Republicans, who occupied the White House at the time. Subsequent interim revisions lowered the growth rate, which favored the Democrats. The ultimate benchmark revisions reverted close to the initial estimates as being the most accurate.

No formal investigation of tampering was conducted. Also, no evidence emerged at the time or up to this writing in the summer of 2003 of tampering with the data in 1992.

On balance, I believe the above institutional mechanisms of Senate confir-mation of statistical agency heads and of limiting access to the data preparation through the limited access procedure lessen the chances that economic indicators can be compromised. But no system is foolproof when there is a determination to violate it. Thus, these and future measures to protect the integrity of data will reduce, but not eliminate, attempts to contaminate the data for political gain.

Therefore, it is essential that the press and analysts be vigilant in safeguard-ing the integrity of the statistics and sound the alarm when they believe the data may be undermined. This is added insurance for maintaining accurate infor-mation, which is a bulwark of a free, democratic society.

Crime Statistics

In the summer of 2002, two planned changes were reported in the press for the collection and release of crime statistics by the Bureau of Justice Statistics in the U.S. Department of Justice that raised the possibility of political tampering with the data.[24] One is the use of private contractors, euphemistically "outsourc-ing," in the production of crime statistics. The other is the requirement for questions on crime statistics by the press to be forwarded to a Department of Justice public affairs officer for response. While crime statistics are not strictly "economic" data, they have important economic causes and consequences, and therefore are included in this discussion.

As of June 1, 2003, the Justice Department had not put out the contracting of producing crime statistics for private bids. Also as of June 1, 2003, reporters still had direct access to the statisticians in the Bureau of Justice Statistics.

The use of private contractors for producing crime statistics is highly questionable because of their potential susceptibility to politicizing the data by casting the data in a particular light in order to obtain contracts. The lack of direct access of reporters to statisticians limits the benefits of public oversight on attempts to make the data more favorable to the president who is in office at the time. In addition, it would be a huge step backward for maintaining the integrity of the data to have the collection and/or preparation of economic indicators or crime statistics done by private contractors.

Education Statistics

The Commissioner of the Center for Education Statistics in the U.S. Department of Education has long been appointed by the president subject to confirmation by the Senate. A presidential appointment confirmed by the Senate is one institutional method for insulating statistical agencies from political pressure and thus maintaining the integrity of the data, as noted previously.

However, in 2002, legislation was introduced in both houses of Congress that would end the appointment of the Commissioner for Education Statistics by the president and confirmation by the Senate. The proposed legislation was defeated in Congress in 2002, and so the Commissioner for Education Statistics continues to be appointed by the president and confirmed by the Senate. In the congressional debate on the proposed change, opponents of the proposal saw it as a breach of the political independence of the commissioner and thus as a threat to the integrity of education data.[25] The administration did not submit a formal proposal to Congress to end the appointment of the commissioner by the president subject to Senate confirmation. But as I looked into this episode, it became clear that the Department of Education, which is an arm of the administration, was behind the proposal, and got members of Congress to introduce it in education bills in the House of Representatives and in the Senate.

Education data have been politicized by both political parties, as noted by Gerald Bracey and by Diane Ravitch and Chester Finn.[26] While having the Commissioner for Education Statistics appointed by the president and confirmed by the Senate does not insure the objectivity of the data, with the history of education data being distorted, it is essential to maintain this institutional safeguard. When a presidential nominee for commissioner is ideological and partisan, it is only in the Senate confirmation process that this potential for undermining the objectivity of the data can be effectively exposed and rejected.

Education data are not strictly economic. But through their impact on education, and through education's impact on the quality of the workforce, education data are basic to the economic vitality of the nation. Education data should be protected from all attempts to undermine their objectivity.

Congressional Budget Office

While the executive branch of government provides the bulk of economic statistics, economic data are also provided by congressional offices, such as the Congressional Budget Office (CBO). The CBO was created by the Congressional Budget and Control Act of 1974 and began operating in 1975. The CBO described its mission as follows: "CBO's mission is to provide the Congress with the objective, timely, and nonpartisan analyses needed for budget and economic decisions and with the information and estimates required for the congressional budget process."[27] The key words in this mission statement in terms of data integrity are "objective" and "nonpartisan." And the CBO has adhered impeccably to the objective, nonpartisan standards throughout its existence, which in 2003 is into the twenty-ninth year. I have used CBO analyses in this book with the confidence that they represent high-quality substantive work and high integrity.

A threat to the CBO's integrity occurred in 2003, when Congress appointed a new director of CBO for the purpose of making budget projections with a methodology referred to as "dynamic scoring." This methodology incorporates assumed incentive and disincentive effects of tax decreases and tax increases, respectively, on economic growth. It differs from using only the direct revenue effects of changes in the tax laws, which had been the long-standing CBO methodology. Under dynamic scoring, the decreased revenues from a tax cut would be lessened by the greater economic growth and incomes from the incentive effects, resulting in less of a revenue loss than would be estimated only using the direct measure of tax reductions in projecting revenues in future years. On the other hand, a tax increase would result in less tax revenues than would be expected if estimates of tax revenues were limited to a direct measure of the increase, because lower economic growth and incomes from the disincentive effects would lessen the revenue gain in projecting revenues in future years.

The problem with dynamic scoring is that the incentive and disincentive effects of tax changes on economic growth are difficult to quantify, and the subject of considerable disagreement among economists. Thus, by injecting dynamic scoring into the tax revenue projections, the objective, nonpartisan mission of the CBO is compromised. Specifically, dynamic scoring politicizes the budget process, as it is a way of obtaining congressional support for proposed tax cuts and obtaining congressional opposition to proposed tax increases.

The first CBO use of dynamic scoring occurred in March 2003, when it used several different models of direct revenue and dynamic scoring methodologies in projecting the revenue effects ten years into the future of the tax cuts proposed to be enacted into law in 2003. These various projections actually showed little difference in their revenue effects.[28]

The first exercise in using dynamic scoring for estimating the effects of proposed tax cuts on future tax revenues showed little difference in the alternative methodologies. But the future use of dynamic scoring raises the possibility of strong pressure from elected members of Congress on the Congressional Budget Office, when the political party in the majority in Congress favors tax cuts, to provide budget projections that endorse the party's agenda. This undermines the objective, nonpartisan mission of the CBO, which has been a major advance in the preparation of the U.S. budget, and in developing legislation associated with the budget. It also raises the appearance of partisanship in other studies the CBO conducts in the future. Dynamic scoring should be discontinued in order to preserve the integrity of the CBO.

REVIEW QUESTIONS

- How does the United States depoliticize the determination of when a recession begins and ends?
- Can the designation of a recession period be objective if no fixed formulas are used for determining the beginning and ending points of a recession?
- How do growth cycles supplement business cycles in analyzing current economic movements?
- If monthly or quarterly data are not seasonally adjusted, "seasonal" comparisons are sometimes made between the current month or quarter and the corresponding year-earlier period. What are the limitations of this approach?
- Index numbers are a convenient way to summarize masses of data, but they also have an inherent "product mix" problem. Explain the problem.
- What is a sound way of accounting for upcoming data revisions in analyzing current economic movements?
- What is the problem with a statistical survey on which an economic indicator is based for which a sampling error cannot be calculated?
- How can the phase of a business cycle distort the calculation of long-term growth rates?
- Is the divergence between the current dollar and price-adjusted dollar measures of an economic indicator greater during periods of stable or rising prices?

- Why is the underground economy an issue in analyzing economic indicators?
- How do goods industries differ from service industries in their use of transportation facilities?
- Why is the production of economic indicators an issue for economic analysis?
- If there is no foolproof way of preventing the preparation of economic indicators from being politicized, what recourse does the public have?

NOTES

1. For examples of recent interpretations, see Jeffrey C. Fuhrer and Scott Schuh, editors, *Beyond Shocks: What Causes Business Cycles?* Conference Proceedings, Federal Reserve Bank of Boston, June 1998; and Victor Zarnowitz, "Theory and History Behind Business Cycles: Are the 1990s the Onset of a Golden Age?" *Journal of Economic Perspectives,* Spring 1999.
2. Victor Zarnowitz, *Business Cycles: Theory, History, Indicators, and Forecasting* (University of Chicago Press, 1992), chs. 2 and 8.
3. The role of the NBER Business Cycle Dating Committee raises basic questions about the definition of a recession and the role of the committee in determining when a recession begins and ends. See Edward Steinberg, "Who Says the Recession Is Over?" *New Haven Register,* August 21, 2003, p. A4.

    First, when over 9 million people are unemployed, as they were in June and July 2003, with an unemployment rate of over 6 percent, those workers would probably find the word "recovery" to describe the economy as irrelevant. Is there a threshold level of unemployment above which a new definition is needed? Many unemployed workers in 2003 probably view the period as a recession. To economists, a frequently used term is jobless recovery (see chapter 8 under Jobless Recoveries of 1991–92 and 2002–03). *Perhaps jobless recovery or some variant should be given a statistical foundation similar to the different phases of the business cycle discussed in this section.*

    Second, the committee's designation of cyclical turning points becomes part of analyses and forecasts of the economy, which then become part of economic policy formulations that influence macroeconomic growth, employment, and price movements. This is a lot of power given to a panel of experts.
4. Geoffrey H. Moore, *Business Cycles, Inflation and Forecasting,* 2d ed. (Ballinger, 1983), pp. 3–9.
5. Michael P. Niemira and Philip A. Klein, *Forecasting Financial and Economic Cycles* (Wiley, 1994), p. 262.
6. In a conversation with the author, Victor Zarnowitz, who is a member of the NBER Business Cycle Dating Committee, said this was his recollection of the committee's deliberations. He also noted that the dating of the pre-World War II recovery from the depression trough in March 1933 to the peak in May 1937 as a separate business cycle phase was an exception to this guideline, because economic activity at the May 1937 peak was below that at the peak of the previous expansion in August 1929. Following the May 1937 peak, the economy turned down into a recession in June 1937 that culminated at the trough in June 1938.

    (Subsequent to this conversation, revised real gross domestic product data showed that GDP in 1936 was back to the 1929 level, and that in 1937 and 1938, which spanned the 1937–38 recession, GDP exceeded the 1929 levels in both years on an annual basis. The depression year GDP data are available only for annual data. See chapter 3 under Trends Before and After World War II and endnote 6.)

7. Robert D. Hershey, Jr., "This Just In: Recession Ended 21 Months Ago," *New York Times*, December 23, 1992, p. D1.

8. Business Cycle Dating Committee, National Bureau of Economic Research, "The NBER's Recession Dating Procedure," August 26, 2003 (www.nber.org/cycles/recessions.html).

9. Zarnowitz, *Business Cycles*, ch. 7.

10. Christina D. Romer, "Spurious Volatility in Historical Unemployment Data," *Journal of Political Economy*, February 1986; idem, "Is the Stabilization of the Postwar Economy a Figment of the Data?" *American Economic Review*, June 1986; idem, "New Estimates of Prewar Gross National Product and Unemployment," *Journal of Economic History*, June 1986. See also David R. Weir, "The Reliability of Historical Macroeconomic Data for Comparing Cyclical Stability," *Journal of Economic History*, June 1986; Stanley Lebergott, "Discussion," *Journal of Economic History*, June 1986.
The Weir and Lebergott articles are rejoinders to Romer, all three being in the *JEH*. See also Zarnowitz, *Business Cycles*, pp. 77–79, 89, 91, 363.

11. Zarnowitz, *Business Cycles*, Note 2, p. 262.

12. Bureau of International Labor Affairs, U.S. Department of Labor, *The Underground Economy in the United States*, September 1992.

13. Bureau of Economic Analysis, U.S. Department of Commerce, "Improved Estimates of the National Income and Product Accounts for 1959–95: Results of the Comprehensive Revision," *Survey of Current Business*, January/February 1996, pp. 24–25. See also Internal Revenue Service, U.S. Department of the Treasury, *Federal Compliance Research: Individual Income Tax Gap Estimates for 1985, 1988, and 1992*, April 1996.

14. Richard J. McDonald, "The 'underground economy' and BLS statistical data," *Monthly Labor Review*, January 1984.

15. Internal Revenue Service, *Federal Compliance Research*, note 13.

16. Charles O. Rossotti, Commissioner of the Internal Revenue Service, "Report to the IRS Oversight Board: Assessment of the IRS and the Tax System," September 2002; David Cay Johnston, "Hunting Tax Cheats, IRS Vows to Focus More Effort on the Rich," *New York Times*, September 13, 2002, p. A1. In referring to the reporting in previous articles on the IRS in the spring of 2002, Johnston noted that "the agency was looking for tax cheating by wage earners far more carefully than by those whose income comes from their own businesses and investments, which usually provide much greater opportunity to cheat. Other articles showed that the working poor are audited far more often than high-income taxpayers." Idem, "IRS Closes Loophole That Let Rich Hide Income," *New York Times*, September 26, 2002, p. C1; idem, "U.S. Proposes Regulations to Restrict Some Tax Shelters for High-Income People," *New York Times*, October 18, 2002, p. C2; idem, "New Rules Order Companies to Disclose Offshore Moves," *New York Times*, November 13, 2002, p. C2; idem, "Pension Fund to Press Issue of Corporate Offshore Homes," *New York Times*, November 17, 2002, p. 29; idem, "I.R.S. Seeks Injunction Against Income-Tax Resister," *New York Times*, March 14, 2003; idem, "I.R.S. Seeking Buyers' Names in Tax Shelters," *New York Times*, June 20, 2003, p. C1; idem, "U.S. Moves Against Promoter of Tax-Avoidance Maneuver," *New York Times*, June 20, 2003, p. C 14. The backtracking is in idem, "I.R.S. Tightening Rules for Low-Income Tax Credit," *New York Times*, April 25, 2003, p. A1.

17. Office of Management and Budget, Executive Office of the President, "1997 North

American Industry Classification System—1987 Standard Industrial Classification Replacement," *Federal Register*, April 9, 1997.

18. Office of Management and Budget, Executive Office of the President, *Statistical Programs of the United States Government: Fiscal Year 2003*, 2002.

19. An analogy can be made with the difficulty of making a convincing case for funding scientific research, which also is often seen to have limited practical application.

20. Office of Management and Budget, Executive Office of the President, "Statistical Policy Directive No. 3: Compilation, Release, and Evaluation of Principal Economic Indicators," *Federal Register*, September 25, 1985.

21. Joseph P. Goldberg and William T. Moye, *The First Hundred Years of the Bureau of Labor Statistics*, Bulletin 2235, Bureau of Labor Statistics, U.S. Department of Labor, September 1985, pp. 221–26.

22. Robert D. Hershey, Jr., "U.S. Officials Defend Data on Economy," *New York Times*, November 19, 1992, p. C8.

23. The provision by the Bureau of Economic Analysis of timely statements of the judgments used in preparing the gross domestic product estimates was a major recommendation of the *Gross National Product Data Improvement Project Report*. See Report of the Advisory Committee on Gross National Product Data Improvement, *Gross National Product Data Improvement Project Report*, Office of Federal Statistical Policy and Standards, U.S. Department of Commerce, October 1977, p. 8.

24. Fox Butterfield, "Some Experts Fear Political Influence on Crime Data Agencies," *New York Times*, September 22, 2002, p. 23.

25. Lisa Fine Goldstein, "Senate Panel Passes Federal Research Bill," *Education Week*, October 2, 2002.

26. Gerald W. Bracey, "Media and Public Misrepresentation of Public Education," *Best Practices, Best Thinking, and Emerging Issues in School Leadership*, ed. by William A. Owings and Leslie S. Kaplan (Corwin Press, 2003); and Diane Ravitch and Chester E. Finn, Jr., "Time to Save Federal Education Data," *Education Week*, October 15, 2002.

27. Congressional Budget Office, *The Congressional Budget Office: Who We Are and What We Do*, n.d., p. 2.

28. Edmund L. Andrews, "Study Says Tax Cuts Will Make Deficit Soar," *New York Times*, March 26, 2003, p. A12. See also U.S. House of Representatives, Committee on the Budget, *Congressional Budget Office's Analysis of the President's Fiscal Year 2004 Budget*, Committee Hearings of the U.S. House of Representatives, March 25, 2003.

2

Framework for Macroeconomic Analysis and Policies

This chapter provides an overview of how the economic indicators discussed in the following chapters are interrelated for use in analyzing and forecasting the economy. The relationships are limited to the most "macro" indicators. This has the virtue of giving a concise view of the forest from the trees, with fairly extensive explanations of the interrelationships between indicators. The chapter briefly notes the substance of each indicator. Subsequent chapters explain the meaning of these and other indicators, and how their movements shed light on the strengths and weaknesses of the economy. The later chapters give a more complete view of how economists analyze and forecast the economy. Thus, the reader starts in this chapter with a top-down orientation to the indicators as a group, which gives a context for proceeding through the entire book.

Statistical relationships between certain economic indicators are generally, but not always, consistent with theoretical notions of what the relationships are thought to be, such as between economic growth and unemployment, inflation and unemployment, and interest rates and economic growth. These relationships are attempts to summarize the effect of underlying factors that drive the economy but which are not fully understood. They are proxies for complex interrelationships affecting domestic and international commodity, service, labor, and financial markets; impacts of economic and political actions of governments on the economy; and the psychological moods of optimism and pessimism among households and businesses.

This chapter has two main components. The analytic section provides a system for assessing the direction and momentum of the economy. The policy section covers the role of fiscal, monetary, and incomes policies.

ANALYTIC SYSTEM

The system for evaluating recent and long-term economic movements is based on analyzing the following interrelationships of economic indicators and policies: economic growth vs. unemployment; unemployment vs. inflation; interest rates vs. economic growth; and fiscal, monetary, and incomes policies.

Economic growth represents trends in the output of goods and services in the overall economy. It is a key factor affecting unemployment: rapid economic growth lowers unemployment, and slow or negative growth raises unemployment. The relationship between economic growth and unemployment compares economic growth, as reflected by movements in the real gross domestic product, to changes in the unemployment rate, with the constraint that rapid economic growth not lead to rising price inflation. The relationship is referred to as "Okun's Law," after Arthur Okun, who developed it in the 1960s.[1]

Okun's Law and the NAIRU

There is more than one methodological formulation of Okun's Law. One way to view it is to break it into three aspects: (a) the break-even point, which indicates the economic growth rate required for maintaining a stable unemployment rate, (b) the unemployment effects of growth rates above and below the break-even point, and (c) the constraint of limiting the pace of economic growth so that price inflation does not accelerate. As noted above, economic growth is represented by the price-adjusted gross domestic product (real GDP). Unemployment is defined as the number of persons without jobs who are available for and actively seeking work. The unemployment rate (UR) is the percentage that unemployed persons are of the labor force; the labor force is the sum of employed and unemployed persons. The inflation rate is the consumer price index (CPI). Chapters 3, 9, and 11 detail the gross domestic product, unemployment, and inflation concepts and measures, respectively.

The break-even point can be understood with the following example. Assume the UR is 6 percent, the labor force grows by 1 percent per year, and labor productivity (output per worker) increases 2 percent annually. Then the real GDP must grow by at least 3 percent annually to absorb 94 percent of the labor force growth and thus maintain the UR of 6 percent.

The break-even point in the early 2000s is approximated at an annual real GDP growth rate of 2 percent. At the 2 percent rate, the UR tends to be stable. And for every percentage point of annual GDP growth above or below 2 percent, the UR tends to decrease (increase) by 0.5 percentage point over the year. In addition, at the 2 percent real GDP growth rate, the CPI may increase from period to period, but the rate of increase does not accelerate.

Okun's Law is based initially on the concept of the gap between the actual GDP output of goods and services and the potential output of goods and services. The gap represents the difference in total levels of output in a period as well as changes in the gap from period to period. The potential GDP is determined by the labor hours worked by employed persons, the accumulation of capital equipment and structures used in production, and the combination of all other factors not accounted for by the labor input and the capital facilities components.[2] The latter "all other" category is referred to as multifactor productivity or total factor productivity, and includes but is not limited to skills and work effort of workers, executive direction and managerial abilities, technology, and the quality of materials (see chapter 10 on productivity). This potential GDP measure is then cyclically adjusted to remove the shorter-term effects of the business cycle when the actual labor, capital, and multifactor productivity components are above or below the long-term trend. In addition, as part of the methodology, potential output represents the maximum level of activity the economy can sustain without causing inflation to accelerate. Stated differently, potential output is associated with a steady rate of inflation, though the inflation rate may decelerate at potential output.

To accommodate the inflation restraint, Okun's Law is linked to an inflation restraint called the nonaccelerating inflation rate of unemployment (NAIRU). The NAIRU is based on the expected future rate of inflation, and is not tied to any specific rate of inflation. This means the same NAIRU can exist at different rates of inflation, depending on the economic environment at a particular time. The corollary is that when unemployment exceeds the NAIRU, the rate of inflation tends to decrease, and when unemployment drops below the NAIRU, the rate of inflation tends to increase.

The theory is associated with changes in a business's costs of production, with higher production costs being passed on in higher prices for the items the business sells, and modest or even declining production costs leading to smaller price increases or even price decreases. Thus, when the economy is robust and unemployment relatively low, businesses use more of their older, outmoded, and less efficient equipment and structures facilities, and the shortage of workers may lead to a bidding up of wage rates faster than increases in worker productivity. The resultant higher production costs will lead to higher prices unless businesses absorb the higher costs in lower profit margins. By contrast, when the economy is slack and unemployment is relatively high, production costs tend to rise slowly, if at all, because of zero or small increases in worker wage rates (and in some cases wage cuts), and because the underutilization of existing capital facilities of structures and equipment allows businesses to use the more modern and efficient of their capital facilities rather than the older, outmoded, and less efficient facilities. Consequently, there is little likelihood of accelerating inflation.

Figure 2.1 shows the GDP/UR relationship from 1960 to 2002. Each black diamond represents the intersection of the GDP growth rate and the UR for a year, and the line of white diamonds is the long-term average relationship based on a linear statistical regression. The concept reflects a long-term average inverse relationship: as the GDP increases at sufficient rates, the UR falls, and vice

Figure 2.1 **Okun's Law: 1960–2002**

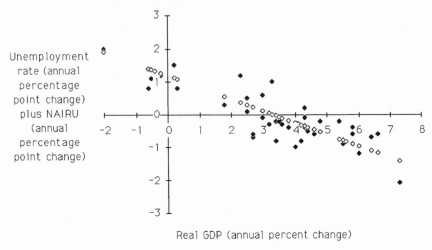

Real GDP (annual percent change)

| • Real GDP & unemployment rate   ◦ Long-term average (linear |
| yearly intersection   regression) |

Note: Based on U.S. Bureau of Economic Analysis, U.S. Bureau of Labor Statistics, and Congressional Budget Office data.

versa. Graphically, this appears in the direction of the straight line that slopes downward to the right. When the relationship departs from the theory, such as when the GDP increases but at a lower rate than the break-even point associated with a stable UR, both the GDP and the UR increase.

Two caveats are in order when using Okun's Law to analyze the current economy. First, the law changes over time. For example, the break-even point in the early 1980s was a real GDP growth rate of about 3 percent annually, compared with 2 percent in the early 2000s, and the change in the annual UR for every percentage point of annual real GDP growth above or below the break-even point is about 0.5 percentage point in the early 2000s. The decline in the break-even point resulted in large part from the declining proportion of the labor force made up by teens (16–19 years old) in the labor force, who have very high unemployment rates.

Second, the break-even numbers are multiyear average relationships that typically do not hold in any single year. This is apparent in Figure 2.1, which shows that most years diverge from the long-term average relationship, being either above or below the long-term line. This divergence results from the fact that GDP growth is driven by employment, hours worked, and productivity, none of which necessarily moves in tandem with the UR.

With these caveats, Okun's Law provides an overall perspective for linking economic growth and unemployment. In assessing these trends, the analyst should observe special conditions that may cause a large divergence from the long-term trend for particular years. In addition, the break-even point should be reviewed every few years to determine if there are significant changes (attributable to changes in the growth rate of the labor force and/or productivity) that should be brought into the analysis.

NAIRU's Evolving Characteristics

Changing economic environments have resulted in fluctuating NAIRU estimates over time. While analysts differ on the specific NAIRU for any particular time period, these variations typically are within a range of one percentage point, and the changes estimated in the NAIRU by various analysts from one period to the next are typically in the same direction. Thus, NAIRU estimates rose from a range of 3 to 4 percent in the 1960s to 6 to 7 percent in the 1970s, and then declined to 5 to 6 percent by the mid-1990s and to 5 percent in the early 2000s.

These fluctuations are ascribed mainly to the rising teenage share of the labor force that peaked in the late 1970s, and subsequently declined into the early 2000s. Because teens (16–19 years old) have a higher UR than other workers, a rising teenage share of the labor force tends to raise the NAIRU, while a declining teenage share of the labor force tends to lower the NAIRU. In 2002, when the UR for all workers was 5.8 percent, for workers aged 20 years and older it was 4.9 percent, and the UR for teenage workers was 16.5 percent. The teen share of the labor force declined from 8.8 percent in 1980 to 5.2 percent in 2001.

A much smaller effect has been attributed to the increase in working women, whose UR before the 1980s was typically in a range of 1.0 to 1.5 percentage points higher than that for men, though in some years the differential was below or above this range. But from the 1980s to the early 2000s, the differential disappeared, with men having higher URs in some years and women having higher URs in other years. Within these year-to-year variations, there is a general pattern of men's URs being lower than women's URs when the economy is robust and jobs are easier to find, and of women's URs being lower than men's URs during recessions and when the economy is growing slowly and jobs are harder to find. This pattern exists because recessions have a disproportionate effect on industries (such as auto production) whose work forces are predominately male. The depiction of long-term demographic shifts in the labor force dominating the NAIRU is a widely accepted view, although not universal, as seen in Geoffrey Tootell's analysis.[3]

In addition, a combination of institutional factors appears to have lowered the NAIRU by about one percentage point in the 1990s.[4] These include the increased prison population, increased use of temporary labor, the effect of welfare reform, and the increased use of the Internet for job searches.

The decline in working teenagers noted above followed the decreasing number of children under 5 years old in the 1960s and 1970s. The under-5-year-old population rose modestly in the 1980s and the mid-1990s, and then declined through 2000.[5] Based on these demographic trends, the break-even point in Okun's Law of 2 percent in real GDP growth in the early 2000s will, in the next decade or so, rise from an increase in the number of teen workers only if the relatively stable number of children under 5 years old is bolstered by increasing numbers of immigrant children who subsequently enter the labor force as 16–19 year olds.

NAIRU estimates are discussed further below under Fiscal Policy: Structural Budget and under Monetary Policy.

Unemployment vs. Inflation: Phillips Curve

The most direct measure of the relationship between unemployment and inflation is the Phillips Curve. It is named for A.W. Phillips, who in the 1950s assessed the relationship between unemployment and wage rates in England over a 100–year period. It showed a generally inverse relationship (although not one-to-one) with lower unemployment raising wages and higher unemployment lowering wages.[6] In today's analyses, the wage-rate component has been replaced by prices, but the Phillips Curve encompasses the same concept as the original formulation. The shift to prices reflects the fact that wages are an important cost of production that affects prices, as businesses aim to maintain or increase profit margins.

The Phillips Curve is a graph that depicts the idea of an inverse relationship between unemployment and inflation: as unemployment decreases, inflation increases, and vice versa. The reason is that declining unemployment leads to higher production costs, as less-productive workers are employed and more outmoded and inefficient machinery is used. Also, when unemployment is low or declining, unions and workers generally tend to get higher wage increases because they are in a stronger bargaining position. Conversely, when unemployment is high or rising, wages and production costs increase more slowly or may even decline.

In addition, changes in the position of the Phillips Curve indicate if the unemployment-inflation long-term tradeoff has improved or worsened between two periods. The tradeoff improves when unemployment in both the past and current periods is unchanged and inflation lessens in the current period. The tradeoff worsens when unemployment is unchanged in both periods and inflation increases in the current period. Chapters 9 and 11 focus on unemployment and inflation, respectively.

Figures 2.2a through 2.2e show Phillips Curve trends for approximate decades of the 1950s through the early 2000s. The UR is shown one year before the change in the CPI on the premise that changes in the UR do not immediately affect prices—for example, changes in the UR in 2000 affect the CPI in 2001.

The figures differ from other formulations of the Phillips Curve in two ways. First, earlier depictions of the Phillips Curve consolidate longer periods of several decades in one time frame. The breakdown by decade is used here because distinct differences appear in the decade-by-decade relationships. Second, a commonly used version is referred to as the "expectations-augmented Phillips Curve."[7] It assumes a shifting Phillips Curve that links different rates of economic growth based on the real gross domestic product to the "short-run expected change in the rate of inflation," and compares that with the "long-run correct expectations of inflation." By contrast, Figures 2.2a through 2.2e show the actual year-to-year changes in the unemployment/inflation relationship.

The figures conform to the concept of a trade-off between unemployment and inflation when the long-term average line of the yearly white diamonds slopes downward to the right. This theoretical inverse relationship was most evident in the 1960s, though it was a more extreme vertical version in the latter part of the decade with the accelerating inflation. Experience was contrary to

Figure 2.2a **Phillips Curve: 1950–59**

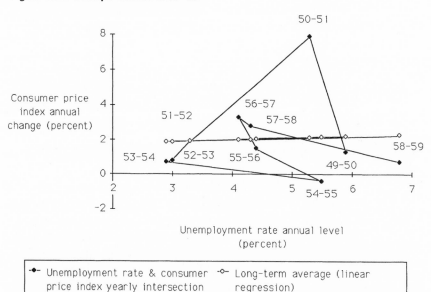

Note: Unemployment rate of previous year corresponds to CPI change of current year (e.g., UR 1958 and CPI 1959).

Figure 2.2b **Phillips Curve: 1960–69**

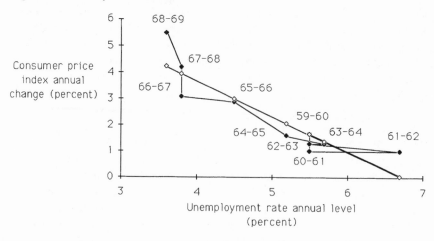

Note: Unemployment rate of previous year corresponds to CPI change of current year (e.g., UR 1968 and CPI 1969).

Figure 2.2c **Phillips Curve: 1970–79**

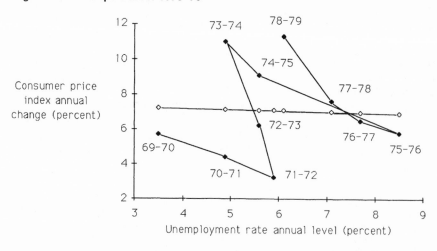

Note: Unemployment rate of previous year corresponds to CPI change of current year (e.g., UR 1978 and CPI 1979).

Figure 2.2d **Phillips Curve: 1980–89**

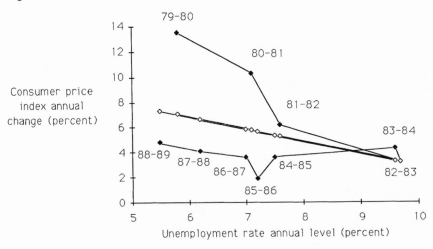

Note: Unemployment rate of previous year corresponds to CPI change of current year (e.g., UR 1988 and CPI 1989).

Figure 2.2e **Phillips Curve: 1990–2002**

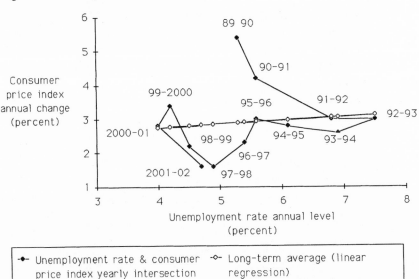

Note: Unemployment rate of previous year corresponds to CPI change of current year (e.g., UR 2001 and CPI 2002).

the theory in the 1950s, 1970s, and 1990s to early 2000s, when there was a slight direct relationship (upward-sloping line to the right). In addition, the unemployment/inflation tradeoff worsened during the 1970s, as the Phillips Curve continually shifted to the right from the early 1970s to the late 1970s, with both unemployment and inflation rising. A generally inverse relationship appeared in the 1980s, with the trade-off improving over the decade as the curve shifted to the left. A slight direct relationship appeared in the 1990s to early 2000s (long-term average line sloping upward to the right), although several subperiods showed an inverse relationship. The trade-off improved over the period, as the curve shifted to the left, similar to the experience of the 1980s.

Given the half century of significant, and even momentus, political and economic events that underlie this depiction, in retrospect it would be exceptional if the Phillips Curve had not varied considerably over five decades from the 1950s to the early 2000s. A simple listing of the events speaks for itself: the cold war and post-cold war periods; the Korean, Vietnam, and Persian Gulf wars; the Arab oil embargo, Iranian revolution, and emergence of the Organization of Petroleum Exporting Countries (OPEC) cartel; the civil rights, women's, and environmental revolutions; long-term economic growth peaking in the 1960s, and decelerating in the subsequent decades; varying cyclical recession periods, with three recessions in the 1950s, one recession in the 1960s, and one beginning at the end of the decade, two recessions and accelerating inflation in the 1970s, two back-to-back recessions in the 1980s with the second being the most serious one since the depression of the 1930s, one recession in the 1990s to 2000, and a recession in 2001; and the generally decelerating inflation from the 1980s to the early 2000s.

The Phillips Curve theoretically provides approximations of the NAIRU, and of the implications of a zero inflation rate for unemployment and of a zero unemployment rate for inflation. The NAIRU is implicit in the long-term trend line for each time period in the figures. It is obtained from any point on the trend line by comparing the intersection of the unemployment rate on the horizontal (X) axis with the corresponding inflation rate on the vertical (Y) axis at that point. Thus, unemployment at any point on the long-term average line is associated with a nonaccelerating inflation rate at that point.

Phillips Curve Trade-off

Shifts in the trade-off between unemployment and inflation toward an improvement or worsening can result from a variety of factors. For example, production cost decreases resulting from rising productivity, a weakening of the cartel pricing powers of OPEC, or increasing global competition improve the trade-off, but when these items move in the opposite direction, the trade-off worsens.

The theoretical Phillips Curve trade-off is most apparent in practice when inflation and unemployment are in relatively low ranges. During other periods, the experience often diverges from the theory. For example, low unemployment and high inflation may not be compatible over sustained periods, as spending by households and businesses is moderated or lowered because the higher prices reduce the purchasing power of their incomes, leading to lower economic growth and higher unemployment. On the other hand, high unemployment and low inflation may lead to a prolonged period of stagnating economic growth. And the worst of both worlds, high unemployment and high inflation, lowers living conditions, inhibits business investment, and causes social discord.

By contrast, low unemployment and low inflation may be compatible up to a point as a result of continuing workplace production efficiencies, global competition, and increasing returns to scale. Increasing returns to scale reflect the situation when higher employment and higher utilization of capital equipment and structures facilities result in a proportionately greater increase in output. This is accentuated by overhead costs (fixed costs), such as minimum maintenance crews, that are essential regardless of the level of output, and that are not increased with every increase in employment or capacity utilization. Thus, as the fixed costs are spread over a greater volume of items produced, the unit costs of production are lessened. This continues until the increased use of workers and capital facilities leads to inefficiencies, as shortages of workers and capital facilities necessitate hiring less productive workers and bringing outmoded and less efficient equipment into production, in which case decreasing returns to scale set in.

Application of the Phillips Curve to Economic Analysis

The divergence between the theory and experience indicates that, for the most part, the economy is too complex for simple Phillips Curve relationships. Most obvious is that there was a direct, rather than an inverse relationship, between unemployment and inflation in the 1950s, 1970s, and 1990s to early 2000s. This was heightened in the 1970s when both inflation and unemployment were relatively high. The direct relationship reflected the substantial increase in inflationary expectations, which became self-fulfilling when they led to spiraling price and wage increases as businesses and workers tried to make up for declines in real incomes.

The implications of zero inflation or of zero unemployment appear by extending the trend line in Figures 2.2a to 2.2e to the X and Y axes. Zero inflation is reached where the long-term average line touches the X axis, and the corresponding unemployment rate at zero inflation is read at that point on the X axis. Analogously, zero unemployment is reached when the long-term average line touches the Y axis, and the corresponding inflation rate is read at that point on the Y axis. The extension of the long-term line in this manner results in very high unemployment rates at zero inflation, and in very high inflation rates at zero unemployment. Even if this oversimplified technique were valid analytically, the results are too extreme to be sustained politically as a matter of public policy.

Also, this simplistic application of the trend line to zero inflation and unemployment rates gives potentially reasonable estimates only when there is a long-term pronounced inverse relationship between unemployment and inflation, which at best was evident in the 1960s, except for the latter years in the decade when the accelerating inflation was accompanied by only slight declines in unemployment. The application intuitively gives nonsense estimates when there is a direct relationship between unemployment and inflation, negative unemployment rates at zero inflation, and high inflation with high unemployment, except for the aberration of the 1970s.

The analyst should consider Phillips Curve analyses of inflation and unemployment most relevant during periods when both unemployment and inflation are relatively low. The assessment should include qualitative judgments of the effect of long-term structural changes in the economy on the trade-off between unemployment and inflation. In general, the graphic depictions of the changing trade-offs between unemployment and inflation provided by the Phillips Curve are useful for exposing fault lines in the economy that may be remedied or worsened by economic events and policies affecting the shift in the trade-off.

FISCAL, MONETARY, AND INCOMES POLICIES

The federal government and the Federal Reserve attempt on a continuing basis through fiscal and monetary policies, respectively, to moderate cyclical fluctuations and maintain steady long-term economic growth. Fiscal policy refers to the influence of federal government spending and taxation by the president and Congress. Monetary policy is the influence of the Federal Reserve on bank credit, interest rates, and the money supply. The federal government also occasionally uses incomes policies to curb inflation through voluntary guidelines or mandatory controls on prices and wages.

Although there is considerable sophistication in analyzing the effects of fiscal, monetary, and incomes policies, the causes of and remedies for business cycles and economic growth are complex, and the application of these policies is in part quantitative but also includes considerable qualitative judgment. Economic policies explicitly or implicitly take many factors into account: purely economic considerations such as balancing sales, production, employment, investment, prices, and interest rates; and political and other influences such as wars, harvests, household and business optimism and pessimism, international tensions, cartels, and protectionism.

Perhaps the major achievement of these policy tools is that no recession since

World War II has degenerated into a cataclysm such as the depression of the 1930s.[8] In addition, the 1961–69 period went nine years without a recession, the 1982–90 period approached eight years without a recession, and the 1991–2000 period went nine years without a recession. By historical standards, these expansions are very long. The first two periods, however, were tarnished by large increases in military spending that bolstered production and employment (in the 1960s for the Vietnam War and in the 1980s for the cold war). By contrast, the expansion of the 1990s to 2000 occurred after the cold war ended in the late 1980s and military spending subsequently declined until the late 1990s. The first two periods had fueled the hope that fiscal and monetary policies can maintain steady growth without recession or inflation. But the hope was dashed by the recessions and inflation in the 1970s and early 1980s and the recession in the early 1990s. The recession of 2001 reaffirmed the difficulty of preventing recessions through fiscal and monetary policies because the economy is far too complex and unpredictable for problems to be diagnosed sufficiently far in advance and for the fiscal and monetary remedies to be timely enough to elicit the necessary response in the private sector to turn a pending recession into a mere slowdown in economic growth.

Fiscal, monetary, and incomes policies impact the economy in different ways. Before proceeding with the substantive aspects of the policies, it is useful background to contrast the institutional differences among them that affect the way they are carried out.

Fiscal policy is conducted through federal spending and taxes, which are aimed at influencing the long-term growth and cyclical movements of the economy. But fiscal policy is developed in the broader context of the role of government in the life of the nation. In the free, democratic society of the United States, the federal, state, and local governments provide the institutions and services for enhancing the well-being of the nation's inhabitants. What governments do is ultimately determined at the ballot box when citizens elect their representatives. In general, governments are responsible for activities that in whole or in part are best done collectively for the common good, such as defense, elections, police, courts, health, education, transportation, income maintenance, environment, and other foundations of life. Taxation aims to finance that spending consistent with concepts of ability-to-pay, work and investment incentives, and efficient tax collection. When spending exceeds tax collections, the deficit is financed by borrowing, which in turn leads to spending in later years for the interest payments on the loans used to finance the deficit.

Thus, fiscal policies are developed as a subtext to the federal government's budget priorities for particular programs and taxes. The federal government, in contrast to state and local governments, is most suited to conduct fiscal policies, as noted below. Also, there is a long lag before the spending and tax changes impact the economy because of a lengthy process in putting them into effect.

First, the negotiation process between Congress and the president usually takes over a year to resolve to complete each year's fiscal budget. Second, these legislated changes then go through additional steps to make them operational: on the spending side, federal agencies must obligate funds to be spent, sign contracts, and make other provisions for the work to be done, and pay for the work done before the new spending enters the income stream; on the revenue side, the Internal Revenue Service must write regulations and design tax forms to conform to the new laws before the new taxes can be collected.

By contrast, monetary policies aim solely at influencing the economy's growth rate, and in this respect pay particular attention to the employment and inflationary aspects of economic growth rates at different stages of the business cycle. They affect the economy through their influence on bank credit, interest rates, and the money supply. Monetary policies are modified throughout the year by the Federal Reserve, and can be and often are put into immediate effect when policy changes are adopted.

Because incomes policies interfere with the marketplace in determining prices and wages, they are used only when an upward spiral in prices is so great that the traditional fiscal and monetary policies are considered inadequate for getting inflation under control. The corollary is that incomes policies are always treated as a temporary emergency measure that is ended when the inflation crisis is over.

Differences in implementing the three types of policies due to their institutional differences may be summarized as follows. First, fiscal policy is derived as an outgrowth of spending priorities for government programs and tax legislation, while the primary purpose of monetary and incomes policies is to influence the economy. Second, monetary policy is more flexible than fiscal policy because changes in Federal Reserve actions affecting bank credit and interest rates can be made quickly, while spending and tax changes require a lengthy political and operational process. Third, incomes policies are only temporary, while fiscal and monetary polices are ongoing, and changes are easier to make in incomes policies than in fiscal policy, but changes in incomes policies are less flexible than those in monetary policy.

Fiscal Policy

Fiscal policy is use of the overall federal government budget spending and taxation levels to foster economic growth without leading to inflation or a recession. The limitation of fiscal policy to the federal government, as distinct from state and local governments, reflects the fact that there is no national control over the spending and taxing actions of state and local governments. However, while there is no national policy direction to the fiscal actions of state and local governments, their budgets impact the economy, and estimates of the effects of these governments' fiscal actions are included here.

A budget surplus (receipts exceed spending) results in the government taking money out of the income stream of households and businesses, a budget deficit (spending exceeds receipts) puts money into the income stream, and a balanced budget (receipts equal spending) has no effect on the income stream. Thus, the first order effects of the federal budget are: a surplus restrains economic growth through the reduction in income and related spending, a deficit stimulates economic growth through the increase in income and related spending, and a balanced budget is neutral with regard to growth because total income and spending is unaffected.

This generalization is modified and may even be reversed by several secondary effects of the budget position. First, when considering the effects of changes in the budget position on economic growth over time, the analyst should consider not only the absolute levels, but also whether they are increasing or decreasing. Thus, if a budget surplus in period 1 becomes smaller in period 2, the budget is less restraining in period 2 because it takes a smaller amount of money out of the income stream; analogously, if a budget deficit in period 1 becomes smaller in period 2, the budget is less stimulative in period 2. Second, a budget deficit tends to lead to higher interest rates than a budget surplus, since the government must borrow money to finance the deficit. And the higher interest rates restrain spending by other borrowers, in turn leading to a lower growth rate, in contrast to the first-order effect of a higher growth rate. Analogously, a budget surplus tends to lower interest rates as the government does not need to borrow funds for the current year's budget (it may still borrow funds for its existing debt that cumulated from previous deficits). And the lower interest rates stimulate spending by other borrowers, leading to a higher growth rate than the first-order effect. Third, contrary to general perceptions, a balanced budget actually stimulates spending in subsequent rounds of spending, cumulating over time to the total amount of the first-order spending through what is known as the balanced-budget multiplier.

This discussion of fiscal policy has centered on government spending and taxes as influencing economic growth. But economic growth also influences government spending and taxes. Thus, there is a two-way street between the federal budget and economic growth. The budgetary aspects of cyclical expansions and recessions are called "automatic stabilizers." The longer-term economic growth that spans several business cycles is called the "structural budget."

Automatic Stabilizers

Automatic stabilizers are built-in institutionalized countercyclical aspects of government budgets that cause government spending and tax collections, without direct intervention of new government programs, to move in the opposite direction or in less extreme patterns than trends in the overall economy. For example, the inherent nature of unemployment insurance is to put more money in the income stream in recessions than in expansions. Budget outlays for unemployment insurance rise in recessions and decline in expansions. The progressive income tax removes proportionately more income from households in expansions and less in recessions. Thus, these stabilizers automatically move consumer purchasing power in a countercyclical direction, lowering the growth of purchasing power during expansions and raising the growth of purchasing power during recessions. This is a two-step process, in which the economy initially impacts the budget, and then in a second-round feedback, the modified budget impacts the economy.

Figures 2.3a and 2.3b show this experience separately for the combined total of all governments, the federal government, and the aggregate of all state and local governments during the business cycles in the 1980s and the 1990s to early 2000s. The two long expansions of the period are disaggregated into the first and second halves of each multiyear period. In relating government budgets to the overall economy, the figures depict the change in the budget surplus or deficit for each expansion (from trough to peak) and for each recession (from peak to trough) in relation to the average gross domestic product in the period.

Figure 2.3a **Shift in Government Budgets toward a Surplus (+) or Deficit (−) as a Percentage of the Gross Domestic Product, 1980s to Early 2000s: Expansions**

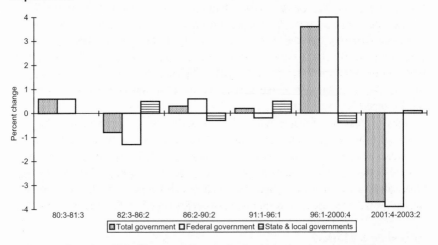

Source: Based on U.S. Bureau of Economic Analysis data in current dollars.

Note: Number after colon is quarter of year. State and local budgets had a zero change in 1980–81.

Figure 2.3b **Shift in Government Budgets toward a Surplus (+) or Deficit (−) as a Percentage of the Gross Domestic Product, 1980s to 2001: Recessions**

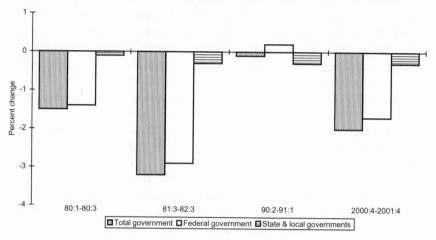

Source: Based on U.S. Bureau of Economic Analysis data.

Note: Number after colon is quarter of year.

If the budget surplus increases or the deficit decreases, the change is positive; and if the deficit increases or the surplus decreases, the change is negative.

Thus, the analysis focuses on the direction of the change of the surplus or deficit during the expansion or recession, not on whether the budget was in surplus or deficit.

Government budgets typically restrain income growth in expansions and boost incomes in recessions, which fits the concept of the stabilizing role. These patterns reflect the combined effects of economic growth, the tax laws, and inflation on tax receipts and spending.

During the expansions of the 1980s and 1990s to 2000, budgets for the combined total of all governments moved in a stabilizing, that is, restraining, direction in all cases except the first half of the 1982–90 expansion, when the total budget stimulated economic growth in a destabilizing direction. In the first half of both the 1982–90 and 1991–2000 expansions, the federal budget stimulated the economy, that is, was destabilizing, while the state and local budgets restrained the economy and were stabilizing. In the second half of both of these expansions, the reverse occurred with the federal budget restraining economic growth in a stabilizing direction, while the state and local budgets stimulated economic growth in a destabilizing direction. The total government budget and the federal budget restraint were much greater in the second half of the 1991–2000 expansion than in the second half of the 1982–90 expansion.

The governmental budget positions in the short recovery/expansion of 1980–

81 and the recovery of 2002 were too close to the preceding recessions to apply the "stabilizing" and "destabilizing" characterizations as during longer cyclical expansions. In fact, because of the need for stimulus in both recoveries, the movement toward budget deficits would be stabilizing. In the 1980–81 recovery/ expansion of one year, the total and federal budgets moved in a restraining direction and thus were destabilizing, while the state and local budgets showed zero change and thus had a neutral cyclical effect. And in the 2002–03 recovery, the total and the federal budgets were stimulating and thus stabilizing, while state and local budgets were restraining and thus destabilizing.

During the four recessions from the 1980s to the early 2000s, budgets for the combined total of all governments were stimulating that is, stabilizing, on all occasions, although the stimulus in the 1990–91 recession was very small. Overall, the federal budget was far more stimulating than state and local budgets, except for the 1990–91 recession when it was restraining. The greatest stimulus was in the 2001 recession, occurring at all three government levels, though primarily at the total government and the federal levels.

The generally stabilizing movements of both the federal and the state and local budgets result from different patterns of spending and receipts. At both levels of government, expenditures increased in both expansions and recessions. In addition, while unemployment insurance is a joint federal-state program, un-employment taxes paid by employers are held in a federal trust fund and thus are counted as receipts in the federal budget, and unemployment insurance ben-efit payments are part of the federal budget and thus raise federal outlays in recessions (the unemployment insurance system, including its effect on moder-ating recessions, is discussed in chapter 9 on unemployment).

But for revenues, the federal and the state and local patterns diverge. Federal receipts fall in some recessions because personal and corporate income taxes are the dominant source of federal revenue, with high unemployment and low busi-ness profits causing tax collections to drop. The dominance of income taxes occurs despite continuing increases in Social Security taxes, excise taxes, cus-toms duties, and miscellaneous receipts. The decline in federal income tax re-ceipts in recessions is heightened because of the progressivity in the federal income tax law, in which proportionately lower taxes are paid as income de-creases (analogously, during expansions proportionately higher taxes are paid as income increases).

By contrast, a much greater share of state and local tax collections comes from sales and property taxes, which are not as cyclically sensitive as income taxes. For example, in 2002, personal and corporate income taxes accounted for 54 percent of federal receipts and only 18 percent of state and local receipts. This reliance on income taxes, together with the unemployment insurance benefit payments coming from the federal budget, strengthens the stabilizing impact of the federal budget in recessions and accounts for much of the disparity between the federal and the state and local budgets in stimulating the economy during recessions noted above.

Government budgets generally, but not always, have a stabilizing effect on the economy, restraining economic growth during expansions and stimulating it during recessions. The analyst should monitor these patterns to determine to what extent the budgets impact the economy at different phases of the business cycle. This should be done for the total of all governments and separately for the federal and the aggregate of all state and local governments to assess what stabilizing or destabilizing effects of government budgets are emerging.

Structural Budget

The structural budget of the federal government is the size of the budget surplus or deficit independent of whether the economy is in an expansion or recession. It is a hypothetical budget that focuses on whether the budget inherently stimulates or restrains overall economic activity, initially through its effect on the income stream of households and businesses, and subsequently on their spending and investments and the resultant economic growth. It is stimulative when it is in deficit because more money is added to than is removed from the income stream, and it is restraining when it is in surplus because more money is removed from than is added to the income stream.

The structural budget published by the Congressional Budget Office is referred to as the standardized budget. The standardized budget assumes the economy is operating at its highest potential without leading to a greater rate of inflation. This is the concept of the potential GDP, which is linked to the NAIRU, discussed earlier under Okun's Law and the NAIRU. In abstracting from short-term cyclical movements above and below the potential GDP, the standardized budget excludes the amounts of budget surpluses and deficits attributable to the cyclical differentials from the potential GDP. By contrast, the actual budget represents the receipts and outlays coming into and going out of the U.S. Treasury.

The effect of the budget on the income stream occurs as a first-order result of changes in the budget position. Secondary impacts related to shifts in the direction of the surplus or deficit and the effect of the budget on interest rates may modify or reverse the first-round impacts on economic growth.

Table 2.1 shows the budget surplus/deficit positions of both the actual and the standardized budgets from 1990 to 2002. It indicates a stark shift in the surplus/deficit positions of the two budgets. From 1990 to 1996, the actual budget had a noticeably larger deficit than the standardized budget, although the differential lessened over the period. But from 1997 to 2001, the actual budget shifted to a lower deficit and then to earlier and larger surpluses than the standardized budget. However, in 2002, both budgets swung to approximately equiv-

Table 2.1

Actual and Standardized Federal Budgets: Fiscal Years 1990–2002 (billions of dollars)

Surplus or Deficit (−)

	Actual budget	Standardized budget
1990	−221	−121
1991	−269	−147
1992	−290	−185
1993	−255	−185
1994	−203	−145
1995	−164	−144
1996	107	−99
1997	−22	−73
1998	69	−37
1999	126	−3
2000	236	99
2001	127	80
2002	−158	−153

Source: Congressional Budget Office, *The Budget and Economic Outlook: Fiscal Years 2004–2013*, Appendix F, Table F-12, January 2003, p. 159.

Note: The actual budget represents receipts and outlays coming into and going out of the U.S. Treasury. The standardized budget is cyclically-adjusted to exclude receipts and outlays that result from an actual level of output that is above or below the potential output of the economy. See text.

alent deficit positions. These reversals in the positions of the actual and standardized budgets reflect the accelerated economic growth above the potential GDP that took hold in the latter part of the 1990s, which was followed by the depressed growth in the recession of 2001 and the low economic growth in the recovery of 2002.

The concept of the structural budget is limited to the federal government. In the American federal system, it is impractical to use state and local budgets as a fiscal policy tool because: (a) institutional aspects vary considerably—there are different constitutional limitations on debt, legislatures meet at different times of the year, and fiscal years cover different twelve-month periods; and (b) it is not politically feasible to have a coordinated fiscal policy for even the five or ten largest states (abstracting from the other states and the over three thousand localities), as the complexity resulting from the independence of the large number of states and local jurisdictions is far greater than for the federal budget, which itself is quite complicated merely in negotiating between Congress and the president.

Economic concepts about how best to balance robust economic growth through fiscal policy with low inflation have evolved over the years. In the 1960s, a "full employment surplus" (defined as 3 to 4 percent unemployment) was regarded as desirable, and full employment surplus budgets were developed and used as a fiscal policy tool. Because the budget surplus generated from such high employment was found to be a "fiscal drag" on economic growth, it was a basic rationale for the tax cuts of the early 1960s. During the 1970s, the model was modified as the "high employment budget," which raised the NAIRU from 6 to 7 percent. In the 1980s, the model was further changed to the "cyclically adjusted budget," which specified the budget position based on the economic growth trend at 6 percent unemployment. And in the 1990s, the concept of the standardized budget was developed.

The effect of the structural budget on the economy is driven in the first instance by whether the budget is in a surplus, deficit, or balanced position. However, as with the above automatic stabilizers, the greater policy interest is in the change in the budget from one period to the next. Thus, the budget exerts a greater stimulus to economic growth when the surplus is reduced or the deficit is increased, and analogously it has a greater restraining effect on economic growth when the surplus becomes higher or the deficit becomes lower.

It is useful to compare the levels and movements of the actual and standardized federal budgets to assess the differential impacts that both budgets have on the economy, as well as the effect of the economy on the budgets. Prospective changes in the federal budget arising from tax and spending legislation should be included in the analysis.

Frequency of Changes in the Tax Structure

Tax rates and how the different types of taxes affect individuals and businesses of different incomes and wealth are ultimately based on political considerations of the role of the government in society, fairness, and the efficiency of collecting taxes. These considerations change with the outcomes of presidential and congressional elections.

Because the tax structure affects individuals and businesses in their spending, saving, and investments, there is a general virtue in having a degree of certainty about future taxes. This enables actions taken on spending, saving, and investments to be made with a sufficiently long time horizon so that individuals and businesses will feel that their economic decisions will not be adversely affected shortly after they are made. Such stability in the tax structure encourages economic decisions to be made more on their merits than on speculation about future tax changes.

I believe that maintaining an existing tax structure for at least a few years has a positive effect on economic growth because it provides an environment of stability. Such stability gives individuals and businesses confidence that their economic actions of today will not be affected by tax changes in the immediate years ahead.

Monetary Policy

Monetary policy is associated with actions of the Federal Reserve System (FRS) that affect the reserves of commercial banks that are available for extending credit to households and businesses. Changes in bank reserves in turn impact the availability of bank loans to individuals and businesses and interest rates. Chapter 12 gives a more comprehensive explanation of the institutional framework of the FRS and its conduct of monetary policy.

Federal Open Market Committee

The FRS monetary policies are determined by the Federal Open Market Committee (FOMC). The FOMC has twelve voting members: the seven governors of the Federal Reserve Board in Washington, D.C., and the president of the Federal Reserve Bank of New York are permanent voting members, and the presidents of the eleven other Federal Reserve banks have one-year terms as voting members on a rotating basis, with four of them voting in any one year. All twelve members vote on what should happen to interest rates. Their decisions are carried out through open market operations.

The FOMC meets eight times a year on a regular basis, and on other occasions as needed. It submits two reports to Congress every year, one in February and one in July. The reports include the FOMC's assessment of the economy and general plans for monetary policy.

Tools of Monetary Policy

The FOMC uses three main tools in conducting monetary policy: open market operations, reserve requirements, and the discount rate. Open market operations are the purchase and sale by the FRS of existing U.S. government securities. The purchase and sale of these securities affect bank reserves, bank loans, and interest rates. Open market operations are the main tool for conducting monetary policy, and are typically conducted several days each week.

Reserve requirements are varying percentages of different types of deposits that banks must hold as reserves. The discount rate is the interest rate that the twelve regional Federal Reserve banks charge the banks in their region for loans. Changes in reserve requirements and the discount rate are not as significant as open market operations in conducting monetary policy, and they are also made much less frequently than open market operations. The seven governors of the Federal Reserve Board have direct authority, independent of the FOMC, over reserve requirements. The discount rate is set by each Federal Reserve bank, subject to board approval, though the board not only reacts to proposed rate changes by the banks, but at times encourages the banks to initiate a proposed rate change.

Monetary policies impact both economic growth and prices. When the FOMC acts to increase the amount of bank credit available for loans, it does so by increasing commercial bank reserves by buying federal government securities in its open market operations. This raises the price of the securities, or lessens the decline in their price. It leads banks and other investors to sell at least part of their holdings of federal securities, either to realize a profit or lessen their losses on the original purchase price of the securities. By selling their securities, banks increase their reserves. The increase in reserves causes interest rates to decline or rise more slowly because banks make money by lending money, and when they have an increased amount of money to lend, they have a greater incentive to lower interest rates in order to increase the amount of loans they make, since they do not make money when their funds are idle. At the same time, when interest rates are lower, households and businesses have a greater incentive to borrow funds to finance purchases of housing, cars, vacations, machinery, inventories, etc., all of which stimulate production and economic growth.

The reverse process occurs when the FOMC acts to decrease or slow down the growth of bank credit available by reducing bank reserves through selling federal government securities. The decrease in reserves causes interest rates to rise or decline more slowly, and households and businesses have less of an incentive to borrow money, which lowers production and economic growth.

Federal Funds

The most sensitive indicator of changes in monetary policy is the federal funds interest rate, which is the interest rate charged on loans between commercial banks.[9] The loans are usually for overnight, but they also include loans for a few days to over one year. The FOMC uses the federal funds rate as its main operating mechanism in influencing the amount of bank reserves available for credit. It does this by targeting the federal funds rate it desires based on its assessment of the need for stimulating or restraining economic growth. Changes in federal funds rates indicate a change in FOMC policy, with higher rates pointing to a desired slowdown in economic growth and lower rates to a desired speedup in economic growth.

While traditionally the FOMC has focused on the federal funds rate, it has pushed short-term interest rates so low during 2002 and 2003 that further efforts to stimulate the economy may require changes in long-term rates. Long-term rates are more important than short-term rates in influencing household purchases of housing and business and government purchases of equipment and structures.

Interest Rates, Economic Growth, and Price Change

The general relationships between interest rates and economic growth and between interest rates and price change have some qualifiers. *First*, during periods of high inflation, a greater availability of credit may lead to higher rather than to lower interest rates. This reflects the expectation that the greater credit availability will stimulate borrowing and spending above the economy's capacity to produce, and thus lead to growth rates that overheat the economy and cause accelerating inflation. Because lenders must consider the price levels that will prevail when their loans are paid back, interest rates include an "inflation premium," which is the expected increase in prices from the time the loan is made to the time it is paid back, and an expectation of higher inflation in turn raises interest rates. *Second*, FOMC policy changes on bank credit and interest rates affect the economy with long, imprecise, and differential lags on economic growth on the one hand, and on inflation on the other. A rule of thumb is that changes in interest rates affect economic growth and employment one to two years after they occur, while they affect inflation about three years later. *Third*, nonmonetary factors, such as the federal budget deficit, foreign investment, the international value of the dollar, household and business moods of optimism and pessimism, and very high unemployment or inflation, complicate and may override monetary policies. The limited power of FOMC policies in the face of these nonmonetary factors is suggested by the expressions "pulling the string" and "pushing the string." Generally, the FOMC is considered to be more effective at slowing economic activity by raising interest rates (pulling the string) than at quickening economic activity by lowering interest rates (pushing the string).

In their overall thrust, the FOMC's actions and pronouncements emphasize the containment of inflation more than the lowering of unemployment, except during periods of high unemployment. This reflects the view that price stability, defined variously as an inflation rate of 0 to 2 percent inflation, does not distort economic decisions made by households and businesses. A zero inflation rate means that the overall price level for all goods and services, such as the consumer price index, does not change from one period to the next, although component items such as food and housing may rise or fall.

The idea is that the natural generative forces of American life are most likely to bring about the desirable goals of a growing number of jobs, high wages, and robust profits in an environment of price stability. The perception affects the conduct of monetary policy. Generally, members of the FOMC consider the economy to have a greater inflationary potential than some other analysts. Therefore, during cyclical expansions, the FOMC tends to restrain economic growth at higher unemployment levels and with greater restraint than some other analysts would. Analogously, during cyclical recessions, the FOMC tends to stimulate economic growth at higher unemployment levels and with less stimulus than some other analysts.

These other analysts believe that aiming for a zero inflation rate is too restrictive for promoting economic growth and maintaining or lowering unemployment. For example, in the mid-1990s, George Akerlof, William Dickens, and George Perry found that a steady inflation rate of 3 percent annually would allow for an unemployment rate of 5.2 percent, while actions taken to reduce the inflation rate of 3 percent to zero would raise the unemployment rate by 2.6 percentage points.[10] An innovative feature of this study is that it incorporates the "real world" tendency for workers to resist reductions in wages, while recognizing that wage cuts do occur. Resistance to wage cuts results in a permanent shock to production costs, which is inflationary at the relatively low inflation rates considered in the study. Unemployment would remain steady if the Federal Reserve succeeded in its attempts to accommodate the higher inflation through expanding the amount of bank credit available and thus keeping interest rates from rising. Or unemployment would rise if the Federal Reserve decided not to accommodate the higher inflation and succeeds in restraining bank credit and rising interest rates. The authors concluded that because of wage rigidity, there is no unique NAIRU, a subject discussed previously under Okun's Law. In the early 2000s, Akerlof reiterated this concern that during periods of low inflation, firms that need to cut their real wages (wages adjusted for inflation) in order to compete in the marketplace may be averse to cutting nominal wages.[11]

The issue of price deflation is discussed in chapter 11 under Concern about Deflation: Common Stock and Housing Asset Prices and the CPI.

Voting Patterns of FOMC Members

Within the FOMC, individual members have varying degrees of concern about inflation, including response to advance signs of a possible acceleration in inflation and of striving toward zero inflation. The starkest differences are between "hawks," who take a hard line in fighting a possible inflationary acceleration and in lowering inflation to zero, and "doves," who require more evidence of a possible inflationary acceleration and are more hesitant to strive toward zero inflation because of its possible consequences of higher unemployment.

Each member of the FOMC has individual views of the economy and votes accordingly on what monetary policy should be. For most members, their typical predilection in conducting monetary policy is an eclectic approach, in which a variety of economic indicators is assessed, and based on this review, votes are cast on whether monetary policies should be changed, and if so, in what direction.

However, this eclectic approach is not universal among FOMC members. There is another approach to monetary policy, called monetarism, which advocates following a steady growth rate in the money supply (checking deposits and currency in circulation) regardless of changes in economic conditions and their effect on interest rates. This is based on the premise that little is known about forecasting economic activity, and that frequent changes in monetary policies cause undue uncertainty in the business community with the attendant volatility in interest rates and economic activity. By contrast, steady and predictable growth in the money supply is conducive to a more certain economic environment encouraging more business investment and a higher rate of long-term economic growth. A minority of FOMC members typically follows the monetarist approach.

Opponents of monetarism contend that it is based on a simplistic view of the economy that would hamstring the FOMC in its job of fostering economic growth and employment and moderating inflation. In chapter 12, "Finance," I argue that the money supply is intrinsically a passive factor in credit markets. Of course, at any particular point in time, the makeup of the FOMC membership determines whether the committee as a whole follows the eclectic or monetarist approach.

The FOMC as an entity does not use the NAIRU, discussed previously, as an underlying tool in its deliberations. However, some FOMC members may include the NAIRU concept in their analyses, although they may be based on varying estimates of the NAIRU. If the economy is operating below its NAIRU potential and inflation is not accelerating, those members following the eclectic approach and using a NAIRU analysis would call for stimulating the economy through increasing the amount of credit that banks have to lend, which in turn tends to lower interest rates and stimulate economic growth. But if the economy is approaching or above its NAIRU potential and inflation is accelerating or is expected to accelerate, these same members would call for lessening the amount or slowing the growth of available bank credit to raise interest rates and slow economic growth. Still, in the dynamics of the FOMC meetings, individual predilections for eclecticism and monetarism, varying views on the actual level of the NAIRU and forecasts of economic growth and inflation, and hawk-dove attitudes on inflation are subject to modification in the discussions and persuasiveness of opposing arguments, depending on the strength of the predilections held and on the particular issue at hand.

In assessing the prospects for future movements in interest rates, the analyst should consider the outlook for both economic growth and inflation. Possible changes in monetary policies should also be monitored for their effect on interest rates. In addition, because the Federal Reserve use of the federal funds rate in conducting monetary policy is inherently limited to short-term interest rates, the analyst should supplement this with an assessment of the outlook for long-term interest rates.

Interaction of Fiscal Policy and Monetary Policy

The above discussions of fiscal policy and monetary policy appear as separate topics. However, they are not independent of each other. Changes in the federal budget surplus/deficit positions affected by new laws passed by Congress and the president lead to changes in federal government borrowing to finance the resultant budgetary effects and their impact on interest rates.

Thus, a growing federal budget surplus lessens the need for federal borrowing which, abstracting from the vitality of the economy, tends to lower interest rates. In contrast, a growing federal budget deficit increases the need for federal borrowing which, abstracting from the vitality of the economy, tends to raise interest rates.

But the fiscal/monetary interaction is not independent of the vitality of the economy. In prosperous times of robust economic growth, increased federal borrowing needs are more likely to result in higher interest rates than when the economy is depressed. Analogously, when the economy is depressed, a lessening of federal borrowing needs is less likely to lower interest rates than when the economy is prosperous.

In evaluating the impacts of fiscal and monetary policy interactions, the analyst should include the current and future expectations of economic growth.

HUMPHREY-HAWKINS ACT UNEMPLOYMENT AND INFLATION GOALS

The specifics of balancing unemployment and inflation have been and probably always will be subject to vibrant debate. The debate reflects the predilections of those who place a greater weight on lowering unemployment and those who stress the greater importance of lowering inflation.

The Full Employment and Balance Growth Act of 1978, referred to as the Humphrey-Hawkins Act (HH), established the first legislated numerical national goals for unemployment and inflation. These were unemployment of 4 percent and inflation (based on the consumer price index) of 3 percent by 1983, with a further reduction of inflation to zero by 1988; however, the act permits the inflation goals to be relaxed if pursuing them would hinder achieving the unemployment goal. As noted previously, zero inflation means no change in overall prices, although prices for particular goods and services may increase or decrease. The goals were not met by the target dates: in 1983 unemployment was 9.6 percent and inflation was 3.2 percent, and in 1988 unemployment was 5.5 percent and inflation was 4.1 percent.

The HH goals came closest to being met during 1998–2000, when unemployment was in the 4.0–4.5 range, and inflation was in the 1.6–3.4 range. The act's goals continue in effect, even though the timetables have passed, unless the legislation is modified or repealed in the future.

As a matter of public policy, the question becomes, "What purpose do the HH goals serve?" Such goals may be more important for their intangible effect on the nation's outlook than on their tangible results. On the one hand, the goals represent a clearly defined objective for the nation, one that will bring significant improvements in living conditions and that encourages the nation to continue to strive to do better, even if the results at any time are below expectations. On the other hand, if the goals are unrealistic, they will not only be disregarded but also may lead to cynicism that discourages efforts for improvement, and thereby have a negative effect.

The HH Act also requires the Federal Reserve chairman to report semiannually to Congress on the outlook for the economy and the Federal Reserve's general plans for monetary policy. While maintaining the independence of the Federal Reserve from political interference, the requirement to report to Congress brings a modicum of accountability on its actions every six months (see chapter 12, under Appendix: Federal Reserve Organization and Independence).

Developing meaningful goals requires balancing ideal aspirations and feasible achievements. In my opinion, the Humphrey-Hawkins goal of zero inflation is unrealistic. If the HH goals are to be credible for conducting fiscal and monetary policies, the zero inflation goal should be reassessed.

INCOMES POLICIES

From time to time, fiscal and monetary policies are supplemented with incomes policies, a euphemism for either voluntary price-wage guidelines or mandatory price-wage controls. Incomes policies diverge from the complete market determination of prices and wages, and they are instituted only when it is thought that fiscal and monetary policies are too blunt to have the desired effect in curbing inflationary behavior at the micro level by businesses and labor unions. They are resorted to as a temporary device to break the inflationary psychology engendered when prices and wages spiral upward with no end in sight, and when it is believed that a recession and high unemployment caused by restrictive fiscal and monetary policies are too high a price to pay for breaking the inflationary environment.

Mandatory price and wage controls were used in World War II, part of the Korean War (1950–51), and part of the Vietnam War (1971–73). Voluntary price-wage guidelines were used in 1962–65 and 1978–79. Economists debate their effectiveness. Some say they distort price, wage, and profit relationships among products, industries, and companies, and result in higher inflation after they are removed. Others say they hold inflation below what it would have been, without undue interference with market determined prices and wages, so long as they are temporary.

In implementing incomes policies, government agencies are set up to develop standards for allowable price and wage increases, with variations for particular industries. Efforts to obtain compliance with voluntary price and wage guidelines have incentives such as being a prerequisite for bidding on government contracts, while compliance with mandatory incomes policies requires a much larger enforcement bureaucracy that includes penalties for violating the price and wage controls. In addition, there is an institutional imbalance between businesses and workers in monitoring the price and wage standards that can undermine compliance with the standards and consequently the entire program. Thus, it is easy for businesses to monitor wages because they know what wages they pay to their workers, while it is difficult for workers to monitor the prices of the various products sold by their employers.

Because of their sporadic use, incomes policies are not analyzed in this book. But if they are used in the future, they will have to address the critical problem of compliance, because it is easier for businesses to monitor wage increases of their employees than it is for workers to monitor price increases of the various products sold by their employers. Neither business nor labor favors price and wage standards, but if standards are imposed, the standards can be effective only if both sides feel they are treated fairly.

REVIEW QUESTIONS

- Why is the NAIRU used in developing Okun's Law?
- Using a formulation of Okun's Law that puts the break-even point for unemployment at an annual growth rate in the real GDP of 2.0 percent, the change in the unemployment rate of 0.5 percentage point for every one percentage point change in the annual growth of the real GDP above and below the break-even point, and a current unemployment rate of 5.0 percent, calculate the new unemployment rate for:

Annual GDP growth	New unemployment rate
4.0%	_____
3.0%	_____
2.0%	_____
0.0%	_____
−1.0%	_____

- The Phillips Curve inverse relationship between unemployment and inflation breaks down in two economic environments: (a) when both unemployment and inflation are high, and (b) when both unemployment and inflation are declining. What causes the breakdowns during these periods?
- Characterize the difference between automatic stabilizers and the structural budget of the federal government budget for their effects on the economy.
- Why is there sometimes great uncertainty about actions the Federal Reserve FOMC will take on monetary policy?
- What is your opinion of the usefulness of the NAIRU concept for fiscal and monetary policymaking? Explain.
- Which goal of the Full Employment and Balanced Growth Act of 1978 (Humphrey-Hawkins Act) is more likely to be realized, a 4 percent unemployment rate or a zero inflation rate? Explain.

Extra Credit

- We will see in the next chapter that the reported growth rate of the real GDP is subject to periodic long-term revisions. What does that say about Okun's Law?
- What developments in the next decade might push the Phillips Curve leftward? Rightward?

NOTES

1. Arthur M. Okun, "Potential GNP: Its Measurement and Significance," *Proceedings of the Business and Economic Statistics Section*, American Statistical Association, 1962. Reprinted, with slight changes, in Arthur M. Okun, *The Political Economy of Prosperity* (Norton, 1970), Appendix.
2. Congressional Budget Office, *CBO's Method for Estimating Potential Output: An Update*, A CBO Paper, August 2001. This is a comprehensive methodology, although not the only one used by economists.
3. Geoffrey M. B. Tootell, "Restructuring, the NAIRU, and the Phillips Curve," *New England Economic Review*, Federal Reserve Bank of Boston, September/October 1994.
4. Congressional Budget Office, *The Effect of Changes in Labor Markets on the Natural Rate of Unemployment*, A CBO Paper, April 2002.
5. *Economic Report of the President*, Appendix Table B-34, February 2003.
6. A. W. Phillips, "The Relation between Unemployment and the Rate of Change of Money Wage Rates in the United Kingdom, 1861–1957," *Economica*, November 1958.
7. Robert J. Gordon, *Macroeconomics*, 6th ed. (HarperCollins College Publishers, 1993), pp. 241–44.
8. Besides fiscal and monetary policies, other factors preventing a depression include unemployment insurance and other income maintenance programs that provide a

floor during recessions, bank deposit insurance, and active government intervention to stem a widespread financial collapse by failing banks.

9. For a good discussion of federal funds, see Federal Reserve Bank of Richmond, *Instruments of the Money Market*, 7th ed., 1993, ch. 2. The 8th edition is available only on the Federal Reserve Bank of Richmond's Web site: www.rich.frb.org.

10. George A. Akerlof, William T. Dickens, and George L. Perry, "The Macroeconomics of Low Inflation," *Brookings Papers on Economic Activity* 1, 1996.

11. George A. Akerlof, "Behavioral Macroeconomics and Macroeconomic Behavior," *American Economic Review*, June 2002, p. 421.

3

Economic Growth

The overall performance of the economy is reflected in its economic growth. This is the percentage increase from one period to the next in which the nation's workers and enterprises produce goods and services. Growth of the American economy is generally positive, as it rises in many more calendar quarters and years than it declines. The growth and employment increases also vary during rising periods, in some years above and in others below the average rate. The onset of recessions and the accompanying declines in employment result in low or negative growth rates. Such periods typically are no longer than twelve months (see chapter 1 under Business Cycles and Economic Growth).

Economic growth is important because it affects the material well-being and social harmony of the population, as well as U.S. influence in world affairs. Material well-being relates to basic aspects of life such as food, shelter, clothing, health, transportation, education, and the environment. Because a faster growth rate usually translates into greater employment, the higher the growth rate is, the greater is the purchasing power of the incomes of the working and non-working population. Higher real incomes tend to lessen social tensions through the improved living conditions they bring, although economic discontent is not the only cause of these tensions. Thus, greater material well-being may bring a greater emotional happiness and social harmony, but it does not necessarily do so. In world affairs, while the United States has a unique prestige as the only superpower, its influence in obtaining international agreement for its economic, environmental, social, diplomatic, and military policies is probably heightened when its own economy is perceived as being on a sound and robust footing.

In referring to economic growth, President John Kennedy said that a rising tide lifts all boats. The analogy for persons is only generally true, because not everyone benefits from economic growth. Thus, one of the needs of economic policy is to help those workers and households who do not share in the prosperity of a robustly growing economy.

This chapter highlights the gross domestic product (GDP) as the primary measure of economic growth. Because the GDP construct is so large, the chapter focuses on its aggregate dimensions, while its major components of households, business, government, international, and investment-saving transactions are detailed in chapters 4 to 8.

In addition to the overall perspective on long-term and cyclical aspects of economic growth, the chapter contrasts the demand and supply attributes of economic growth, relates manufacturing to growth in the overall economy, and gives an assessment of economic growth in the first decade of the twenty-first century. The GDP is central to economic analysis, and I believe it will be beneficial for those not familiar with basic GDP concepts to spend some time getting an overall grasp of the GDP framework in the following methodology section.

GDP METHODOLOGY

The GDP data are prepared quarterly by the Bureau of Economic Analysis (BEA) in the U.S. Department of Commerce. The data are published in the BEA monthly journal, the *Survey of Current Business* (www.bea.doc.gov). The initial estimate for each quarter is published about one month after the quarter. This is followed by a series of revisions: they begin with revised estimates in the two subsequent months; the next revisions are published annually in the three succeeding years, usually in July; and lastly, the benchmark revision is prepared on a periodic five-year schedule. For five-year benchmark revisions, definitional, classification, and statistical changes are carried back to 1929, thus maintaining a consistent GDP series from 1929 forward.

The GDP summarizes in a single number the nation's total economic output valued in dollars. It is derived by organizing the various sectors of the economy—the household, business, government, and international sectors—into a system of spending and income accounts. These are referred to as the "national income and product accounts," "national economic accounts," or simply the "national accounts."

The summary GDP number consolidates spending and its counterpart income flows to represent the nation's output from two perspectives, the differing components of demand and supply. The *demand* concept (known as the "product side") refers to the end-use markets for goods and services produced in the United States. It appears in the national accounts as sales of these items to households, businesses, governments, and foreigners. The *supply* concept (known as the "income side") refers to the incomes and costs involved in producing these goods and services. It is shown in the accounts as sum of employee compensation, business profits, interest payments, rental income, depreciation allowances for structures, equipment, and computer software, and sales and property taxes.[1]

The product and income sides are economic counterparts that have strong interrelationships. At the simplest level, the incomes generated on the income side are the source of spending on the product side. Moreover, this is a continuing process as the spending for goods and services in turn generates income for their production, and so the process continues from income to spending to income, etc. These interrelationships between income and spending are discussed in various chapters for the enrichment they give to the analysis.

Table 3.1 shows the product and income sides of the GDP in 2002 and their major components. The total value of goods and services produced in 2002 was $10.4 trillion. The table indicates the dominance of consumer expenditures on the product side with 70 percent of the GDP, and employee compensation on the income side with 57 percent of the GDP. As discussed below under Analysis of Trends, these and other components move at different rates over the business cycle.

Meaning of Production

The GDP is defined on a "value-added" basis. This means that as goods pass through the various stages of production—from raw materials to semifinished goods to final products—only the value that is added in each stage is counted for GDP purposes. If goods and services purchased from other businesses for use in production were included, their value would be endlessly recounted. The value-added method counts only the total resources used in producing the final item, as represented in the wage, profit, and other income-side components, and the final markets of the product side. This prevents double counting of items on the product side. The income-side methodology, itself, prevents double counting on the income side.

Another key point in defining production is that the GDP excludes capital gains and losses in the sale of securities, land, and used goods. These are considered valuation changes in the transfer of assets, and while they may have effects on future production, they do not change output at the time of the transfer. But brokerage charges associated with these transactions are in the GDP because the broker's service is current production.

The GDP measures production in terms of dollar costs, without making value judgments on the differential worth to society of the activities measured. Equal weight is given to purchases of goods and services for everyday living, investment for future production, and public services—food, housing, machinery, inventories, education, defense, etc., are all valued strictly in dollar terms. Similarly, the labor and capital resources necessary to produce this output are measured strictly in dollar amounts as workers' wages and business profits. This objective measure of the nation's output may be contrasted to measures that could account for the nation's "welfare" or "well-being" by assigning a positive or negative value to activities based, not only on their marketplace value, but also on their intrinsic worth.

A GDP that accounted for welfare would measure the nonmaterial effects of activities by deducting from production for "bad" items and adding for "good" items over and above their value in the marketplace. Such a computation would assign greater value to industrial activity that protects the environment than to an equal amount of production that harms the environment. Similarly, defense spending that deters war would be valued more highly than defense spending that results in destructive or war-provoking actions, although in practice such a distinction would be very difficult to make. A GDP that took welfare into account would also include the value of many "products" currently not valued in dollar terms, such as the increased leisure time resulting from a shorter work week, the greater security resulting from improved police protection, and the market value of unpaid labor services of homemakers, parents, and volunteers. Such a GDP measure would also evaluate consumer goods like autos, furniture, and appliances differently to incorporate the value of their services over the years of their useful life, as well as the actual dollar amount involved in producing the goods, which is included in the traditional GDP measure. In the 1970s, the Bureau of Economic Analysis began to develop estimates of such items that economists could use to modify the traditional GDP measures, but the project was discontinued for lack of funding.

Because the market value of unpaid labor services of homemakers is not included in the GDP, the long-term shift of women working as homemakers for no pay to working at paying jobs in the market economy has overstated the growth rate of the GDP. The result is that increasing amounts of work previously done within the family for no money wages such as housekeeping, food preparation, child care, and care of the elderly are increasingly done and paid for in the marketplace, which are added to the GDP. Thus, with the passage of time, the GDP has increased simply because of the change in the societal way work is done. However, no estimates are available of the effect of this societal change on the economic growth rate.

At the same time, some nonmarket-type activities are included as "imputed" estimates in the GDP. The main ones are the rental value of owner-occupied housing, employer-paid health and life insurance premiums, and services provided by financial intermediaries without payment. Imputed items accounted for 15 percent of the GDP in 2001, of which the rental value of owner-occupied housing is 7.5 percent (data on imputations for 2002 will become available with the five-year benchmark revisions planned for December 2003).

Real GDP and Price Change

"Nominal" and "real" are the terms commonly used to denote the distinction in GDP measures of the treatment of prices. The "GDP in current dollars" repre-

Table 3.1

Gross Domestic Product and Main Components: 2002

	Product side ($ billions)	Income side (percent)
Gross domestic product	10,446.2	100.0
Personal consumption expenditures	7,303.7	69.9
Durable goods	871.9	8.3
Nondurable goods	2,115.0	20.2
Services	4,316.8	41.3
Gross private domestic investment	1,593.2	15.7
Nonresidential[a]	1,117	10.7
Residential[b]	471.9	4.5
Inventory change	3.9	—
Net exports	−423.6	−4.1
Exports	1,014.9	9.7
Imports	1,438.5	13.8
Government consumption expenditures and gross investment	1,972.9	18.9
Federal	693.7	6.6
State and local	1,279.2	12.2

Source: Bureau of Economic Analysis, U.S. Department of Commerce, *Survey of Current Business*, April 2003.

a. Business purchases of structures, equipment, and software.

b. New housing construction and improvements.

c. Profits of unincorporated businesses.

d. Mainly sales and property taxes.

e. Mainly depreciation allowances.

f. Income receipts from the rest of the world (exports) less income payments to the rest of the world (imports): profit-type income of (dividends, reinvested earnings, and interest) received from and paid to foreign residents including corporations, and compensation paid to persons who work in foreign countries.

g. Mainly depreciation allowances with capital consumption adjustment.

h. Income receipts from the rest of the world less income payments to the rest of the world.

i. Product-side total less income-side components shown above. Balancing item between product-side and income-side totals.

(*continued*)

Table 3.1 (*continued*)

	Product side ($ billions)	Income side (percent)
Gross domestic product	10,446.2	100.0
Compensation of employees	5,977.4	57.2
Wages and salaries	5,003.7	47.9
Supplements	973.7	9.3
Proprietors' income[c]	756.5	7.2
Farm	12.9	0.1
Nonfarm	743.7	7.1
Rental income[d]	142.4	1.4
Corporate profits[e]	787.4	7.5
Net interest	684.2	6.5
Indirect business taxes[f]	800.4	7.7
Consumption of fixed capital[g]	1,393.5	13.3
Business transfer payments	44.1	0.4
Less: Government subsidies less surplus of government enterprises	32.5	−0.3
Rest of the world[h]	9.6	0.1
Statistical discrepancy[i]	−116.7	−1.1

sents the actual prices of the goods and services bought and sold in each period in market transactions, and is referred to as "nominal GDP." The "GDP in chained dollars" eliminates the effects of rising or declining prices from a base period, and is referred to as "real GDP."[2]

Real GDP, which technically is "GDP in chained [year—e.g., 1996] dollars," represents the quantity of goods and services produced abstracted from price increases or decreases from quarter to quarter and year to year. "Chained" dollars refers to the procedure of changing the proportions of the expenditures for various goods and services items every year in calculating indexes of price change, which are referred to as weights (see chapter 1 under Index Numbers). To correct for any bias in these calculations due to using the prices of the individual items in year 1 or year 2, the prices of both years are "chained" by multiplying them together and averaging them by a geometric mean. The base period is the reference period from which before and after all movements are calculated, which at the time of this writing is 1996.

The real GDP measures have little relevance in absolute terms, as they are difficult to relate to over time; for example, in 2004, it is difficult to think of spending in 1996 dollars. But real GDP data are the most important measures of the *rate of change in percentage terms* of the quantity of economic output from quarter to quarter and year to year. Thus, real GDP is the most comprehensive and widely accepted indicator of economic growth.

In its simplest form, GDP in current dollars is converted to real GDP by dividing the current-dollar data by one plus the price change from one quarter to the next (or annually from one year to the next) for each of the detailed goods and services items in the GDP. The real GDP data also provide measures of price change. These indexes of inflation (rising prices) and deflation (falling prices) are based on the percent distribution of the expenditure patterns of the component goods and service items used as weights to calculate price change from one period to the next. There are two variants of the GDP price measures. One is the chain-type price index discussed above. The other is the "implicit price deflator," which is derived by dividing current-dollar GDP by the chained-dollar GDP. The deflator reflects continuing shifts in tastes and spending patterns because it accounts for actual spending as new or substitute products replace old ones and as consumers choose between higher- and lower-priced products or between items with slow or rapid price increases. Thus, the expenditure weights continually change from one period to the next in this price measure, as in the chain-price index, but the method of calculating the weight change differs in the two measures.

These alternative price measures are very close in magnitude. In practice, the two measures of price change are often identical or differ by no more that 0.1 percentage point, except for the most recent quarter. Therefore, the two different estimates of GDP price change are not a problem for economic analysis.

The preparation of price indexes has the ongoing problem of accounting adequately for changes in the characteristics of the goods and services being priced. The indexes purport to measure price changes that result solely from a price increase or decrease, not from changes in the quality or specifications of the item. For example, if a loaf of bread increases in price without a change in quality or size, that is a price increase for purposes of GDP measurement. If the loaf increases in size as much as in price, there is no price change for GDP measurement. Or if the price of the bread is unchanged but the loaf is now larger or contains a nutritious new ingredient, a price decrease will be registered.

Price measurement issues are discussed more fully in chapter 11, "Inflation and Deflation." They are noted here to indicate that price measurement, and the price-derived GDP in chained dollars (real GDP), are imprecise measures.

Government Budgets

Federal, state, and local government spending in the GDP is composed of consumption expenditures and gross investment. Consumption expenditures cover employee compensation of government workers, purchases of goods and services from private industry, and depreciation charges on existing capital structures, equipment, and computer software. Gross investment covers capital outlays for newly acquired structures, equipment, and computer software from private industry.

The GDP measurement of government consumption and gross investment is less inclusive than that of expenditures in federal, state, and local official budgets. Thus, government consumption and gross investment exclude transfer payments to individuals for Social Security, unemployment benefits, and other income maintenance programs, federal grants to state and local governments and state grants to local governments, interest on government debt, foreign economic aid, and government loans less repayments—all of which are included as spending in official government budgets. The spending generated by these transfer-type payments typically is reflected in the GDP in subsequent rounds as the income received as transfers is used to buy goods and services in the same or later periods (excluding foreign aid except for the part that is spent in the United States). For example, Social Security and other income maintenance payments when spent become consumer expenditures; state and local government spending of federal grants appears in state and local consumption and investment; foreign spending of economic aid on U.S. production appears in net exports; and interest payments on government debt and government loans and subsidies appear in the spending by the recipients of these funds in the domestic and foreign components of the GDP. Thus, while these transfer-type items are excluded from government consumption and investment in the GDP, they are accounted for subsequently in all GDP components, except to the extent they are used to increase saving, reduce debt, or for the foreign aid spent on non-U.S. output.

Nevertheless, the exclusion of these items from the GDP accounting of the government sector limits one's view of the economic impact of government. For example, federal government consumption and investment expenditures in the GDP of $694 billion represented only 32 percent of all federal government outlays in 2002. One way to more fully analyze the economic impact of governments in the GDP framework is to use supplementary data in the national accounts on government statistical budgets which include transfer payments as well as consumption and investment, plus tax and other receipts collected by governments. These are similar to the official budgets, but are modified to make them more useful for estimating the effects of expenditures, receipts, and the budget surplus or deficit on economic activity.

Selected Technical Topics

This section addresses several technical aspects of the GDP relevant to interpreting economic trends: alternative summary measures, seasonally adjusted annual rate, error range, the statistical discrepancy, net exports, and valuation adjustments.

Alternative Summary Measures

In addition to the GDP, other summary measures of the national accounts are available to better reflect special circumstances in the domestic or international economies. These measures are final sales of domestic product, gross domestic purchases, final sales to domestic purchasers, gross national product, and command-basis GDP. Another alternative GDP measure, GDP on the income side, is discussed in the statistical discrepancy section below.

Final sales of domestic product is the GDP excluding inventory change. In deriving final sales, an inventory increase is deducted from the GDP or an inventory decrease is added to the GDP. Inventory movements arise from differences between production and sales—inventories increase when production is larger than sales, and they decrease when sales are greater than production. Businesses augment or cut back on their stock of goods based on their perceptions of future sales and prices, or because of unexpected market developments such as substantially greater-than-anticipated rises or falls in sales, in which case the subsequent inventory depletion or accumulation is referred to as "unplanned." The unplanned changes may in turn generate deliberate actions to bring inventories into a desired balance with sales. Short-term inventory movements can be important signals that future production may increase because inventories are low in relation to sales, or that production may decrease because inventories are relatively high.

It is also informative to assess the economy's performance independent of inventory movements by focusing on the strength of demand in all GDP markets as evidenced in final sales. For example, if sales are level or falling but production is adding to inventories, the overall GDP growth rate may not be sustainable. Or if sales are increasing and inventories are being depleted because of production bottlenecks, the GDP growth rate may fall below the longer-term sustainable level. The purpose of the final sales measure is to capture this underlying demand.

Gross domestic purchases is the GDP minus exports and plus imports. It focuses on the demand for goods and services in the United States, regardless of the country that produces the items. By excluding exports, it abstracts from foreign demand for American production, and by including imports, it includes American domestic demand that is not being met by American industry. Thus, it focuses on purchases of goods and services in the United States.

Final sales to domestic purchasers is final sales minus exports and plus imports. It measures underlying demand in the U.S. domestic economy by excluding inventory movements from gross domestic purchases.

Gross national product (GNP) is the GDP adjusted to include the effect of profits (dividends and retained earnings) and interest derived from foreign investments and of wages and salaries received from working in foreign countries. These are referred to as "factor income." The GNP is a residency concept, in contrast to the GDP, which is a geographic location concept of the fifty states and the District of Columbia. The GNP treats multinational corporations' profits according to the nationality of the company's ownership, and foreign workers' wages according to the nationality of the worker. In the GNP, profits and interest from foreign operations of U.S.-owned companies are included as business income, while profits from operations in the United States of foreign-owned companies are excluded from business income. Analogously, wages and salaries of U.S. residents working abroad are included in GNP, and wages and salaries of foreign residents working in the United States are excluded from GNP.

For some analyses of the American economy, the generation of incomes of U.S. companies and workers based on residency is most significant. Thus, foreign workers send some of their wage income to relatives in their home country, although they also spend money in the nation where they are working. And profits of a multinational company with affiliates in several countries accrue to the parent company in the home country, and thus affect the company's business decisions on investment and operations worldwide, although the profits are in part generated from production and employment outside the home country. In sum, the GNP includes the profits of U.S.-owned companies earned from foreign operations and wages of U.S. residents employed abroad, and excludes profits of foreign-owned companies from their U.S. operations and wages of foreign workers employed in the United States. This reverses their treatment in the GDP.

Command-basis GNP represents the "command" by U.S. residents over goods and services produced. It responds to the problem that as prices for exported and imported items diverge and substantially change the terms of trade (the ratio of export prices to import prices), the conventional deflation of exports and imports by their respective price indexes distorts real GNP growth rates and thus gives U.S. residents a misleading higher or lower claim on U.S. production than actually exists. The problem results from the accounting need to subtract imports from exports and payments of factor income from receipts of factor income in the net foreign transaction component of the GNP. This is done to offset the inclusion of imports in the other product-side GNP components of consumer expenditures, business investment, and government consumption and investment. If imports were not subtracted from exports, GNP would be overstated because it would include foreign production, and the product and income sides of the GNP would not balance because income-side wages and profits do not exist for imports (this also applies to the GDP and is discussed more fully in the later section on net exports). The command-basis measure is prepared for the GNP rather than the GDP because the GNP national concept is considered more relevant to the command-basis idea than the GDP concept of incomes derived from economic activity within the fifty states and the District of Columbia.

The problem occurs when important internationally traded items such as crude oil have relatively large price changes. For example, during the Arab oil embargo of 1973–75 and during the Iranian revolution of 1979–81, when the price of imported oil rose very sharply, chained-dollar imports were much lower than current-dollar imports. This in turn raised chained-dollar net exports (net exports are exports minus imports) and therefore real GNP. It suggested that Americans had a greater supply from which to "command" goods and services because of the higher import prices. This is an anomaly of the accounting need to deduct imports, because higher import prices actually lower the availability of goods and services for consumption. Analogously, the oil price decline during 1982–86 falsely suggested a lower command of goods and services over that period in the conventional GNP.

Command-basis GNP handles such problems by changing the deflation of prices of net exports in real GNP. The conventional GNP method deflates exports and imports separately by export and import prices, and then subtracts chained-dollar imports from chained-dollar exports. Command-basis GNP deflates net exports in a single step, using import prices as the only deflator (export prices as the single deflator would yield similar results). This device tends to moderate the anomalies produced by the accounting need to subtract imports in the net export component.

Seasonally Adjusted Annual Rate

Two steps are involved in calculating the seasonally adjusted annual rate. The first is the GDP absolute level for the quarter at an annual rate, and the second is the percentage change in this level from the preceding quarter at an annual rate. In step 1, the GDP is estimated quarterly, but the number for each quarter is published as if the activity in the quarter were at an annual level (seasonality is discussed in chapter 1 under Seasonality). In step 2, the annual rate shows how much the economy would grow over a year, if it continued growing for the next three quarters at the same rate as it grew in the latest quarter. This facilitates comparison of the economy's current volume with past and projected annual levels.

Specifically, the GDP level is the sum of the seasonally adjusted data for the three months of the quarter, multiplied by four to raise it to an annual level. For example, for the first quarter of the year, the seasonally adjusted data for January, February, and March are summed, and the total is multiplied by four. The resulting number is the quarterly GDP at a seasonally adjusted annual rate. Because the quarter includes activity for three months, the GDP in a particular month of a quarter can decline (or rise) even if it rises (or declines) for the quarter as a whole.

Then, to derive an annual percentage rate of change in the current-quarter GDP from the preceding quarter, the relative change for the present quarter is compounded to represent an annual rate. The procedure is to raise the rate of growth or decline in the current quarter to the fourth power, subtract 1.0, and multiply by 100, as follows:

$$\left(\frac{\text{Seasonally adjusted annual GDP (current quarter)}}{\text{Seasonally adjusted annual GDP (previous quarter)}} \right)^4 -1.0 \times 100$$

Percentage changes from quarter to quarter or year to year are published for major GDP aggregates except inventory change and net exports, because these components of the GDP can be either positive or negative, and a percentage change is not relevant between two periods that do not have the same sign, or for two periods that both have negative signs. To avoid confusion, the BEA reports only measures of economic activity that can be calculated on a regular basis. Thus, percentage changes for exports and imports are published separately.

Evaluation of Reliability

Because the GDP is developed from a variety of data sources, it is not possible to develop a statistical measure of reliability (chapter 1 under Revisions). But two indirect estimates of the accuracy of the GDP are useful to the analyst, revisions to the early data, and the statistical discrepancy.

Revision Error Range

Table 3.2 shows that the contemporaneous GDP estimates published in each of the three months after each quarter are provisional, as is evident from the size of the revisions made as more complete and accurate information becomes available. Experience with these revisions indicates that, in nine cases out of ten, their likely effect on seasonally adjusted annual growth rates for quarterly real GDP is in the ranges indicated in Table 3.2. For example, in nine of ten cases, the revision between the advance estimate of GDP and the latest estimate was between minus 1.5 percentage points and plus 3.2 percentage points. Thus, when the real GDP for the first quarter of 2003 was first reported (advance estimate) to have increased at an annual rate of 1.6 percent, the chances were nine out of ten that the latest estimate would fall somewhere between 0.1 and 4.8 percent. There is also a tendency for revisions, which incorporate new and additional data, to raise growth rates or lower the rate of decline.

The table shows two sets of revision ranges. One set of early estimates focuses on the revisions that occur on a contemporaneous basis. These are revisions made between the advance estimate published one month after the quarter, and the preliminary and final GDP estimates which are published two and three months after the quarter. The other set of estimates focuses on subsequent revisions of the three early estimates based on the annual revision that is prepared every July and on the still later five-year benchmark GDP revisions, both of which are distant from the quarter in question.

Both sets of revisions are sizable, but as would be expected, those resulting from the annual and five-year benchmark revisions are greater than those between the GDP published one to three months after the quarter. However, policymakers responsible for setting fiscal and monetary policies to influence the economy clearly cannot apply such high revision ranges in their analyses of the current rate of economic growth. Further, to be timely, economic policymakers must respond to trends based on contemporaneous GDP measures, long before the annual and five-year benchmark revisions become available. For current policy analysis, then, a more workable measure of revision range is the average without regard to sign, also shown in Table 3.2. These data, which average the revision ranges into a single number and thus eliminate the extremes appearing in the actual ranges, indicate notably lower error ranges of approximately plus or minus 0.6 percentage point between the one-month and three month estimates, and plus or minus 1.3 to 1.4 percentage points between the three month estimate and the annual and five-year benchmark revisions.

In contrast to the high error ranges associated with the revisions, the average

Table 3.2

Probable Revisions to Real GDP Quarterly Annualized Growth Rates: Nine of Ten Revisions (percentage points)

Vintage comparisons	Average without regard to sign (plus or minus)	Range
Advance to preliminary	0.5	−0.9 to 1.2
Advance to final	0.6	−1.0 to 1.3
Preliminary to final	0.3	−0.5 to 0.6
Advance to latest	1.4	−1.5 to 3.2
Preliminary to latest	1.3	−1.7 to 2.8
Final to latest	1.4	−1.7 to 3.0

Source: Bureau of Economic Analysis, U.S. Department of Commerce, "Gross Domestic Product: First Quarter 2003 (Advance)," *BEA News*, April 25, 2003.

Notes: Based on the period from 1978 through 2001 for the first three lines and from 1978 through 1999 for the last three lines.
Advance: One month after the quarter
Preliminary: Two months after the quarter
Final: Three months after the quarter
Latest: Most recent annual or five-year benchmark revision

without regard to sign provides at least a workable error range. However, whether one uses the revision ranges or the average without regard to sign, the error range for revisions to the GDP is still high, which underscores the need to observe the trend for at least two consecutive quarters before using it as a basis for changing economic policies. But even current trends of three consecutive quarters can be misleading for economic policy analysis, as occurred in 2001 (see chapter 1 under "Revisions"). In general, one should also wait for the final estimate three months after the quarter before concluding that the numbers reflect the actual circumstances of the quarter. The overall lesson is that no single GDP number should be interpreted to indicate a new trend or validate an existing one, but rather should be viewed in the context of trends for previous quarters to determine whether a change is occurring.

While the direction and extent of future revisions are unpredictable, two aspects of the gross national product (GNP) revisions have been differentiated into "noise" and "news" in a 1986 analysis based on data for the 1975–82 period (the GNP rather than the GDP was the featured measure at that time).[3] Noise is related to errors in the variety of survey and other data used in preparing the GDP estimates. News refers to other information that is available at the time the early estimates are prepared that is used to modify the survey data on the supposition that the survey data will be revised. Thus, use of the available news in preparing the early GDP estimates aims at improving the accuracy of the early estimates, with the implied objective of lessening the size of future revisions when the more complete and accurate survey data become available. The analysis concluded that the revisions were not predictable, and characterized the procedures used in preparing the early GDP estimates as being an efficient process.

Statistical Discrepancy

Conceptually, the grand totals of the product and income sides of the GDP represent the equivalent output of goods and services, although arrived at from different perspectives and data sources. In practice, limitations in the underlying data mean that the totals are rarely equal. The data are obtained from a variety of surveys, tax records, and other sources that have varying comparability with the GDP concepts. They also have varying degrees of accuracy, because the survey samples are not necessarily representative and the respondents may provide erroneous information.

The difference between the output totals on the product and income sides is the net effect of these inconsistencies and inaccuracies, and is referred to as the "statistical discrepancy." The discrepancy is not systematic from quarter to quarter, as different data problems continually occur. By convention, the discrepancy is calculated as the product side minus the income side, and this number appears as a balancing item on the income side of the accounts. Because of the likely overstatement and understatement among the individual data items, the statistical discrepancy is smaller than if the gross deficiencies were added without regard to their over- or understatement, that is without regard to sign.

While there is nothing that would inherently favor the product or income side as being more accurate, it seems that based on the data available for preparing both estimates, a stronger case can be made that the product side is more accurate.[4] Still, from the user's perspective, the discrepancy allows alternative GDP growth rates to be calculated from the product- and income-side information. These upper and lower bounds recognize that, given the data shortcomings in general, "reality" is probably more a range than a precise number, with the analyst considering for each period whether the upper or lower part of the range is more appropriate.

For analytical purposes, the user should be aware that a noticeable change in the discrepancy could affect the growth rate. For example, in a $10 trillion GDP, assume a change in the statistical discrepancy from −$10 billion in the first quarter to $40 billion in the second quarter of the year, for a swing from the first to the second quarters of $50 billion. If the GDP on the product side grows at an annual rate of 2 percent in the second quarter, the alternative growth rate on the income side (adjusted for the statistical discrepancy) for the second quarter is zero. Based on Okun's Law discussed in chapter 2, the product-side growth rate of 2 percent maintains a stable unemployment rate, while a growth rate of zero raises the unemployment rate by about one percentage point per year. Such alternative estimates suggest a weaker economy than that shown only by the product side estimate in this illustration, though the product side seems to have a stronger data base, as noted above.

Net Exports

"Net exports of goods and services" is the GDP component that represents U.S. transactions with other countries. It is derived by subtracting imports from exports. The net concept is necessary to keep the product and income sides of the GDP in balance, due to the special situation of imports. Exports and imports are detailed in chapter 7.

Because imports are produced abroad, their production does not generate wages and profits in the United States, and thus no income-side payments are associated with their production. However, imported items do appear on the product side as households, businesses, and governments buy the imported goods and services. If nothing were done to offset the import purchases in the consumption, investment, and government components on the product side, that side would be overstated and higher than the income side, as it would appear that imports are produced in the U.S. Therefore, imports are deducted from exports in the net export because imports are not produced in the United States.

The deduction of imports, however, causes the net export component to appear as a deceptively small share of the GDP. In 2002, for example, net exports were –$424 billion ($1015 billion of exports minus $1439 billion of imports), or –4.1 percent of the GDP. This relatively small net number masks the much higher actual economic impact of exports and imports separately, as exports were 9.7 percent and imports were 13.8 percent of the GDP in 2002.

While net exports give an overall view of the differential effect of exports and imports and of money flows between the United States and other countries (and can be important for foreign exchange values and U.S. monetary policies), exports and imports taken separately are more relevant for assessing the impact of international trade on American production and prices. Exports and imports affect and are affected by employment and inflation in the United States, American competitiveness in international markets, the value of the dollar, and the pace of the American and world economies.

Valuation Adjustments for Inventories and Depreciation

Special adjustments are made for the effect of price changes on inventories and on depreciation allowances for equipment and structures as conventionally accounted for by companies. These adjustments are particularly important during periods of high inflation and when depreciation allowances in the tax laws differ substantially from the use of capital facilities in business practice.

In both cases, the purpose of the adjustments is to reflect the replacement cost of inventories and capital facilities based on prices when they are used up, as distinct from prices at the time the inventories and capital facilities were acquired (their historical cost). Doing so eliminates the effect of valuation gains and losses on inventories due to price increases and decreases of capital goods since they were acquired. And for capital facilities, the adjustment provides a truer picture of the actual cost used up during the accounting period as compared with the depreciation deductions allowed in income tax laws.

The *inventory valuation adjustment* (IVA) converts the change in inventory book value to the GDP concept, which is called the "change in private inventories" on the product side. The GDP concept is the change in the physical volume of inventories valued at the average acquisition cost during the accounting period. On the income side, the IVA converts business profits from a valuation based on the book value charge against inventories to the GDP concept.

During periods of rising inventory prices, the IVA is negative to offset inventory profits when goods are sold; when prices are falling the IVA is positive to offset the inventory losses. Since prices generally are rising, the IVA is typically negative, although the amounts vary considerably depending on the inflation rate. For example, the IVA moved from –$7.2 billion in 1999 to –$22.5 billion in 2000 to $13.6 billion in 2001 to –$10.7 in 2002. These trends reflect changes in the rate of price increases and decreases of various commodities in the producer price indexes prepared by the U.S. Bureau of Labor Statistics for crude materials, intermediate materials, and finished goods.

The data cited here refer to the IVA on the product side. The product- and income-side estimates of the IVA differ because they represent different accounting systems. The levels are of the same general magnitude and the year-to-year movements are almost always the same. Because inventories are continually replenished and sold at current prices, the IVA provides a more realistic assessment of actual inventory buildups and depletions and of business profits.

The *capital consumption adjustment* (CCAdj) affects the income side of the GDP, and appears as an offsetting item, with different signs, to business profits and capital consumption allowances (mainly depreciation). Thus, the CCAdj does not affect total GDP, but it does affect the distribution between profits and depreciation. The CCAdj reflects the fact that the actual usage of capital facilities by business (known as economic depreciation) differs from the depreciation based on tax law provisions (known as tax depreciation). While tax depreciation is based on statutorily defined schedules, economic depreciation is a closer approximation of actual depreciation in industry practice both in terms of the expected lifetime of the asset and the rate at which it is depreciated over the years. Estimates of economic depreciation are based on actual service lives for various types of equipment and structures as indicated by industry surveys conducted in the 1970s by the U.S. Department of the Treasury, by information collected from regulatory agencies, and from studies of prices on used equipment and structures in resale markets.

The CCAdj is affected by the tax laws and inflation. When the tax laws allow accelerated depreciation schedules, which permit businesses to recoup the original cost of capital facilities faster than businesses actually use them up, the CCAdj appears as a positive item in business profits and a negative item in capital consumption allowances. When prices of capital goods are rising and thus raising the cost of new capital facilities, the CCAdj deducts from profits and adds to capital consumption allowances. The opposite occurs when the tax laws require slower depreciation rates than those at which business tends to use up capital facilities or when capital goods prices are falling. The CCAdj tends to be smaller when the tax laws have few investment incentives or disincentives in their own right, and larger when tax-generated investment incentives and disincentives are great. Thus, the smaller the CCAdj is, the closer the depreciation assumptions of the tax laws are to economic reality.

The CCAdj for unincorporated farm businesses and rental income of persons reflects changes in the capital goods inflation rate, but does not include differentials between tax law depreciation and actual business practice in the "using up" of capital facilities. The reasons for this difference are: (a) there are limited reliable data to prepare such estimates for unincorporated farm businesses and rental property income, and (b) rental income is composed mainly of "rent" for owner-occupied dwellings that is imputed as if it were a cash payment to a landlord, but for which no depreciation is taken on the individual income tax return.

ANALYSIS OF TRENDS

This part of the chapter covers the main patterns shown by American business cycles from the 1945–48 expansion to the 1991–2000 expansion, and the subsequent 2001 recession and recovery in 2002–03. It highlights the major factors driving these trends. The period represents a major change from the depression of the 1930s and World War II both in the nature of the economy and the tools available for moderating business cycles. In addition to the patterns of economic growth as represented by the economy-wide GDP, this part addresses the following topics: (a) the GDP component demand markets of households, business, and governments; (b) alternative macro measures of the GDP; (c) the labor, capital facilities, and productivity supply perspective of the GDP; (d) manufacturing and economic growth; and (e) assessment of economic growth in the first decade of the twenty-first century.

As mentioned in chapter 1 under Determining Business Cycle Phases, there have been ten expansions and ten recessions since the end of World War II in 1945, from the expansion of 1945–48 to the 2001 recession. There was a recession from February to October 1945, but because it was so closely linked to the war and the demobilization, it is not included in this analysis. The subsequent expansion from 1945 to 1948 was affected by the pent-up demand for housing and consumer durables which were produced at very low levels both in the depression of the 1930s due to the low incomes then, and during World War II, when the concentration was on military production. This demand backlog, coupled with the higher incomes derived from wartime production in the place of production for the civilian economy, resulted in large amounts of household savings at the end of the war. Thus, the war had an important, although indirect, effect. The 1948–49 recession was the first postwar cyclical movement that was sufficiently removed from the war not to have been affected by the war's aftermath.

Table 3.3 shows the beginning and ending quarters of expansions and recessions for the business cycles since the end of World War II. The turning point used here to mark the peak of expansions and the trough of recessions is the change in direction of the real GDP. It is based on the cyclical turning points established by the National Bureau of Economic Research (NBER) discussed in chapter 1. Because the NBER cyclical turning points are on a monthly basis, and the GDP is prepared on a calendar-quarter basis, there is an ambiguity in dovetailing the monthly and quarterly turning points. Thus, one month in the quarter can be the peak of the expansion and the next month in the same quarter can be the beginning of the recession (the same situation occurs when the trough month of the recession and the following first month of the recovery are in the same quarter). To limit this ambiguity, the convention adopted here is to use the quarter closest to the NBER monthly turning point in which the real GDP changed directions.

The postwar period expansions averaged four years in peacetime and four and one-half years including wartime cycles, and recessions averaged one year in both cases, as noted in chapter 1. However, the duration of individual cycles varies widely around these averages. The expansion of the 1960s lasted nine years, the expansion of the 1980s lasted eight years, and the expansion of the 1990s to 2000 lasted ten years. There were very short expansions of two years and one year in the 1950s and 1980s, respectively.

Trends Before and After World War II

To put the period in a longer context, the discussion first briefly contrasts trends in economic growth during the twentieth century before and after World War

Table 3.3

Duration of Expansions and Recessions Related to the Real Gross Domestic Product

Expansions		Recessions	
	Duration (quarters)		Duration (quarters)
1945:4T-48:4P[a]	12	1948:4P-49:4T	4
1949:4T-53:3P	15	1953:3P-54:2T	3
1954:2T-57:3P	13	1957:3P-58:2T	3
1958:2T-60:1P	7	1960:1P-60:4T	3
1960:4T-69:3P	35	1969:3P-70:4T	5
1970:4T-73:4P	12	1973:4P-75:1T	5
1975:1T-80:1P	20	1980:1P-80:3T	2
1980:3T-81:3P	4	1981:3P-82:3T	4
1982:3T-90:2P	31	1990:2P-91:1T	3
1991:IT-2001:1P	40	2001:1P-01:4T[b]	3

Source: Monthly cyclical turning points established by the National Bureau of Economic Research were adapted by the author to quarterly GDP measures. See text.

Notes: Number after colon is quarter of year.
P-peak. High point of expansion before economy turns down into recession.
T-trough. Low point of recession before economy turns up into recovery.
a. Quarterly real GDP data are not available before 1947. Use of 1945:4 as the start of the 1945–48 expansion follows the designation by the National Bureau of Economic Research of November 1945 as the beginning of the expansion.
b. The recession that began in 2001:2 was not designated as ending as of this writing in the spring of 2003. The table assumes that the recession ended in 2001:4.

II. Table 3.4 shows long-term trends in real GDP during the twentieth century.[5] The first part of the century, from 1901–29, included the period before and after World War I, culminating with the high point of 1929 before the depression of the 1930s. The subsequent periods from the 1930s to the early 2000s had considerably varied economic conditions.

The 1929–39 period was dominated by the depression of the 1930s. In an example of how changes in the methodology used in preparing the real GDP estimates can affect measures of economic growth, the revised methodology adopted in the 1990s showed that real GDP regained its 1929 level in 1936, rather than 1939.[6]

The 1939–48 years comprised World War II and the transition after the war to a peacetime economy. Incomes were bolstered considerably by the employment growth associated with the high wartime production, but because there was little construction of housing and production of consumer durables, households

Table 3.4

Annual Growth of Real GDP: 1901–2000

	Percent
1901–29	3.0
1929–39	0.9
1939–48	6.3
1948–59	3.7
1959–69	4.4
1969–79	3.2
1979–89	3.0
1989–2000	3.1

Sources: 1901–29: Michael P. Niemira and Phillip A. Klein, *Forecasting Financial and Economic Cycles* (Wiley, 1994), Appendix A. The 1901–29 data represent the gross national product (GNP), not the gross domestic product (GDP). This definitional difference is insignificant for long-term trends generally, and specifically because such definitional differences are overwhelmed by the large statistical gaps in the early estimates. See text.

Data for 1929–2000 are prepared by the Bureau of Economic Analysis, U.S. Department of Commerce.

Note: The author calculated the compounded annual rates.

had large amounts of savings after the war. Thus, the peacetime transition during 1945–48 reflected large increases in the demand for new housing and consumer durables stemming from backlogs created by (a) the low output and low incomes of the depression, and (b) the curtailment of output for the civilian economy during the war years. These backlogs, together with the much greater household incomes and savings available after the war, coalesced for the greatly increased spending on housing and consumer durables after the war.

The decades from the 1950s to 2000 each had substantially different rates of economic growth, peaking in the 1960s at 4.4 percent and dropping to the 3 percent level from the 1970s to 2000. They were also preoccupied internationally with the cold war until the early 1990s.

Long-term trends in real GDP that span several business cycles show distinct shifts in the annual growth rate. Generally, 1901–29, 1939–48, the 1950s, and the 1960s showed the highest growth rates, and the 1930s, 1970s, 1980s, and 1990s to 2000 had the lowest growth rates. The highest growth rate for the entire period occurred during 1939–48, but that was a great exaggeration because it started from the low base at the end of the 1930s and was boosted by World War II and the immediate postwar period. The lower growth rates from the 1970s to 2000 were accompanied by periods of long and short expansions, as noted previously.

A theoretical case could be made that fewer or possibly more uniform cyclical fluctuations result in faster economic growth or vice versa. Looking more closely at the second half of the twentieth century, however, the evidence on the growth-cyclical relationship is inconclusive. The highest growth rate occurred during the expansion of the 1960s. But the 1950s had the second highest growth rate and had three recessions, the most in any decade. This was discussed over a much longer time span in chapter 1 under Business Cycles and Economic Growth.

Such long-term comparisons are inherently tentative because the increasing accuracy of GDP measures over time limits the statistical comparability, particularly between the first and second halves of the century (see chapter 1 under Changing Characteristics of Business Cycles Since the Nineteenth Century). Also, there is little documentation of the statistical methodology used in developing the estimates from 1901 to 1929. They were prepared by private researchers outside of the U.S. Bureau of Economic Analysis.

Overall Cyclical Movements

This analysis of real GDP and its main components focuses on their movements from the 1980s to the early 2000s. The main components are highly summarized to give a broad overview at this stage, as they are detailed in subsequent chapters. Each of the two long expansions of the period is separated into halves, four years each for the 1980s and five years each for the 1990s to 2000. This points up the evolving nature of long-term expansions that would not be apparent in viewing the entire expansion as a whole. Exports and imports are not included here because they are heavily influenced by the world economy (see chapter 7, "The United States in the World Economy").

Figures 3.1a and 3.1b show these movements for expansions and recessions, respectively. *During expansions*, there was one short upturn of only one year from 1980 to 1981, which I characterize as an aborted expansion. Another short-term upturn was in progess from the recovery of 2002 to the second quarter of 2003 as of this writing. There was an overall difference between the long expansion of the 1980s and that of the 1990s to 2000. During the 1980s, economic growth *decelerated* in the last half of the expansion, while during the 1990s to 2000, economic growth *accelerated* in the last half of the expansion.

Consumer expenditures for goods and services have movements very similar to those in GDP. While they account for the dominant share of the GDP (typi-

Figure 3.1a **Business Cycle Movements of Real Gross Domestic Product and Selected Components, 1980s to Early 2000s: Expansions**

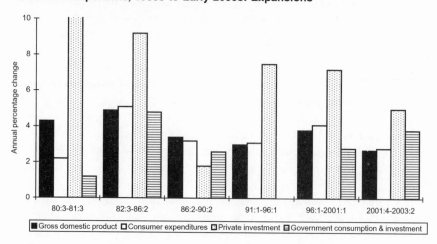

Source: Based on U.S. Bureau of Economic Analysis data in chained (1996) dollars.

Note: Number after colon is quarter of year. Private investment in 80:3–81:3 is truncated. Government spending was zero change in 91:1–96:1.

Figure 3.1b **Business Cycle Movements of Real Gross Domestic Product and Selected Components, 1980s to Early 2000s: Recessions**

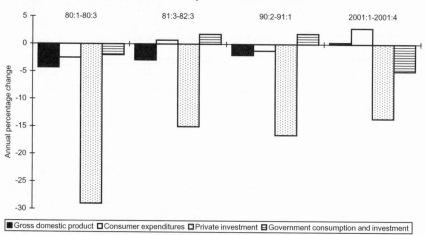

Source: Based on U.S. Bureau of Economic Analysis data in chained (1996) dollars.

Note: Number after colon is quarter of year.

cally 66–68 percent), reaching 70 percent in the sluggish recovery year of 2002 (Table 3.1), other components also influence the overall growth rate. Consumer expenditures are detailed in chapter 4.

Private investment for nonresidential equipment and structures, housing, and inventory accumulation and depletion have much larger increases and decreases than the GDP, and in general constitute the most volatile cyclical component of the GDP. In fact, the sharp increases in investment in the short 1980–81 expansion and in the 2002–03 recovery are deceptive in that they reflect the boost from the low recession base rather than from a robust rise. Private investment is detailed in chapter 5.

Outlays for consumption and investment by the aggregate of federal, state, and local governments increase less than GDP. But this pattern is not the full story of the government impact on the economy because of the definition of government in the GDP. The government component of the GDP covers *direct* consumption and investment of the nation's goods and services, but excludes *indirect* transfer payments for Social Security, unemployment benefits and various other income maintenance programs, federal government grants to state and local governments, interest on government debt, foreign aid, and government loans minus repayments, as noted in the methodology section under Government Budgets. Thus, the government component of the GDP considerably understates the impact of government outlays on the economy. In fact, based on the GDP definition, real government spending did not change during the first five years of the 1990s expansion (Figure 3.1a). Federal, state, and local government spending and taxes are detailed in chapter 6.

During recessions, consumer expenditures typically decline less than the GDP and in one case (1981–82) even rose. This countercyclical tendency is important for lessening economic declines. Government consumption and investment typically has an even greater countercyclical effect. But the 2001 recession was a major exception to this pattern, when consumer expenditures and government consumption and investment both declined more than the GDP, thus exacerbating the recession. Private investment declines much more than the GDP, and accounts for the bulk of the fall in the GDP during recessions.

The contrasting movements of consumer expenditures and private investment during expansions and recessions reflect their intrinsically different characteristics. Consumer expenditures include a large component of necessities such as food, housing occupancy, and transportation, which are not drastically changed when incomes increase or decline in expansions and recessions, while the share of cyclically volatile consumer durable goods is much smaller than the above items (discussed further in chapter 4). By contrast, private investment includes a larger amount of discretionary items for nonresidential equipment and structures and housing construction that are more readily deferred when incomes decline in recessions, but which have above average increases when incomes rise in expansions.

At the time of this writing, the sluggish recovery of 2002 and mid-2003 were of major concern. Preventing another possible decline in the GDP were gains in consumer expenditures and housing construction (housing construction is covered in chapter 5 under Housing).

Alternative GDP Measures of Economic Growth

The GDP numbers are subject to various sources of imprecision because they are prepared from a wide range of underlying data that do not necessarily match the GDP definitions and that reflect varying degrees of accuracy. The inherent statistical error in the GDP due to these limitations in the source data is not known. Differences between the GDP on the product and income sides are compounded because the two measures are prepared from many different data sources, which in itself introduces an unknown amount of inconsistency between them. Theoretically, if both measures were prepared from the same data sources, they would show the same GDP. Even here, it may not be so, because the component data items such as sales and payrolls obtained from the same survey may be reported by a different number of survey respondents and with varying accuracy.

The result is that the GDP estimates on the product and income sides vary continually. The difference is called the "statistical discrepancy," which conventionally is calculated as the product-side estimate minus the income-side estimate, as discussed in the Methodology section. The GDP on the income side is referred to as the gross domestic income (GDI). The GDP and the GDI are different measures of economic growth, though the GDP is considered to be more accurate statistically. Differences in the growth rates from one period to the next tend to be magnified when, in period 1 the product side is higher than the income side, and in period 2 the income side is higher than the product side. Generally the differential growth rates are larger on a quarterly than on an annual and multiyear basis, which probably results from offsetting inconsistencies and errors over time.

In addition, alternative definitional variations are prepared as slight modifications to the GDP for analytical purposes, as noted in the Methodology section. These include final sales of domestic product, gross domestic purchases, final sales to domestic purchasers, gross national product, and command-basis gross national product.

Figure 3.2 illustrates the varying growth rates on a quarterly basis from 1999 to mid-2003 of three alternative measures: GDP, final sales of domestic product, and GDI. These differences tend to offset over a few quarters, but there sometimes are noticeable differences on an annual basis. For example, Table 3.5

Figure 3.2 **Alternative Real Gross Domestic Product Measures, Quarterly at Annual Rate: 1999:1–2003:2**

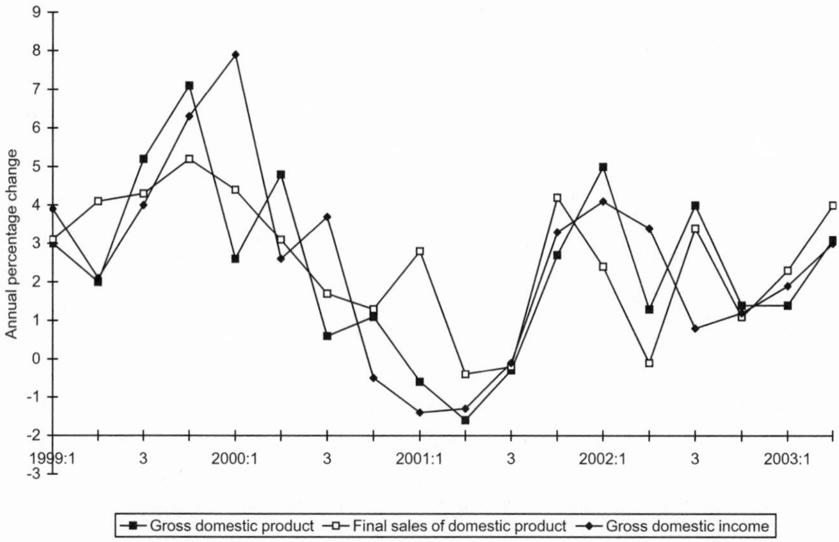

Source: Based on U.S. Bureau of Economic Analysis data in chained (1996) dollars.

Note: Number after colon is quarter of year.

shows that the GDI growth in 2000 was one percentage point higher than that of the GDP and final sales, the 2001 growth of final sales exceeded that of the GDP and GDI by one percentage point, and the GDP and GDI growth in 2002 exceeded that of final sales by one-half percentage point.

Because one measure is intrinsically no more accurate than the other, no single number represents reality. One way to resolve the difference is to treat each quarterly growth rate as being in a range between the upper and lower bounds. It is also useful to compare final sales with the GDP to determine if underlying demand represented by final sales is stronger or weaker than the GDP, because final sales exclude inventory change.

Supply Perspective of Economic Growth

The nation's output of goods and services is produced by the combined effect of three supply resources: (1) labor contribution of workers, (2) services contribution of capital physical facilities, and (3) productivity (efficiency). Thus, the GDP represents the combined effects of the quantity and quality of the labor and capital resources used in production plus the overall productivity of the economy. Estimates of the three components of production in this section are

Table 3.5

Alternative Real GDP Measures: 1999–2002
(annual percent change)

	Gross domestic product	Gross domestic income	Final sales of domestic product
1999	4.1	4.2	4.3
2000	3.8	4.7	3.7
2001	0.3	0.1	1.5
2002	2.4	2.3	1.8

Source: U.S. Bureau of Economic Analysis.

based on the multifactor productivity measures prepared by the U.S. Bureau of Labor Statistics.[7] The labor, capital, and productivity components are discussed more fully in chapter 10 on productivity. This differs from the earlier discussion of the household, business, and government components of the GDP, which represent the markets for goods and services, that is from the demand perspective.

Mathematically, the weighted three growth components sum to business GDP in all periods as follows:

% change in business GDP = % change in labor inputs × labor's share of costs (labor contribution)
+ % change in capital inputs × capital's share of costs (capital contribution)
+ % change in multifactor productivity

The GDP measure used in these estimates represents the private business sector only. It excludes the output, which is primarily the compensation of government employees and of paid employees of households, operating expenses of nonprofit institutions, and the rental value of owner-occupied housing. This modification of the traditional GDP is made because output is not measured independently of inputs, especially labor inputs, as needed for productivity measurement. Implicit within some of these sectors is the assumption that output per hour, or labor productivity, does not change over time. Incorporating an obviously inaccurate assumption within the data would result in a biased measure of productivity.

The labor measure represents the hours at work of employees, self-employed proprietors, and unpaid family workers. These are weighted to account for shifts to workers with more education and experience, or to relative increases in the compensation of these workers, which leads to greater measured labor input. The weights differ because the hours of workers with more schooling or experience are weighted more heavily to reflect differences in capabilities between workers. Thus, the weights differentiate among different groups of workers as separate and distinct inputs in the production process. *These adjustments implicitly reflect the changing efficiency of the nation's work force.*

The capital services measure represents the stocks of physical assets used in production—business equipment, structures, inventories, and land. These are weighted by the income derived from their use in production. The income associated with these capital facilities in turn is based on a market rental value when the enterprise rents the items, or by an implicit rental value when the facilities are owned by the enterprise. Financial assets and owner-occupied housing are excluded because they do not directly involve the production of goods and services, although they have important indirect effects. *The adjustments to the physical assets implicitly reflect the changing efficiency of the nation's capital facilities.*

Multifactor productivity is a combination of many known and unknown elements that contribute to the efficiency of the economy. They include such items as managerial know-how, technology, quality of materials, utilization of productive capacity of firms, energy usage, transportation and distribution systems, and the interaction of these and all other factors. Changes in efficiencies associated with multifactor productivity often involve fundamental changes in efficiency that take relatively long to filter through the broad spectrum of industries in the economy.

Economic growth comes from the combined effects of the labor contribution (labor inputs and efficiency), the capital contribution (capital inputs and efficiency), and multifactor productivity. Figure 3.3 shows the labor contribution, the capital contribution, and multifactor productivity, which sum to business GDP, from 1979 to 2000.[8] Three periods of annual growth are shown separately over the twenty-one-year period: 1979–90, 1990–95, and 1995–2000.

Figure 3.3 indicates that the labor, capital, and multifactor productivity components each contributed to growth in business GDP. Labor and capital each had the largest proportions of the increase in the GDP, though multifactor productivity rose in relative importance from the 1980s to the 1990s to 2000.

In monitoring growth patterns of the GDP, the analyst should include an assessment of the supply components of economic growth. Generally, economic growth will be sustained if the rate of increase in the labor, capital, and multifactor productivity components are at least maintained, while more rapid growth depends on an acceleration of some or all of the components.

Figure 3.3 **Supply Components of Economic Growth: 1948–2000**

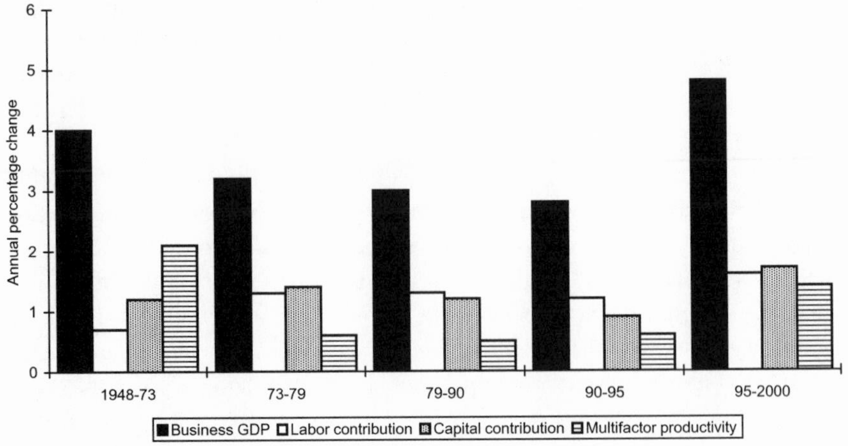

Source: Based on U.S. Bureau of Labor Statistics data.

Manufacturing and Economic Growth

Manufacturing's share of the GDP has been declining over the years, falling to 14 percent in 2001.[9] While manufacturing has become less important, it is still a potent component of the economy. The 14 percent share of the GDP represents manufacturing's *direct* impact on the economy. But it also has significant and wide secondary effects that reverberate throughout the economy.

First, manufacturing in one industry generates direct purchases of goods from selected other manufacturing industries, agriculture, mining, utility, and transportation industries, wholesale and retail trade, and communication, finance, insurance, repairs, and other service industries. These then generate indirect second and subsequent rounds of purchases from all of the above. Second, because manufacturing industries account for a major share of investment in equipment and structures, these investments result in markets for the production of machinery, trucks, and building materials, and the employment of construction workers. Third, because average incomes of workers in manufacturing industries are higher than those in other industries, consumer spending is stimulated proportionately more by the same numbers of manufacturing workers as workers in other industries.

Figure 3.4 shows the annual movements of real GDP and manufacturing production from 1972 to 2002. Manufacturing production is based on the industrial production index prepared by the Federal Reserve Board. The two data series differ methodologically—the industrial production index is calculated on a gross output basis that includes the inputs of purchased materials and serv-

Figure 3.4 **Real Gross Domestic Product versus Manufacturing Production: 1972–2002**

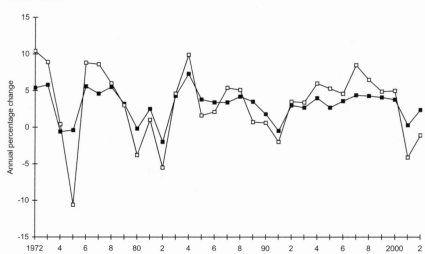

Source: Based on U.S. Bureau of Economic Analysis and Federal Reserve Board data.

ices, while the GDP data are calculated on a net output basis (value added) that excludes the double counting of the inputs of purchased goods and services.

Manufacturing is more volatile than the GDP in the year-to-year movements, with manufacturing typically having sharper increases and decreases than the GDP. This reflects the fact that manufacturing does not include the more stable service industries and government functions that are part of the GDP. Over periods of several years, however, the two series have broadly similar upward and downward patterns.

The above noted decline over the years in manufacturing's share of the GDP in part reflects the rising needs of households and businesses for services, and in part reflects the result of American manufacturing companies continuing to shift more of their production of goods to low-wage countries. This transfer of manufacturing to other countries erodes the manufacturing base of the United States, which is detrimental to economic growth. The problem and a recommended remedy are discussed in the next section, Assessment of Economic Growth in the First Decade of the Twenty-first Century.

Manufacturing has an important bearing on economic growth. The analyst should monitor the health of manufacturing for clues to the future course of the overall economy.

ASSESSMENT OF ECONOMIC GROWTH IN THE FIRST
DECADE OF THE TWENTY-FIRST CENTURY

In January 2001, I overheard a couple discussing the sudden weakness in the economy. She said, "How did this happen?" He gave a rambling response that reflected the incomprehensibility of the fall-off in the economy.

This overview contains seven categories that give my assessment of what happened leading up to the recession, and where the economy is headed from the recovery of 2002–03 to the end of the decade. It also includes my ideas for putting the economy on a more robust path during the decade.

The basic premise of this assessment is that the economic recovery of 2002–03 and later years is faced with a major obstacle not present in previous recoveries. The obstacle is the enormous drag that the collapse of the telecommunications companies left on the overall economy. To remedy this, American business executives will have to focus on producing more goods in the United States in order to get economic growth on a robust upward trajectory.

Collapse of the Telecommunications Companies

First, many new telecommunications companies were created in the 1990s that were unprofitable and vastly overrated in their economic potential and in their stock market values. When the mirage could no longer be contained, some became much smaller and some went out of business. There were substantial job losses that were not limited to those companies. The job losses first spread to other industries from which the telecommunications firms directly purchased various goods and services. They then spiraled to a wider number of industries that were indirectly dependent on the viability and growth of the sharply downsized or failed telecommunication companies, such as computer hardware and software companies.

The impact widened to a broader array of economic ventures that newly emerged or of existing enterprises that expanded because of the general lift to the economy and from the telecommunications boom. These are shopping centers, resorts, airlines, financial companies, artistic enterprises, and other ventures that were seemingly removed from the telecommunications impulse, but in fact would have been undertaken only because of the higher economic growth rate emanating largely from the boom in telecommunications. Overlaid on this was the greatly inflated stock values of these enterprises that generated the financial bubble of paper wealth on an unsound economic base. The stock market euphoria in turn generated an overly optimistic outlook for economic ventures, and the seeming inexhaustible financial resources to undertake the ventures. This perception unraveled into reality in less than a year during 2001, when the affected companies could no longer withstand the withering losses in their income statements and balance sheets.

This depiction of the transmission of the telecommunications collapse throughout the economy cannot be systematically quantified due to methodological limitations. However, an analysis of the jobless recovery of 2002–03 suggests that this widespread and permanent job loss occurred from the 2001 recession. This is discussed in chapter 8 under Jobless Recoveries of 1991–92 and 2002–03.

Nature of the 2001 Recession

Second, the 2001 recession was different *in kind* from previous ones because it was triggered and deeply impacted by the collapse of many telecommunications companies. In the 1990s to 2000 expansion, the telecommunications industries had become imbedded throughout the economy, and in fact propelled the economy to higher levels than would have occurred in their absence. This widening influence of the telecommunications industries resulted in the entire economy being vulnerable to their collapse.

By contrast, previous recessions did not occur in the context of such dependence on particular industries, and so their recoveries were not hindered by such an overhang. In previous recessions, the economy turned up more smoothly, though slowly and in fits and starts, from the snowballing effects of high and persistent unemployment, declining household incomes and business profits, unsold inventories of goods, and productive overcapacity in factories, stores, and offices. Thus, as the downward momentum bottomed out, households and businesses began buying replacements for older items that they had deferred buying during the recession. Even the aftereffects of the terrorist attacks of 2001, which were a tremendous shock, are not in the same league as the decline of the imbedded telecommunications industries (the terrorist attacks are noted further below).

An indicator of the different nature of the 2001 recession is the lower interest rate levels in the 2002 recovery compared with those in the 1992 recovery following the 1990–91 recession. Short-term and long-term interest rates in 2002 were typically 1.5 to 2.0 percentage points lower than they were in 1992. But despite the noticeably lower 2002 rates, the 2002 recovery was weak. (The Federal Reserve moved vigorously in 2001 and 2002 to lower interest rates, but its policies preceding the 2001 recession were wrong, as discussed below.)

Need for American-Made New and Existing Products

Third, the problem with the sluggish recovery in 2002–03 is that new products or the revitalization of American-made products did not materialize to replace the diminished telecommunications stimulus. The hybrid car, powered alternately at different speeds by an internal combustion gasoline engine and an electric motor running on batteries, is an example of a new product that has an enormous market potential. The car would bolster the economy if manufactured in the United States. American car companies have plans to produce hybrid cars in the mid- and late 2000s. It is important that they adhere to the plans and that they market the cars aggressively. High-definition TV is another example of a new product with a tremendous market potential, but unlike hybrid cars, television sets are no longer made in the United States.[10]

This raises a basic question of the economic importance of manufacturing. Manufacturing has significant direct and indirect impacts on the economy, as noted in the previous section. One way for the economy to become robust over the long run is for American companies to get back in the game of manufacturing. Rather than continuing to produce increasing numbers of products in low-wage countries abroad, or cede the market for computers, electronics, kitchen and other household appliances, railroad cars, clothing, shoes, and other products to foreign companies, American company executives should utilize their know-how and ingenuity to employ the skilled, productive, and talented American workers in manufacturing high-quality products in the United States.

In my opinion, if American companies develop products made in the United States that are recognized worldwide for their excellence in performance, safety, and repairs, they will gain large markets and high profits. By contrast, continuing the race to the bottom results in moving ever more production to low-wage countries that leads to a further abdication of the manufacturing base. This is a road with no end in sight that diminishes economic growth, employment and worker incomes, and business profits below what they would be with the establishment of American-made high quality products. It is noteworthy in this regard that the race to the bottom of lower and lower wages proceeds with no interruption. When it became apparent in 2002 that even the low wages of Mexican workers were not considered to be low enough, the production of some items made in Mexico was shifted to China, where wages are still lower.

Federal Reserve Policies Preceding the 2001 Recession

Fourth, in order to lower inflation by slowing economic growth, the Federal Reserve acted to raise the federal funds interest rate continuously from 4.6 percent in January 1999 to 6.5 percent in July 2000. The federal funds rate continued at this high level of 6.5 percent through November 2000, after which it declined through mid-2003. Federal funds indicate the Federal Reserve stance on monetary policy (see chapter 12 under Implementing Monetary Policies).

Thus, the Federal Reserve reversed course over the next two and one-half years to counteract the weakened economy by lowering the federal funds rate preceding the 2001 recession, during the recession, and during the subsequent sluggish recovery in 2002 and 2003. This was reflected in the long-term decline in the federal funds rate beginning in December 2000 to historic lows of 1.25 percent from January to May 2003 and further down to 1 percent in June 2003.

Many analysts dismiss the higher interest rates as one factor leading to the 2001 recession. I disagree. Economic growth was lower during the first three quarters of 2000. Stock market prices and long-term interest rates also declined slightly during this period. This was not the sign of an overheating economy needing restraint.

While prices had risen slightly in 2000, they were within the accepted range of modest inflation. The actions to raise interest rates were taken as a preventive to ward off future inflation, but their actual effect was to slow economic growth. Moreover, the prime sources of the price increases were the rising costs of health care and of gasoline and oil prices, which were not efficient targets for the Federal Reserve monetary policies. The gasoline and oil price hikes reflected the supply constraints of the Organization of Petroleum Exporting Countries (OPEC) cartel in which the member countries showed a more-than-usual adherence to the OPEC production quotas. Underlying this market power, which violates competitive antitrust principles, is the growing preference of households for gas guzzling sport utility vehicles and pickup trucks. Neither OPEC nor the consumer preference for gas guzzlers is likely to respond to higher interest rates. Similarly, higher health care costs have more fundamental causes than the blunt tools of higher interest rates can address.

In addition, the Federal Reserve chairman made pronouncements in the late 1990s of the "irrational exuberance" of the inflated stock market. But the Federal Reserve took no action to cool the stock market speculation. Thus, it did not use its authority to raise margin requirements on stock market credit that is used to purchase securities. The Federal Reserve's regulatory authority applies to credit extended by brokers and dealers, banks, and other lenders including those overseas. By not raising margin requirements from the existing 50 percent level to, say 75 percent or more, the Federal Reserve missed a chance to lessen the speculation driving the stock market. While the effect of such an increase in margin requirements cannot be known, the lack of action accomplished nothing. This is another example of where the Federal Reserve acted incorrectly in the period preceding the onset of the 2001 recession.

Terrorist Attacks, Iraq War, and SARS

Fifth, at the time of the terrorist attacks of September 11, 2001, the recession had been underway since March 2001. For a time in 2002, the terrorist attacks aggravated the sluggishness of the economic recovery, particularly in reduced airline travel and vacations, but this had largely dissipated by the summer of

2002. The Iraq War and the breakout of the Severe Acute Respiratory Syndrome (SARS) in 2003 caused a subsequent decline in airline travel. But even if the terrorist attacks, Iraq War, and SARS had not occurred, there would still be a need for a robust and sustained infusion of American-made new products as outlined above.

In this respect, previous recessions and recoveries also were not free of disruptive outside shocks, such as the sharp rise in crude oil prices resulting from the Arab oil embargo of 1973–75 and subsequently resulting from the Iranian revolution of 1979–81. From 1973 to 1981, these events led to over a quintupling of crude oil prices, compared with slightly more than a doubling of prices of finished producer goods in the producer price indexes prepared by the U.S. Bureau of Labor Statistics, as finished goods prices also have imbedded in them the higher crude oil prices. The spillover of sharp changes in energy prices into the nonenergy sectors is discussed in chapter 11 under Core Price Change.

As part of a broader analysis of sixteen shocks from the 1960s to the early 2000s, including the terrorist attacks of September 11, that could have impacted the economy, Victor Zarnowitz and Jacinto Torres concluded that only the reverberations from the oil price shocks of the 1970s and early 1980s noted above had longer effects beyond the immediate period when they occurred (see Chapter 13 under External Shocks).[11] The linkage of terrorism to productivity is discussed in chapter 10 under Effect on Productivity of Private Industry Spending to Combat Terrorism.

Supply Perspective of Economic Growth

Sixth, economic growth from the GDP supply perspective of labor, capital facilities, and productivity differs *in kind* from the demand perspective of the household, business, and government markets of the GDP discussed in the above assessments. The productive capacity of the American economy includes continuing increases in inputs and efficiencies that have led to the long-term rising standard of living of the American people. The ability of the economy to meet rising demands without igniting inflation was apparent in the 1990s to 2000 expansion. Thus, the problem for long-term growth is not the ability to produce goods and services, but the market demand of households, businesses, and governments to purchase the items that the economy can produce.

Federal, State, and Local Finances

Seventh, the decline in economic growth and concomitant decline in tax receipts of state and local governments have resulted in undesirable cutbacks in the education, health, housing, criminal justice, and other vital services provided by these governments as well as layoffs of government workers (chapter 6 covers government finances). Thus, in addition to the debilitating effects of unemployment on those out of work and the negative effect that unemployment has on reviving the economy, the sluggish economy and budget shortfalls of state and local governments have impacted the well-being of the everyday lives of persons in all walks of life around the country.

There will be large demands for increased federal spending during 2004–10 to alleviate the shortfalls in state and local budgets, and for the domestic war on terrorism, new military technologies, the war in Afghanistan and its aftermath, the Iraq war and its aftermath, and the domestic needs of health care, corporate regulation, and other public services. These will have to be reconciled with alternative ways to finance them—increased taxes, lower spending, or a lower rate of increased spending for some items, increased borrowing, or a combination of all three.

AN ACTION PLAN

The result of this assessment is that the recession of 2001, the recovery of 2002, and their aftermath are different in kind from previous recessions and recoveries. The reason is that there has been no replacement for the shrinkage and demise of telecommunications companies that were imbedded, directly and indirectly, in a wide range of industries in the late 1990s and 2000. This implies a much lower rate of economic growth from the early 2000s to the end of the decade than prevailed before the onset of the recession. Specifically, based on my expectations for employment and productivity growth, I envision average annual growth in the 2.0–2.5 percent range from the early 2000s to the end of the decade. This compares with average annual growth of 3 percent from the 1980s to 2000, but which included an acceleration to 4 percent from 1996 to 2000. The projected lower economic growth also points toward an average unemployment rate of 5.5 to 6.0 percent during the first decade of the twenty-first century.

To convert the anticipated low growth and high unemployment into robust economic growth and lower unemployment, I recommend the following actions by American businesses and the federal government during the mid- and late 2000s.

Reclaiming American Manufacturing

The above outlook presumes there will be only a limited resurgence of American-made products during the decade, primarily associated with the production of hybrid cars. The outlook for the mid and late 2000s would be brighter, however, if American company executives actively reasserted the excellence of products made in the United States in performance, safety, and repairs.

The need is to break the conventional wisdom that producing in low-wage countries is necessary because it is the only way companies can compete. I do not find the low-wage argument persuasive. Besides hurting the U.S. economy in the short run, the argument also leads down a losing road because foreign nationals who supply the foreign low-wage labor employed by American companies abroad today can easily replace the American companies once they have acquired the know-how and combine it with domestic or imported capital facilities and technology to produce the same products on their own tomorrow. There is, in fact, anecdotal evidence that this has been occurring.

Surely, American business can, in enlightened self-interest, combine the skills, talents, and work ethic of American workers, including training in the particular skills needed to work on products that are no longer produced in the United States or only produced in small numbers, with American technology, design, and management in innovative ways to compete in the global marketplace. This new direction will have to come from the recognition by American businesses that producing in the United States will lead to greater and growing markets and profits from the initial production of goods made in the United States. It will require the chief executive officers and the boards of directors of manufacturing companies to lay out plans for making quality products in the United States, and to actively implement such plans. This fundamental redirection would be bolstered nationwide by the Business Roundtable, composed of the chief executives of the largest American companies, together with the National Association of Manufacturers, to develop a course of action that would benefit companies that produce a variety of products in the United States as a major way of revitalizing the economic health of American industry.

The case of hybrid cars is instructive here. American companies only got into the market after Japanese companies pioneered and began producing them. This is a defensive action that runs the risk of not being pursued energetically. It is a minimalist approach when a vigorous marketing program is needed, as noted previously under Need for American-Made New and Existing Products. Thus, development and promotion of the hybrid car should not be a public relations project to prevent tougher fuel economy standards, nor should the potential development of an environmentally cleaner hydrogen-fueled car in the 2020s be used now to deflect attention from actively competing in the hybrid car market.

The issue involves two attitudinal problems among CEOs and corporate boards of directors. One is the need to promote the innovation of desirable new products rather than following the pioneering new product developments of foreign competitors in a defensive pattern, such as is occurring with hybrid cars. The other is to acknowledge that a major reason for producing goods abroad is to utilize low-wage labor there. But according to the U.S. Chamber of Commerce, low wages are not a factor. Thus, in the Chamber's listing of "The Twelve

Commandments for International Investors," which itemizes twelve considerations for a company's overseas investment decisions, the one relating to labor notes only "the quality of the indigenous work force."[12] It does not mention wage levels. The other considerations relate to the size and potential of the internal market, government interference in entering a country's market, availability of local-country raw materials, protection from currency devaluation, real and intangible property rights protection, and so on.

The problem of not acknowledging the role of low wages abroad is that it is a rationale for continuing the attitude of accepting this practice as inevitable, rather than focusing on producing American-made high-quality products of performance, safety, and repair that would lead to greater markets and profits.

U.S. Support of International Labor Standards

What can the U.S. government do to lessen the extent to which substandard wages abroad undermine the health of U.S. manufacturing? A potentially important vehicle involves the ratification and enforcement of certain international labor standards of the International Labor Organization (ILO).

The ILO has eight core conventions on international labor standards. Many nations have ratified them, though the United States has ratified only two. The following itemizes those the United States has and has not ratified.

Ratified by the United States

- Eliminate forced labor which was not offered voluntarily under the menace of penalty, other than for military service or normal civil obligations.
- Eliminate worst form of child labor, such as sale and trafficking in children, debt bondage, compulsory recruitment for armed conflict, prostitution, pornography, and drug trafficking.

Not Ratified by the United States

- Freedom of association of workers to join an organization of their choice.
- Right of workers to organize and bargain collectively.
- Abolition of child labor below certain minimum ages.
- Establish minimum wage fixing machinery to adopt minimum wages.
- Eliminate discrimination in employment, training, and working conditions based on race, color, sex, religion, political opinion, national extraction, and social origin.
- Equal pay for men and women for work of equal value.

Of course, all standards, even if adopted, are meaningless unless they are enforced. But as a first step, it is necessary that standards be adopted in order for them to be put into practice.

The U.S. ratification of the ILO standards on forced labor and the worst form of child labor is good. But these are not enough to address the problem of substandard wages. The right of free association of workers and of the right to organize into labor unions and bargain collectively are fundamental to raising the wages of workers in substandard wage countries. Yet unions by themselves are not capable of dealing with loopholes that propagate substandard wages by permitting the hiring of very young children for work, not having minimum wages that afford a floor of decency below which market determined wages cannot go, applying demographic and cultural prejudices in the workplace, and creating a situation where work typically performed by women is paid much less than work that requires a similar level of skill and risk of health and safety, but which is typically performed by men.

All of the above items that have not been ratified by the United States are part of American labor law, except for the one on equal pay for work of equal value. The United States would become more credible in its efforts to get other countries to comply with the ILO standards by ratifying those standards that are part of American law. The rationales for not ratifying the standards are: (a) the standards are inconsistent with certain aspects of federal and state laws, and (b) U.S. treaties with other countries are the "supreme Law of the Land" that override those aspects of federal and state laws that conflict with the specifications in the treaties (U.S. Constitution, Article VI).[13] The main opposition to ratifying the standards comes from businesses and from those states that discourage unions through their "right-to-work" laws. There has been a long-standing U.S. policy, formalized in the late-1980s, of ratifying only those ILO standards that do not conflict with existing federal or state laws.

To implement higher labor standards affecting American companies abroad, the U.S. government would have to become actively involved with the foreign governments. Specifically, the U.S. government would have to work diplomatically on (a) enforcing existing labor laws in countries that meet ILO standards, (b) raising labor standards in those countries that do not meet ILO conventions and enforcing them, and (c) requiring U.S.-owned companies operating abroad to pay a living wage.

In a comprehensive study of international labor standards, Kimberly Elliott and Richard Freeman note that the major criticism of the ILO has been its lack of enforcement power.[14] And they recognize that the United States has a major role in helping the ILO to raise labor standards around the world.[15]

In assessing ways to raise wages in low-wage countries, John Miller notes that enforcing country labor laws that meet ILO standards in those countries that have such laws would be of some help, but such enforcement is not likely to be systematically applied by those governments.[16] Miller also points to a more direct approach that would require multinational companies to pay a living wage in those countries.

The U.S. Department of Labor studied wage conditions in the low-wage apparel and footwear industries in thirty-five major exporting countries that manufacture those products and in the United States.[17] The study provides a wealth of information on the minimum wage, prevailing average wage, non-wage benefits, measures of workers' basic needs (the poverty line), and the extent to which wages meet such needs in those countries.

In order to stanch the hemorrhaging of U.S. manufacturing companies moving their production abroad, the U.S. government should do the following: (a) look into the feasibility of ways to ratify those ILO core standards that the United States has not ratified, (b) work diplomatically on a sustained basis with the governments in countries having substandard wages to both ratify and enforce the ILO labor standards in their countries, and (c) require U.S.-owned companies operating in all countries to comply with ILO labor standards, with active U.S. enforcement and strong penalties for noncompliance. This will take the political will of the U.S. government to ameliorate the problem. The U.S. Department of Labor study on wages in low-wage countries would be a useful analytic starting point for an active U.S. role in implementing ILO labor standards in all exporting industries in low-wage countries.

Federal Grants-in-Aid to State and Local Governments

Because shortfalls in state and local budgets are likely to continue for several years, the federal government has an urgent responsibility to support state and local budgets during 2004–10. It should provide state and local governments with grant moneys that become part of their budget revenue base, not loans that must be repaid, to fund their essential public service programs.

Limit Federal Deficits

In addition to the vital state and local governments needs, there are substantial spending increases in store for the federal government to finance the domestic and international wars on terrorism, and the domestic needs of health care, corporate regulation, and other public services. Therefore, no net federal tax cuts should be made in the first decade of the twenty-first century beyond those that were established in 2001. This does not preclude tax increases and decreases for different income groups or between households and businesses, but the net effect of such changes should maintain the same level of existing revenues— that is, any tax changes should be revenue neutral.

REVIEW QUESTIONS

- The GDP on the "product side" and the "income side" is the same in total, except for statistical problems. However, the components of the two measures differ substantively. What is the nature of the difference?
- What type of additional information would be needed to develop supplementary GDP measures that reflect a concept of well-being, in contrast to the existing concept of production?
- GDP data are provided in absolute current dollars, absolute dollars adjusted for price change (real GDP), and rates of change of both.
    - a. Why is the main interest in rates of change of real GDP?
    - b. Give examples of analytical uses of the absolute GDP data in both current and price-adjusted dollars.
- Government consumption and investment in the GDP exclude transfer payments such as Social Security and unemployment benefits, even though they are part of government budgets and affect the economy.
    - a. Why are transfer payments excluded?
    - b. How is this limited measure of government dealt with in economic analysis?
- Why is it deceptive to look only at "net exports" (exports minus imports) in the GDP without considering the export and import components separately?
- Why are valuation adjustments for inventories and depreciation allowances more important during highly inflationary period than when prices rise slowly?
- How do movements in economic growth differ between the periods before and after World War II? What are the statistical problems with these comparisons?
- During cyclical expansion and recession periods, why are consumer expenditures less volatile than private investment?
- There are several alternative GDP measures: gross domestic income, final sales of domestic product, gross domestic purchases, final sales to domestic purchasers, gross national product, and command-basis GNP.
    - a. How does gross domestic income differ from the alternative measures?
    - b. How are the alternative measures used in economic analysis?
- Why are labor and capital contributions to economic growth associated with working harder, and multifactor productivity associated with working smarter?

Extra Credit

- For what reasons is real GDP a less-than-perfect measure of the output of the U.S. economy?
- Why is manufacturing important to economic growth?
- To what extent is the GDP framework sufficient for analyzing the macro economy? What other economic elements should be taken into account? Explain.

NOTES

1. Use of demand and supply terminology refers to the distinction between the components of the GDP on the product and income sides. In total, both sides measure "production." The difference between the two is in the demand and supply nature of the components. The sum totals into a single number of the product and income side components are conceptually equivalent, though they are based on independent data sources, and only by chance would be statistically equal (the difference, called the "statistical discrepancy," is discussed below). A third measure of the summary GDP that is conceptually equivalent is based on the input-output accounts of interindustry transactions; it is available only annually, and is also prepared by the Bureau of Economic Analysis. The input-output measure of the GDP, referred to as "value added," is derived as the difference between sales and purchases industry-by-industry, and the sum of the value added for all industries is the GDP. Because the input-output measure is based on still different data sources, its summary GDP differs statistically from the product and income side numbers.
2. Some may object to these words as misleading. There is nothing nominal about the GDP in current dollars because this represents the actual market prices in which items are bought and sold. And there is nothing real about GDP in chained dollars that are adjusted for rising or declining prices because in the everyday world, items are bought and sold in today's price, not in the unchanged prices from a particular base year.
3. N. Gregory Mankiw and Matthew D. Shapiro, "News or Noise: An Analysis of GNP Revisions," *Survey of Current Business*, May 1986. A later study found that the GDP revisions for the United States are "very slightly predictable." See Jon Faust, John H. Rogers, and Jonathan H. Wright, "News and Noise in G-7 GDP Announcements," *International Finance Discussion Papers* 690, Board of Governors of the Federal Reserve System, December 2000.
4. The income side is not included as part of the first GDP estimate for each quarter because the data for corporate profits are not available in time. For the fourth quarter of each year, the income side is not included for the first and second estimates for the same reason. For the annual and benchmark estimates, several income items are based on tax return and other government administrative record data, where the data are byproducts of revenue collection and not strictly statistical programs. Also, income for tax purposes has become more difficult to define.
5. Because the growth rates are calculated from similar phases of the business cycle in which the beginning and end years of the comparison—1901, 1929, 1939, 1948, 1959, 1969, 1979, 1989, and 2000—are years of economic expansion, they provide a consistent representation of long-term trends. Calculating the rates from terminal

years that include both expansion and recession years would distort the averages (chapter 1 under Calculating and Presenting Growth Rates).

6. The effect on the real GDP growth trend during the depression is noted in Angus Maddison, *The World Economy: A Millennial Perspective* (Organization for Economic Cooperation and Development, 2001), Box 3–1, p. 138. The revised methodology affected the weighting procedure for averaging the GDP components between five-year benchmarks. The previous procedure of holding the price weights of the various goods and services in each benchmark year constant in the following years until the next benchmark was changed to using the geometric mean of the benchmark price weights for the years between the benchmarks. See Allan H. Young, "Alternative Measures of Change in Real Output and Prices, Quarterly Estimates for 1959–92," *Survey of Current Business*, March 1993.

   This earlier recovery to the 1929 level in 1936 was still very long, though it gives a more positive picture of the effect of the New Deal on economic growth. Previously, it appeared that the economy exceeded the pre-depression level only with the massive increase in military spending beginning in 1940 for World War II. However, in terms of employment, the 1929 level was still first exceeded in 1940.

7. Bureau of Labor Statistics, U.S. Department of Labor, "Multifactor Productivity Trends, 2000," *News Release*, March 12, 2002.

8. These productivity data do not reflect the annual GDP revisions published in the August 2002 *Survey of Current Business*. It is unlikely, however, that the revised data change the overall patterns discussed here.

9. Robert J. McCahill and Brian C. Moyer, "Gross Domestic Product by Industry for 1999–2001," *Survey of Current Business*, November 2002, Table 2, p. 32.

10. High-definition TV has a still longer time horizon than hybrid cars. Thus, the high-definition TV market cannot burgeon until there is a wide adoption of a digital broadcasting system, which does not seem likely until 2007 or later. Moreover, even when the digital system is adopted, it will have little effect on economic growth, because no television sets are produced in the United States. Thus, for the American economy to benefit from the inroads of high-definition TV, American company executives will have to restore the manufacture of television sets into the United States.

11. Victor Zarnowitz and Jacinto Torres, Jr., "Economic Context and Consequences of 9/11, a Year Later," *Business Cycle Indicators,* September 2002.

12. U.S. Chamber of Commerce, "What Goes into a U.S. Company's Decision on Whether to Invest Overseas?" or "The Twelve Commandments for International Investors," n.d.

13. Article VI of the U.S. Constitution establishes that all U.S. treaties with other countries take precedence over federal and state laws in adjudicating conflicts between the provisions of a treaty and existing federal and state laws.

    U.S. Constitution, Article VI, Clause 2: "This Constitution, and the Laws of the United States which shall be made in Pursuance thereof; and all Treaties made, or which shall be made, under the Authority of the United States, shall be the supreme Law of the Land; and the Judges in every State shall be bound thereby, any Thing in the Constitution or Laws of any State to the Contrary notwithstanding."

14. Kimberly Ann Elliott and Richard B. Freeman, *Can Labor Standards Improve Under Globalization?* (Institute for International Economics, June 2003), p. 102.

15. Ibid., p. 107.

16. John Miller, "Why Economists Are Wrong about Sweatshops and the Antisweatshop Movement," *Challenge,* January-February 2003.

17. Bureau of International Labor Affairs, U.S. Department of Labor, *Wages, Benefits, Poverty Line, and Meeting Workers' Needs in the Apparel and Footwear Industries of Selected Countries*, February 2000.

4

Household Income, Saving, and Expenditures

The primary reason people work is to provide for the material well-being (that is, the living conditions) of themselves and their families. Work also gives a feeling of self-worth. Material well-being is represented by the incomes of households and the spending of their incomes to obtain goods and services for everyday living, such as housing, food, clothing, health, education, transportation, business, and personal services, entertainment, art, crafts, music, and other cultural pursuits. The trade-off between work and leisure time varies among households, with some giving more importance to work and income and others giving more importance to leisure and the pursuit of their interests.

The personal income and expenditures of households are a major driving force of the nation's economic growth (chapter 3). They affect and are affected by employment and wages (chapter 9), and impact investment in structures and equipment (chapter 5), which in turn are determinants of productivity (chapter 11). By contrast, in a Garden of Eden environment in which all material needs are abundantly available without one's having to work for them, we would not speak about "the economy," or the accompanying topics of employment, inflation, investment, saving, and productivity.

Households buy goods and services using income obtained in the current period and from income obtained in previous periods which was not spent but accumulated as savings or other wealth assets. Purchases of goods and services are also financed from borrowing that is paid off in later periods. This continuing circular flow from income to expenditure to income to expenditure is the focal point of assessing the current status and future outlook of the household sector of the economy.

Households have a dual role of allocating their incomes (a) as consumers for their current needs in the purchase of housing accommodations as renters or as owner occupants, food, and other needs of material well-being noted above, and (b) as savers and investors for future benefits such as buying real estate and financial stocks and bonds. This dual role can be elusive, and the procedures of

119

how they are integrated in the data are discussed in the following methodology section.

METHODOLOGY

The personal income and expenditure measures are prepared monthly by the Bureau of Economic Analysis (BEA) in the U.S. Department of Commerce, as part of the national income and product accounts (NIPAs) and the gross domestic product (GDP) covered in chapter 3. The data are published in the BEA monthly journal, the *Survey of Current Business* (www.bea.doc.gov). This section highlights the content and measurement used in preparing the personal income and expenditure data. It also includes personal saving, borrowing, and debt, which are importantly linked to income and expenditure.

Personal Income

Personal income (PI) is the main source of household power used to buy goods and services. It primarily represents the income received by households and comprises income derived from current production, investments, and transfer payments. Income from production covers money wages and salaries, fringe benefits, and profits from self-employment. Income from investments covers rent, interest, and dividends. Income from transfer payments covers Social Security, unemployment insurance, food stamps, Medicare, Medicaid, and other income maintenance programs. Social Security taxes paid by employees and employers are excluded from personal income. In addition to households, PI includes the rental, dividend, and interest income from property assets of private nonprofit organizations, life insurance companies, noninsured pension funds, and trust funds. Separate data are provided for the household and nonprofit organization components of personal income.

Table 4.1 shows that in 2002, income from production accounted for 71.3 percent of personal income, income from investments for 18.9 percent, and income from government transfers for 14.4 percent. The total of these items, minus the 4.3 percent of employee contributions for Social Security, sums to 100 percent.

Disposable personal income (DPI) represents the actual purchasing power available to consumers from current income. It is personal income after the payment of income, estate, and gift taxes, and miscellaneous fines and penalty taxes (as noted, Social Security taxes paid by the employer and employee are excluded from personal income). Personal taxes and nontax payments accounted for 12.5 percent of personal income in 2002. Theoretically, DPI is more cyclically stable than PI because of the progressive income tax, a main attribute of the federal income tax law. Under the progressive income tax, a higher propor-

Table 4.1

Personal Income: 2002

	Billions of dollars	Percentage distribution
Total	8,929.1	100.0
Income from production	*6,370.8*	*71.3*
Wages and salaries	5,003.7	56.0
Fringe benefits	610.6	6.8
Self-employment	756.5	8.5
Income from investments	*1,654.7*	*18.5*
Rent	142.4	1.6
Dividends	433.8	4.9
Interest	1,078.5	12.1
Income from government transfers	*1,288.1*	*14.4*
Social Security	699.8	7.8
Unemployment insurance	62.9	0.7
Veterans benefits	29.6	0.3
Other (government employees retirement, aid to families with dependent children, Medicare, Medicaid, food stamps, other)	495.8	5.6
Less: Personal contributions for Social Security	*(384.5)*	*(4.3)*

Source: Bureau of Economic Analysis, U.S. Department of Commerce, *Survey of Current Business*, April 2003, Table 2.1, p. D-7.

Note: Author grouped the categories of income from production, investments, and government transfers, and calculated the percentage distribution.

tion of income is paid as taxes as income of the recipient increases; and conversely, as recipient income declines, a lower proportion is paid in taxes. This progressiveness should result in proportionately less of an increase in DPI than in PI during expansions, and in proportionately less of a decrease in DPI than in PI during recessions. The effect during expansions is to restrain income and spending growth, thus moderating economic growth and inflation. The effect during recessions is to shore up income and spending, thus moderating the declines in output and employment.

Household Purchasing Power

Household purchasing power refers to consumers' capability to finance spending. It encompasses personal income noted above, consumer installment loans, household savings in bank deposits, financial assets (money market accounts, stocks, bonds, etc.), and less liquid assets such as real estate. In addition to income, all of these sources may be used to finance consumer spending and repay consumer debt by liquidating savings and other assets, or by using these assets as collateral for further loans.

Alternative Personal Saving Measures

Personal saving is what is left of disposable personal income after all personal outlays. Personal outlays consist mainly of consumer spending for goods and services (93.5 percent of disposable personal income in 2002), but also include interest on loans paid by households to business, excluding home mortgage interest (2.4 percent), and net personal payments by U.S. households to foreigners (0.4 percent). The personal saving rate measures saving as a percentage of disposable personal income. In 2002, the personal saving rate was 3.7 percent. The personal saving data are prepared as part of the NIPAs covered in chapter 3.

Another measure of personal saving developed by the Federal Reserve Board as part of the flow of funds accounts, is based on the change in net worth of financial and tangible assets of households—that is, assets less liabilities. Other differences between the flow of funds and NIPA saving measures include the treatment of capital gains and losses, which are included in the flow of funds and excluded from the NIPA personal saving; the services derived from the use of consumer durables—cars, furniture, appliances, etc.—as measured by depreciation of the consumer durables are included in the flow of funds and excluded from the NIPA personal saving; and the net worth of unincorporated businesses is included in the flow of funds and excluded from NIPA personal saving. The two saving measures cannot be reconciled statistically because the various sources of the differences cannot be quantified. Differences in the uses of the two measures include: NIPA personal saving derived by subtracting personal outlays from disposable personal income seems more relevant for assessing the contribution of personal saving to national saving, while the flow of funds measure of the change in net worth of households seems more relevant for assessing whether households in the aggregate are preparing adequately for the financial needs of retirement, as Maria Perozek and Marshall Reinsdorf note.[1]

Table 4.2 shows the NIPA and flow of funds saving measures from 1998 to 2002. The services derived from the use of consumer durables are excluded from the flow of funds saving in order to provide a more definitional consistency between the two measures. The addendum to the table shows the flow of funds saving measure that includes the use of consumer durables.

The differential in the two saving measures ranged from 0.1 to 1.7 percentage points over the 1998 to 2002 period. The NIPA saving exceeded the flow of funds saving by 0.2 and 0.1 percentage point in 1999 and 2002, respectively,

Table 4.2

Alternative Measures of Personal Saving: 1998–2002
(saving as a percentage of disposable personal income)

	1 NIPAs	2 Flow of funds	3 Difference (1)−(2)
1998	4.7	6.2	−1.4
1999	2.6	2.4	0.2
2000	2.8	1.1	1.7
2001	2.3	3.9	−1.6
2002	3.7	3.6	0.1

Addendum: Flow of funds saving including consumer durables

1998	9.4
1999	5.7
2000	4.5
2001	7.5
2002	6.7

Source: U.S. Bureau of Economic Analysis and Federal Reserve Board.

Note: Excludes estimates of consumer durables savings. Detail may not sum to totals due to rounding.

and by 1.7 percentage points in 2000. The flow of funds saving exceed the NIPA saving by 1.4 and 1.6 percentage points in 1998 and 2001, respectively. The inclusion of the services derived from consumer durables in the flow of funds saving measure increased that measure by approximately 3 percentage points.

There is no definitive answer as to what is the better saving measure for economic analysis. The personal saving rate derived from the NIPAs is used in this book. It has the advantage of being consistent with the definitions and data base of the national accounts because the accounts are the foundation of much economic analysis and forecasting. But the NIPA saving rate does not represent all aspects of household saving relied on for consumer spending.

William Gale and John Sabelhaus recommend broadening the flow of funds for personal saving estimates to include retirement savings, capital gains and losses, adjustments for inflation, and adjustments for income tax accruals.[2] Their broader estimates of saving show no long-term decline in the saving rate, contrary to the long-term declines in the saving rates of both the NIPA and the flow of funds accounts.

Gale and Sabelhaus do not advocate the adoption of a particular saving measure. They maintain that the saving measure used should be determined by the nature of each analysis. But they conclude that the broader saving measure would enrich studies of saving in theoretical, empirical, and policy contexts.

Another study attributed the decline in the NIPA personal saving rate to the effect of excluding capital gains and losses from the NIPA personal saving, as noted by Richard Peach and Charles Steindel.[3] They also conclude that the NIPA saving decline occurs primarily in the wealthier stratum of households that have financed an increased proportion of spending from income derived from non-wage incomes such as dividends, interest, rents, and unincorporated business profits as a way of tapping the capital gains from the stock market. By contrast, Peach and Steindel believe that the majority of households, which depend on wages and salaries for income, probably has not tended to spend more freely, and thus the saving rate for these households has not declined.

Still another study attributed the decline in the NIPA personal saving to the explosion in medical care expenditures, as noted by Lynn Browne and Joshua Gleeson.[4] They conclude that the sharp increase in medical expenditures in the NIPAs has raised consumer spending and lowered personal saving in the NIPAs. This occurred after allowing for out-of-pocket expenditures for medical expenditures by households and the financing of a large part of medical expenditures by Medicare, Medicaid, and private health insurance through taxes and employer and household health insurance premiums.

Financing Personal Outlays

Personal outlays are financed by personal income plus other sources of consumer purchasing power—installment credit, existing savings, and loans obtained on real estate and other financial assets. Therefore, personal saving is affected by the use of credit, existing savings, and sale of existing assets, as well as by current personal income. The total value of items bought on credit is included as spending when the purchase is made; in later periods, repayments of the principal of the loan are included as saving. In addition, while personal outlays exclude household purchases of homes and investments such as stocks, bonds, money market instruments, and real estate, personal saving includes the equity in these housing and investment transactions if they are financed from current income (the change in equity is discussed below).[5] However, these items are not included in saving to the extent that they are financed by selling homes or other assets to other households or by interpersonal gifts (e.g., from parents to children). In general, personal saving is affected by transactions between households on the one hand, and businesses, governments, and foreigners on the other, but personal saving is not affected by transactions between households.

The net effect on saving of the use of loans and existing assets to finance consumer expenditures has the following attributes. Saving is reduced when a loan is used for spending, and saving is increased when the loan is paid off. Saving is reduced when consumers finance spending from existing savings or by selling real estate and financial assets to businesses, governments, or foreigners. And saving is increased when households build up equity in housing and in real estate and financial investments such as stocks and bonds, and as they pay off mortgage and other loans associated with the assets (changes in equity do not reflect price appreciation or depreciation of homes or investments). Saving is not affected by gifts between households, such as when parents give a house to their children; or by sales of homes, cars, and other assets between households, except for payments to intermediaries such as brokers' commissions and used car dealer markups.

Nonmarket Imputations in Consumer Expenditures

In addition to goods and service items bought for money in a market transaction, consumer expenditures include an imputed value for certain nonmarket items that are acquired for no payment. The largest nonmarket imputed items are the rental value of owner-occupied housing, certain services provided without charge by financial intermediaries, and the value of employer contributions for health and life insurance. All imputations accounted for 12.5 percent of consumer expenditures in 2001, of which owner-occupied housing accounted for 10.9 percent (data on imputations for 2002 were not available at the time of this writing).

ANALYSIS OF TRENDS

Household expenditures for goods and services are the dominant component of the overall economy, accounting for 70 percent of the GDP in 2002 (the GDP is detailed in chapter 3). Table 4.3 shows that consumer expenditures fluctuated within 62 to 65 percent of the GDP from the 1950s to the 1980s, and rose to 68 percent in 2000 and 70 percent in 2002. The years shown represent the peak years of business expansions by decade, plus the 2001 recession and the 2002 recovery years.

Household decisions to spend are affected by two broad considerations. One is the overall environment of economic growth, employment, and inflation discussed in chapters 3, 8, and 11. The other is the individual consumer's purchasing power as reflected in personal income, saving, borrowing, debt, and wealth.

Employment and price trends weigh heavily in the timing and types of consumer spending. Households in which workers are currently employed with little likelihood of being unemployed are among the best candidates to spend in the near future, both for necessities and deferrable items. By contrast, households in which workers are employed but expect to be unemployed, or in which they

Table 4.3

Personal Consumption Expenditures as a Percentage of the Gross Domestic Product: 1948–2002

	Percent
1948	65.1
1959	62.7
1969	61.5
1979	62.2
1989	65.5
2000	68.0
2001	69.3
2002	69.9

Source: Based on U.S. Bureau of Economic Analysis data.

Note: The author calculated the percentage distributions.

are unemployed with low expectations of finding a job, are likely to curtail spending sharply for deferrable items, such as a new car, clothing, or recreation, while maintaining or somewhat reducing outlays for necessities. These households are far more constrained, both by a currently limited income and by the need to save for future spending, than are households with more secure job situations.

Household spending decisions are also affected by current and anticipated price movements. Ideally, consumers time their purchases to buy at the lowest price. For deferrable items, if prices are rising rapidly and inflation is expected to continue at a high rate, consumers are likely to feel it is better to buy immediately. If prices are rising now but are expected to decline within a certain period, consumers may defer some purchases. In addition to affecting timing, prices can also affect the overall amount of spending, depending on relative prices between necessities and deferrable items. For example, a sharp rise in gasoline prices may curtail spending for other items. Or if deferrable items (say, television sets) drop sharply in price, spending for these items may increase.

Shifts in Importance of Consumer Expenditure Components

Within overall consumer expenditures, the most striking change has been a long-term shift in the share of total outlays from nondurable goods to the more labor-intensive services. The shift reflects the rising importance of such services as

Table 4.4

Component Shares of Personal Consumption Expenditures: 1948–2002
(percent)

	Total PCE	Durable goods	Nondurable goods	Services
1948	100.0	13.1	55.1	31.9
1959	100.0	13.4	46.7	39.9
1969	100.0	14.2	41.8	44.0
1979	100.0	13.4	39.1	47.4
1989	100.0	13.0	32.4	54.6
2000	100.0	12.0	29.5	58.5
2001	100.0	12.0	29.2	58.8
2002	100.0	11.9	29.0	59.1

Source: Based on U.S. Bureau of Economic Analysis data.

Note: The author calculated the percentage distributions.

housing costs, health care, and transportation services compared with the declining shares of food, clothing, and fuel products. Durable goods declined only slightly in relative importance.

Table 4.4 shows the relative shares of total consumer spending accounted for by durables, nondurables, and services from 1948 to 2002. The years shown represent the peak years of business expansions by decade, plus the 2001 recession and the 2002 recovery years. The shift from nondurables to services occurred in all decades, though it slowed in the 1990s. In 2002, durables accounted for 12 percent, nondurables 29 percent, and services for 59 percent of all consumer expenditures.

Volatility of Consumer Durable Goods Spending

Consumer spending for all goods and services shows similar movements to the gross domestic product during cyclical expansions, and less volatility than the GDP during cyclical recessions, as noted in chapter 3. The cyclical patterns of consumer expenditures and the GDP during expansions are similar. But during recessions, consumer expenditures cushion the effects of declining output from other sectors of the economy. While consumer expenditures account for the bulk of the GDP (70 percent in 2002), the other components do influence the GDP movements.

However, there are large cyclical differences among the three broad categories of consumer expenditures due to distinguishing natures of the items—durable goods, nondurable goods, and services. Durable goods represent items intended to last three or more years, such as cars, furniture, and household appliances. Nondurable goods, such as food, clothing, and gasoline, last less than three years, though much clothing is often used longer than three years. Services are noncommodity items such as housing rent (including both tenant rentals and nonmarket imputed rent for owner-occupied housing), utilities, public transportation, private education, medical care, and recreation that comprise labor-intensive functions.

While durable goods account for the smallest share of consumer outlays, typically ranging from 12 to 13 percent of the total, they are the most volatile of the major components of consumer spending over the business cycle. This reflects the longer life of these items, as it is easier for households to defer purchasing them when economic conditions, such as wage earnings, unemployment, or inflation, are adverse. Figures 4.1a and 4.1b indicate this volatility in both the expansion and recession phases of the business cycle from the 1980s to the early 2000s. Each of the two long expansions of the period is separated into halves, four years each for the 1980s and five years each for the 1990s to 2000. This breakdown indicates the evolving nature of the long-term expansions that would not be apparent in the entire expansion as a whole.

During expansions (Figure 4.1a), durable goods spending increased substantially more than did spending for nondurables and services in all six periods. *During recessions* (Figure 4.1b), durable goods spending declined in three of

Figure 4.1a **Business Cycle Movements of Real GDP and Consumer Expenditures, 1980s to Early 2000s: Expansions**

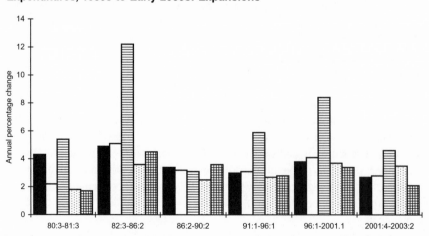

Source: Based on U.S. Bureau of Economic Analysis data in chained (1996) dollars.

Note: Number after colon is quarter of year.

Figure 4.1b **Business Cycle Movements of Real GDP and Consumer Expenditures, 1980s to Early 2000s: Recessions**

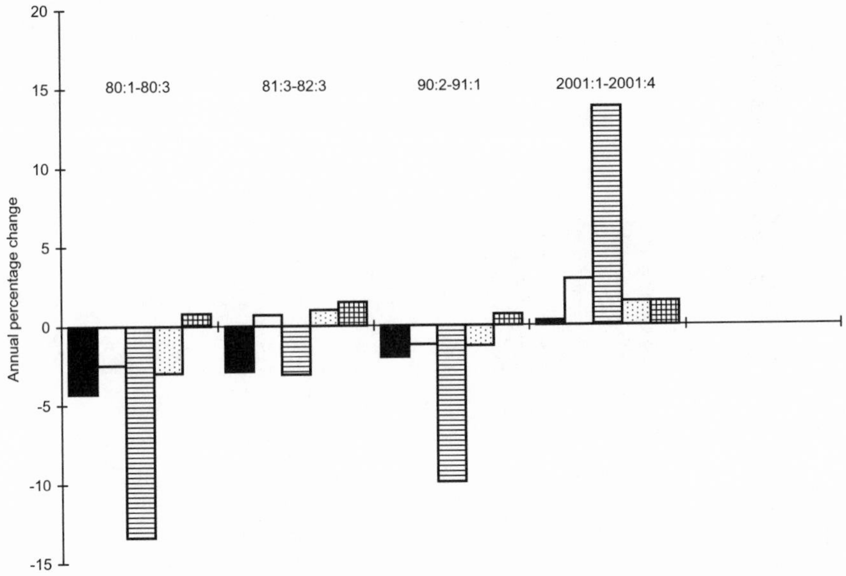

Source: Based on U.S. Bureau of Economic Analysis data in chained (1996) dollars.

Note: Number after colon is quarter of year.

the four recessions, the exception being the 2001 recession. Nondurable goods purchases declined in three of the four recessions.

Personal Income

Figures 4.2a and 4.2b show the cyclical movements of gross domestic income (GDI), PI, and DPI from the 1980s to the early 2000s. The GDI is the GDP plus the statistical discrepancy, also referred to as the GDP on the income side (see the Methodology section of chapter 3). *During expansions* (Figure 4.2a), the expected patterns of GDI increasing more than PI, and of PI rising more than DPI, occurred fully in 1980–81 and 1991–96, and partially consistent in 1982–86, 1986–90, 1996–2000, and the 2002–03 recovery. Thus, in the six expansions, the income measures were consistent with the theory in two instances, and partially consistent in four instances.

During recessions (Figure 4.2b), the three income measures appear as increasing because they are in current dollars, and thus include price changes which on an overall basis were rising. But the increases were much smaller than those during expansions in Figure 4.1a, which distinguishes them as recessions.

Figure 4.2a **Business Cycle Movements of Gross Domestic Income, Personal Income, and Disposable Personal Income, 1980s to Early 2000s: Expansions**

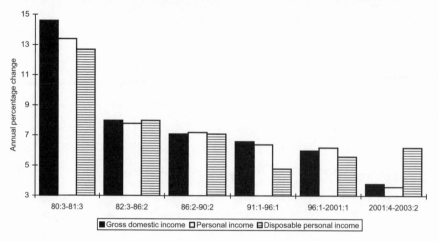

Source: Based on U.S. Bureau of Economic Analysis data in current dollars.

Note: Number after colon is quarter of year.

Figure 4.2b **Business Cycle Movements of Gross Domestic Income, Personal Income, and Disposable Personal Income, 1980s to Early 2000s: Recessions**

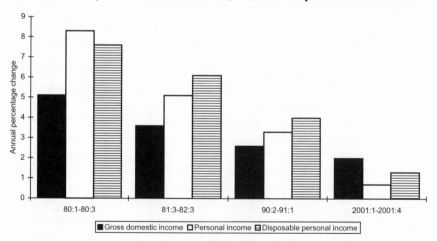

Source: Based on U.S. Bureau of Economic Analysis data in current dollars.

Note: Number after colon is quarter of year.

The expected patterns of PI increasing more than GDI and DPI increasing more than PI occurred fully in 1981–82 and 1990–91, and partially in 1980 and 2001. Thus, of the four recession periods, the movements were consistent with the theory in two cases, and partially consistent in two cases.

In focusing solely on the relationship between PI and DPI (i.e., abstracting from the economic growth aspect of GDI), the expected pattern in expansions is of increases in PI being larger than those in DPI, while in recessions the expected pattern is of increases in DPI being larger than those in DPI. In *expansions*, the expected patterns occurred in 1980–81, 1986–90, 1991–96, and 1996–2000, while 1982–86 and 2002–03 were contrary to the expected patterns. Thus, the movements were consistent with the theory in four of the six expansions. And in *recessions*, the movements were consistent with the theory in three of the four cases, the exception being the 1980 recession.

Overall, the movements of GDI, PI, and DPI during the expansions and recessions from the 1980s to the early 2000s generally were more consistent with the countercyclical stabilizing theory in the relationship of personal income to disposable personal income, than when the economic growth dimension of GDI is included.

The analyst should monitor the movements of the GDI, PI, and DPI to determine if they are following their expected patterns of cyclical stability. A break with expected patterns lessens the prospects for economy-wide cyclical stability.

Personal Saving

Personal saving is what is left of disposable income after all personal outlays are made, as noted in the Methodology section. The saving rate measures saving as a percentage of disposable personal income. Thus, personal saving in the current period is the residual of what is left over from current income after personal spending in the current period. In part, the saving may reflect conscious decisions to defer spending to a future period. But this distinction cannot be extracted from the data.

Figure 4.3 shows the saving rate from 1980 to 2002. It has declined noticeably over the period. It also showed no differential patterns in expansion and recession periods. It is volatile from year to year, and has varied considerably from the decades of the 1960s to the 1990s. Generally, the saving rate was in the 9 to 11 percent range in the early 1980s, the 8 percent level in the mid- and late 1980s, the 5 to 8 percent range in the early to mid-1990s, and it declined from 5 percent in the mid 1990s to a low of 2.3 percent in 2001, followed by a rebound to 3.7 percent in 2002. Over the 1992–01 period, preliminary estimates indicate that the decline in personal saving from 1992 to 1998 was attributable solely to the household sector, but from 1998 to 2001, the nonprofit

Figure 4.3 **Personal Saving Rate: 1980–2002**

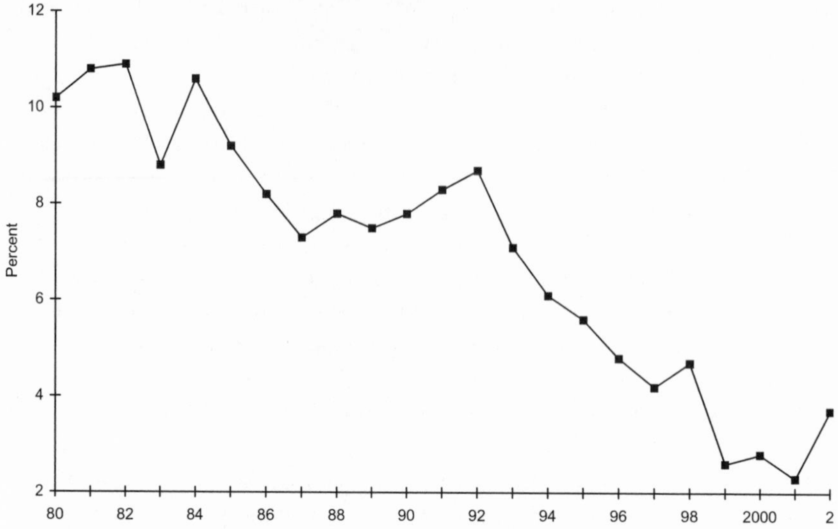

Source: Based on U.S. Bureau of Economic Analysis data.

Note: Personal saving as a percentage of disposable personal income.

sector also contributed to the saving decline, as noted by Charles Mead, Clinton McCully, and Marshall Reinsdorf.[6]

These long-term and year-to-year movements are difficult to forecast. This adds to the uncertainty of forecasting consumer expenditures, because changes of one to two percentage points in the saving rate result in substantially different spending rates, assuming the same level of DPI. In addition, the decision to spend or save is a chicken and egg question of which came first. Both are probably involved in household actions.

In projecting saving rates to anticipate consumer spending, the analyst should prepare saving rates that appear appropriate for that phase of the business cycle. These projections require considerable judgment regarding consumer behavior, including the use of consumer installment credit and existing assets to finance spending, because over the years consumer behavior has not displayed the re- petitive patterns that are essential for developing quantitative relationships.

Wealth Effect

The income derived from the rise in the stock market in the 1990s and the associated capital gains have been widely cited as stimulating consumer spend- ing, even with the decline in stock prices in the 2001 recession, and the subsequent fluctuating stock market prices in the 2002 and 2003 recovery. An analogous, though continuous rise without interruption in housing prices from the 1990s into the early 2000s including 2003, led homeowners to buy more expensive housing, or to use the higher housing valuations as collateral for home equity loans. These increases in the asset values of stocks and housing are referred to as the "wealth effect."

The Methodology section discussed alternative measures of personal saving to that derived from the NIPAs, which excludes capital gains and losses on the sale of stock market and real estate assets. These alternative measures include capital gains and losses as part of personal saving.

Dean Maki and Michael Palumbo assessed the effects of capital gains and losses in stocks and housing on different income and education demographic groups from 1992 to 2000.[7] Their study focused on the wealth effect in each quintile of the income distribution, from the lowest fifth to the highest fifth. In order to test whether shifts of households from one income group to another over time could affect the analysis, they also analyzed the wealth effect of households with different education levels over time, because education levels remain relatively constant over time. The education levels are less than high school, high school graduate, some college, and college graduate.

Maki and Palumbo conclude that the wealth effect was concentrated in the richest group of households, that is, in the top fifth of the income distribution. The study also showed that the wealth effect dominated households with the highest education levels.

Another study, by Karl Case, John Quigley, and Robert Shiller, compared the wealth effect of the capital gains in the stock market and the housing market.[8] They included one set of estimates for each state within in the United States based on quarterly data from 1982 to 1999, and one set based on Canada and twelve European countries based on annual data from 1975 to 1996. More data estimation was required for developing comparable measures among the U.S. states than was required for the country distinction in the international estimates.

Case, Quigley, and Shiller found a greater wealth effect on consumer expenditures from the capital gains in housing than those from the stock market. This difference occurred in both the United States and the international estimates. In a general assessment of what factors lead some household holders of different kinds of wealth to spend more on consumption than others, the authors include such considerations as which assets are considered temporary or uncertain, which assets may have a bequest motive at death, which assets are treated as an accumulation of wealth as an end in itself, which asset values are more readily known than others, and an overall mental category in which households consider some assets more appropriate for consumer expenditures than others. This listing of general factors probably varies among households, but the statistical finding of housing wealth having a greater effect on consumer expenditures than the stock market represents the effects of all of the factors in the aggregate.

Tax Rebate of 2001

As part of the Economic Growth and Tax Relief Reconciliation Act of 2001, income tax rebates of $300 for single individuals and up to $600 for a married couple filing a joint return were sent to taxpayers from the last week in July through the last week in September of 2001. Based on a telephone survey of households conducted from August through October 2001, Matthew Shapiro and Joel Slemrod estimated that 22 percent of the households receiving the rebate had spent, or expected to spend, more because of the rebate.[9] The survey respondents who said they would not spend more because of the rebate divided into 59 percent expecting to repay debt and 41 percent expecting to increase saving. The total rebate was $38 billion, accounting for about 0.4 percent of the GDP.

At the macro level, the effect of the rebate was to increase personal income, spending, and saving in 2001. The rebate was subject to the payment of income taxes in 2002 on the 2001 income tax return. As William Gale and Samara Potter noted, "Even if half of it [the rebate] were spent, the stimulus would have been small."[10]

Consumer Credit and Debt

Consumer credit loans augment consumer purchasing power and thus increase consumer expenditures. When an item is purchased on credit, the entire cost of the item is counted as a consumer expenditure at the time of the purchase, and as the loan is paid off, the repayments are counted as personal saving, as noted in the Methodology section. The other side of consumer credit is that it is a debt, which is a depressant on future spending because of the need to pay off the debt.

Consumer Credit

Consumer credit data provided by the Federal Reserve Board encompass loans to households by banks, credit companies, and retail stores. The loans cover automobiles and other motor vehicles, credit cards, and other items such as mobile homes, home improvements, education, and vacations. They include loans with an option to repay in two or more monthly payments, plus those scheduled to be repaid in a lump sum, including single-payment loans, charge accounts, and service credit. Secured and unsecured loans are included, except those with secured real estate. Securitized consumer loans—loans made by finance companies, banks, and retailers that are sold as securities—are included. The data exclude home mortgages, revolving home equity loans, and automobile leasing.

Figure 4.4a shows the relationship between the annual percentage change in consumer credit outstanding and the annual change in consumer expenditures that encompass durable goods, nondurable goods, and services from 1990 to 2002. Figure 4.4b shows the same relationship between consumer credit outstanding and consumer durable goods only. Consumer durables are items that last three or more years, such as cars, furniture, and appliances.

Over the period, there was a weak direct relationship between the growth in credit outstanding and the growth in consumer spending in Figure 4.4a, as reflected in the long-term average trend line that slopes upward to the right. This means that on average, when consumer credit increases, so do consumer expenditures, while a decline in consumer credit is associated with a slowdown in the increase in consumer expenditures. However, there also are wide year-to-year variations in the relationship, as indicated by the dispersion of the individual years (black diamonds) around the average long-term trend line (white diamonds). Thus, while consumer credit is important in financing consumer spend-

Figure 4.4a **Consumer Credit Outstanding versus Consumer Expenditures: 1990–2002**

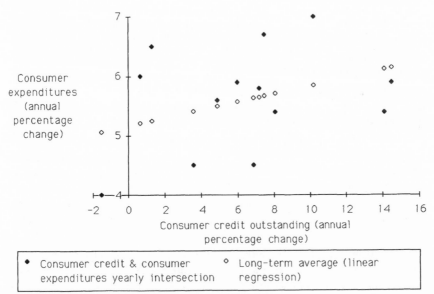

Source: Based on Federal Reserve Board and U.S. Bureau of Economic Analysis data in current dollars.

Figure 4.4b **Consumer Credit Outstanding versus Consumer Durable Goods Expenditures: 1990–2002**

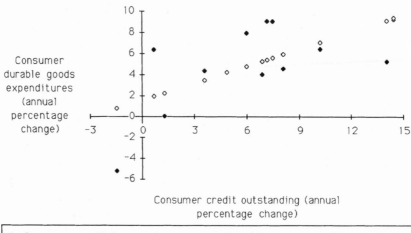

Consumer credit outstanding (annual percentage change)

| • | Consumer credit & consumer durable goods expenditures yearly intersection | ○ | Long-term average (linear regression) |

Source: Based on Federal Reserve Board and U.S. Bureau of Economic Analysis data in current dollars.

ing, other factors, such as personal income, savings, and prices also weigh heavily, with gauges of consumer confidence (discussed below) seeming to have less importance.

But the relationship in Figure 4.4b for consumer durable goods spending only and consumer credit outstanding is stronger than that for all consumer expenditures in Figure 4.4a, that includes all consumer expenditures, as apparent in the dispersion of the individual years around the long-term average. This reflects the fact that much of consumer credit is for the purchase of consumer durables.

The influence of consumer credit was apparent in the 2001 recession and the 2002 recovery, when low and even zero interest loans stimulated purchases of automobiles, pickup trucks, and SUVs.

Consumer Debt

While consumer credit is a source of financing for consumer expenditures, it also creates a debt burden that at times inhibits household spending. The ratio of consumer installment credit to disposable personal income is an overall measure of the debt burden. As the ratio increases, there probably is a threshold level when households retrench in spending because of an unwillingness to take

Figure 4.5 **Consumer Credit Outstanding as a Percentage of Disposable Personal Income: 1990–2002**

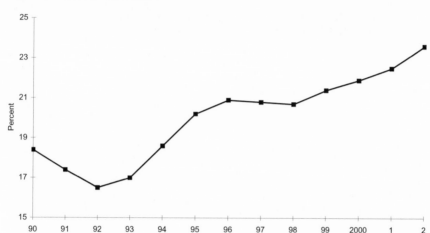

Source: Based on Federal Reserve Board and U.S. Bureau of Economic analysis data.

Note: Consumer credit represents December of each year, and disposable personal income represents the yearly total. The author calculated the percentages.

on additional debt, or because lenders, noting the higher debt burdens and associated increase in loan delinquencies, become stricter in extending credit to consumers. However, it is difficult to infer from historical experience what that threshold is. A tentative indicator of such a threshold is noted below.

There is a complex interaction among household incomes, debt burden, and delinquencies, as Jonathan McCarthy notes.[11] Households change their spending patterns more in line with changes in their incomes and income prospects than with their debt burden. This is reflected in the tendency for consumer spending to change direction before directional changes in household financial liabilities. Concomitantly, banks use their knowledge of customers' income prospects to decide on the creditworthiness of their customers. Thus, the confluence of more stringent credit rationing by banks and higher delinquency rates on consumer loans may have a common linkage in the perception of lower income prospects of bank customers.[12]

Figure 4.5 shows the consumer credit outstanding as a percentage of disposable personal income for 1992, 1995, 1998, and 2001.[13] After declining to a low of 16.5 percent in 1992, the ratio rose gradually to a high of 23.6 percent in 2002.

Table 4.5 shows the ratio of scheduled debt payments for consumer loans and mortgages as a percentage of family income for 1992, 1995, 1998, and

Table 4.5

Scheduled Family Debt Payments as a Percentage of Family Income: 1992, 1995, 1998, and 2001

	All families with debts payments (percent)	Families with debt payments greater than 40 percent of family income (percent)
1992	14.0	10.8
1995	13.6	10.6
1998	14.4	12.8
2001	12.5	11.0

Source: Ana M. Aizcorbe, Arthur B. Kennickell, and Kevin B. Moore, "Recent Changes in U.S. Family Finances: Evidence from the 1998 and 2001 Survey of Consumer Finances," *Federal Reserve Bulletin*, Table 14, January 2003.

2001, as prepared by the Federal Reserve Board.[14] The scheduled payments include principal and interest ranging from monthly to annual depending on the contractual terms of the loans. Families include couples living together (whether they are married or living together as partners) and individuals. Data are shown separately for all families and for families with debt payments exceeding 40 percent of income.

The data for all families fluctuated over the four selected years, peaking at 14.4 percent in 1998 and declining to a low of 12.5 percent in 2001. Families with debt payments exceeding 40 percent of income account for the bulk of all families, ranging from 10.6 percent in 1995 to 12.8 percent in 1998. The differential between all families and families with debt payments exceeding 40 percent of income declined over the 1992 to 2001 period, from 3.2 percentage points in 1992 to 1.5 percentage points in 2001.

The decline in the differential from 1992 to 2001 indicates that families with scheduled debt exceeding 40 percent of income became a rising share of all families, including those having no debt. Stated differently, the proportion of families with debt below 40 percent of income declined.

The decline in the percentages of both data series from 1998 to 2001 also may be a tentative indicator of some threshold level of family debt acting as a restraint on household spending. But because 2001 was a recession year, further light on such a threshold may appear in the Federal Reserve 2004 survey data that will be published in early 2006. (Federal Reserve data on household debt service burden are available quarterly on an up-to-date basis, though the long-term trends in those data vary from those in the periodic survey data cited here.)

Table 4.6

Family Debt for Investments Except Real Estate as a Percentage of Total Family Debt: 1992, 1995, 1998, and 2001

	Percent
1992	1.8
1995	1.0
1998	3.3
2001	2.8

Source: Ana M. Aizcorbe, Arthur B. Kennickell, and Kevin B. Moore, "Recent Changes in U.S. Family Finances: Evidence from the 1998 and 2001 Survey of Consumer Finances," *Federal Reserve Bulletin*, Table 14, January 2003.

Table 4.6 shows the debt of all families associated with investments, excluding real estate investments, as a percentage of total family debt for selected years from 1992 to 2001 (the data were prepared by the Federal Reserve Board).[15] Non-real-estate investment encompasses such items as stocks, bonds, IRA deposits, gold, and investments in unincorporated businesses.

The debt related to investments excluding real estate fluctuated with a general upward trend, peaking at 3.3 percent in 1998 and receding to 2.8 percent in 2001. Some of the increase may represent consumer credit used for the stock market, but the extent of this usage is not known.

The analyst should include consumer credit and debt as a supplement to personal income, saving, and spending patterns for durable goods, nondurables, and services in assessing the strength of the household sector of the economy. In particular, household credit and debt should be monitored for any tendency to overheat the economy during cyclical expansions or intensify the decline during cyclical recessions.

Personal Bankruptcy

Personal bankruptcy, as distinct from business bankruptcy, is another signal of household debt burden problems.[16] Persons are declared to be in bankruptcy in federal courts, which arrange for creditors to obtain some monetary compensation. For the debtors, bankruptcy is a procedure for getting their lives together and reversing the treadmill of going deeper into debt.

While personal bankruptcy is affected by economic conditions such as failing businesses, other personal factors unique to households that face, or are in bankruptcy, are important and in many instances dominate. These include households spending beyond their means that result in being saddled with excessive debt, credit card companies issuing credit cards to noncreditworthy households, the lessening social stigma of bankruptcy, accidents, sickness, divorce, or other unexpected personal events that diminish incomes or raise expenses.

Thus, bankruptcy is often the culmination of a variety of factors in the personal lives of households. With these personal factors as the backdrop, slack or depressed general economic conditions may spark or aggravate the personal factors that lead to bankruptcy.

In short, bankruptcy is not a typical macroeconomic phenomenon. It could become one if the economy were to go into a deep slump. But at the time of this writing, the economic conditions of the first decade of the twenty-first century do not fit that outlook.

CONSUMER OPTIMISM AND PESSIMISM OPINION SURVEYS

Two monthly surveys about how households perceive current and future economic conditions and their own economic situation are widely reported in newspapers and on radio and television. The aim of the surveys is to gauge whether households are optimistic or pessimistic about the economy and how this may affect their spending for consumer goods and services both currently and in their plans for the future. Because of the importance of consumer expenditures in the overall economy, interest in these surveys extends to the information they provide on the outlook for overall economic growth.

Both surveys register opinions of households regarding their optimism or pessimism for the economy, and the survey responses are combined into statistical indexes. One is the "index of consumer sentiment" prepared by the University of Michigan's Survey Research Center, and the other is the "consumer confidence index" prepared by The Conference Board. The indexes differ in the content and wording of the questions asked, in the survey sample, both in size and the use of the telephone or mail inquiries, and in the mathematical method of weighting the survey responses. Despite these technical differences, the monthly movements of both surveys are similar. Anecdotally, it appears that the monthly survey opinion responses in both indexes are heavily influenced by household perceptions of the overall economy and recent movements in the stock market.

In an analysis of the usefulness of the surveys for forecasting the overall economy, Alan Garner concluded that at best they provide only slight improvements in the forecasts.[17] This assessment was based on comparing simple statistical models with and without the consumer confidence and sentiment indexes. It also was consistent with previous research by other analysts.

Garner extended this analysis to the effect of four outside shocks on the confidence/sentiment indexes—the 1993 World Trade Center bombing, Oklahoma City bombing, Persian Gulf War, and September 11, 2001, terrorist attacks. The analysis suggested that households did not consider the World Trade Center and Oklahoma City bombings as significantly affecting the overall economy. But the impact of the Persian Gulf War reduced the confidence and the sentiment indexes by about 14 and 8 points, respectively.

In the analysis of the aftermath of the September 11 terrorist attacks, the attacks did not appear to significantly affect the movements of the two indexes. However, Garner noted that the statistical significance estimate of the confidence index "is small enough that many analysts would not completely dismiss the view that the terrorist attacks lowered consumer confidence. But the fourth-quarter decline in consumer confidence can largely be attributed to worsening economic conditions in the third quarter and earlier. The fourth-quarter movements of the confidence indexes apparently did not contain much information on the economic impact of September 11."

The consumer sentiment and confidence indexes are useful to the analyst on a current basis for confirming or contradicting the movements of other macroeconomic indicators. The indexes provide only marginal improvements in forecasts of the overall economy.

REVIEW QUESTIONS

- Household spending is important in moderating the extremes of cyclical expansions and recessions.
    - a. What factors are responsible for this?
    - b. Give an example of what could change this in the future.
- Both unemployment benefits and the progressive income tax give greater stability to disposable personal income over business cycles.
    - a. Explain.
    - b. How can the indexing of inflation in the tax laws affect this in highly inflationary periods?
- Why is the saving rate problematic in short-term forecasts of household spending?
- Give examples of how household debt can adversely affect economic growth.
- When does a sharp rise in bankruptcies become a macroeconomic concern?
- What relevance do measures of consumer confidence have for economic analysis?

Extra Credit

- Services have grown from 32 percent of consumer expenditures in 1948 to 59 percent in 2002. What factors are responsible for this growth?

NOTES

1. Maria G. Perozek and Marshall B. Reinsdorf, "Alternative Measures of Personal Saving," *Survey of Current Business*, April 2002, pp. 13–14.
2. William G. Gale and John Sabelhaus, "Perspectives on the Household Saving Rate," *Brookings Papers on Economic Activity* 1, 1999.
3. Richard Peach and Charles Steindel, "A Nation of Spendthrifts? An Analysis of Trends in Personal and Gross Saving," *Current Issues in Economics and Finance*, Federal Reserve Bank of New York, September 2000.
4. Lynn Elaine Browne with Joshua Gleeson, "The Saving Mystery, or Where Did the Money Go?" *New England Economic Review*, Federal Reserve Bank of Boston, September/October 1996.
5. Residential construction is defined as investment in the gross domestic product (chapters 3 and 5).
6. Charles Ian Mead, Clinton P. McCully, and Marshall B. Reinsdorf, "Income and Outlays of Households and of Nonprofit Institutions Serving Households," *Survey of Current Business*, April 2003, p. 15.
7. Dean M. Maki and Michael G. Palumbo, "Disentangling the Wealth Effect: A Cohort Analysis of Household Saving in the 1990s," *Finance and Economics Discussion Series Working Papers* 2001–21, Federal Reserve Board, April 2001.
8. Karl E. Case, John M. Quigley, and Robert J. Shiller, "Comparing Wealth Effects: The Stock Market versus the Housing Market," Working Paper 8600, National Bureau of Economic Research, November 2001.
9. Matthew D. Shapiro and Joel Slemrod, "Consumer Response to Tax Rebates," National Bureau of Economic Research Working Paper No. 8672, National Bureau of Economic Research, December 2001. The survey was conducted as a rider on the University of Michigan Survey Research Center's monthly Survey of Consumers.
10. William G. Gale and Samara R. Potter, "An Economic Evaluation of the Economic Growth and Tax Relief Reconciliation Act of 2001," *National Tax Journal*, March 2002.
11. Jonathan McCarthy, "Debt, Delinquencies, and Consumer Spending," *Current Issues in Economics and Finance*, Federal Reserve Bank of New York, February 1997.
12. Consumer credit delinquency data are collected and published quarterly by the American Bankers Association in *Consumer Credit Delinquency Bulletin*.
13. Use of disposable personal income instead of personal income in the denominator of the consumer debt burden measure raises the proportion by 2 to 3 percentage points, but the movements over time are similar in both measures.
14. Ana M. Aizcorbe, Arthur B. Kennickell, and Kevin B. Moore, "Recent Changes in U.S. Family Finances: Evidence from the 1998 and 2001 Survey of Consumer Finances," *Federal Reserve Bulletin*, January 2003, pp. 26–29 (including Table 14).
15. Ibid., pp. 25–26 (including Table 12).
16. Bankruptcy data are collected and published quarterly by the Administrative Office of the United States Courts, Statistics Division, *Statistical Tables for the Federal Judiciary*.
17. C. Alan Garner, "Consumer Confidence after September 11," *Economic Review*, Federal Reserve Bank of Kansas City, Second Quarter 2002.

5

Business Profits, Nonresidential Investment, and Housing

This chapter has two parts: (1) the relationship between business profits and nonresidential investment in structures and equipment, and (2) the short-term and long-terms factors affecting new housing construction.

The data on profits, investment, and housing are components of the gross domestic product (chapter 3). They are prepared quarterly by the Bureau of Economic Analysis (BEA) in the U.S. Department of Commerce and are published in the monthly BEA journal, the *Survey of Current Business* (www.bea. doc.gov). Other data sources used in analyzing investment and housing are noted in the chapter.

GDP, NONRESIDENTIAL INVESTMENT, AND BUSINESS PROFITS

Business investment in nonresidential structures and equipment provides the industrial capacity to produce goods and services for household, business, government, and export markets. These capital investments raise economic growth and productivity (chapters 3 and 10). They cover all privately owned buildings (e.g., factories, offices, stores), non-building structures (e.g., roads, power plants, telephone lines, oil and gas well drilling), machinery, vehicles, computers, furniture, and other equipment lasting two or more years. The structures and equipment are used for first-time investments in new businesses and to expand, replace, and modernize existing capital facilities in for-profit, not-for-profit, farm, and nonfarm activities. The dollar value of the purchased structures and equipment depreciates over the life-span of each item and thus becomes an annual cost of production, which appears as depreciation allowances on business income tax returns and in the income side of the gross domestic product (GDP).

Figure 5.1 shows the share of the GDP accounted for by nonresidential investment and net nonresidential investment on the product side of the GDP, and business profits on the income side of the GDP, from 1979 to 2002. Nonresi-

Figure 5.1 **Nonresidential Fixed Investment and Business Profits as a Percentage of GDP: 1979–2002**

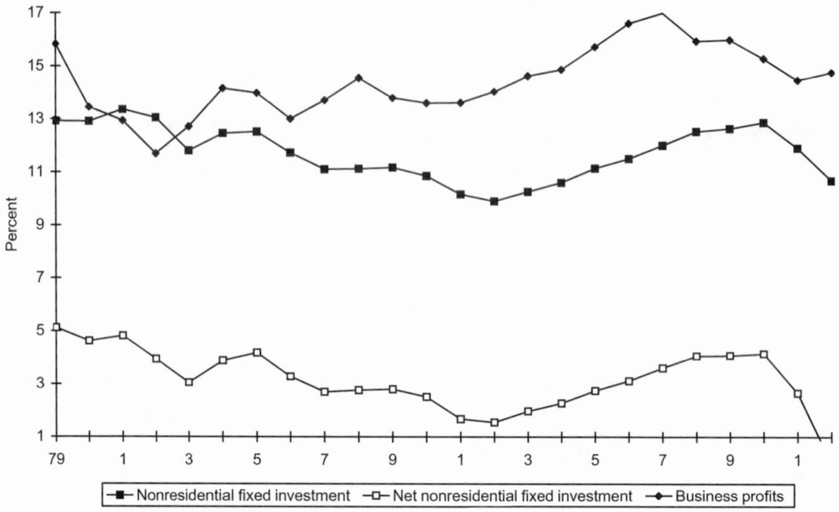

Source: Based on U.S. Bureau of Economic Analysis data

Note: Nonresidential investment is in structures and equipment. Net investment is after capital consumption allowances (see text for 2002). Profits cover corporations and unincorporated businesses.

dential investment in structures and equipment (referred to as nonresidential fixed investment because it excludes inventory change) fluctuated within 10 to 13 percent of the GDP over the period. The proportion peaked in 1981 and 1982, declined to a low in 1992, rose to another high in 2000, and declined in 2001 and 2002.

Net nonresidential investment represents investment after the deduction for depreciation and adjustments for the current cost of replacing the existing capital facilities from their original purchase cost. Data for net investment were not available for 2002 at the time of this writing. Net nonresidential investment ranged from 1.5 to 5 percent of the GDP over the period, peaking in 1979, declining to a low in 1992, rising to another high during 1998–2000, and declining in 2001. Net nonresidential investment showed the same pattern of annual movements as nonresidential investment. But net nonresidential investment was typically only 20 to 30 percent as large as nonresidential investment.

Business profits cover income of corporations and unincorporated businesses before the payment of income taxes. These fluctuated within 13 to 16 percent of the GDP over the period, except for 1982 (12 percent) and 1996 and 1997

(17 percent). Profits as a percentage of the GDP peaked in 1997, and then declined by 2002 to the lower levels of the early 1990s.

As a percentage of the GDP, profits were consistently larger than investment, except for 1981 and 1982, over the 1979–2002 period. The differential rose from 1 to 3 percentage points in the 1980s to 4 to 5 percentage points in the 1990s, and then receded to 3 to 4 percentage points in the early 2000s.

Figures 5.2a and 5.2b show the cyclical movements of the GDP, nonresidential investment, and business profits in current dollars from the 1980s to the early 2000s.[1] Each of the two long expansions of the period is separated into halves, four years each for the 1980s and five years each for the 1990s to 2000. This indicates the evolving nature of the long-term expansions that would not be apparent in the entire expansion as a whole.

During expansions, investment spending rose more than the GDP in three of the five upturns. *During recessions*, investment spending declined in all four downturns, while the GDP in current dollars rose in all four recessions. The differential cyclical patterns of investment and the GDP arise because such investment is often deferrable, as businesses can often make do with existing facilities. Deferring investments may result in lower profits than the optimum potential for businesses because older facilities are less efficient than more modern technology, and because businesses may have insufficient productive capacity to meet sudden surges in demand. The ebbs and flows in sales of a firm's products result in waves of optimism and pessimism, which in turn lead to

Figure 5.2a **Business Cycle Movements of GDP, Nonresidential Investment, and Business Profits, 1980s to Early 2000s: Expansions**

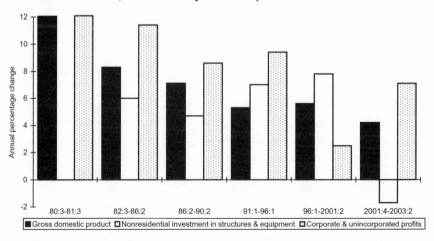

Source: Based on U.S. Bureau of Economic Analysis data in current dollars.

Note: Number after colon is quarter of year. Data for 80:3–81:3 are truncated.

Figure 5.2b **Business Cycle Movements of GDP, Nonresidential Investment, and Business Profits, 1980s to Early 2000s: Recessions**

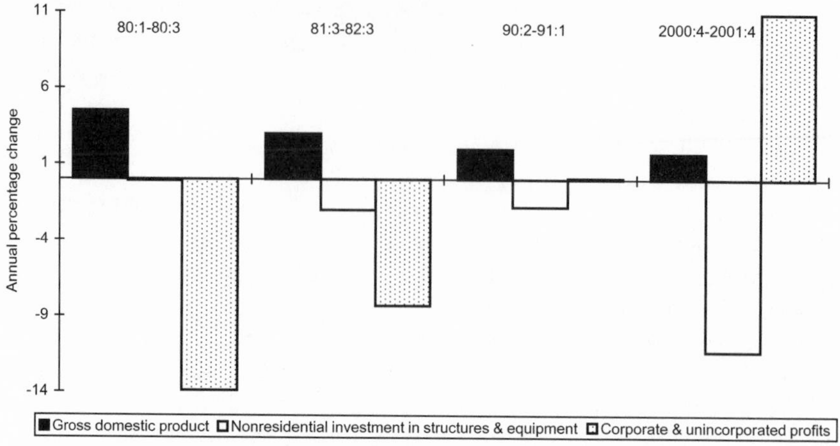

Source: Based on U.S. Bureau of Economic Analysis data in current dollars.

Note: Number after colon is quarter of year.

substantial additions of capital facilities during expansions, only to be followed by over-capacity in recessions and accompanying deep cutbacks in investment outlays.

The Role of Profits

Because the basic purpose of a business is to make a profit, anticipated profits are the engine that drives investments in nonresidential capital facilities. Anticipated profits are affected by perceptions of whether trends in past profits will continue at similar rates or if the future movements will turn decidedly higher or lower.

Profits of firms are sales of goods and services less the costs of producing the goods and services, and as a residual reflect the movements of both sales and costs. Sales are the outcome of the demand and price for a firm's product. Costs represent the firm's purchases of materials and services, wages paid to its workers, and other expenses. If profits are rising and markets are expanding, a business tends to be optimistic that markets for its products will grow, and it is thus encouraged to invest in new facilities to supply those markets. In contrast, during periods of declining profits and shrinking markets, there is little urgency to expand productive capacity, and a greater share of capital investments is used for replacing and modernizing existing facilities in order to lower production costs.

Profits provide financing for structures and equipment investments in two ways. First, as internally generated funds from company operations that are retained in the company rather than paid out in dividends to corporate stockholders or as compensation to unincorporated business owners, profits provide money to buy the capital facilities. Second, a business's profits are a key factor in lenders' and investors' decisions to provide external funds through bank loans, debt instruments (e.g., bonds), and equity capital (e.g., stock).

During expansions, Figures 5.2a and 5.2b show that the increase in business profits was greater than the increase in the GDP in four of the six upturns, and that the increase in profits exceeded that of nonresidential investment in three of the six upturns. During recessions, profits declined in two of the four downturns, while investment declined in all four downturns.

GDP and Profits versus Nonresidential Investment

The growth of the economy represented by the GDP, together with private enterprise incentives represented by business profits, are underlying macroeconomic factors affecting investment in nonresidential structures and equipment. Figures 5.3a and 5.3b show the long-term relationships from 1980 to 2002 between the GDP and nonresidential investment. Figure 5.2a represents the price-adjusted dollar levels of the GDP and nonresidential investment, and Figure 5.2b represents the annual percentage change in the price-adjusted GDP and nonresidential investment. The black diamonds are the actual plotting points of the individual years at which the GDP on the horizontal axis intersects nonresidential investment on the vertical axis. The white diamonds represent the long-term average relationship.

Both figures indicate a direct relationship between the GDP and investment, which is reflected in the long-term average line sloping upward to the right. That is, the GDP and nonresidential investment typically move in the same direction. Generally, there is a closer relationship between the GDP and nonresidential investment in Figure 5.3a than in Figure 5.3b. This is apparent in the dispersion of the individual years around the long-term average line, where the black diamonds are closer to the white diamonds in Figure 5.3a than they are in Figure 5.3b. It suggests that the impact of the overall volume of economic activity of the GDP on the level of nonresidential investment is a more stable relationship than the year-to-year movements alone of both variables. Thus, the GDP and investment levels also have the properties of year-to-year movements.

Figure 5.4a, which represents the overall dollar levels of profits and investment, has a closer relationship in the two variables than the relationship in Figure 5.4b, which compares the year-to-year percentage changes in both variables. This parallels the patterns in 5.3a and 5.3b noted above.

Figure 5.3a **Real GDP versus Private Nonresidential Structures and Equipment Investment, Annual Levels: 1980–2002**

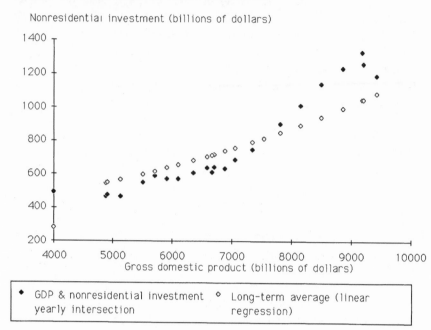

Nonresidentiai investment (billions of dollars)

Gross domestic product (billions of dollars)

| • | GDP & nonresidential investment yearly intersection | ◦ | Long-term average (linear regression) |

Source: Based on U.S. Bureau of Economic Analysis data in billions of chained (1996) dollars.

Capacity Utilization and Nonresidential Investment

As a supplement to the GDP and business profits, capacity utilization rates (CURs) in the manufacturing, mining, and electric and gas utilities industries provide an additional perspective on the factors driving nonresidential invest-ment. The CURs indicate the proportion of capacity in structures and equipment facilities used in production. For example, if a factory with the capacity to produce 1,000 cans of paint a month actually produces 800 cans a month, its utilization rate is 80 percent. Mathematically, the CUR is the ratio of production in the numerator and capacity in the denominator. The measure of unused ca-pacity is obtained by subtracting the utilization rate from 100 percent. In prac-tice, preparation of the capacity measures in the various industries is often indirect and represents only a broad order of magnitude. The CUR measures are prepared monthly by the Federal Reserve Board.[2]

Theoretically, the direction and level of CURs indicate the demand for non-residential investment and the degree of inflationary pressure in the economy. Rising CURs tend to reduce unit costs of production for a time, as the existing

Figure 5.3b **Real GDP versus Private Nonresidential Structures and Equipment Investment, Annual Percentage Change: 1980–2002**

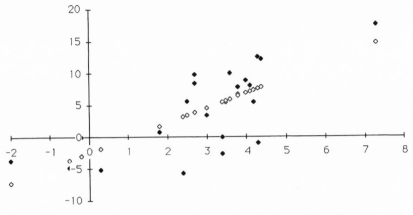

Nonresidential investment (annual percentage change)

Gross domestic product (annual percentage change)

| • | GDP & nonresidential investment yearly intersection | ○ | Long-term average (linear regression) |

Source: Based on U.S. Bureau of Economic Analysis data in chained (1996) dollars.

stock of structures and equipment produces a greater volume of goods. The cost advantage of the larger volume (increasing returns to scale) continues until the utilization rate reaches a level at which further increases in production raise unit costs because of machinery breakdowns, increasing use of outmoded and less reliable equipment, hiring of less-productive workers as unemployment falls, and laxness by managements in holding down costs.[3]

The specific point at which the turnaround threshold occurs on costs, and consequently on structures and equipment investment, varies among industries and is hard to quantify precisely. The observed turnaround zone is based on movements of the data—it does not mean that company decisions to invest or change prices are linked to a particular CUR level. The rising production costs at the higher utilization rates spur companies to reduce costs by increasing capacity through new investment in structures and equipment. By contrast, relatively low and falling CURs reduce business incentives to expand capacity, and replacements of run-down and outmoded capacity account for greater shares of nonresidential investment during such periods. Analogously, increasing production costs foster higher prices, and decreasing costs foster stable or declining prices.

Figure 5.4a **Business Profits versus Nonresidential Structures and Equipment Investment, Annual Levels: 1980–2002**

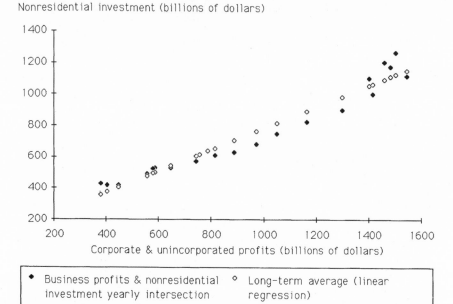

Nonresidential investment (billions of dollars)

Corporate & unincorporated profits (billions of dollars)

| • | Business profits & nonresidential investment yearly intersection | ○ | Long-term average (linear regression) |

Source: Based on U.S. Bureau of Economic Analysis data in billions of current dollars.

CURs are provided only for the manufacturing, mining, and utilities industries. Although these industries cover a limited part of the overall economy, they are capital intensive and so have a significant impact on capital investment. For example, these industries accounted for 18 percent of the GDP and 28 percent of nonresidential investment in 2001 (excluding owner- and tenant-occupied housing and the real estate industry that mainly reflect investments in structures).

Figure 5.5 shows the relationship between the CUR for the total of all manufacturing, mining, and utilities industries and the annual percentage change in the inflation-adjusted nonresidential investment in structures and equipment from 1980 to 2002. The CUR is on the horizontal axis and nonresidential investment is on the vertical axis. The black diamonds are the actual plotting points of the individual years at which the CUR on the horizontal axis intersects nonresidential investment on the vertical axis. The long-term average line of white diamonds slopes upward to the right, indicating a direct relationship between the CUR and investment in which both indicators typically move in the same direction, which would be theoretically expected.

The individual years are widely dispersed around the long-term average line,

Figure 5.4b Business Profits versus Nonresidential Structures and Equipment Investment, Annual Percentage Change: 1980–2002

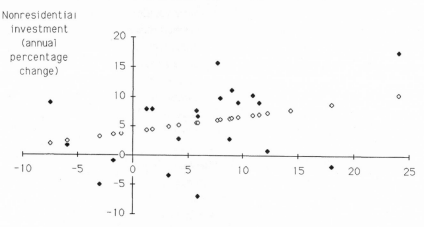

Corporate & unincorporated profits (annual percentage change)

♦	Business profits & nonresidential investment yearly intersection	○	Long-term average (linear regression)

Source: Based on U.S. Bureau of Economic Analysis data in current dollars.

which means that the relationship varies widely from year to year. Other relationships were tried that varied the absolute levels and the annual changes, and having the CUR lead investment by one year. However, the closest relationship was that in Figure 5.5 shown here. In general, however, the loose relationship undoubtedly reflects the fact that manufacturing, mining, and utilities industries, though capital intensive, account for a minor share of all nonresidential investment (as noted above, 28 percent in 2001).

Another factor complicating the relationship between the CUR and investment is the CUR's tendency to function as a threshold in this relationship, or what is sometimes referred to as a "flash point." That is, above a particular CUR level, businesses are assumed to increase structures and equipment expenditures substantially to expand capacity in order to meet the increased demand for their products, while below the threshold businesses are assumed to retrench capital spending and concentrate on modernizing by replacing inefficient and outmoded facilities rather than on expanding capacity. The CUR threshold for all manufacturing industries is sometimes thought to be in the 83 to 85 percent zone. However, statistical analyses of such thresholds are at best very weak.

Figure 5.5 **Capacity Utilization in Manufacturing, Mining, and Utilities Industries versus Nonresidential Investment: 1980–2002**

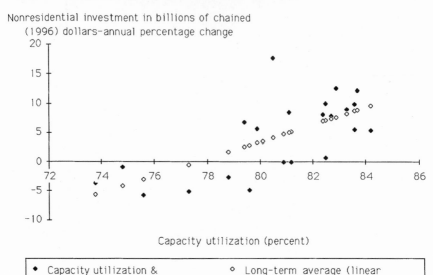

Nonresidential investment in billions of chained (1996) dollars-annual percentage change

Capacity utilization (percent)

♦ Capacity utilization & nonresidential investment yearly intersection	○ Long-term average (linear regression)

Source: Based on Federal Reserve Board and U.S. Bureau of Economic Analysis data.

Orders for Nondefense Capital Equipment

The most concrete short-term advance indicator of nonresidential investments is the commitment of company funds to begin work on an investment project. Such information is included in the Census Bureau survey data on orders received by manufacturers of nondefense capital goods. These monthly data are used by The Conference Board in preparing the leading indicators system (chapter 13).

The reader should keep in mind a few basic differences between the data on equipment orders on the one hand, and those on nonresidential investments on the other. First, the equipment orders data exclude construction work on structures. Second, the orders data are for part or all of an investment project, but they do not specify when the spending for the project will occur. This is particularly pertinent for large-scale projects with lead times of more than one year. Third, the orders data do not give precise coverage of equipment purchases by American business because they exclude U.S. imports of capital equipment, while they include U.S. exports of capital equipment that are not part of investment in the United States.

Table 5.1

Average Age of Private Nonresidential Equipment and Structures: 1990–2001

	Years		
	1990	1995	2001
Equipment and software	7.0	7.0	6.3
Information processing equipment and software	4.2	4.3	3.8
Industrial equipment	9.3	9.6	9.2
Transportation equipment	7.8	7.0	6.0
Other equipment	6.0	6.1	5.6
Structures	20.2	21.2	20.8
Nonresidential buildings, excluding farm	16.2	17.5	18.0
Utilities	30.1	31.1	29.6
Farm	29.5	32.2	33.8
Mining exploration, shafts, and wells	12.2	13.5	13.1
Other nonfarm structures	19.2	18.3	19.9

Source: Bureau of Economic Analysis, U.S. Department of Commerce, "Fixed Assets Tables."

The Age of Structures and Equipment

A basic attribute of nonresidential structures and equipment is that they last several years. They are typically replaced for two reasons: (a) after they have deteriorated and it doesn't pay to repair them, or (b) after they become outmoded and are no longer efficient in terms of current technologies. Annual age data in years on these facilities are based on the capital stock estimates prepared by the Bureau of Economic Analysis in the U.S. Department of Commerce.[4] They are calculated as the depreciated value of the structures and equipment assets, which is referred to as net stocks. Net stocks are the cumulative value of the purchased capital facilities (gross investment) in past years minus the cumulative value of the past depreciation. Depreciation covers wear and tear, obsolescence, accidental damage, and aging.

Table 5.1 shows the average age of broad categories of private nonresidential equipment and structures for 1990, 1995, and 2001. The data indicate little change in the average ages. While purchases of equipment and structures declined in the recession and recovery years of 2000 and 2001, it is unlikely that the lower purchases will affect the average age measures significantly.

Because capital stocks are used for long periods, the average age changes slowly. Thus, in the years preceding 1990 (not shown in Table 5.1), the average age for all equipment reached in the late 1940s continued with little change to the early 2000s. For structures, the average age reached in the late 1960s continued with little change to the early 2000s. The average age was higher for equipment before the late 1940s and for structures before the late 1960s because of the low levels of investment during the depression of the 1930s and in the 1940s until World War II ended in 1945.

The investment declines in 2001 and 2002 were far smaller than the investment deficits of the depression and World War II. Also, an aging of the capital stock does not show in the broad item categories in Table 5.1, nor in the more detailed items not shown in the table. Thus, a significant aging of the capital stock is not evident in the early 2000s that would create an investment stimulus in the mid- and late 2000s.

Reclaiming American Manufacturing

Chapter 3 on Economic Growth included a discussion of ways for American manufacturers to produce many more goods in the United States (see section entitled Assessment of Economic Growth in the First Decade of the twenty-first Century). This would reverse the trend of moving production facilities to low-wage countries abroad and also ceding markets for manufactured items to foreign producers.

If such a change were to occur, there would be considerably more investment in manufacturing structures and equipment in the United States. Many of the capital facilities previously used in producing goods in the United States no longer exist or are in abandoned buildings. Thus, a revitalization of American manufacturing would also stimulate new nonresidential investment in the United States.

The analyst should follow several steps in monitoring the strength and outlook for nonresidential investment. The first is to focus on the movements of the GDP and business profits. The linkage is closer when the GDP, profits, and investment data are expressed in dollar levels than in the year-to-year percentage change in the dollar levels. The relationship between capacity utilization and investment is weaker than the relationship of the dollar levels of the GDP and profits on investment, though the capacity utilization data provide a broad check on the other variables. On the most current basis, the data on manufacturers' orders for capital goods are an early indicator of concrete company actions taken on equipment investment. In using the orders data, the analyst should recognize the definitional differences between the orders and the investment data in forecasting equipment investment. The age of the capital stock of structures and equipment in the early 2000s does not indicate a backlog of aging facilities that need to be replaced in the mid- and late 2000s.

Table 5.2

Residential Investment: 2002

	Billions of dollars	Percent
Total	462.4	100.0
New housing units	289.2	62.5
Single-family and townhouses	247.0	53.4
Multifamily	33.6	7.3
Mobile homes	8.6	1.9
Nonhousekeeping	1.9	0.4
Improvements	107.0	23.1
Brokers' commissions	66.9	14.5
Net purchase of used structures by the private sector from the public sector	(2.6)	(0.6)

Source: U.S. Bureau of Economic Analysis, U.S. Department of Commerce.

Note: Details may not sum to totals due to rounding.

HOUSING

The housing component of private investment covers the value of new construction of privately-owned single-family (including townhouse) and multifamily (apartment buildings) permanent-site housing units, mobile home housing units, nonhousekeeping dormitories, fraternity and sorority houses, and doctors' and nurses' homes, and improvements consisting of additions, alterations, and major replacements to existing residential structures. The residential investment category of the GDP also includes brokers' commissions on the sale of new and existing housing, and the net purchase of existing residential structures by the private sector from the public sector. After reviewing overall trends based on all residential investment, this section will focus on the new housing unit component—single-family homes, townhouses, apartments, and mobile homes.

Table 5.2 shows that the component shares of residential investment are dominated by new housing units, accounting for 62.5 percent of the total in 2002. The next largest are improvements (23.1 percent) and brokers' real estate commissions (14.5 percent).

Cyclical Behavior of Residential Investment

Residential investment as a share of the GDP fluctuated within 3 to 5 percent from the 1980s to the early 2000s. The typical proportion is 4.0 to 4.5 percent.

The cyclical impact has two aspects. In terms of timing, the number of housing starts, building permits issued by local governments for housing construction, and the value of residential investment in price-adjusted dollars are all classified as leading indicators of the overall economy—turning up in a recession before the recovery begins and turning down in an expansion before the recession begins (chapter 13). In a short-term perspective, this tends to stabilize the cyclical aspects of the economy.

But a different picture appears when viewing residential investment over the entire course of business cycle expansions and recessions. Figure 5.6a (expansions) and Figure 5.6b (recessions) show the cyclical movements of residential investment and the GDP from the 1980s to the early 2000s. Each of the two long expansions of the period is separated into halves, four years each for the 1980s and five years each for the 1990s to 2000. This indicates the evolving nature of the long-term expansions that would not be apparent in the entire expansion as a whole.

During expansions, residential investment increased more than the GDP in two of the five upturns, in both cases in the first half of the long expansions. *During recessions*, residential investment declined sharply while the GDP increased in three of the four downturns. And in the 2001 recession, residential investment increased less than the GDP, which also was destabilizing, though

Figure 5.6a Business Cycle Movements of Real GDP and Residential Investment, 1980s to Early 2000s: Expansions

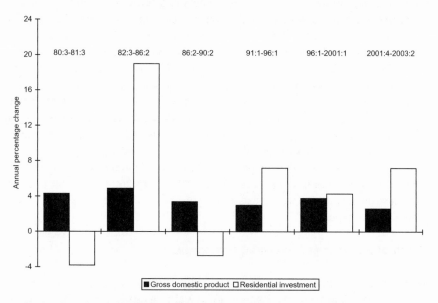

Source: Based on U.S. Bureau of Economic Analysis data in chained (1996) dollars.

Note: Number after colon is quarter of year.

Figure 5.6b **Business Cycle Movements of Real GDP and Residential Investment, 1980s to Early 2000s: Recessions**

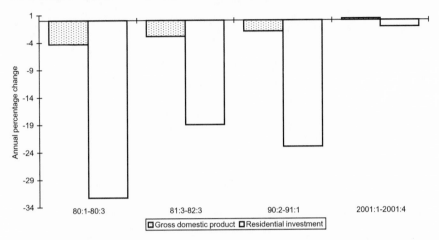

Source: Based on U.S. Bureau of Economic Analysis data in chained (1996) dollars.

Note: Number after colon is quarter of year.

not nearly as much as the decline in nonresidential investment (see previous section).

Housing Starts

A housing start occurs in the month when the excavation work begins for the foundation of the building. Each single-family house (including townhouses) and apartment in a multifamily building is counted as a housing start. Because of differences in the size, amenities, and structural aspects of various types of buildings, the amount of construction work done is measured in the dollar value of housing construction.

Figure 5.7 shows the movement of housing starts from 1980 to 2002. The annual average for the period is 1.45 million starts. The year-to-year levels are volatile, peaking at 1.7 to 1.8 million units during 1983–86, having lower peaks of 1.6 million units during 1998–2001 and 1.7 million in 2002, and having lows of 1.1 to 1.3 million units during 1980–82 and 1.0 to 1.3 million units during 1990–93.

Secondary Spending Impact of Home Purchases

Although the residential investment share of the GDP is small compared with other components, it has secondary impacts that are not apparent from size

Figure 5.7 **Private Housing Starts: 1980–2002**

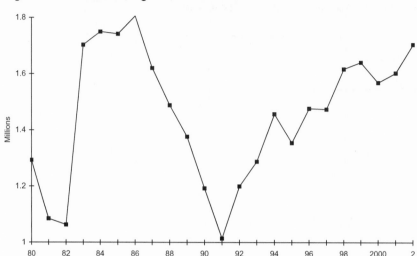

Source: Based on U.S. Bureau of the Census data.

alone. The secondary impacts result from the tendency for purchases of a new home to generate additional spending on a wide range of consumer durables, such as household appliances, furniture, carpets and other furnishings, computers, and lawn mowers, and on structural alterations and repairs to the house.[5]

Paul Emrath analyzed consumer expenditure data following the purchase of a house by both the new homeowners and by homeowners who did not move.[6] The study was based on quarterly consumer expenditures data provided in the consumer expenditures survey of the U.S. Bureau of Labor Statistics from the first quarter of 1995 to the first quarter of 1998 (thirteen quarters) and converted to 1999 dollars by the consumer price index. The study found that in the first year after purchasing a house, the homeowners spent an average of approximately $8,600 on consumer durables and structural improvements on homes built before 1990 and $6,500 on homes built after 1990, compared with $3,000 by non-moving owners of a house. Importantly, the study also found that the new spending appears to have been financed from savings rather than by cutting back on other household outlays, thus increasing overall consumer spending.

In addition, the study included a statistical model that held the demographic and income characteristics constant for a hypothetical married couple with a child between 6 and 17 years, an annual income of $60,000, and in which the male was 35 to 44 years, white, and employed as a manager (characteristics typical of buyers of homes built from 1990 to 1997). The model was developed to determine if the overall average spending estimates based on the survey results, which did not distinguish among demographic and income groups, masked differential spending patterns between purchasers of houses and non-moving homeowners. The model estimates showed that during the 1995–98 period of thirteen quarters noted above, in the first year after the house was purchased, spending on consumer durables and structural improvements was approximately $8,900 by the owner of a house built from 1990 to 1997 and $7,700 on a house built between 1980 and 1989, and such spending by a non-moving owner of a house was $4,000. The model estimates also include consumer durable and structural improvement spending in the second year after the purchase of a house. These show lower spending of slightly above $4,000 for house buyers and the same $4,000 for non-moving owners.

The methodologies of the survey data and the statistical model are significantly different. For example, the survey data are based on overall averages of buyers in *all* demographic and income groups and distinguish between houses built from 1990 to 1997 and in *all* years before 1990. By contrast, the statistical model focuses on a single category of a demographic and income group that was typical of buyers of houses built between 1990 and 1997, and compared their spending with buyers of houses that were built only between 1980 and 1989. Yet the survey data and the statistical model result in estimates of spending for consumer durables and structural improvements that are roughly similar. This suggests that such spending is an economic stimulus, given the study's finding that the spending does not appear to detract from household spending on other items.

The inclusion of purchases of existing houses in this section results from their financial effect on the purchase of newly constructed houses and the subsequent impact of the new house purchase on secondary spending. In contrast to the value of a newly constructed house, which is part of the GDP, the only aspect of the purchase of an existing house that is part of the GDP is the broker's commission on the sale. But purchases of newly constructed and existing houses are interrelated, because the financing of a newly constructed house is often based on the sale of an existing house. This means that expenditures for consumer durables and structural alterations and repairs by purchasers of existing houses are at least in part linked to purchases of newly constructed houses.

New Housing Demand

The market for new housing reflects both long-term and short-term factors. The long-term factors determine the number and cost of housing units needed over a period of about a decade, and the short-term factors affect the yearly movements that vary around the average annual levels implied by the long-term needs.

Long-Term Factors

Over the long run, the market for new housing construction is driven mainly by demographic trends of population and households that include both national totals and geographic subnational migrations. Population trends are associated with birth and death rates, immigration and emigration between the United States and other countries, and regional migration between localities within the United States. Household formation reflects the tendency for individuals to set up separate living quarters (a household includes a family, a single person living alone, or unrelated persons sharing a house or apartment). The number of households is determined by marriage and divorce rates, adult children moving out of their parents' homes or moving back with their parents, unrelated individuals sharing a house or apartment, and immigration minus emigration.

Based on these demographic factors, the number of households is expected to increase by 1.1 to 1.3 million annually from 2000 to 2020.[7] The range reflects alternative assumptions regarding the rate of immigration.

Secondary long-term factors for new housing include the replacement of existing housing removed from the housing inventory. The lost housing results from destruction due to natural disasters such as fires, floods, hurricanes, and earthquakes, deliberate demolition of substandard housing, and the net effects of conversions between residential and nonresidential use and between single-family and multifamily housing. The secondary new housing demand also includes the market for second homes. The effect of the housing stock removals and the second-home market is projected at an additional 300 thousand housing units annually from 2000 to 2020.

The combination of 1.1 to 1.3 million new households plus the 300 thousand housing units associated with replacements of the lost housing stock and the demand for second homes leads to an annual average market for 1.4 to 1.6 million new housing units from 2000 to 2020. However, because the household projections represent national totals, they do not include the effect of new housing demand due to geographic migration within the United States. Allowing for an additional 200,000 housing units to accommodate households that move from one community to another, when some communities gain more households than they lose to other communities, the total annual level of new housing units needed from 2000 to 2020 is 1.6 to 1.8 million.[8] This is similar to the highs of 1.7 to 1.8 million units in the mid-1980s and the 1.6 to 1.7 million units during 1998–2002 noted previously (Figure 5.6).

In addition to the above factors that focus on the number of housing units, the size and amenities of the housing units determine their construction costs and thus the residential investment dollar expenditures. These are affected by the demand for single-family housing and townhouses in contrast to apartment dwellings and mobile homes, as single-family and townhouse structures have higher per-unit construction costs than apartment housing and mobile homes. Generally, the demand for single-family housing and townhouses is greatest for households in the 35–54-year age group, while that for apartment housing is largest in the 34-year-and-under and the 55-year-and-over age groups. Projected household trends indicate a marked shift in the proportion of households in the 55-and-over age group, from 34 percent in 2000, to 41 percent in 2010, to 50 percent in 2020.

The size and amenities of permanent-site housing units and mobile homes, such as the number of rooms, bathrooms, and comfort features, are reflected in the number of persons and the income levels of households. With the shift to more apartment dwellings to accommodate the growing number of 55-year-and-over households from the mid 2000s to 2020, it is likely that construction expenditures per housing unit on average will decline over the period. An opposite trend in average housing construction costs is evident in the shift to large single-family houses ("MacMansions" are the most striking example) as well as more amenities in apartment units. Overall, given the stable level of annual housing starts of 1.6 to 1.8 million units over the period, plus the divergent average construction costs of apartment and single-family dwellings, residential investment as a share of the GDP will likely continue in the 4.0 to 4.5 percent range over the period.

Short-Term Factors

While housing demand from year to year reflects the long-term factors noted above, it also fluctuates in the short term. These movements include the effects of business cycle expansions and recessions on employment, interest rates, and inflation. In expansions, as employment and incomes rise, more households have sufficient income to qualify for mortgage loans to buy housing or to rent costlier new apartments, both of which stimulate residential investment. This increase in purchasing power is partially offset during expansions by higher inflation and mortgage interest rates and the resultant higher cost of housing, but the net effect is increased housing demand and residential investment, though at a lower and even negative rate in the latter part of long expansions, as noted previously (Figure 5.6a). The opposite occurs in recessions when falling employment lessens the demand for housing, although the decline during recessions is tempered by restraints on house price increases and lower interest rates.

Figures 5.8a and 5.8b show the relationship of mortgage interest rates and housing starts from 1980 to 1990 and from 1991 to 2002, respectively. The interest rate data reflect the annual average rate charged on mortgages for new single-family homes (interest rates for new apartment housing have similar movements). Each black diamond shows the average mortgage interest rate (horizontally) and the number of housing starts (vertically) for a particular year

Figure 5.8a **Mortgage Interest Rates versus Private Housing Starts: 1980–90**

Private housing starts (thousands)

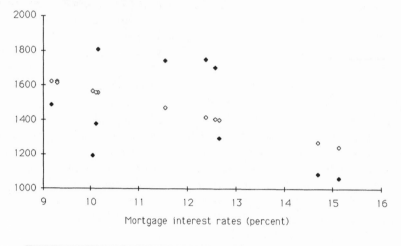

Mortgage interest rates (percent)

◆ Mortgage interest rates & housing starts yearly intersection	◦ Long-term average (linear regression)

Source: Based on Federal Housing Finance Board and U.S. Bureau of the Census data.

during the period. The long-term average of white diamonds slopes downward to the right, indicating an inverse relationship in which interest rates and housing starts typically move in opposite directions, which would be expected theoretically.

However, the individual years vary widely around the long-term line, though much less in Figure 5.8b than in Figure 5.8a. This suggests that mortgage interest rates had a greater impact on housing starts from 1991 to 2002 than from 1980 to 1990.

Figures 5.9a and 5.9b show the relationship between unemployment and housing starts from 1980 to 1990 and from 1991 to 2002, respectively. The relationship between unemployment and housing starts was stronger from 1991 to 2002 (Figure 5.9b) than from 1980 to 1990 (Figure 5.9a), similar to the experience with interest rates.

It isn't readily apparent why such underlying factors as mortgage interest rates and unemployment showed closer relationships with housing starts during 1991–2002 than during 1980–90. A possible reason for this difference is the movement of housing affordability in the two periods. Figure 5.10 shows the housing affordability index (HAI) from 1980 to 2002.[9] The HAI is calculated

Figure 5.8b Mortgage Interest Rates versus Private Housing Starts: 1991–2002

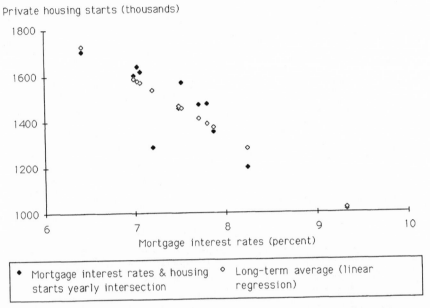

Source: Based on Federal Housing Finance Board and U.S. Bureau of the Census data.

as the ratio of median family gross income to the median-price house for a single-family existing house. It is based on a down payment of 20 percent and a financial standard to obtain conventional loans for thirty-year fixed-rate mortgages and for adjustable-rate mortgages, which requires that the monthly principal and interest payments not exceed 25 percent of the mortgage applicant's monthly gross family income. The HAI threshold number is 100, in which the median-price house is exactly affordable for the median-income family. When the index is above 100, say 120, the median-income family has 20 percent more income than is required to obtain a mortgage, and conversely when the index is below 100, say 90, the median-income family has 10 percent less income than is required to obtain a mortgage.

Figure 5.10 indicates that from lows at the 70 level in 1981–82, the HAI rose to close to the 140 level in 1993 (preceded by little change around the 115 level during 1987–91), and then fluctuated within the 130 to 141 level from 1994 to 2002. Thus, there was a sharp rise from the early 1980s to the early 1990s, and then stability at the higher level through the early 2000s. The possible effect of this pattern on the relationship between mortgage interest rates and unemployment with housing starts is that the sharp rise in the HAI from the early 1980s

Figure 5.9a **Unemployment Rate versus Private Housing Starts: 1980–90**

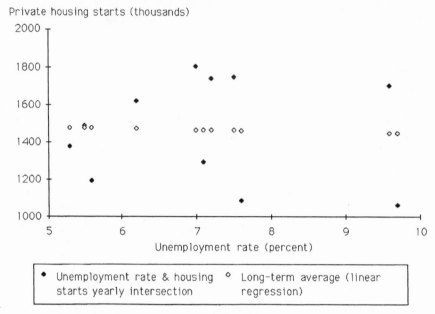

Private housing starts (thousands)

| | Unemployment rate & housing starts yearly intersection | | Long-term average (linear regression) |

Source: Based on U.S. Bureau of Labor Statistics and U.S. Bureau of the Census data.

to the early 1990s was a stimulus to housing starts that lessened the dominance of interest rates and unemployment, and then with the relative stabilization of the HAI at the higher 130 to 141 levels from the early 1990s to the early 2000s, interest rates and unemployment became more prominent. In considering this as a possible element, it should be recognized that the HAI is not completely independent of mortgage interest rates and unemployment, which introduces some overlap, although indirect, among the three factors. Thus, the family income and financial requirement for obtaining a mortgage components of the HAI are related to unemployment through the effect of unemployment on income, and to mortgage interest rates through the monthly interest payments included in the requirement to obtain a mortgage.

Yet even with the stronger relationships during 1991–2002, the variations of the individual years around the long-term average line indicates that the short-term housing market is far more complex than would be evident in comparisons of single economic indicators with housing starts.

Figure 5.9b **Unemployment Rate versus Private Housing Starts: 1991–2002**

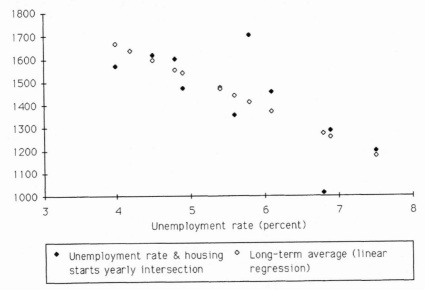

Source: Based on U.S. Bureau of Labor Statistics and U.S. Bureau of the Census data.

Figure 5.10 **Housing Affordability Index: 1980–2002**

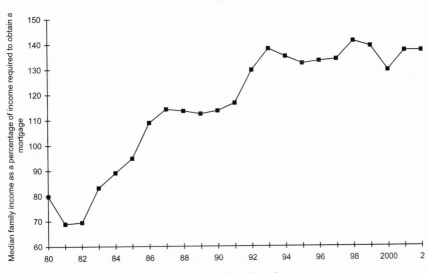

Source: Based on National Association of Realtors data.

General Complexity of Housing Markets

The complexity of the interacting factors in housing markets is illuminated by Ling He.[10] From models developed by He, distinct differences appear in the factors affecting sales of new housing and existing housing. The general distinction reflects a difference between the economic status of buyers of newly constructed houses and that of buyers of existing houses. Buyers of new houses typically are wealthier and own more corporate stock than buyers of existing houses. Buyers of new houses also have less concern about housing prices and unemployment than buyers of existing houses.

The He analysis notes that both new home sales and existing home sales respond to changes in mortgage interest rates and disposable personal income. But sales of new housing are also heavily influenced by returns on the stock market. By contrast, sales of existing housing are also heavily influenced by changes in housing prices and unemployment, and they are impacted by a possible indirect effect from returns on the stock market.

The new and existing home markets are not separate and distinct, but in fact interact with each other. For example, owners of existing homes finance down payments on more expensive newly constructed houses from the capital gains they receive in selling their existing homes. This all occurs in the context of sales in the existing home market being much greater than sales of new housing.

In anticipating the future demand for housing, the analyst should consider both long-term factors such as demographic trends, and short-term cyclical movements in the economy. Unless substantial changes are expected in household formation or in private or government programs to replace substandard housing, the long-term demand is shaped largely by demographic trends.

By contrast, short-term cyclical forecasts of housing demand are subject to much greater uncertainty because of the complexity of the interactions among the factors affecting the short-term movements. The experience of the 1991-2002 period suggests that the traditional short-term factors of interest rates and unemployment have become more dominant, and thus more efficient in forecasting housing starts, though still leading to forecasts in individual years that substantially miss the target.

REVIEW QUESTIONS

- What makes investments in nonresidential structures and equipment have extreme cyclical movements?
- Distinguish the differing roles of the GDP and business profits in influencing nonresidential investment.
- Why is capacity utilization a useful indicator of nonresidential investment if it covers only 17 percent of the overall economy?

- How do manufacturers' orders for capital equipment differ in nature from the GDP, profits, and capacity utilization as indicators of nonresidential investment?
- Residential investment accounts for only 4.0 to 4.5 percent of the GDP, but it gets a lot of analytic attention. Why?
- Why is the distinction made between short-term and long-term factors affecting housing forecasts?
- Although demographic trends are not typically a critical factor affecting short-term housing forecasts, give an example of when demographic movements can have a noticeable impact on such forecasts.
- Under what conditions do movements in the housing affordability index seem to have most influence on housing starts?

Extra Credit

- Why is the relationship between manufacturing capacity utilization and unit manufacturing costs not a simple one?
- Explain why homebuilding activity slows more than the GDP before the end of a cyclical expansion, and turns up more robustly during the recovery.

NOTES

1. The data in Figures 5.2a and 5.2b are expressed in current dollars because there is no price index for converting business profits to inflation-adjusted constant dollars. It would beg the question to convert profits to constant dollars by the GDP chain price index.
2. See chapter 11 on Inflation and Deflation for a further description of the CUR methodology. The reader will also find the following article helpful in understanding the CUR methodology: Carol Corrado and Joe Mattey, "Capacity Utilization," *Journal of Economic Perspectives*, Winter 1997.
3. In prosperous times, managers probably have less pressure to seek more efficient operations than in periods of slow growth or recessions, when businesses tend to be more aggressive in cutting costs. These practices over the business cycle are difficult to quantify, but they are intuitively plausible and also appear anecdotally in the press. They are related in the economic literature to the idea of "X-efficiency," which typically associates differences in competitive pressures in monopolistic and more competitive industries. See Harvey Leibenstein, "Allocative Efficiency vs. 'X-Efficiency,'" *American Economic Review*, June 1966; and F. M. Scherer, *Industrial Market Structure and Economic Performance*, 2d ed. (Rand McNally, 1980), pp. 464–466.
4. For a detailed explanation of the capital stock estimates, see Bureau of Economic Analysis, U.S. Department of Commerce, *Fixed Reproducible Tangible Wealth in the United States, 1925–94*, 1999.
5. Technically, residential investment in the GDP is represented by the construction of new housing units and additions and alterations to existing housing. The reference

in the text is to purchases of housing because the purchase is associated with the new homeowner, who also buys consumer durables and improvements to existing structures.

6. Paul Emrath, "What Else Home Buyers Buy," *Housing Economics*, National Association of Home Builders, April 2000.

7. Joint Center for Housing Studies of Harvard University, *The State of the Nation's Housing 2002*, 2002.

8. This geographic movement includes several housing market adjustments in the areas that have a net decline in households. For example, some housing left behind is converted to office and retail use. There may be higher housing vacancy rates. And some houses may be sold at distressed prices.

9. The housing affordability index is prepared monthly by the National Association of Realtors.

10. Ling T. He, "The Effects of Real Stock Returns on Sales of New and Existing Homes," *Journal of Housing Research* 13, no. 2, 2003.

6

Government

Federal, state, and local governments profoundly affect the well-being of the American people and the American economy. The major part of the economy is in the private sector that functions within the market system, and this undoubtedly has been important in bringing the high level of material well-being to the nation. But this achievement has not happened in a vacuum. Many needs of the people and of the private sector are best performed by the public sector. Even the market system does not proceed unbridled, but is regulated to assure adherence to accepted standards of economic and social behavior.

A free democratic society, national defense, homeland security, progressive income taxes, courts, police, education, health, transportation, water, garbage disposal, income maintenance, labor laws, environmental protection, food and drug laws, mail delivery, and a money and banking system are examples of government activities that underlie the quality of life of the nation. Government activities provide the tangible essentials and the overall climate for workers, businesses, not-for-profit organizations, and governments to produce the nation's goods and services energetically, efficiently, and innovatively. Aesthetically, park land set aside by governments for noncommercial use sometimes results in unique development in the surrounding areas, as in the case of Central Park in New York City.

The effects of governmental activities are often observable, but because of their complexity, are also often difficult to quantify. At the macroeconomic level of this book, the government's role is highlighted in the federal, state, and local government budgets of spending, taxes, borrowing, and debt.

This chapter focuses on the following aspects of government budgets: (a) growth in the aggregates and shifts in the components over time, (b) studies of the impacts of spending and taxes on economic growth, and (c) the effect of taxes on work effort. As background, the reader may find it helpful to review chapter 2, "Framework for Macroeconomic Analysis and Policies," especially the discussions of automatic stabilizers and the structural nature of government budgets.

BUDGET AGGREGATES AND COMPONENTS

This section covers government expenditures and receipts, budget surpluses or deficits, and debt. The data on expenditures, receipts, and budget surpluses or deficits are based on statistical budgets that are part of the national income and product accounts (NIPAs) prepared by the Bureau of Economic Analysis (BEA) in the U.S. Department of Commerce (see chapter 3, "Economic Growth"), and are published in the BEA journal, the *Survey of Current Business* (www.bea. doc.gov). They are of the same order of magnitude as data in the official government budgets, though there are differences in item content and timing. The debt data for the federal government are based on the official budget of the U.S. Office of Management and Budget, and for the state and local governments, the debt data are obtained from the various state and local government financial agencies by the U.S. Bureau of the Census and published in *Government Finances*.

The government's role in the economy is based on two definitional measures that are important to distinguish (noted previously in chapter 3 under the methodology section). One measure is restricted to consumption expenditures and gross investment. It reflects the direct government impact on production through expenditures for goods and services used in current production, investment expenditures for longer-lasting structures, equipment and software, and compensation of government workers.

The other is based on government budgets that reflect a comprehensive view of government effects on the economy. It includes expenditures for benefit payment transfers such as Social Security, Medicare, Medicaid, and unemployment insurance and federal grants-in-aid to state and local governments, as well as the consumption, investment, and compensation expenditures cited above. In addition, this definition includes the financing of government expenditures through taxes and nontax receipts, and through borrowing and the associated debt creation. Thus, the expenditures and receipts budget gives a fuller picture of the government's impacts on the economy because it shows the funneling of transfer payments that become incomes of households and governments, which then are available for subsequent spending by the recipient households and governments. At the same time, it shows how household and business incomes are lowered through the payment of taxes, and thus illustrates the effects of expenditures and taxes on the incomes of all sectors of the economy.

Government Expenditures

Tables 6.1a and 6.1b show the two measures of government expenditures as a percentage of the gross domestic product (GDP), separately for the aggregate

Table 6.1a

Government Consumption Expenditures and Gross Investment as a Percentage of the GDP: Selected Years, 1980–2002

	Total	Federal	State and local
1980	20.4	8.8	11.6
1985	20.8	9.8	11.0
1990	20.4	8.8	11.6
1995	18.5	7.0	11.5
2000	17.8	6.0	11.8
2001	18.4	6.2	12.2
2002	18.9	6.6	12.2

Table 6.1b

Government Current Expenditures and Gross Investment as a Percentage of the GDP: Selected Years, 1980–2002

	Total	Federal	State and local
1980	35.2	21.9	13.3
1985	36.3	23.7	12.6
1990	36.3	22.7	13.6
1995	36.7	22.4	14.3
2000	34.0	19.6	14.4
2001	35.4	20.2	15.2
2002	36.2	20.9	15.3

Source: Based on U.S. Bureau of Economic Analysis data in current dollars.

Note: Consumption expenditures are mainly purchases of goods and services, compensation of government employees, and depreciation of structures and equipment.

Gross investment is purchases minus sales of structures and equipment.

Current expenditures are mainly consumption expenditures, transfer benefit payments for Social Security, Medicare, Medicaid, unemployment insurance, and other government programs, interest paid minus interest received, and federal grants-in-aid to state and local governments.

Details may not sum to totals due to rounding.

government sector, the federal government, and the total of all state and local governments. They appear for selected years from 1980 to 2002: 1980, 1985, 1990, 1995, 2000, 2001, and 2002. There are three cyclical expansion years (1985, 1995, and 2000), three recession years (1980, 1990, and 2001), and one recovery year (2002). The same years are used in subsequent tables on government receipts and the surplus/deficit position.

Table 6.1a is the limited government role that is tied to the GDP. For the aggregate government sector, the government share of the GDP declined from the 20 percent range in 1980–90 to the 18 to 19 percent range in 1995–2002. The decline occurred entirely in the federal government share, while the state and local share increased slightly over the twenty-two-year period. In the early 2000s, the federal government accounted for 6 percent and state and local governments accounted for 12 percent of the GDP.

Table 6.1b uses the comprehensive definition of government expenditures that goes beyond the GDP to the overall effects on the economy. The aggregate government sector fluctuated around 35 percent of the GDP over the twenty-two-year period, with a high of 36.7 percent in 1995 and a low of 34 percent in 2000. In general, the federal share declined and the state and local share rose over the period, similar to the pattern of the limited government definition in Table 6.1a. In the early 2000s, the federal share was 20 percent of the GDP and the state and local share was 15 percent. This contrasts with the greater state and local share in Table 6.1a.

To summarize Tables 6.1a and 6.1b: government outlays in the early 2000s accounted for 18 percent of the GDP in the limited definition, and 35 percent of the GDP in the comprehensive definition. For the aggregate government sector, the limited-definition share declined from the 1980–90 period to the 1995–2002 period, while the comprehensive definition share fluctuated within a limited range with no upward or downward trend over the entire twenty-two-year period. The federal share declined and the state and local share rose in both definitions over the twenty-two-year period. As a proportion of the overall economy, the state and local share was greater in the limited definition and the federal share was greater in the comprehensive definition.

Government Receipts

Table 6.2 shows government receipts as a percentage of the GDP for the same government levels and selected years as in Tables 6.1a and 6.1b (see the designation of expansion and recession years there). Government receipts cover all activities of governments, and thus are consistent with the comprehensive measure of government expenditures in Table 6.1b.

For the aggregate government sector, the receipts share of the GDP rose from 29 to 30 percent in 1980–90 to 30 to 33 percent in 1995–2002. Over the twenty-

Table 6.2

Government Current Receipts of Taxes and Nontaxes as a Percentage of the GDP: Selected Years, 1980– 2002

	Total	Federal	State and local
1980	30.0	18.7	11.3
1985	28.9	17.7	11.1
1990	29.6	18.2	11.4
1995	31.1	18.7	12.4
2000	33.1	20.7	12.4
2001	32.4	19.9	12.5
2002	30.4	18.0	12.5

Source: Based on U.S. Bureau of Economic Analysis data in current dollars.

Note: Taxes are mainly personal and corporate income taxes, Social Security and Medicare insurance taxes, and sales and property taxes.

Nontaxes include donations, fees, fines and forfeitures, rents, and royalties. Details may not sum to totals due to rounding.

two-year period, the high point was 33 percent in 2000 and the low point was 29 percent in 1985. Both federal and state and local receipts showed the same general pattern of higher shares of the GDP in 1995–2002 compared with those in the 1980–90 period. In the early 2000s, the federal share fluctuated around 20 percent and the state and local share was 12.5 percent. This compares with the federal share of expenditures of 20 percent and the state and local share of 15 percent of the GDP in Table 6.1b.

From an overall perspective of government receipts and expenditures as a percentage of the GDP in the early 2000s, the aggregate government sector showed receipts fluctuating around 30 to 33 percent and expenditures fluctuating around 34 to 36 percent. These proportions rose by 2 percentage points for receipts from 1980–90 to 1995–2002, and were stable for expenditures over the entire twenty-two-year period. Federal receipts peaked at 20.7 percent in 2000 and declined to 18.0 percent in 2002, and federal expenditures bottomed at 19.6 percent in 2000 and rose to 20.9 percent in 2002. State and local receipts were stable at 12.4 to 12.5 percent from 2000 to 2002, and state and local expenditures rose from 14.5 percent in 2000 to 15.3 percent in 2002.

Budget Surpluses and Deficits

The government surplus or deficit $(-)$ measures are calculated as current receipts (Table 6.2) minus current expenditures (Table 6.1b). These "current" data exclude both revenue, from the sale of bonds, real estate, and other assets, and investment expenditures for structures and equipment.

Table 6.3 shows the government budget surplus or deficit position as a percentage of the GDP for the same selected years from 1980 to 2002 as in the previous tables, plus 1992 when the budget deficit rose to its peak and 1998 when the federal budget first shifted to a surplus. For the aggregate government sector, deficits as a percentage of the GDP ranged from 1.6 percent in 1980 to 4.8 percent in 1992. The surpluses of 2.3 percent in 2000 and 0.4 percent in 2001 became a deficit of 2.4 percent in 2002.

The shift from a deficit to a surplus in the federal budget in 1998 created the surplus in the aggregate government sector in that year. The state and local governments' total showed a surplus in all years until deficits appeared in 2001 and 2002.

Prospects for the federal and state and local budget positions in the mid-2000s are discussed in the later section on Prospects for Government Surplus/ Deficit Positions.

Government Debt

Government debt reflects the borrowing cumulated from previous years and the current year, plus borrowing in anticipation of future capital construction projects by new bond offerings of state and local governments. Debt resulting from this borrowing is represented in the value of outstanding interest-bearing securities such as bills, notes, and bonds of the federal and the state and local governments. Intergovernmental loans from the federal to the state governments and from the state to the local governments are excluded from the debt data.

Federal debt securities are a vehicle for obtaining interest income that is comparatively low but provides risk-free private investments. State and local debt securities have the incentive of exemptions of the interest income from federal income taxes, though they are subject to investment risks of temporary or permanent defaults by the issuing government. An issue of great interest to economists is the effect of government debt on interest rates. This will be discussed in chapter 12, "Finance."

Table 6.3 shows government debt as a percentage of the GDP from 1980 to 2002 for the same selected years as in Tables 6.1a and 6.1b. The federal debt data appear in two categories: (a) gross debt held by the public comprising individuals, businesses, pension funds, foreigners, and the Federal Reserve, plus debt held by government trust funds such as Social Security, Medicare, federal worker retirement, and unemployment insurance, and (b) debt held by the public only. State and local debt is shown only at the gross level of debt held by the public together with insurance trust funds such as unemployment insurance, state and local worker retirement, and workers' compensation.

Table 6.3

Government Budget Surplus or Deficit (−) and Debt as a Percentage of the GDP: Selected Years, 1980–2002

	Surplus or deficit (−)[a]		
	Total	Federal	State and local
1980	−1.6	−1.9	0.3
1985	−3.7	−4.2	0.5
1990	−2.9	−3.0	0.0
1992	−4.8	−4.7	−0.1
1995	−2.4	−2.6	0.2
1998	1.0	0.5	0.5
2000	2.3	2.1	0.2
2001	0.4	0.7	−0.3
2002	−2.4	−1.9	−0.5

	Federal debt[b]		*State and local debt*[e]
	Gross[c]	Held by public[d]	Gross[f]
1980	33.3	26.1	12.0
1985	43.9	36.4	13.5
1990	55.9	42.0	14.8
1995	67.2	49.2	15.1
2000	57.9	35.1	14.8
2001	57.6	33.1	15.4
2002	60.0	34.3	NA

Sources: Surplus or deficit based on U.S. Bureau of Economic Analysis data.

Debt based on U.S. Department of the Treasury, U.S. Office of Management and Budget, U.S. Bureau of Economic Analysis, and U.S. Bureau of the Census data.

Note: All data are in current dollars. Details may not sum to totals due to rounding.

a. Current receipts minus current expenditures, calendar year.

b. Represents debt at end of fiscal year on September 30.

c. Securities owned by individuals, businesses, pension funds, foreigners, the Federal Reserve, and by government trust funds such as Social Security, Medicare, federal worker retirement, unemployment insurance, highways, and mass transit.

d. Securities owned by individuals, businesses, pension funds, foreigners, and the Federal Reserve.

e. Represents debt of state and local governments with varying fiscal years ending between July 1 and the following June 30—e.g., the year 2000 represents the debt of governments with fiscal years ending between July 1, 1999, and June 30, 2000.

f. Securities owned by the public and by insurance trust funds such as unemployment insurance, state and local worker retirement, and workers' compensation.

NA: Not available at time of writing.

Federal debt as a percentage of the GDP rose from 1980 to a peak in 1995, declined through 2001, and rose in 2002. Federal debt has been three to four times greater than state and local debt. Federal debt held by the public fluctuates more with government borrowing needs than does debt held by government trust funds, as noted by the Congressional Budget Office.[1]

Expenditure Components

Table 6.4 shows selected components of government current expenditure and gross investment as a percentage of the GDP from 1980 to 2002 for the same years as those in Tables 6.1a and 6.1b. For the aggregate government sector, consumption and transfers shares of the GDP were significantly larger than net interest, grants-in-aid, and gross investment in 2002. Consumption expenditures fluctuated around 15 percent and transfers fluctuated around 11 percent of the GDP. The smaller items of net interest, grants-in-aid, and gross investment fluctuated within 2 to 4 percent of the GDP.

Consumption expenditures declined as a percentage of the GDP from 1980 to 2000, and rose in 2001 and 2002, while transfers rose over the entire twenty-two-year period. Net interest peaked in 1995, and declined in the following years to 2002. Grants-in-aid bottomed in 1985 and 1990, and generally rose in the subsequent years to 2002. Gross investment peaked in 1985, bottomed in 1995, and then rose slightly in the following years to 2002.

Differences between the federal and state and local proportions reflect the varying emphasis in the functions and the budget surplus/deficit positions of the two government levels. State and local governments had larger outlays for consumption and gross investment than the federal government. This reflects the more direct provision of services by state and local governments.

By contrast, the federal government had larger outlays for transfers to persons and net interest, while grants-in-aid flowed in only one direction from the federal government to the state and local governments. Federal transfers of Social Security and Medicare are the dominant transfer items. The greater federal net interest payments reflect the greater federal debt than state and local debt. The grants-in-aid end up mainly as state and local consumption and gross investment outlays.[2]

Receipts Components

Table 6.5 shows selected components of current receipts as a percentage of the GDP for the same selected years as those in Table 6.2. For the aggregate government sector, personal taxes and nontaxes were the largest sources of revenue at 10 to 13 percent of the GDP, followed by indirect business taxes at 8 percent,

Table 6.4

Selected Components of Government Current Expenditures Plus Gross Investment as a Percentage of the GDP: Selected Years, 1980–2002

Total government

	Current expenditures				Gross
	Consumption[a]	Transfers[b]	Net interest[c]	Grants-in-aid[d]	investment[e]
1980	16.8	9.8	1.9	2.6	3.6
1985	17.1	9.8	3.2	1.9	3.8
1990	16.6	10.0	3.5	1.9	3.7
1995	15.3	11.8	3.6	2.5	3.2
2000	14.6	10.7	2.6	2.5	3.3
2001	15.1	11.4	2.3	2.8	3.3
2002	15.5	12.1	2.0	2.9	3.4

Federal

	Current expenditures				Gross
	Consumption[a]	Transfers[b]	Net interest[c]	Grants-in-aid[d]	investment[e]
1980	7.5	8.0	2.1	2.6	1.3
1985	8.0	8.0	3.4	1.9	1.8
1990	7.2	7.8	3.6	1.9	1.5
1995	5.9	8.8	3.6	2.5	1.1
2000	5.0	7.9	2.7	2.5	1.0
2001	5.2	8.4	2.4	2.8	1.0
2002	5.6	8.9	2.0	2.9	1.0

State and local

	Current expenditures				Gross
	Consumption[a]	Transfers[b]	Net interest[c]	Grants-in-aid[d]	investment[e]
1980	9.3	1.8	−0.2	—	2.3
1985	9.0	1.8	−0.2	—	2.0
1990	9.4	2.2	−0.1	—	2.2
1995	9.4	2.9	0.0	—	2.1
2000	9.5	2.8	0.0	—	2.3
2001	9.9	3.0	0.0	—	2.3
2002	9.9	3.2	0.0	—	2.3

Source: Based on U.S. Bureau of Economic Analysis data in current dollars.

Note: Details may not sum to totals due to rounding.

a. Mainly purchase of goods and services, compensation of government employees, and depreciation of structures and equipment.

b. Mainly benefit payments to persons for Social Security, Medicare, Medicaid, unemployment insurance, and other government programs.

c. Mainly monetary interest paid on public debt minus monetary and imputed interest received on loans and investments. Because state and local governments are combined into one sector, state grants to local governments end up mainly as consumption and gross investment outlays of state and local governments.

d. Federal payments to state and local governments.

e. Mainly purchase minus sales of structures and equipment.

Table 6.5

Selected Components of Government Current Receipts as a Percentage of the GDP: 1980–2002

Total government

	Personal taxes and nontaxes[a]	Corporate profits taxes[b]	Indirect business taxes[c]	Social insurance taxes[d]	Grants-in-aid[e]
1980	10.9	3.6	7.6	5.9	2.6
1985	10.2	2.3	7.8	6.7	1.9
1990	10.5	2.4	7.7	7.1	1.9
1995	10.5	2.9	8.0	7.2	2.5
2000	13.1	2.6	7.7	7.1	2.5
2001	12.8	2.0	7.7	7.2	2.8
2002	10.7	2.0	7.7	7.2	2.9

Federal

	Personal taxes and nontaxes[a]	Corporate profits taxes[b]	Indirect business taxes[c]	Social insurance taxes[d]	Grants-in-aid[e]
1980	8.9	2.5	1.4	5.8	—
1985	8.0	1.8	1.4	6.6	—
1990	8.2	2.0	1.1	6.9	—
1995	8.0	2.4	1.3	7.0	—
2000	10.3	2.3	1.1	7.0	—
2001	10.0	1.7	1.1	7.1	—
2002	9.1	1.7	1.1	7.1	—

(continued)

Table 6.5 (*continued*)

State and local

	Personal taxes and nontaxes[a]	Corporate profits taxes[b]	Indirect business taxes[c]	Social insurance taxes[d]	Grants-in-aid[e]
1980	1.9	0.5	6.2	0.1	2.6
1985	2.2	0.5	6.5	0.1	1.9
1990	2.3	0.4	6.6	0.2	1.9
1995	2.5	0.4	6.8	0.2	2.5
2000	2.8	0.4	6.6	0.1	2.5
2001	2.8	0.3	6.6	0.1	2.8
2002	2.6	0.3	6.6	0.1	2.9

Source: Based on U.S. Bureau of Economic Analysis date in current dollars.

Note: Details may not sum to totals due to rounding.

a. Personal income taxes, net of refunds on a payments basis, and personal property taxes. Nontaxes include donations, fees, fines, forfeitures, rents, and royalties.

b. Profits taxes are on an accrual (liability), not a payments, basis.

c. Mainly sales and real property taxes.

d. Federal: Mainly Social Security and Medicare. State and Local: Mainly unemployment insurance and workers' compensation.

e. Federal payments to state and local governments. There are no state and local grants to the federal government.

social insurance taxes around 7 percent, corporate profits taxes in the 2 to 3 percent range, and grants-in-aid at 2 percent over the twenty-two-year period.

There are distinct differences in government receipts between the federal and the state and local governments. Federal receipts of personal taxes and nontaxes (mainly income taxes), corporate profits taxes, and social insurance taxes were much greater than state and local receipts of these taxes. By contrast, state and local receipts of indirect business taxes (mainly sales and property taxes) were much greater than the federal receipts of these taxes.

In general over the twenty-two-year period, personal taxes and nontaxes fluctuated with an upward drift, except for noticeable declines in 1985 and 2002; social insurance taxes rose over the period; corporate profits taxes fluctuated with a downward drift; indirect business taxes fluctuated with no upward or downward trend; and grants-in-aid bottomed in 1985 and 1990 and then drifted upward. Because grants-in-aid flow in only one direction—from the federal government to state and local governments—there are no federal grants-in-aid receipts.

PROSPECTS FOR GOVERNMENT SURPLUS/DEFICIT POSITIONS IN THE MID-2000s

This section focuses on future budget surplus/deficit positions of the federal and the total of state and local governments.

Federal Government

The federal budget surplus/deficit position shifted from rising surpluses in the late 1990s to 2000 to a decline in the surplus in 2001 and a deficit of 1.9 percent of the GDP in 2002 (Table 6.3). This resulted from the low economic growth and concomitant slowdown in tax receipts and the increase in defense spending (Tables 6.2, 6.5, and 6.6). Preceding this shift, there were long-term projections of rising surpluses. For example, the Congressional Budget Office projected rising federal surpluses in fiscal years 2002 to 2011 cumulating to $5.6 trillion.[3] I estimate the deficit in 2003 will be about 3 percent of the GDP, which is 1.5 percentage points lower than the deficit in 1992 (1992, as 1993, was a recovery year from a recession).

Unless there is a return to robust economic growth in 2004 and later years, the prospects are for deficits during 2004–10 to rise to 5 percent of the GDP, similar to the levels of the mid-1980s.[4] Factors contributing to the rising deficits include the prospects for large multiyear postwar U.S. expenditures for rebuilding the political and economic base in Iraq and Afghanistan, growing military involvement around the world, future cuts in individual and business income taxes, and increased spending for homeland security and for Medicare prescrip-

Table 6.6

National Defense Expenditures as a Percentage of the GDP: Selected Years, 1980–2002

1980	6.1
1985	7.4
1990	6.5
1995	4.7
2000	3.8
2001	4.0
2002	4.3

Source: Based on U.S. Bureau of Economic Analysis data in current dollars.

tion drugs. These would have to be largely offset by significant reductions in spending on other programs and recisions of previous tax cuts to stop the increase in future deficits.

Problem of Nonpayment of Federal Income Taxes

A long-standing problem in the federal budget surplus/deficit position has been the nonpayment of federal individual and business income taxes. As noted in chapter 1 under The Underground Economy and note 13 to chapter 1, the Internal Revenue Service has long allowed some wealthy individuals and some corporations not to pay taxes by not auditing and pursuing them. Instead, the IRS has focused on auditing individuals of modest and low incomes, including the working poor.

This practice was heightened in 2003, when the IRS was reported to be planning to aggressively audit individuals who apply for the earned-income tax credit (EITC), with limited pursuit of the wealthy tax cheats and corporations who pay little or no taxes through offshore accounts and other evasions of the tax laws. The rigorous enforcement of the EITC was estimated as saving $10 billion per year. This compares with the estimated cumulated avoided, evaded, or unpaid taxes by individuals of $132 billion, including $70 billion in offshore accounts, and $46 billion by corporations.[5]

State and Local Governments

The total of state and local budgets has typically been in surplus, but it fell into its largest deficit positions in 2001 and 2002 (Table 6.3). This was a shift from a budget surplus of 0.2 percent of the GDP in 2000, to a deficit of 0.3 percent of the GDP in 2001, to a deficit of 0.5 percent of the GDP in 2002. I estimate the state and local budget deficit will rise to 0.6 percent of the GDP in 2003.

State and local constitutions typically require balanced budgets, so these governments are obligated to limit deficits, when they occur, to short periods. Thus, there have been strong pressures in 2002 and 2003 to cut state and local spending and/or raise taxes. It appears that if a federal law is passed in the mid-2000s creating uniform national standards for electronic on-line state sales taxes that would authorize states to collect these taxes, it would be too late to alleviate the likely deficits in the mid-2000s.

In assessing prospects for future government budget surpluses or deficits, the analyst should monitor both the expenditure and receipts components of the budgets. These budget data should be considered in the context of the overall economy, as a percentage of the GDP, to give a historical perspective with previous years, and also to put the severity of a deficit into perspective.

FISCAL POLICY INITIATIVES TO STIMULATE ECONOMIC GROWTH

The overall effect of government budget expenditures, revenues, and the surplus/deficit position was covered in chapter 2, "Framework for Macroeconomic Analysis and Policies."

Using that framework as a starting point, many studies have been made of the impact on economic growth of changes in federal government spending and taxes that were made over the years.[6] But the conclusions of the studies vary widely. For example, consider evaluations of the cyclical expansions of the 1980s and of the 1990s to 2000. Analyses of the differential economic impacts of the tax cut in 1981 accompanied by the sharp increase in defense spending and the weakening of regulations on health and safety in the workplace and environmental protection in the 1980s on the one hand, and the tax increase in 1993 accompanied by the decline in defense spending in the 1990s and strengthening of regulations on health and safety in the workplace and environmental protection in the 1990s to 2000 on the other, either praise or disparage the results of one or the other of these diametrically opposed fiscal and regulatory policies.

In evaluating such studies, the analyst should verify the beginning and ending dates bracketing the periods used to measure economic growth to determine if they are consistent in terms of peaks and troughs of the business cycle. Other factors that give a more comprehensive view of the periods should also be evaluated, including employment, inflation, real incomes, income distribution, government budget surplus/deficit positions, and interest rates. Cause-and-effect relationships are difficult to determine statistically using regression analysis, as noted in the Preface. But an informed judgment can be reached by considering a wide range of outcome indicators, as suggested here.

TAXES AND WORK EFFORT

One aspect of the impact of taxes is their possible effect on work effort. Depending on the level of taxation, it can be argued that, at some point, taxes take so much income from workers and entrepreneurs that it is no longer worth their while to work to obtain more income (disincentive effect). But it could also be argued that by reducing after-tax income, increased taxes lead workers and entrepreneurs to work longer hours to make up for the lost income (incentive effect). Another possibility is that, in some circumstances, a tax cut is a work disincentive as workers would substitute leisure time for additional income (leisure effect).

Tables 6.7a and 6.7b provide data on average weekly hours of workers for selected years. The data cover selected years from the 1970s to the early 2000s, a period during which three major changes to the federal income tax laws were made. In 1981, federal income taxes were lowered; in 1993, federal income taxes were raised; and in 2001, federal income taxes were lowered for higher income workers.

Table 6.7a

Average Weekly Hours at Work by Employment Status: 1976 and 1993
(percent distribution)

	Total	1 to 34 hours	35 to 39 hours	40 hours	41 to 48 hours	48 hours or more
Nonfarm wage and salary workers						
1976	100.0	24.5	7.3	44.6	10.6	13.0
1993	100.0	24.0	6.7	40.3	10.6	18.5
Nonfarm self-employed workers						
1976	100.0	27.4	4.4	22.8	9.0	36.4
1993	100.0	30.9	4.9	23.3	7.0	33.8
Farm workers						
1976	100.0	30.7	4.8	14.4	8.2	42.0
1993	100.0	29.4	4.9	22.3	7.6	35.8

Source: Philip L. Rones, Randy E. Ilg, and Jennifer M. Gardner, "Trends in Hours of Work since the Mid-1970s," *Monthly Labor Review*, April 1997, Table 3, p. 10.

Note: Details may not sum to totals due to rounding.

Table 6.7b

Average Weekly Hours at Work by Occupation: 1995, 2000, 2001, and 2002

	Total	Usually work full time	Usually work part time
All nonfarm occupations			
1995	39.2	43.0	NA
2000	39.7	43.3	20.9
2001	39.2	42.8	20.9
2002	39.1	42.8	20.9
Managerial and professional			
2000	42.2	44.9	20.9
2001	41.5	44.2	20.7
2002	41.5	44.2	20.7
Farming, forestry, and fishing			
2000	41.4	46.9	18.6
2001	41.5	46.9	18.9
2002	40.9	46.1	19.0

Sources: 1995 data—Same article as in table 6.7a. Within that article, the 1995 data are from Table 1, p. 4.

2000, 2001, 2002 data—U.S. Bureau of Labor Statistics, Table 30B, Persons at work by actual hours of work at all jobs in the reference week, annual average. Unpublished data from the Current Population Survey.

NA: Not available.

Table 6.7a shows the percent distribution of average weekly hours worked for nonfarm wage and salary workers, nonfarm self-employed workers, and farm workers for 1976 and 1993. For nonfarm wage and salary workers, re-ductions in hours worked occurred mainly in the forty hour workweek category and to a smaller extent in the workweek categories of 35 to 39 hours and 1 to 34 hours, while an increase in hours worked occurred in the category of 48 hours or more. Nonfarm self-employed workers showed an opposite pattern, in which work hours rose in the workweek categories of 40 hours, 35 to 39 hours, and 1 to 34 hours, while work hours declined for the workweek categories of 41 to 48 hours and 48 hours or more. For farm workers, a third pattern emerged, in which a large increase in hours worked occurred in the 40–hour week category, while a large decrease occurred in the workweek category of 48 hours or more, and smaller declines occurred in the 1 to 34 hour and 41 to 48 hour categories.

Table 6.7b shows average weekly hours worked for all nonfarm occupations, managerial and professional workers, and farming, forestry, and fishery workers classified by full-time and part-time work status, selectively for 1995, 2000, 2001, and 2002. The data cover both wage and salary workers and self-employed workers. For all nonfarm occupations, weekly hours increased from 1995 to 2000, declined in 2001, and were unchanged in 2002. This pattern was limited to full-time workers, as hours worked for part-time workers were unchanged. For managerial and professional workers, weekly hours declined from 2000 to 2001 and were unchanged in 2002. This pattern occurred for both full-time and part-time workers. For farming, forestry, and fishing workers, the workweek fell from 2000 to 2001 and was unchanged in 2002 for full-time workers, while the workweek rose during this period for part-time workers.

It is difficult to isolate the effects of changes in the tax laws on the workweek data. For example, in Table 6.7a, the tax cuts of 1981 were dominant over the 1976–93 period, except for the tax increase of 1993 which was in effect only for the last year of the period. During this period, one would expect an incentive effect in the categories of 41 to 48 hours and 48 hours or more. This occurred for wage and salary workers in the 48 hours or more category, but hours worked declined for self-employed workers in both the 41 to 48 hours and the 48 hours or more categories. And in Table 6.7b, which reflected the tax cuts of 2001, the workweek declined for all nonfarm occupations and for managerial and profes-sional workers in 2001 for full-time workers. In this case, it would seem that any work incentive effect was trumped by declining demand associated with the 2001 recession.

For farm, forestry, and fishing workers, the hours-worked data may be more affected by changes in industry markets and unionization than in tax law changes.

Obviously, many factors affect changes in the length of the workweek other than tax law changes. The data show apparently contradictory trends that would otherwise be surmised from effects solely related to changes in the tax laws. Moreover, hypothetical incentive and disincentive effects of tax law changes can reasonably be stated in many variations, as noted in the introduction to this section. Thus, the possible effects of taxes on work effort are a complex topic that needs more empirical analysis to determine the existence and nature of such effects.

REVIEW QUESTIONS

- Why is it important to distinguish between government expenditures in the GDP and government budgets?
- Assess the impacts of government spending and taxes on economic growth. Distinguish between the federal government and the total of state and local governments.

- Assess the impacts of transfer payments and defense spending on economic growth.
- To what extent are changes in income tax laws relevant to data on hours at work?

Extra Credit

- How can the nonpayment of federal income taxes affect fiscal policy?
- Review the articles cited in note 6 in light of the varying fiscal policies used during the expansions of the 1980s and the 1990s to 2000. What common themes and what differences appear in these analyses? Which ones are most persuasive? Explain.

NOTES

1. Congressional Budget Office, *The Budget and Economic Outlook: Fiscal Years 2004–2013*, January 2003, p. 16.
2. For data showing state government budgets separately from local government budgets, including the flow of grants between state and local governments, see Bruce E. Baker, "Receipts and Expenditures of State Governments and of Local Governments, 1959–2001," *Survey of Current Business*, June 2003.
3. Congressional Budget Office, *The Budget and Economic Outlook: Fiscal Years 2002–2011*, January 2001.
4. Federal government debt as a percentage of the GDP in the mid-1980s (fiscal years):
   1982 4.0%
   1983 6.0%
   1984 4.8%
   1985 5.1%
   1986 5.0%
   Source: *Economic Report of the President*, February 2003, Table B-79, p. 370.
5. Mary Williams Walsh, "I.R.S. Tightening Rules for Low-Income Tax Credit," *New York Times*, April 25, 2003. p. A1.
6. Here is a sample of such studies: Oliver Blanchard and Roberto Perotti, "An Empirical Characterization of the Dynamic Effects of Changes in Government Spending and Taxes on Output," *Quarterly Journal of Economics*, November 2002; Douglas W. Elmendorf and David L. Reifschneider, "Short-Run Effects of Fiscal Policy with Forward-Looking Financial Markets," *National Tax Journal*, September 2002; Martin Feldstein, "Supply Side Economics: Old Truths and New Claims," *AEA Papers and Proceedings*, American Economic Association, May 1986; and Benjamin M. Friedman, "What Have We Learned from the Reagan Deficits and Their Disappearance?" NBER Working Paper 7647, National Bureau of Economic Research, April 2000.

7

The United States in the World Economy

The globalization of the U.S. economy encompasses the growing interdependence of the U.S. economy and those of other nations in three major ways. One is the exports of goods and services produced in the United States and sold abroad, and the imports of goods and services produced in other countries and bought by U.S. residents. The second is the output and employment generated by foreign investments of U.S.-owned companies abroad and by foreign-owned companies in the United States. The third is financial investments in stocks and bonds by U.S. residents in foreign securities and by foreign residents in U.S. securities.

Foreign trade and foreign investments bring increasing competition and efficiencies into the U.S. economy, though they also bring dislocations of workers and firms. Increasing internationalization also increases the sensitivity of the U.S. economy to foreign economic and political developments.

This chapter first summarizes the methodological characteristics of the data on international transactions in the balance of payments measures, and their integration within the gross domestic product (GDP). It then highlights the analytic factors surrounding exports and imports of goods, services, and investment income, their relationship to international investments and the value of the dollar, and the sustainability of continued balance of payments deficits and the growing net international debtor position of the United States.

INTERNATIONAL TRANSACTIONS METHODOLOGY

The data on international economic transactions comprise exports and imports of goods and services, income on foreign investments, and the international flows of money that pay for the foreign trade in goods and services and for the foreign investments in the United States and abroad. The international transactions data are often referred to as the balance of payments. The statistical measures are prepared quarterly by the Bureau of Economic Analysis (BEA) in the

U.S. Department of Commerce, and are published in the BEA monthly journal, the *Survey of Current Business* (www.bea.doc.gov).

Foreign trade in goods covers agricultural, mineral, and manufactured items produced in the United States and sold abroad (exports), and such items produced in other countries and bought in the United States (imports). Foreign trade in services covers travel, transportation, royalties and license fees, insurance, telecommunications, and business services sold abroad by U.S. companies, and such services that foreign parties sell to the United States. It also covers U.S. military sales contracts, direct defense expenditures, and miscellaneous U.S. government services.

Foreign investment refers to purchases by U.S.-owned companies and U.S. residents of assets in other countries, and by foreign residents of assets in the United States. There are two broad categories of foreign investments. Foreign *direct* investment is defined as ownership or control, direct or indirect, by residents of one country of 10 percent or more of the voting securities of a corporation or the equivalent interest in an unincorporated enterprise in another country. Foreign *portfolio* investment is the ownership or control of less than 10 percent of a company's voting securities, plus foreign party holdings of company and government bonds. Income on foreign investments covers the profits from direct investment, dividends on stocks, and interest. Income receipts represent returns to U.S. residents on U.S. investments abroad (exports), and income payments are returns to foreign residents on their investments in the United States (imports).

The balance of international economic transactions, which is referred to as the balance of payments, is calculated as exports minus imports. Thus, when exports exceed imports, the balance is positive (i.e., a surplus position), and when imports exceed exports, the balance is negative (i.e., a deficit position). Table 7.1 shows the U.S. international transactions for goods, services, and investment income for 2002. Goods accounted for the major share: 55 percent of exports and 71 percent of imports. The total balance on goods, services, and income was –$422 billion, which reflected the overall negative balance that was only partially reduced by the positive balance on services.

Conceptually, the sum of foreign trade in goods and services, income on foreign investments, and unilateral transfers abroad such as personal remittances that foreign workers send home and government-to-government grants on the one hand, must equal the capital flows between nations that are used to finance these transactions on the other. However, in practice these opposite sides of the coin do not equal each other due to statistical limitations in the data. The difference is referred to as the statistical discrepancy. A positive statistical discrepancy means that net capital inflows of money into the United States exceed those indicated by the data on trade, investment income, and unilateral transfers, while a negative statistical discrepancy indicates that net capital outflows of money

Table 7.1

U.S. International Economic Transactions: 2002 (billions of dollars)

	Goods	Services	Investment income	Goods, services, and income
Exports	681.9	292.2	255.5	1,229.6
Imports	1,164.7	227.4	259.5	1,651.6
Balance (exports minus imports)	−82.9	64.8	−4.0	−422.0

Source: U.S. Bureau of Economic Analysis.

Note: Details do not sum to totals due to rounding.

from the United States exceed that indicated by the trade, investment, and unilateral transactions. The statistical discrepancy reflects omissions in all categories, but the major problem is generally considered to be in the capital rather than the trade transactions. The statistical discrepancy is a net figure of the sum of the individual categories, some of which overstate and some of which understate the true values. Thus, some of the errors are offsetting, which means that the statistical discrepancy is smaller than would appear if all the errors both above and below the true values were aggregated, that is, if they were summed without regard to sign. But such a number cannot be calculated because the true values are not known.

Table 7.2 shows the statistical discrepancy in the international economic accounts, as distinct from the statistical discrepancy in the GDP in chapter 3, from 1993 to 2002. It ranged from −$91 billion in 1997 to $130 billion in 1998. Such large yearly swings reflect a fair amount of inconsistency in the data underlying the measures from year to year.

Goods and Services

Exports and imports of goods and services also enter into the calculation of the GDP. As discussed in chapter 3, "Economic Growth," exports and imports are counted in the GDP as a net number, exports minus imports. The net number has been constantly negative from 1976 to 2002, meaning that imports have exceeded imports every year over the twenty-seven year period. The net number is a bookkeeping technique to avoid double counting in the GDP, because the GDP includes imports within the consumption, investment, and government categories. The net number grossly understates the importance of foreign trade in the economy. For example, as a percentage of the GDP, in 2002 net exports

Table 7.2

Statistical Discrepancy in the U.S.
Balance of Payments: 1993–2002
(billions of dollars)

1993	1.8
1994	−10.5
1995	19.6
1996	−19.3
1997	−90.5
1998	129.7
1999	59.1
2000	−44.1
2001	−20.8
2002	−45.9

Source: U.S. Bureau of Economic Analysis.

were −4.1 percent, while exports were 9.7 percent and imports were 13.8 percent. But the net number is relevant for assessing America's competitive position in the world economy, the foreign exchange value of the dollar, and potentially the extent of protectionist sentiment. These factors, in turn, influence the volumes of exports and imports.

The international transactions data on goods and services are modified slightly for inclusion in the GDP. The differences in order of descending importance are: the geographic coverage of U.S. territories and Puerto Rico, imputed interest for certain financial services provided without payment, and the treatment of gold. Other international transactions in the balance of payments cover capital movements for foreign investments, bank and nonbank financial transactions, and government official reserve assets. While these capital movements are not part of the GDP, they reflect economic activity that affects the foreign exchange value of the dollar, which in turn influences exports and imports of goods and services, and thereby the GDP.

Investment Income

Within the national income and product accounts, there is a difference in the treatment of incomes associated with multinational companies and foreign workers between the GDP and the gross national product (GNP), as noted in chapter 3. The GDP includes the profits of foreign-owned companies operating in the U.S. and the wages, salaries, and fringe benefits of foreigners working in the

United States, and excludes the profits of U.S.-owned companies operating abroad and the employee compensation of Americans working abroad.

The GNP does the reverse, by including the profits of American-owned companies operating abroad and the employee compensation of Americans working abroad, and excluding the profits of foreign-owned companies operating in the United States and the employee compensation of foreigners working in the United States. *The GNP definition of profits of multinational companies is the same as that in the balance of payments accounts.*

DEMAND FOR EXPORTS AND IMPORTS

The growth of exports and imports is determined by three general economic factors: economic growth at home (for imports) and abroad (for exports), relative domestic prices for competing U.S. and foreign goods and services, and the foreign exchange value of the U.S. dollar in relation to other national currencies. Table 7.3 summarizes these factors. In addition, exports and imports are affected by the quality and the perception of the quality of U.S. and foreign goods and services, plus other nonprice factors, including tariffs, quotas, and nontariff barriers such as domestic-content laws requiring that imported goods contain minimum amounts of domestically produced items.

The foreign trade of the United States has become increasingly important in the overall economy from the 1960s to the 1990s to early 2000s. As a proportion of the GDP, exports of goods and services were 10 to 11 percent and imports rose from 11 to 14 percent of the GDP during 1990–2002 (reaching 15 percent in 2000). This compares with 4 to 5 percent for exports and 5 percent for imports in the 1960s. In 2002, the volume of both exports and imports was larger than

---

Table 7.3

Directional Impact of Factors Affecting U.S. Exports and Imports of Goods and Services

Demand factor	Exports	Imports
Economic growth abroad	Higher growth, higher U.S. exports	—
Economic growth in U.S.	—	Higher growth, higher imports
U.S. prices relative to foreign prices for the same item	Higher U.S. prices, lower exports	Higher U.S. prices, higher imports
Value of U.S. dollar	Higher dollar, lower exports	Higher dollar, higher imports

consumer spending for durable goods, housing investment, and federal government consumption and gross investment outlays, and the volume of imports only was larger than nonresidential investment and state and local government consumption and gross investment outlays.

VALUE OF THE U.S. DOLLAR

The foreign exchange value of the U.S. dollar is the price of the U.S. dollar in relation to the currency unit of other countries. That is, it is the amount of a foreign currency that can be purchased with a dollar. For example, the value of the dollar is the number of Japanese yen or of Mexican pesos that will be exchanged for a dollar.

In one respect, the value of the dollar represents the stock valuation of the United States as a corporation that is traded on the stock market. As perceptions of the health of the U.S. economy change relative to those of the health of other economies, so does the value of the dollar.

Changes in the value of the dollar affect relative prices between the United States and other countries. Conceptually, changes in the dollar have the same relative importance to economic activity as was noted above for prices. However, changes in prices and in the value of the dollar do not always show the same movements. Prices are affected by other factors, including the desire of businesses to maintain or increase market shares in export markets, the effect of price changes on profit margins, and the willingness of sellers to allow prices to be dictated by fluctuations in the value of the dollar. One method for calculating the extent that changes in the value of the dollar affect export and import prices is the "passthrough rate," which estimates the percentage of an increase or decrease in the dollar that is passed through to change the prices of exports and imports. For example, if the dollar declines in value by 20 percent, and prices of U.S. exports (in foreign currency terms) decline by 15 percent, the passthrough is 75 percent (15 divided by 20). Using this same decline of 20 percent in the value of the dollar for U.S. imports, if the dollar price of U.S. imports rises by 10 percent, the passthrough is 50 percent (10 divided by 20).

Passthrough estimates previously could be calculated from foreign exchange rates between the United States and other countries weighted by export and import trade volumes, which were provided as supplementary tables to the U.S. import and export price indexes prepared by the U.S. Bureau of Labor Statistics. Unfortunately, these data are no longer available due to budget cutbacks in statistical programs. Estimates of passthrough rates presently are typically based on coefficients derived from statistical regressions. In both cases, the passthrough estimates exclude exports and imports of fuels because sharp fluctuations in oil prices can distort the analysis.

Purchasing Power Parity

According to one widely cited theory, over the long run the value of the dollar is determined according to the concept of purchasing power parity (PPP). This theory starts with a hypothesized period in which the American and other economies are considered to be in balance with the existing unemployment, inflation, and foreign trade balances consistent with a sustainable steady rate of economic growth. The prices of goods and services in the United States and other countries, which are reflected in the value of the dollar in relation to currencies of those countries during this "equilibrium" period, are used as the base from which to calculate future price changes. As subsequent price movements in the United States and in foreign countries diverge (for example, U.S. prices rise faster than prices in England), the value of the dollar would fall proportionately to the relative rise of American prices in order to maintain the PPP of the base period between the dollar and the pound.

Despite the appeal of the theory, it is difficult to argue that foreign currency values typically move in accord with the PPP concept because (a) it is difficult to determine the base period when economies were in balance, and (b) the base period may become obsolete due to productivity changes, investment opportunities, resource supplies (such as discoveries of oil), interest rates, and political stability. Hence, the PPP concept is difficult to apply to economic events, particularly during periods when international economic relationships change substantially.

The theoretical PPP concept works perfectly if the real value of the dollar, which is adjusted to differential price movements between countries, is constant over time.[1] However, the real value of the dollar varies considerably over time, as noted below. Thus, the PPP is of little value in determining if the dollar is "overvalued" and likely to depreciate, or if it is "undervalued" and likely to appreciate.

Actual Value-of-the-Dollar Measures

Value-of-the-dollar measures between the United States and other countries are developed by grouping selected countries into an overall index. Thus, value-of-the-dollar indexes vary depending on the particular countries included in each index.

The value-of-the-dollar indexes are prepared in both nominal and real terms. The nominal value is the familiar one based on the daily transactions in foreign currency markets. The real value is the nominal rate adjusted for consumer price changes in the United States and other nations. Trade-weighted nominal and real value-of-the-dollar indexes are calculated by combining the dollar exchange rates for several nations into a single number by using the export and import trade volumes of the United States and the other nations as weights.

The Federal Reserve Board prepares three values of the dollar indexes, each in nominal and real terms: (a) the broad index, (b) the major currencies index, and (c) the other important trading partners (OITP) index. The major currencies and the OITP indexes are subsets of the broad index, and together comprise the broad index. The broad index represents the major trading partners of the United States. It encompasses twenty-six national currencies, of which the euro is one.[2]

The major currencies index is based on countries in the single-currency euro area, Australia, Britain, Canada, Japan, Sweden, and Switzerland. In addition to the fact that the currencies of these countries represent competition to U.S. products from the major industrialized countries, they reflect financial pressures on the U.S. dollar because they are "traded in deep and relatively liquid financial markets and for which short- and long-term interest rates are readily available," as Michael Leahy notes.[3] Leahy also notes that these currencies, like the U.S. dollar, have not been subject to high inflation rates, and so do not pose problems of high inflation currencies dominating a nominal index. It may be recalled, however, that the United States and the other major currency countries experienced high inflation rates in the 1970s and early 1980s, though they were low relative to the hyperinflation occurring at various times in other countries.

The OITP index includes Mexico and selected countries in South America, Europe, and Asia. The currencies of these countries are not heavily traded outside their home markets. They are also subject to spells of high inflation.

Figure 7.1 shows Federal Reserve Board trade-weighted nominal and real value of the dollar indexes from 1981 to 2002 for the major currencies index and the broad index. The OITP index is not shown separately, but its impact is apparent in the broad index, as noted below. A rise in the indexes reflects an appreciation in the value of the dollar, and a decline in the indexes reflects a depreciation in the dollar.

In the major currencies index, both the nominal and the real indexes fluctuated widely and in similar patterns. Following the peak values in 1985, the index declined in the next few years, and the subsequent fluctuations were within a narrow band, until a gradual rise that began in the late 1990s was interrupted in 2002. Thus, the real dollar index has not been constant, as would be the case if the value of the dollar were determined by purchasing power parity, as discussed above. The relatively close correspondence between the nominal and real exchange rates means that price inflation in the United States and other nations tends to be similar.

In the broad index, the nominal value showed a large long-term rise over the twenty-one-year period. This reflects the high inflation in the OITP countries that are part of the broad index. By contrast, the real value followed the general

Figure 7.1 **Value-of-the-Dollar Indexes: 1981–2002**

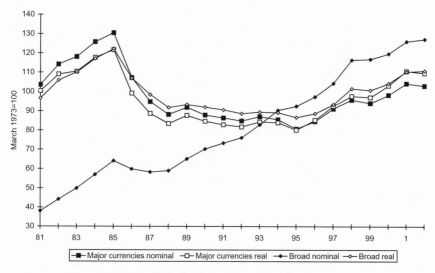

Source: Based on Federal Reserve Board data.

Note: Major currencies index is a subset of the broad index. Real is nominal adjusted for relative consumer price changes in U.S. and abroad.

pattern of the major currencies index, though with a greater rise from the mid-1990s to 2002.

GLOBALIZATION OF PRODUCTION

Globalization of production refers to a long-term manufacturing trend in which some companies whose basic ownership and operations are in one country establish production plants in foreign countries. Examples are when a U.S. automaker (for example, General Motors) produces cars in Brazil and when a German automaker (for example, Daimler Benz) produces cars in the United States. American cars produced in Brazil are not a U.S. export, and German cars produced in the United States are not a U.S. import. But the components and parts for these cars that are produced in the company's home country are exports and imports—the parts and components produced in the United States and incorporated into the cars made in Brazil are a U.S. export, and the parts and components produced in Japan and incorporated into the cars made in the United States are a U.S. import. Also, the profits attributable to these companies' foreign operations are incorporated in the income components of the balance of payments and the GNP (but not in the GDP as noted previously), with profits of U.S. companies in Brazil being a U.S. receipt of factor income, and profits of German companies in the United States being a U.S. payment of factor income.

While relatively small, the globalization of production as part of the overall output of the U.S. economy has been gradually rising. Foreign companies operating in the United States accounted for 7 percent of the U.S. private-industry gross domestic business product in 2000, rising from under 3 percent in the late 1970s and 5 percent in the late 1980s, as William Zeile notes.[4] Employment in these foreign companies followed a pattern similar to that of the gross product. For example, as a proportion of all nonbank private employment in the United States, foreign companies averaged 5.5 percent in 1999 and 2000, compared with 5.0 percent during 1989–98. Not reflected in these measures, however, is that most of the top jobs in a foreign-owned company are held by foreign nationals rather than by U.S. citizens.

Domestic Content

The gross output of a company's product is the value of its intermediate purchases of goods and services from other companies or imports from abroad, plus the company's value added of employee compensation, profits, depreciation on structures and equipment, interest payments, and sales and property taxes. The "domestic content" of the gross output excludes the value of imported goods. Based on the same composition of manufacturing industries, in 1994 the domestic content of foreign-owned companies operating in the United States was 84 percent of gross output, compared with U.S.-owned companies of 93 percent of gross output, as William Zeile notes.[5] As a percentage of intermediate purchases of goods and services for these same manufacturing industries, imports accounted for 21 percent for foreign-owned companies and 11 percent for U.S.-owned companies. Thus, foreign companies utilized imports by 9 to 10 percentage points more than U.S.-owned companies in these measures of domestic content.

GOODS, SERVICES, AND INCOME BALANCES

The balance of payments is calculated as exports minus imports, so that when exports exceed imports, the balance is positive, and when imports exceed exports, the balance is negative. Figure 7.2 shows the balance of payments separately for goods, services, investment income, and the aggregate of all three from 1980 to 2002.

The goods, services, and investment income aggregate balance was positive until 1982, but from 1983 to 2002 it was consistently negative. With the exception of a lessening of the deficit during 1988–91, the deficit generally was grow-

Figure 7.2 **Balances on Goods, Services, and Investment Income, Surplus (+) or Deficit (−): 1980–2002**

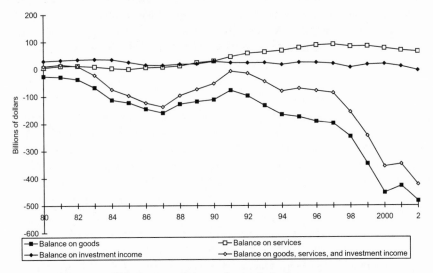

Source: Based on U.S. Bureau of Economic Analysis data.

ing. The deficit grew from $21 billion in 1983 to $422 billion in 2002, rising from 0.6 percent of the GDP to 4.0 percent of the GDP over the period.

The balance on current account, goods, services, investment income, and unilateral transfers grew from $6 billion in 1982 to $481 in 2002, rising from 0.2 percent of the GDP to 4.6 percent of the GDP over the period (not shown in Figure 7.2). Thus, unilateral transfers added 0.6 percentage points as a percentage of the GDP in 2002 (4.6 minus 4.0 of the above balance excluding the transfers). Unilateral transfers are transactions between residents of the United States and residents of other countries for which nothing of economic value is received in return. Examples are individuals and nonprofit organizations sending money gifts abroad, U.S. government military grants to other nations (although these may include a provision for payment terms that are agreed to after the transfer occurs), and pension payments to retired American workers living in foreign countries. Because unilateral transfers reflect a flow of money out of the United States, they can affect the value of the dollar in currency markets, although they are not associated with production for world markets.

Goods cover agricultural, mineral, and manufactured products. Goods began having a decided negative balance in the late 1970s, which generally grew larger into the early 2000s, reaching a high of $483 billion in 2002. Goods in total are the dominant item affecting the overall balance of payments, as the total goods, services, and investment income balance had the same pattern as that for goods. Also, there was a noticeable difference within the goods total between capital goods and industrial supplies and materials on the one hand, and consumer goods and autos on the other, as Catherine Mann notes.[6] Thus, capital goods and industrial materials and supplies showed positive and cyclical movements associated with investment cycles. But this was overridden by the larger and generally growing negative balances for consumer goods and autos.

International services include travel, transportation, insurance, telecommunications, business services, royalties and license fees, and government defense purchases, military sales, and miscellaneous services. The balance on services was positive from 1980 to 2002, rising from $6 billion in 1980 to a high of $91 billion in 1997, and declining in subsequent years to $65 billion in 2002.

International investment income covers both direct and portfolio investments. Direct investment represents the ownership or control of at least 10 percent of a company's voting securities. Portfolio investment is ownership or control of less than 10 percent of a company's voting securities, plus holdings of company and government bonds. The balance on investment income was positive, though declining from 1980 to 2001, and became negative in 2002 (–$4 billion). The investment income balance exceeded the services balance from 1980 to 1988, and then became less than the services balance from 1989 to 2002.

In general, economic growth in the United States affects U.S. imports, and economic growth abroad affects U.S. exports (Table 7.3). Studies of these relationships have found differential patterns of the impacts of growth and foreign trade between the United States and other nations, as Catherine Mann notes.[7] The basic difference is that U.S. imports are far more sensitive to economic growth in the United States than U.S. exports are to economic growth abroad. This "asymmetry" has been suggested as stemming from the following factors: (a) greater competition from new production facilities abroad; (b) the large number of immigrants in the United States and their continued preference for items from the home country; and (c) the younger U.S. population compared with the older population in other countries, in which younger people tend to consume more in goods that are often imported, while older people tend to consume more in services such as health care that are produced domestically.

This asymmetry does not hold for services. In fact, economic growth differentials in the United States and abroad show greater effects on U.S. exports than on U.S. imports of services. A possible cause of this is the tendency of economically developing countries to utilize more services as they become more technologically advanced.

Changes in the value of the dollar have undoubtedly influenced U.S. exports and imports. For example, a visual comparison of Figure 7.1 on the value of the dollar with Figure 7.2 on the balances of exports, imports, and investment income suggests an inverse relationship.

Ownership-Based Foreign Trade Data

A supplementary measure of the balance of payments for goods and services is associated with foreign direct investment income. Foreign direct investment represents ownership or control by residents of one country of 10 percent or more of the voting securities of a corporation or the equivalent interest in an unincorporated enterprise in another country, as noted previously. Companies invest in production facilities abroad to be more competitive in selling their products to foreigners for such reasons as efficiency, lower transport costs, and lower trade barriers. Such sales of goods and services are not recorded in the export and import trade data. For example, Toyota cars produced in the United States and sold in American markets are not counted as Japanese exports to the United States, and Ford cars produced in England and sold in European markets are not counted as U.S. exports to Europe. This is consistent with much of the costs of production of these cars, because the intermediate purchased materials and services and the value added employee compensation, depreciation of structures and equipment, and sales and property taxes largely account for work done in the host country.

However, the profits derived from this production in the host country are included in the profits of the company, and in the balance of payments these profits accrue to the country in which the company is domiciled. In the above example, the Toyota profits appear as investment income to Japan, and the Ford profits appear as investment income to the United States. But these profits can also be thought of as exports of goods, because profits are a component of the value added in producing the cars. An approach to this dichotomy is to allocate these profits of Toyota to Japan's goods exports and U.S. goods imports, and to allocate the related Ford profits to U.S. goods exports and European goods imports.

For the balance of payments as a whole, direct investment income earned by U.S.-owned companies abroad exceeded direct investment income of foreign-owned companies in the United States by $102.6 billion in 2001 (this investment income positive balance declined to $77.9 billion in 2002). By allocating this balance to the U.S. balance on goods and services, the goods and services deficit in 2001 was reduced from $358.3 billion to $255.7 billion, as Jeffrey Lowe notes.[8] At the same time, the investment income surplus of $14.4 billion became a deficit of $88.2 billion (algebraically, the swing from +14.4 to −88.2 is 102.6). *Thus, this ownership-based definition reallocates balances between goods and services and investment income, but it does not change the overall balance of payments.*

The direct investment in this ownership definition of goods and services reflects an active management role in influencing income, in contrast to the passive role of holders of portfolio investments in stocks and bonds. *For some economic analyses, the ownership reclassification may be useful in tracing product demands in world markets.*

INVESTMENT POSITION OF THE UNITED STATES

The international investment position of the United States reflects the difference between holdings of foreign direct and portfolio investment assets by U.S. residents minus the holdings of U.S. direct and portfolio investment assets by foreign residents. There are two methods of valuing the investment position that differ in their treatment of the direct investment component. One is based on the valuation of direct investment in current replacement costs, in which the direct tangible assets of structures, equipment, and land are valued in the prices of replacing them in the current period. The other is based on the stock market value of the direct investment tangible and intangible assets, which reflects the stock market prices of companies that hold the direct investments. In addition to the tangible assets in the current replacement cost valuation, the stock market valuation includes the value of intangible assets such as patents, trademarks, management, and name recognition.

Figure 7.3 shows the U.S. international investment position from 1982 to

Figure 7.3 **U.S. Net International Investment Position, Alternative Measures: 1982–2002**

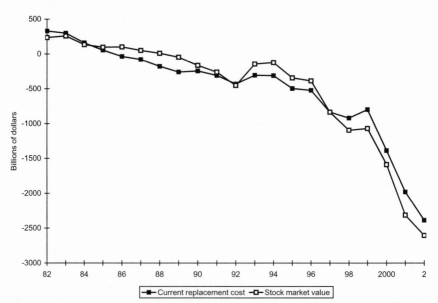

Source: Based on U.S. Bureau of Economic Analysis data.

2001. As a result of the balance of payments deficits beginning in the early 1980s, foreigners had increasingly greater claims on the United States than the United States had on assets abroad for the first time since before World War I. The net debtor status first appeared in 1987 when it totaled $36 billion based on the current replacement cost valuation, and subsequently in 1989 at $47 billion based on the stock market valuation. This shift to a net debtor status reflected the greater increases in foreign-owned assets in the United States compared with the increases in U.S.-owned assets abroad. The debt grew to $2.3 trillion and $2.6 trillion in 2002 based on the current replacement cost and stock market valuations, respectively. These were 23 percent and 25 percent of the GDP, respectively.

Both measures had the same long-term patterns, though the stock market value had a lower debt from the 1980s to the mid-1990s, and a higher debt from the late 1990s to 2002. This differential change in the two measures stemmed from the sharp rise and fall of stock market prices over the period.

SUSTAINABILITY OF DEFICITS AND DEBTOR STATUS IN THE BALANCE OF PAYMENTS

The continuous large U.S. balance of payments deficits and the resultant growing debtor status of the nation both affect the domestic economy and cannot easily be changed. An economy is not like a driver in a car who, having taken a wrong turn, can simply turn around and drive back to the right road. Thus, the loss of markets by American companies in the United States and abroad has altered the economic landscape. This fundamental problem was discussed previously in chapter 3 on Economic Growth in the context of needed actions to reclaim American manufacturing.

What is the problem with the chronic U.S. balance of payments deficits and growing debtor status? Imports and foreign investments in the United States are not intrinsically bad. In fact, they improve living conditions by competing with American industry through lower prices and higher-quality products.

However, there are three significant problems when international deficits and debt are large. First, because the deficits signify a loss of production and employment in the United States, large deficits suggest that better living conditions due to actual or perceived higher-quality products and lower prices from abroad may be outweighed by the loss of worker and business incomes due to the lower production in the United States. While there are no quantitative measures of when deficits are "large," a problem is evident when American-made products for some items are difficult to find. That has increasingly been the case from the 1980s to the early 2000s.

It has also been the experience of industrialized countries, such as the United States, that they are vulnerable to losing their market positions in some products to industrializing countries. This reflects the ability of industrializing countries to duplicate some products with modern equipment and low wages. Thus, the pressure is continuously on industrialized countries to develop new and better products to maintain their overall positions in domestic and world markets.

Second, the large and growing debt owed to foreigners leads to a net outflow of U.S. interest and profits payments to other nations on their investments in the United States. This outflow reduces domestic incomes available for consumer expenditures and business investment in the United States, ultimately lowering living conditions in the United States.

Third, a large foreign debt lessens U.S. control over its economic affairs because the need to manage the debt burden constrains Federal Reserve actions in influencing the domestic economy. The Federal Reserve typically makes decisions to tighten credit and raise interest rates, or loosen credit and lower interest rates, in response to the state of the domestic economy. However, credit and interest rates also have complex relationships to the value of the dollar. Thus, when foreign debt is large, Federal Reserve decisions become complicated by concerns about how foreign investors will react to proposed actions, and to the actions' impact on the competitive position of American-made products in world markets.

A Definition of Sustainability

The growing U.S. balance of payments deficits and debtor status are overall indicators of the loss in the U.S. competitive position in world markets. The impacts on the domestic economy are, of course, a matter of degree. Thus, if they can be absorbed with little disruption to domestic consumer expenditures and business investment compared with the underlying factors affecting their growth (chapters 4 and 5), the deficits and debtor status are considered sustainable, as Catherine Mann notes.[9]

Mann includes in this definition the international finance aspect of sustainability. Specifically, if international investors include U.S. assets in their portfolios with little concern about changes in the value of the dollar and U.S. interest rates, the deficits and debtor status are sustainable. The opposite conditions naturally follow. Thus, if the deficits and debtor status significantly impact consumer expenditures, business investment, and investors' portfolios, they are not sustainable. In this case, the most obvious short-term change would be a large devaluation of the dollar.

Factors Affecting Sustainability

The overall factors impacting consumer expenditures and business investment in terms of sustainability are the differential economic growth rates in the United

Table 7.4

Foreign Trade Balance in Goods for Selected Areas and Countries, Exports Minus Imports: 2002

	Billions of dollars
All countries	−483
Industrial countries	−211
Of which: Euro area	−69
OPEC countries	−35
Other countries	−237
Selected countries	
China	−103
Japan	−72
Canada	−51
Mexico	−38
Germany	−36

Source: Based on U.S. Bureau of Economic Analysis data.

Note: Exports exceed imports is (+), imports exceed exports is (−). The U.S. net imports from industrial countries, OPEC countries, and other countries comprise the net imports from all countries.

States and other countries, the value of the dollar, relative prices of U.S.-produced goods and foreign-produced goods, and the perception of the quality of U.S.-produced goods versus that of foreign-produced goods.

Table 7.4 shows the U.S. foreign trade balance on goods for selected world geographic regions and countries in 2002. They represent the largest balances in which imports exceed exports. Regionally, the negative balance was dominated by trade with industrial countries and all other countries (except the Organization of Petroleum Exporting Countries). The deficit with OPEC was much smaller.

For individual countries, the negative balance was largest with China, followed by Japan, Canada, Mexico, and Germany in descending order. The economic growth rates of the other countries were generally lower than those in the United States in the 1990s and early 2000s, except for China and Canada. The largest U.S. exports to other countries were to Canada and Mexico (not shown in table).

One puzzle in the general topic of sustainability has been the lower rates of return on foreign direct investments in the United States compared with comparable industry returns for U.S.-owned companies. Thus, profits from current production plus interest paid to investors who provide debt financing as a percentage of total assets was 2.2 percentage points lower for foreign-owned non-financial companies operating in the United States than for U.S.-owned companies from 1988 to 1997, as Raymond Mataloni notes.[10] The gap lessened during the period from 3.1 percentage points in 1990 and 1991 to 1 percentage point in 1997.

Despite these gaps, for which there are no satisfying explanations, foreign companies have continued to increase their direct investments in the United States. Thus, the profitability gap has been discussed in the economic literature, but foreign company executives have yet to determine that the profitability gaps are not in the best interests of the companies. Based on this experience, it seems that declines in foreign direct investment in the United States are unlikely, unless economic growth in the United States weakens for a sustained period.

Overall, the balance of payments and growing net debtor status are indicative of the fact that economic growth in the United States would be greater if they did not exist. For example, as a rough measure of these effects, economic growth as defined by the GDP has been lower than growth as defined by gross domestic purchases. Gross domestic purchases modifies the GDP definition by adding imports and deducting exports, which gives a closer measure of underlying domestic demand. From 1990 to 2002, the annual GDP growth rate was 3.2 percent, while the gross domestic purchases growth rate was 4.1 percent.

Problems with the growing balance of payments deficits and debt were noted above. At this writing, these problems are aggravated by the sluggish economies abroad, which are a depressant on U.S. exports of goods, and the loss of U.S. competitive position in world markets, which fosters U.S. imports of goods. In addition, with low economic growth and low interest rates in the United States, foreign investors may tend toward smaller increases in their direct and portfolio investments in the United States. It is in these lights that the dollar is subject to a decline in the mid- to late 2000s. A lower dollar would make U.S. exports more competitive, but make U.S. imports more costly, and thus aggravate inflation. But such a devaluation of the dollar would probably have to be large, say on the scale of the devaluation in the mid-1980s, to have an observable impact on economic growth and on inflation.

Yet the longer-run structural problem of the United States losing the competitive battle in world markets for manufactured products remains. No amount of devaluation is likely to counteract this without a concerted effort to revitalize manufacturing in the United States.

For example, in another aspect of international currencies that affect the value of the dollar, China has pegged the value of the yuan to the U.S. dollar, which fixes the yuan to changes in the value of the dollar. At this writing, some economists and business people consider the yuan to be undervalued by 20 to 40 percent from what it would be if it were allowed to float freely in world currency markets.[11] Proponents of having the U.S. government pressure China to allow the yuan to float believe that a significant rise in the value of the yuan would noticeably improve the competitive position of U.S. manufactured products in world markets. I question this expectation on two grounds. First, it is uncertain that the yuan would increase in value as much as the 20 to 40 percent range if it were allowed to float. Future movements of the yuan would probably be driven to a considerable extent by perceptions that investors in other countries have of China as a place to invest in terms of prospective returns and risk, which, of course, are an unknown. Second, if the yuan were to increase in value by a significant amount, Chinese manufacturers may accept lower profit margins on their products by maintaining the existing dollar price of their goods, or by increasing the dollar price just enough to still underprice American-made products and retain their market share (see the earlier section in the chapter under Value of the U.S. Dollar with reference to "passthrough rates").

In assessing the sustainability of the balance of payments deficits and the growing debtor status, the analyst should focus on economic growth rates in those countries with which the United States has large net import balances (Table 7.4). If growth rates in those countries revive, those countries may buy more U.S. products and thereby raise U.S. economic growth. And over the long run, the analyst should monitor any steps taken by American companies and the U.S. government to reclaim American manufacturing as outlined in chapter 3.

REVIEW QUESTIONS

- Why are exports more related to economic growth abroad while imports are more related to economic growth in the United States?
- How are product prices in world markets affected by changes in the value of the U.S. dollar?
- Why is the globalization of production a long-term rather than a short-term factor?
- What are the problems with continued large deficits in the U.S. balance of payments and the associated growing U.S. foreign indebtedness?

Extra Credit

- Comment on the following statement: "What is amazing about the foreign-trade component of the GDP is how, both over the course of the business cycle and over the long run, the changes in both exports and imports tend to mirror the changes in GDP." (The statement, of course, is totally wrong.)

- Why does the United States have a trade deficit in goods and a trade surplus in services?
- Why would industrially developing nations be a potential market for U.S. services?

NOTES

1. Jane Marrinan, "Exchange Rate Determination: Sorting Out Theory and Evidence," *New England Economic Review*, Federal Reserve Bank of Boston, November/December 1989, p. 44; Cletus C. Coughlin and Kees Roedijk, "What Do We Know about the Long-Run Real Exchange Rate?" *Review*, The Federal Reserve Bank of St. Louis, January/February 1990, p. 37.
2. The single-currency euro countries are: Austria, Belgium, Finland, France, Germany, Greece, Ireland, Italy, Luxembourg, the Netherlands, Portugal, and Spain.
3. Michael P. Leahy, "New Summary Measures of the Foreign Exchange Value of the Dollar," *Federal Reserve Bulletin*, October 1998.
4. William J. Zeile, "U.S. Affiliates of Foreign Companies: Operations in 2000," *Survey of Current Business*, August 2002.
5. William J. Zeile, "The Domestic Orientation of Production and Sales by U.S. Manufacturing Affiliates of Foreign Companies," *Survey of Current Business*, April 1998.
6. Catherine L. Mann, "Perspectives on the U.S. Current Account Deficit and Sustainability," *Journal of Economic Perspectives*, Summer 2002, pp. 133–34.
7. Ibid., pp. 137–40.
8. Jeffrey H. Lowe, "An Ownership-Based Framework of the U.S. Current Account, 1989–2001," *Survey of Current Business*, January 2003, p. 18.
9. Mann, *Perspectives*, p. 143.
10. Raymond J. Mataloni, Jr., "An Examination of the Low Rates of Return of Foreign-Owned U.S. Companies," *Survey of Current Business*, March 2000, p. 57.
11. Elizabeth Becker and Edmund L. Andrews, "China's Currency Is Emerging in U.S. as Business Issue," *New York Times*, August 26, 2003, p. A1.

8

Employment, Worker Income, and Employer Costs

Employment is basic to people's incomes, to the production of goods and services, and to the economic and social well-being of the nation. Jobs are the primary source of income for workers and their families. Income derived from work also gives people the intangible, but vitally important, feeling of self-esteem and dignity. And the hope of a higher material well-being through stable and higher paying jobs enhances a work ethic of responsibility and pride in the work product, in contrast to a feeling of alienation that comes from hopelessness.

From the employers' perspective, workers are essential in producing the goods and services and the profits of their enterprises. Labor costs of wages and fringe benefits plus all other production expenses must be covered by the prices of goods and services sold for the enterprises to make a profit and stay in business. Consequently, employers have a direct interest in having workers who are productive at pay levels that allow the firms to compete in the marketplace.

This chapter discusses three main topics: employment, worker income, and employer costs. The data series are prepared monthly and quarterly by the Bureau of Labor Statistics (BLS) in the U.S. Department of Labor, and are published in the BLS monthly journals, *Employment and Earnings* and the *Monthly Labor Review* (www.bls.gov).

EMPLOYMENT

Methodology of the Two Employment Surveys

Two surveys provide monthly data on trends in employment: (a) a survey of business and government establishments where the employees work, and (b) a survey of households where the employees live. They generally have parallel movements over time, but because they use different definitions and data collection methods, they sometimes have different monthly and even cyclical patterns. Therefore, it is important to know which data are used in particular analyses. The data in both surveys represent employees during pay periods that include the twelfth day of the month.

There are two basic distinctions between the two surveys. The establishment survey provides a count of jobs, which includes all jobs of multiple jobholders, with the emphasis on the industry and geographic location of the business establishments. By contrast, the household survey counts employed persons, who are counted only once even if they have more than one job, with the emphasis on the demographic and socioeconomic characteristics of the workers.

Establishment Survey

Employment data based on the establishment survey are collected from private nonfarm businesses, the federal government, and state and local governments for all workers on employer payrolls, with the exceptions noted below. The data are derived from a sample of employers for the pay period that includes the twelfth day of the month (the establishment survey is also referred to as the payroll survey). Samples of the establishments (places of work) are surveyed for private businesses and state and local governments by statistical agencies within state departments of labor under a federal/state cooperative agreement with the BLS. The data are collected primarily through touch-tone data entry by the employer. Alternative collection modes are electronic data interchange, voice recognition technology, computer-assisted telephone interview, and mail. Data covering all federal government civilian employees, including the Department of Defense, are provided by the U.S. Office of Personnel Management (uniformed military personnel and employees of the Central Intelligence Agency, Defense Intelligence Agency, and National Security Agency are excluded, but wage and salary civilian jobs held by uniformed military personnel are included).

Data are provided on the number of all workers employed, including those from the lowest pay scales to company executives and officers, both part-time and full-time workers, and workers of all ages. Data are also provided separately for production and nonsupervisory workers in private nonfarm industries.[1] The survey is a count of jobs, and thus includes all jobs, including all jobs held by moonlighters, so long as each job is on an employer's payroll. It includes workers who are on paid sick leave, paid vacations, and paid holidays. The survey excludes the self-employed, farm workers, and workers in private households. It also excludes workers on layoff, and workers on leave without pay, on strike or lockout for the entire pay period of the data collection, as well as persons hired but not yet reported to work.

In 2003, the monthly sample surveyed about 160,000 businesses and government agencies, which represented about 400,000 individual worksites and 43 million jobs, accounting for about 33 percent of nonfarm employment. The monthly data go through two sets of revisions. They are initially published as "preliminary" in each of the first two months after the survey is taken, and as "final" in the third month, based on the most complete returns from the employer sample.

The final monthly estimates during the current year are revised annually to conform to benchmark numbers for the month of March. The benchmark data are obtained from the universe of reports sent by all employers who are required to submit unemployment insurance tax payments to the state government employment offices. The new March levels are then used to revise the previous eleven months, which were based on data obtained from the sample of employers, and extrapolations are carried forward to the most current month as well. The unemployment insurance reports covered approximately 98 percent of all nonagricultural employment in 2001. These are supplemented by other reports for industries exempt from unemployment-insurance laws, such as private schools and hospitals, religious organizations, child daycare workers, and non-office insurance sales workers, which are available from Social Security records. And universe data for interstate railroad workers are obtained from the Railroad Retirement Board.

New Firms Starting in Business

Table 8.1 shows that from 1995 to 2002, the benchmark revisions for all employees ranged from –0.1 percent to 0.5 percent. Despite the relatively small revisions in annual benchmarks, there is a long-standing problem regarding the procedure for the timely updating of the sample of establishments to incorporate new firms starting up in business. Because the data for the new firms starting in business become available for incorporation in the survey sample with a lag of several quarters, the monthly survey data first reflect these firms' employment six to nine months after the firms begin operating.

This potential understatement of employment due to the delayed inclusion of new firms in the sample is avoided by the use of estimates derived from a statistical model of the new firms' additional employment. The increment is based on employment growth over the two most recent quarters and a statistical regression coefficient of the significance of that change.[2] In addition to adjusting for the late introduction of new firms, this procedure implicitly adjusts for other sources of error, including the late identification of firms that have gone out of business and a variety of other differences between the benchmark and monthly estimates.

Based on the results of the annual benchmark revisions, the new firm model adds too many workers in recession or slow growth years and too few workers in expansion years. For example, for the March 1999 to March 2000 expansion year, the model added a monthly average of 30 thousand fewer jobs than re-

Table 8.1

Benchmark Minus Final Monthly Estimate of Employment for the Establishment Survey: 1995–2002

	Percentage difference[a]
1995	0.5
1996	[b]
1997	0.4
1998	b
1999	0.2
2000	0.4
2001	−0.1
2002	0.2

Source: U.S. Bureau of Labor Statistics.

a. Benchmark more than monthly is positive, benchmark less than monthly is negative. The benchmark estimates are based on employment data reported by the universe of employers. The monthly estimates are based on employment data reported by a sample of employers.

b. Less than 0.05 percent.

quired (the annual monthly average growth was 234 thousand jobs during the period), while in the March 2000 to March 2001 slow growth year, the model added 16 thousand more jobs than required (the annual average monthly growth was 79 thousand jobs during the period).

New Probability Sample for the Establishment Survey

In a major advance for the establishment survey's methodology, the sample of employer reporting units was converted from a nonprobability quota sample to a probability sample in 2003.[3] The probability sample of establishments is stratified by state, industry, and employer size, which are representative of their distributions in the universe of establishments. Sampling errors and confidence intervals will be published for the first time in the establishment survey. The probability sampling also provides for regular sample updates that lessen the above noted problem of the time lag in incorporating new firms starting in business into the survey sample.

The BLS began the research for converting to the probability sample in 1995, and introduced probability samples into the establishment survey for selected industries from 2000 to 2003. Probability samples were developed for all private nonfarm industries. The samples of federal, state, and local government establishments were not converted to a probability basis because it was not feasible to include them within the time allocated to complete the project. However, because of the high coverage of employment in the existing sample of federal, state, and local government establishments, the BLS considers the overall establishment survey to be on a probability basis.

In 2003 at the 90 percent confidence level, the monthly change in jobs was plus or minus 105 thousand.

Household Survey

Employment data for nonfarm and farm industries are based on a survey of households obtained from a sample of residences in which the worker or workers live. The household survey counts as employed those persons sixteen years and older who worked at least one hour as paid employees of businesses, governments, or private households, the self-employed, unpaid workers in a family business who worked at least fifteen hours a week, and paid volunteer workers. Thus, the employed population consists of wage earners and those who work for profit, the latter being the self-employed and unpaid workers in family businesses who are assumed to share in the profits. The self employed who incorporate their businesses are included as wage and salary workers because technically they are employees of the corporation. Persons on active duty in the armed forces of the United States are excluded. Employed citizens of foreign countries temporarily in the United States but not living in the premises of the foreign embassies are included.

All persons are counted equally if they are paid for an hour or more per week. If a person has two or more jobs, the job with the most hours worked in the week is the only one counted, and the hours worked for all jobs are assigned to that job. Also, unpublished data are available for the hours worked on each job and for the usual hours worked. Separate data are provided on multiple jobholders, who are defined as persons having two or more wage and salary jobs, those who are self-employed and also have a wage and salary job, and unpaid family-business workers who also have a wage and salary job. Multiple jobholders exclude persons with multiple businesses and multiple jobs as unpaid family workers.

The household survey employment data are obtained from a monthly survey of a sample of about 60,000 occupied households, called the Current Population Survey (CPS), which the Census Bureau conducts for the BLS. Survey responses are actually obtained from about 55,000 households each month. For the remaining 4,500 households, no responses are obtained because the occupants refuse to cooperate, are not at home, or for other reasons after repeated contacts by the survey interviewer.

The survey sample is representative of the distribution of households in small and large metropolitan areas and in rural areas. It undergoes a major revision every ten years to be consistent with the most recent decennial population census. The sample was benchmarked to the 2000 census of population beginning in 2003.[4] The sample is also updated annually on a limited basis to reflect current changes in residential locations associated with new housing construction data prepared by the Census Bureau. In order to reduce the reporting burden on any group of households, the sample is divided into eight subsamples (panels) that are rotated over a sixteen-month period. Each subsample is surveyed for four consecutive months, is then dropped from the survey for eight months, and is subsequently resurveyed for the following four months. At the end of the sixteen months, the subsample is eliminated from the sample and replaced with a new panel of households. The result of this procedure is that every month 25 percent of households in the sample are either new to the survey or are returning to it after an eight-month hiatus. Correspondingly, 25 percent of the sample households drop out of the survey every month.

The survey refers to the individual's employment status during the calendar week that includes the twelfth day of the month. The survey is conducted mainly by telephone interviews, supplemented by personal visits as necessary (see chapter 9 on Unemployment for a summary of the CPS interviewing procedures).

In 2003 at the 90 percent confidence level, the monthly change in workers was plus or minus 290 thousand.

Overall Comparisons of the Two Surveys

The establishment survey counts all paying jobs of nonagricultural employees of all ages, including those under sixteen years old, on employer payrolls in U.S. businesses and governments. It includes all jobs held by each worker (not just the primary one, as in the household survey), residents of Canada and Mexico who commute to the United States for work, institutionalized persons on payroll jobs, and wage and salary civilian jobs held by uniformed military personnel. All of these are excluded from the household survey. By contrast, the establishment survey excludes the self-employed, residents of the United States who commute to jobs in Canada and Mexico, private household, agricultural, and unpaid family-business workers, workers in international organizations such as the United Nations and foreign embassies, workers on the job rolls but temporarily not receiving pay, such as those on strike or locked out, or on unpaid vacations or unpaid sick leave. All of these are in the household survey, with the exception of persons living on the premises of foreign embassies. Also, the monthly reference period for collecting data in the establishment survey is the *pay period* that includes the twelfth day of the month, while in the household survey it is the *calendar week* that includes the twelfth day of the month. Because the pay period for some employers is longer than one week, the establishment survey obtains the data over a longer period than the household survey. More generally, there are substantial differences in the data collection and estimating aspects of the surveys.

The net effect of these differences in coverage is that the household survey shows more employment than the employer survey. In 2002, average employment in the household survey was 136.5 million, compared with 130.4 million in the establishment survey. Reconciliations of both measures, when they are put on as similar a definitional basis as the available data will allow, reduce the difference. For example, on a not seasonally adjusted basis, the reconciliation in February 2003 shifted the number of household-survey workers from being 6.9 million greater than the establishment survey down to the household survey having 1.3 million more workers than the establishment survey, and in the March 2003 reconciliation, the greater number of household workers of 7.2 million was reduced to 676 thousand.

Statistically, both surveys have strengths and weaknesses. In 2003, the establishment survey was based on reports from about 160 thousand businesses and government agencies, which represented about 400 thousand individual worksites and about 43 million jobs, accounting for about 33 percent of nonfarm employment, as noted previously. This was much larger than the sample of 55 thousand households in the household survey. The information source for the establishment survey is also better because the data are obtained from employer payroll records, which are used for tax returns, rather than from answers by household members, which are not documented. A weakness of the establishment survey is the indirect statistical model-based increment to the employment survey data to compensate for the lateness of new firms being incorporated into the survey sample.

A weakness of the household survey is its reliance on a household member to provide the data. Though the survey respondent is an adult member of the household, different members of the household may respond differently to the survey from month to month. Errors associated with the survey respondent's answers to questions are referred to as nonsampling errors. Examples of such nonsampling errors are the inability to obtain information on all persons in the sample, differences in the interpretation of the questions by different respondents in the same household from month to month, inability or unwillingness of respondents to provide correct information, and inability of respondents to recall information.

Experience with the reconciliation data indicates that during periods of robust job growth, the establishment survey has a greater increase in workers than the household survey, while during periods of slow job growth or job declines, the establishment survey has a greater decrease in workers than the household survey. Conjectures on the reasons for these cyclical differences include the effects

on the data stemming from problems with the decennial census population un-
dercounts and maintaining up-to-date population controls in the intercensal years
between decennial censuses for minority young men and undocumented immigrants, and the increasing number of businesses adopting biweekly payroll periods, which would result in more employment change than the one week payroll
period.

Because of school vacations, both surveys have seasonal adjustment problems
during the summer months from June to September. While seasonal problems
may be lessened in future years if year-round schooling increases, seasonal problems currently cause some uncertainty in the monthly employment movements
during the summer. The seasonal problem with the household survey involves
the timing of when students end school in May and June and enter the labor
market, and when students leave the labor market in August and September to
return to school. The difficulty is that the household survey respondent does not
always know when the student members of the household change their schooling
and work status.

The two surveys also differ in the frequency of data revisions. The establishment survey data are revised for both the initial monthly estimates and the annual benchmarks. By contrast, the initial monthly estimates of the household
survey typically are not revised on a current or annual basis, but only with the
decennial population census data, when estimates for the intercensal years are
also revised.

*Over the years, the economics community has considered the establishment
survey to be a better measure of the monthly change in employment than the
household survey. This assessment was bolstered by the conversion of the establishment survey to a full probability sample in 2003.*

ANALYSIS OF EMPLOYMENT TRENDS

Table 8.2 shows the year-to-year employment movements in both surveys from
1990 to 2002, and the average annual employment growth for approximate decades that span recession periods from 1948 to 2000.[5] The establishment survey
measure increased more than the household survey measure during years of
employment growth from 1990 to 2002, except for 1992 and 2000. But in the
years of employment decline, the establishment survey data declined more than
the household survey data. The establishment survey also had greater employment growth in the decades during 1948–2000.

Overall, these patterns indicate that employment movements in the establishment survey are larger than those in the household survey. The most likely
reasons for this difference are associated with the varying definitions and data
collection and estimating procedures between the surveys. Three examples of
the impact of these methodological differences are given here.

Table 8.2

Employment Growth of Establishment and Household Surveys: Annual 1990–2002 and Long-Term 1948–2000 (annual percentage change)

	Establishment survey	Household survey
1990	1.4	1.2
1991	−1.1	−0.9
1992	0.3	0.7
1993	1.9	1.5
1994	3.1	2.3
1995	2.7	1.5
1996	2.1	1.4
1997	2.6	2.2
1998	2.6	1.5
1999	2.4	1.5
2000	2.2	2.5
2001	0.2	0.0
2002	−0.9	−0.3
1948–59	1.6	0.9
1959–69	2.8	1.9
1969–79	2.5	2.4
1979–89	1.8	1.7
1989–2000	1.8	1.4
1948–2000	2.1	1.7

Source: Based on U.S. Bureau of Labor Statistics data.

First, when a multiple jobholder gains or loses a job, it is counted as an employment gain or loss in the establishment survey, but as no change in the household survey, as John Stinson notes.[6] Because moonlighting increases during a business expansion, there is no increase in the number of *workers* counted just once in the household survey, but there is an increase of one or more *jobs* in the establishment survey. Second, self-employment creates situations in which workers who have lost wage and salary jobs but are self-employed are counted as employed with no employment decline in the household survey, while the wage and salary job loss results in a decline in the establishment survey, as Eugene Becker notes.[7] Third, because the persons typically undercounted in household surveys, such as minority males, are those with the greatest cyclical changes in employment, the undercount may reduce that survey's employment fluctuations, as Alexander Korns and Chinhui Juhn and Simon Potter note.[8]

Monthly Volatility

Figures 8.1a and 8.1b show the monthly employment movements for both surveys in 2001 and 2002. The household survey data are clearly more volatile
than the establishment survey data

These monthly differences are problematic because it is not known whether
the labor market is actually represented by the establishment survey's relatively
smooth monthly movements or by the household survey's monthly volatility (the
data in both surveys are seasonally adjusted). Two factors contributing to the
smoother movements of the establishment survey are the size of the samples
and the information sources used in obtaining the employment data.

First, because of the much greater size of the establishment sample, the
monthly sampling error is much smaller in the establishment survey. The smaller
sampling error in the establishment survey results in less volatility in that survey.
In 2003 at the 90 percent confidence level, the monthly change in jobs in the
establishment survey was plus or minus 105 thousand, while the monthly change
in workers in the household survey was plus or minus 290 thousand.

Second, the employment data in the establishment survey are obtained from
employer payroll records, while the employment data in the household survey
are obtained from a member of the household who is available in the survey
week. The household member reporting in the survey relies on memory rather

Figure 8.1a **Establishment and Household Surveys, Monthly Employment
Level: 2001 and 2002**

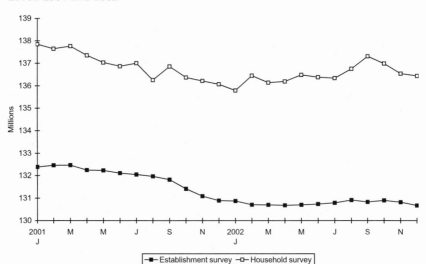

Source: Based on U.S. Bureau of Labor Statistics data.

Figure 8.1b **Establishment and Household Surveys, Monthly Employment Change: 2001 and 2002**

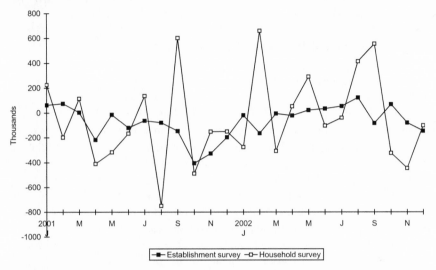

Source: Based on U.S. Bureau of Labor Statistics data.

than on records and also may be replaced by a different household member from month to month. Overall, it is likely that the establishment survey data contain less reporting error than the household survey data. While in the context of obtaining data on employment and unemployment in the household survey, the data on employment are probably more accurate than those on unemployment because it is easier to identify someone who has a job than someone who is unemployed by the survey definitions. The employment data reflect the problems of household reporting noted above. Consequently, there is less "noise" in the establishment survey data attributable to reporting error and in the related monthly volatility of the data than in the household survey data. Different aspects of smoothing in the methodology of both surveys tend to be offsetting. In the establishment survey, the statistical model used to compensate for the six- to nine-month delay in incorporating new firms starting in business adds continuous increments to monthly job growth. In the household survey, the Census Bureau's monthly population estimates are increased by an assumed amount each month, which implicitly increases the monthly employment estimates each month.

These monthly differences point up the lack of perfection in any statistical survey. To deal with this, the analyst should compare the employment patterns of both surveys. If they are similar, they may be considered to confirm the movements. If they differ significantly, definitional and statistical differences between the surveys should be examined to see if there is a reasonable explanation. If there is no plausible explanation, the movement for that short period may be assumed to fall within the lower and upper bounds of both surveys.

Jobless Recoveries of 1991–92 and 2002–03

A primary economic concern at the time of this writing was the loss of 1.0 million jobs during the recovery from the end of the 2001 recession in November 2001 to July 2003, as reported in the establishment survey. This employment decline occurred while economic growth rose at an annual rate of 2.7 percent from the fourth quarter of 2001 to the second quarter of 2003, as measured by the GDP (discussed in chapter 3, "Economic Growth").

Table 8.3 shows the employment movements of the 2001 recession and the 2002–03 recovery for both the establishment and the household surveys. The household survey data shown here refer only to nonfarm wage and salary workers, and so are definitionally consistent with the establishment survey, except that the household survey does not include more than one job held by a worker. These data are on a net basis—job gains minus job losses. The dating points are March 2001 (peak of the 1990s to 2001 expansion), November 2001 (trough of the recession), and July 2003 (latest recovery month at the time of this writing).

For the recession from March 2001 to November 2001, the establishment survey indicated a loss of 1.6 million jobs and the household survey indicated a loss of 1.0 million workers. For the recovery from November 2001 to July 2003, the establishment survey indicated a *loss* of 1.0 million jobs, while the household survey indicated a *gain* of 300 thousand jobs. The employment change for the recession and the recovery combined resulted in a loss of 2.7 million jobs in the establishment survey (unrounded data in Table 8.3), and a loss of 700 thousand workers in the household survey.

Because the household survey data on multiple jobholders are available only on a not seasonally adjusted basis, a comparison of the role of multiple jobholders with the seasonally adjusted establishment and household survey data over the March 2001 to July 2003 period is only an order of magnitude. Multiple jobholders declined by 500 thousand workers from March to November 2001 (recession period), and increased by 150 thousand workers from November 2001 to July 2003 (recovery period). If these movements were similar on a seasonally adjusted basis, they would indicate an additional decline in workers during the recession, making the household survey data more comparable with the establishment survey data, and an additional increase in workers during the recovery, making the household survey data less comparable with the establishment survey data, as shown in Table 8.3.

There is a stark difference in the job change estimates for the recovery period

Table 8.3

Changes in Nonfarm Wage and Salary Employment During the Recession of 2001 and the Recovery of 2002–03: Establishment and Household Surveys

	Establishment survey (thousands of jobs)	Household survey (thousands of workers)
Recession		
March 2001 to November 2001	−1,627	−969
Recovery		
November 2001 to July 2003	−1,030	+285
Recession and recovery		
March 2001 to July 2003	−2,657	−684

Source: U.S. Bureau of Labor Statistics.

between the two surveys. Some workers who lost their jobs during 2001–03 became self-employed or independent contractors, and thus were not included in the establishment survey as employed because that survey only counts workers who are on an employer's payroll, while they would be counted as employed in the household survey. However, this aspect of the difference between the two surveys is relatively small based on the available data, and so it is probably not a major factor accounting for the variation in the data between the two surveys. As discussed in the earlier section on Overall Comparisons of the Two Surveys, the economics community has over the years considered the establishment survey to be a superior measure of employment change. I agree with that assessment. Consequently, I believe the job losses for both the recession and the recovery reported in the establishment survey are more accurate than the smaller job loss in the recession and the job increase in the recovery reported in the household survey.

In an analysis of business cycle recoveries during the twelve months following the end of each recession from the 1960s to the early 2000s, Stacey Schreft and Aarti Singh contrasted the movements of economic growth with those of job growth for the recoveries of 1960–61, 1970–71, 1975–76, 1980–81, and 1982–83 on the one hand, with the recoveries of 1991–92 and 2002 on the other (the analysis does not continue into 2003).[9] The analysis found that the 1991–92 and the 2002 recoveries were jobless, in contrast to the strong job growth in the previous five recoveries. A jobless recovery is defined as an absence of employment growth when economic growth resumes.

The analysis excluded the recoveries of 1949–50, 1954–55, and 1958–59 because comparable labor market data used in the current analysis were not available for those earlier recoveries. But the authors note that due to the strong employment growth during the earlier recoveries, if those recoveries were included in the analysis, the 1991–92 and the 2002 recoveries would appear even more jobless.

Specifically, Schreft and Singh found that economic growth during the first twelve months of the 1991–92 and the 2002 recoveries was 2.3 and 2.9 percent, respectively, which was less than half the average growth rate of the previous five recessions. Concomitantly, employment *declined* by 0.14 percent in the twelve months of the 1991–92 and the 2002 recoveries, while employment *increased* by an average of 2.7 percent in the previous five recoveries. The authors also found that based on historical relationships between economic growth and job growth, employment would have been expected to fall less than it did in both the 1991–92 and the 2002 recoveries. This assessment was based on Okun's Law relationships between economic growth and employment (Okun's Law in terms of economic growth and unemployment is discussed in chapter 2, "Framework for Macroeconomic Analysis and Policies").

In identifying causes of the 1991–92 and the 2002 jobless recoveries, Schreft and Singh concluded the following:

- The economic growth rates during the 1991–92 and the 2002 recoveries were substantially below the average growth rate of the previous five recessions.
- Employers during the 1991–92 and the 2002 recoveries made greater use of overtime work for existing workers rather than hiring new workers.
- Employers during the 1991–92 and the 2002 recoveries made greater use of temporary and part-time workers who have less job stability and work for lower pay and fewer benefits that permanent, full-time workers.

In another assessment of the jobless recoveries during 1991–92 and 2002–03, Erica Groshen and Simon Potter focused on the difference between temporary layoffs and permanent terminations.[10] Temporary layoffs are *cyclical* in nature: they are associated with weak demand, and in them both employers and workers expect that the workers will be rehired when business picks up. By contrast, workers who have lost their jobs permanently, and must find jobs with other firms and often other industries, represent *structural* job losses.

Based on an analysis of job losses and gains among different industries, Groshen and Potter found that job losses during the 1991–92 and the 2002–03 recoveries were proportionately far more structural than were the job losses in previous recoveries. Also, job losses during the 2002–03 recovery were proportionately more structural than those during the 1991–92 recovery.

The authors concluded that structural job losses require more workers to find jobs in different firms and industries than do cyclical job losses. But the process of matching workers who have permanently lost their jobs with newly-created jobs takes longer than the rehiring of workers in their previous jobs. And in the uncertain economic environment of 2002–03, there was a relatively small number of newly created jobs. I believe that the structural job losses in 2002–03 reflected the widespread loss of jobs beyond the contraction and demise of telecommunications companies discussed in chapter 3 under Collapse of the Telecommunications Companies. The job loss was intensified by the increasing trend of U.S. companies to replace workers in certain service occupations, such as high tech computer software and programing and in telephonic scheduling of repair maintenance for failing equipment, with lower paid workers in other countries. This job drainage will be heightened in the future by the expected transfer abroad of radiology analysis of M.R.I. data and stock market company analysis to lower paid workers in other countries.

In assessing job growth in future business cycle recoveries, the analyst should compare economic growth rates with cyclical and structural job losses. When cyclical job losses are dominant, job increases during recoveries are greater than when structural job losses are dominant. During the 1991–92 and the 2002–03 recoveries, increasing structural job losses and small increases in newly created jobs caused the jobless recoveries.

Labor Force Participation Rate and the Employment/ Population Ratio

Two measures of the linkage of the working-age population to job markets are the employment/population ratio (EPR) and the labor force participation rate (LFPR). They represent different aspects of job markets, with the EPR reflecting the demand for workers and the LFPR representing the supply of workers. The EPR is the proportion of the population of working age that has jobs, and the LFPR is the proportion of the population that is working or is seeking a job. Both measures are based on data from the household survey.

Mathematically, they are calculated as:

$$EPR = \frac{Employment}{Civilian\ noninstitutional\ population*}$$

$$LFPR = \frac{Employment + unemployment**}{Civilian\ noninstitutional\ population*}$$

*Persons sixteen years and older who are not in hospitals, nursing homes, jails, etc.
**The labor force is defined as the sum of employment and unemployment.

Figure 8.2 **Labor Force and Employment as a Percentage of the Civilian Noninstitutional Population: 1990–2002**

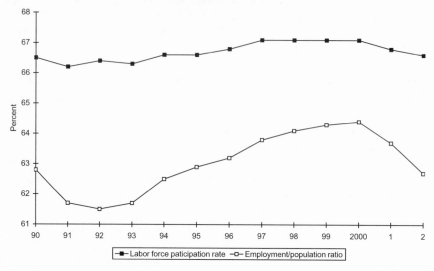

Source: Based on U.S. Bureau of Labor Statistics data.

Because the EPR excludes unemployment, it is not affected by people moving between unemployment and outside the labor force. By contrast, the LFPR reflects these movements into and out of unemployment. Persons are counted as unemployed if they are actively looking for work in the official measure of unemployment (Chapter 9 covers unemployment). Since the civilian noninstitutional population is the denominator in both measures, and it increases steadily over time, the movements of both the EPR and the LFPR are dominated by changes in the numerator.

Figure 8.2 shows the movements of the EPR and the LFPR from 1990 to 2002. The EPR fluctuates far more than the LFPR. This reflects the tendency for the directional change in employment to be muted by the opposite directional change in unemployment. Thus, the offsetting employment and unemployment movements in the LFPR dampen the more pronounced movements of employment in the EPR.

Because the EPR portrays employers' demand for workers, the analyst should focus on the EPR in assessing the momentum of employment growth.

WORKER INCOME

Income from jobs covers money wages and salaries of paid employees and income from self-employment, plus fringe benefits for retirement, health insurance, and life insurance. Money wages and salaries include income from paid vacations, holidays, sick leave, and overtime (whether or not a premium is paid for overtime).

The money wages and salaries data of paid employees are obtained from the establishment survey of the U.S. Bureau of Labor Statistics, which was covered in the previous section on employment. The data represent weekly average earnings for the total of full-time and part-time workers in private nonfarm industries. They are limited to "production workers" in the goods-producing industries and "nonsupervisory workers" in the service-producing industries, which in all industries exclude executives and managers.[11] In manufacturing, construction, and mining industries, workers engaged in professional, technical, office, and sales activities are excluded as well. Thus, the data for workers in the goods-producing industries represent "line" workers, as distinct from administrative and support employees. By contrast, the employment data cover workers in all occupations and levels from the lowest pay scales to executives.

Figure 8.3 shows the percentage change in average weekly money wages and salaries for production and nonsupervisory workers in current and real (price-adjusted) dollars from 1990 to 2002. Price-adjusted wages and salaries indicate the purchasing power of worker incomes after accounting for changes in consumer prices, as measured by the consumer price index (chapter 11, "Inflation and Deflation," discusses the consumer price index). The data represent gross

Figure 8.3 **Money Wages and Salaries Average Weekly Earnings, Annual Percentage Change: 1990–2002**

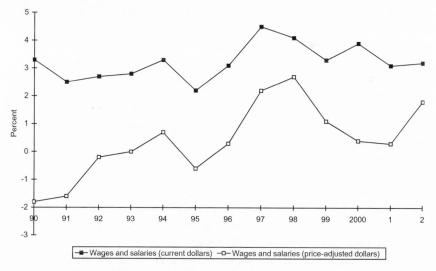

Source: Based on U.S. Bureau of Labor Statistics data.

Figure 8.4 **Job Quality Index, Annual Percentage Change: 1990–2002**

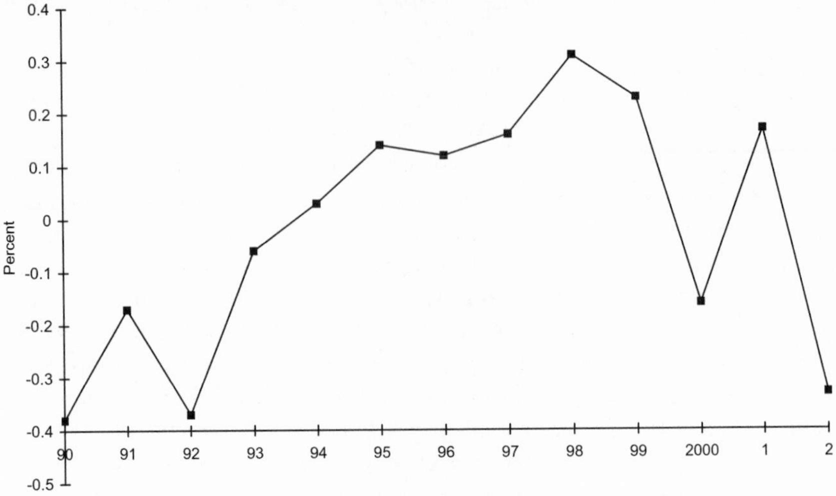

Source: Based on Center for National Policy data.

earnings before the payment of income and Social Security taxes. They exclude the employer share of Social Security taxes, bonuses, retroactive payments, tips, and in-kind payments such as free rent and meals.

Movements in the wage and salary data from period to period reflect shifts in the composition of jobs among industries and occupations. Therefore, the percentage changes in Figure 8.3 include the effect of job shifts between high-paying and low-paying industries and occupations.

Annual increases in current-dollar wages and salaries hovered around 3 percent from 1990 to 1996, and, after rising to a peak of 4.5 percent in 1997, declined to the 3 percent level in 2001 and 2002. Price-adjusted wages and salaries declined during 1990–92 and 1995, which means that the purchasing power and consequently the material well-being of worker incomes worsened in those years. The largest increases in price-adjusted worker incomes, ranging from 1 to under 3 percent, occurred during 1997–99 and 2002. Increases in price-adjusted worker incomes were under 1 percent in the other years, except for zero change in 1993.

The job quality index (JQI) measures shifts in the composition of jobs between high- and low-paying industries and occupations. The JQI is published by the Center for National Policy and is prepared by James Medoff of Harvard University who is also a fellow of the center.

Figure 8.4 shows the JQI from 1990 to 2002. A rise in the JQI indicates a relative increase in high-paying jobs, and a decline in the JQI indicates a fall in high-paying jobs. The decline in the JQI in the early 1990s was followed by a rise that peaked in 2001. This roughly approximates movements of the price-adjusted wages and salaries in Figure 8.3, except for 2001 and 2002. But other factors besides the changing industry and occupation composition of jobs—principally job shortages and surpluses that impact wage rates—affect the movements of price-adjusted wages and salaries.

The analyst should monitor money wages and salaries data for changes in the material well-being of the population derived from worker incomes. Analyses of factors affecting the wage and salary movements should include the relationship between the movements of the price-adjusted wages and salaries data and the patterns of the JQI to assess the impact of shifts between high- and low-paying jobs on worker incomes.

Union and Nonunion Workers

Worker pay rates are determined by many factors, such as relative shortages or surpluses of workers with various skills in local labor markets, confidence of workers about the security of their jobs, union membership, and employers' use of temporary and independent contractor workers.

The bargaining position of workers and employers is also affected by the relative proportions of union workers, nonunion workers, and the employment of temporary workers and independent contractors. Pay scales, retirement and health benefits, health and safety in the workplace, and nondiscrimination in hiring are noticeably better for union members than for the nonunion groups.

Union negotiating strength is directly related to the proportion of workers who are unionized, with worker bargaining power being stronger with large numbers than with small numbers. Union membership as a proportion of wage and salary workers has declined continuously since the end of World War II, from 35.5 percent in 1945, to 23 percent in 1980, to 16 percent in 1990, to 13 percent in 2002.[12] There are also wide variations by industry. In 2002, for example, unionized workers accounted for 2.3 percent of farm workers, 8.7 percent of private nonfarm workers, and 37.5 percent of federal, state, and local government workers. In the late 1990s, unions began drives to unionize more business establishments and thus reverse the long-term decline in the numbers and economic impact of unions, but the decline in union membership continued.

Although unions represent a relatively small share of all American workers, unions influence wage incomes and working conditions of nonunionized workers in a spillover effect. Because unions are the dominant bargaining agent in several industries, their compensation patterns are often a guideline for compensation of nonunion workers in the same industry or company in a class effect. In other cases, some nonunion companies have a policy of raising wages when wages in their union counterpart companies are increased, in order maintain the same differential between union and nonunion wages. This is in response to a threat effect, in which the aim is to reduce the incentive of nonunion workers to join a union.[13]

Beyond the above examples of class and threat effects that occur in particular industries, a more general spillover effect probably permeated the 87 percent of the economy in 2002 that was not unionized. This is a basic factor affecting interstate differentials in per capita personal income when compared with the share of wage and salary employees that are union members in the state.

Generally, unions have an important role as a pacesetter in establishing norms for pay scales, retirement and health benefits, health and safety in the workplace, and nondiscrimination in hiring.

Tables 8.4a and 8.4b show the ten states with the highest per capita personal income and the ten states with the lowest per capita personal income, along with the percentage of employed wage and salary workers that were union members in 2002. Measures of workers *represented* by unions cover members of unions, members of an employee association similar to a union, and workers who are not affiliated with a union, but whose jobs are covered by a union or employee association contract. As a percentage of employed wage and salary workers, this broader measure of union representation is typically 1 to 2 percentage points greater than the share of union members only among the individual states shown in Tables 8.4a and 8.4b.

This ranking shows that the states with the highest personal incomes have

---

Table 8.4a

Per Capita Personal Income and Percentage of Union Workers in Ten States with the Highest Per Capita Income: 2002

State ranked with highest income first	Per capita income (dollars)	Union workers (percentage of employed wage and salary workers)
Connecticut	42,706	16.7
New Jersey	39,453	19.4
Massachusetts	39,244	14.2
Maryland	36,298	14.1
New York	36,043	25.3
New Hampshire	34,334	9.7
Minnesota	34,071	17.6
Illinois	33,404	19.6
Colorado	33,276	7.8
California	32,996	17.5

Sources: Per capita income: U.S. Bureau of Economic Analysis. Union workers: U.S. Bureau of Labor Statistics.

Table 8.4b

Per Capita Personal Income and Percentage of Union Workers in Ten States with the Lowest Per Capita Income: 2002

State ranked with lowest income first	Per capita income (dollars)	Union workers (percentage of employed wage and salary workers)
Mississippi	22,372	6.6
Arkansas	23,512	5.9
West Virginia	23,688	13.3
New Mexico	23,941	6.6
Utah	24,306	6.2
Montana	25,020	14.1
Idaho	25,057	7.1
Alabama	25,128	8.9
South Carolina	25,400	4.9
Louisiana	25,446	8.1

Sources: Per capita income: U.S. Bureau of Economic Analysis. Union workers: U.S. Bureau of Labor Statistics.

percentage shares of union workers in the workforce that are noticeably higher than the union shares in the lowest personal income states. Exceptions to this are New Hampshire and Colorado in the high-income states and West Virginia and Montana in the low-income states.

While many factors contribute to the relative standing of per capital personal incomes among different states, it is hard to ignore the degree of unionization in accounting for the state income differentials.

EMPLOYER COSTS

Viewed from the perspective of the employer, money wages and salaries and fringe benefits are a cost of production that affects the prices of the goods and services produced and the profits of the enterprise. The most appropriate measure of compensation costs is the quarterly employment cost index (ECI) prepared by the U.S. Bureau of Labor Statistics.

The ECI covers money wages and salaries and noncash fringe benefits such as employer-provided health and retirement plans in all private nonfarm industries and state and local governments for workers at all levels of responsibility. The ECI maintains a stable composition of industries and occupations, so that it is not affected by shifts in employment between high- and low-wage industries or between high- and low-wage occupations within industries. The composition is changed every ten years. As of this writing, it is based on the industry and

Figure 8.5a **Employment Cost Index versus Consumer Price Index, Annual Percentage Change: 1990–2002**

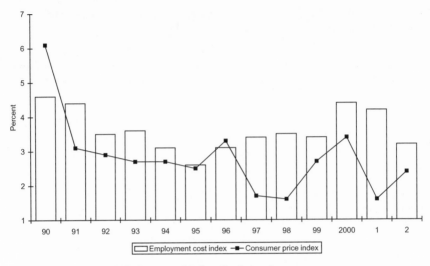

Source: Based on U.S. Bureau of Labor Statistics data.

Note: Annual changes in all series reflect the movements from the fourth quarter of one year to the fourth quarter of the following year (e.g., 2002 change is 2001:4 to 2002:4). See text.

occupational distributions in the 1990 census of population. By contrast, the average weekly earnings data discussed in the previous section are affected by the shifting composition of industries and occupations. Also, the weekly earnings data exclude noncash fringe benefits, contrary to their inclusion in the ECI. (The job quality index discussed previously is the obverse of the ECI.)

Figure 8.5a shows annual changes in the ECI for private nonfarm industries employee compensation (wages, salaries, and fringe benefits) and in the consumer price index (CPI) from 1990 to 2002. Figure 8.5b modifies the ECI to include productivity changes. Because the ECI data are provided only for March, June, September, and December of each year, annual averages of the ECI are not calculated. Therefore, the annual changes in Figures 8.5a and 8.5b represent the movements from the fourth quarter of one year to the fourth quarter of the following year (see chapter 1 under Calculating and Presenting Growth Rates).

The CPI in this perspective is contrasted with the ECI to obtain a notion of changes in profit margins (the CPI is covered in chapter 11, "Inflation and Deflation"). The difference between the CPI and the ECI is the implied movement of profit margins, abstracting from changes in the quantity of goods and services sold, and abstracting, too, from changes in other costs. When the CPI

Figure 8.5b **Employment Cost Index Minus Productivity versus Consumer Price Index, Annual Percentage Change: 1990–2002**

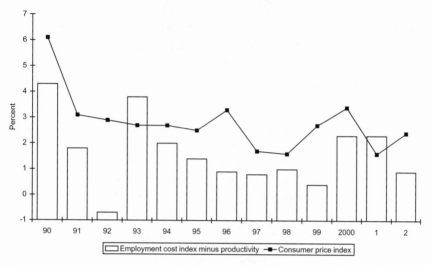

Source: Based on U.S. Bureau of Labor Statistics data.

Note: Annual changes in all series reflect the movements from the fourth quarter of one year to the fourth quarter of the following year (e.g., 2002 change is 2001:4 to 2002:4). See text.

rises more than the ECI, it implies profit margins are rising, and when the CPI rises less than ECI, it implies profit margins are declining. Figure 8.5a indicates that the CPI rose less than the ECI in most years, which suggests that profit margins generally declined over the 1990–2002 period. However, Figure 8.5a does not adjust for productivity, which is a key part of the production of goods and services.

Figure 8.5b adjusts Figure 8.5a for productivity change (chapter 10 covers productivity). Specifically, Figure 8.5b is the ECI minus productivity change. Productivity is the efficiency of the use of materials, services, labor, equipment, and other resources used in producing goods and services. The ECI less productivity is a more realistic assessment of actual changing labor costs in the production process than the ECI without the adjustment, because productivity is an essential ingredient of production by lowering labor costs (when productivity increases) or raising labor costs (when productivity falls).

Figure 8.5a indicates that the CPI rose less than the ECI in most years, which suggests that profit margins generally were not maintained over the 1990–2000 period. But the productivity adjustment included in Figure 8.5b indicates that the CPI increased more than the ECI in most years. This suggests that profit margins generally kept pace with labor costs over the 1990–2002 period, contrary to the above pattern in Figure 8.5a.

Profits are a basic determinant of business investment in equipment and structures, as discussed in chapter 5 on profits, nonresidential investment, and housing. The maintenance of profit margins during the 1990s to 2000 was an important feature in sustaining investment in the 1990s to 2000 expansion.

The analyst should monitor the relationship between the ECI and the ECI adjusted for productivity changes to determine the implied effect on profit margins. Rising profit margins suggest a tendency for businesses to increase investments in equipment and structures and to be less resistant to increasing money wages and salaries and fringe benefits. Declining profit margins have the opposite effect of businesses tending to restrain new investments and increasing worker incomes. Also, increasingly during periods of weak profits there is a tendency to reduce workers' existing pay, referred to as "givebacks," such as occurred during 2001–03.

REVIEW QUESTIONS

- What are the strengths and weaknesses of the establishment and household surveys of employment?
- How do movements of the two measures of employment vary for short-term periods within one year compared with longer periods?
- Why is the employment/population ratio a more significant measure of employers' demand for workers than the labor force participation rate?
- What is the relationship between the job quality index and the average weekly wage and salaries data?
- How are union pay scales related to spillover effects on nonunion workers and the overall economy?
- How does the economic significance of the employment cost index differ from that of the average weekly wage and salary data?
- Why are changes in profit margins implied in the comparative movements of the employment cost index and the consumer price index?

Extra Credit

- What effects may the underground economy have on the accuracy of the household and establishment employment surveys?
- Suppose the next decennial census—in the year 2010—shows that the government has been understating the U.S. population. What would this imply for the relative accuracy of the household and establishment employment measures?

NOTES

1. In manufacturing, mining, and construction, for employees up through the level of working supervisors, "production workers" designates workers who engage directly in the work. The analogous designation in other industries—transportation, utilities, trade, finance, and other services—is "nonsupervisory workers."
2. Bureau of Labor Statistics, U.S. Department of Labor, *Employment and Earnings*, June 2002, pp. 182, 184.
3. In the previously used quota sample, which included certain large establishments with certainty in the sample, the number of small establishments sampled was determined by the proportion of total employment in the industry accounted for by small establishments, with the number of small establishments sampled rising with their share of total employment. Contrary to probability samples, quota samples require a fixed number of sampled units and the units are not necessarily drawn on a random selection basis. Thus, quota samples in the establishment survey did not ensure the representativeness of the universe of establishments by state, industry, and employment size, and so it was not possible to calculate sampling errors and confidence intervals for them. See *Employment and Earnings*, June 2002, pp. 185 and 191.
4. Mary Bowler, Randy E. Ilg, Stephen Miller, Ed Robinson, and Anne Polivka, "Revisions to the Current Population Survey Effective in January 2003," *Employment and Earnings*, February 2003.
5. The approximate decades reflect the calculation of long-term growth rates from peak to peak of cyclical expansions to avoid distorting the growth rates. The treatment here of beginning and ending years of the long-term cyclical expansions of 1948–59 and 1989–2000 results in eleven-year "decades" because of the intermediate recessions of 1949 and 1990. Thus, calculating the growth rate from the trough of the 1948–49 recession in 1949 to the 1959 expansion peak, and from the 1990 depressed level of the 1990–91 recession trough to the 2000 expansion year would overstate each ten–year growth rate. See chapter 1 under Calculating and Presenting Growth Rates, Long-Term Growth Rates.
6. John F. Stinson, Jr., "Comparison of Nonagricultural Employment Estimates from Two Surveys," *Employment and Earnings*, March 1983.
7. Eugene H. Becker, "Self-employed workers: an update to 1983," *Monthly Labor Review*, July 1984.
8. Alexander Korns, "Cyclical Fluctuations in the Difference Between the Payroll and Household Measures of Employment," *Survey of Current Business*, May 1979; and Chinhui Juhn and Simon Potter, "Explaining the Recent Divergence in Payroll and Household Employment Growth," *Current Issues in Economics and Finance*, Federal Reserve Bank of New York, December 1999.
9. Stacey L. Schreft and Aarti Singh, "A Closer Look at Jobless Recoveries," *Economic Review*, Federal Reserve Bank of Kansas City, Second Quarter 2003.
10. Erica L. Groshen and Simon Potter, "Has Structural Change Contributed to a Jobless Recovery?" *Current Issues in Economics and Finance*, Federal Reserve Bank of New York, August 2003.
11. See note 1.
12. For a historical perspective on union membership, see Larry T. Adams, "Changing employment patterns of organized workers," *Monthly Labor Review*, February 1985. Current annual estimates are published in the January issue of *Employment and Earnings*.
13. Jared Bernstein of the Economic Policy Institute distinguished the class and threat effects in a conversation with me.

9

Unemployment

Jobs directly affect the material well-being of workers and their families. To workers out of work, unemployment is not an abstract idea in a theoretical discussion. Thus, voters experiencing unemployment are more likely to vote for politicians who offer different perceptions of how the economy works with the promise of job creation, as noted by Alberto Alesina and Nouriel Roubini.[1]

Unemployment also affects people and the economy in intangible ways, such as its influence on personal satisfaction and social stability. Though personal satisfaction and social stability are not strictly "economic," they can affect economic developments (see chapter 14, "Noneconomic Intangibles").

This chapter covers the official measures of unemployment based on household surveys of the civilian noninstitutional population sixteen years and older, the role of unemployment insurance, matching unemployed workers with job openings, cyclical movements of the labor force, and unemployment goals.

UNEMPLOYMENT DATA

Unemployment data are prepared monthly by the Bureau of Labor Statistics (BLS) in the U.S. Department of Labor based on data obtained from a survey of a sample of households. The data series are published in the BLS monthly journals, *Employment and Earnings* and the *Monthly Labor Review* (www.bls .gov).

The unemployment rate (UR) is defined as the percentage of the nation's civilian noninstitutional labor force sixteen years and older that is out of work, actively looking for a job, and available for work. It is a relative measure of the degree of slack in job markets. At the most simple level, a relatively high UR indicates that production probably can be increased without generating inflation, because the available labor supply will tend to moderate wage rate increases and in some cases reduce wage rates. Conversely, in periods of low unemployment, high economic growth is more likely to raise wages—the tighter labor supply pushes up wages as more experienced and more productive workers are bid away from firm to firm on all steps of the skill ladder, which increases job openings for the less experienced and less productive workers. But the economy has not always conformed to this model (see chapter 2 under Okun's Law and the Phillips Curve). Also, the overall UR may mask significant differences among local markets, occupations, industries, and demographic groups.

METHODOLOGY OF MEASURING UNEMPLOYMENT

There are several measures of unemployment. The basic difference among the various measures is the definition of the unemployed. The framework for all of the measures is civilian noninstitutionalized persons living in the U.S. who are sixteen years or older. They exclude persons who are confined to institutions such as nursing homes, hospitals, or jails, persons on active duty in the armed forces, as well as students in school and others who are not actively seeking employment. The UR measures are defined as civilian unemployment, which excludes persons on active duty in the armed forces.

Mathematically, the UR, which is a percentage, is calculated as follows:

$$UR = \frac{\text{Unemployed persons}}{\text{Employed plus unemployed persons (labor force)}} \times 100$$

The official and most widely accepted UR defines the labor force as consisting of all persons at least sixteen years old who have a job or are actively seeking and available to work. The employment component includes all persons who did any work at all (at least one hour) as paid employees, persons working in their own business (self-employment), persons working at unpaid jobs in a family business for at least fifteen hours a week, as well as those temporarily absent from their job or business due to vacations, illness, or other reasons. Thus, the employed population consists of full-time and part-time wage earners and of those who work for profit, the latter being the self-employed and unpaid workers in family businesses who are assumed to share in the profits of the business. Persons who have more than one job are counted only once, in their primary job, the one in which they work the most hours. Supplementary data are provided on multiple jobholders, those who have more than one job, for analytical use (chapter 8 covers employment).

Unemployed persons are those who had no employment during the survey reference week, were available to work except for temporary illness, and had actively looked for employment sometime during the four-week period ending with the survey reference week. The survey reference week is the week (Sunday to Saturday) that includes the twelfth day of the month. The survey is conducted during the following week. Examples of an active job search are having a job interview; contacting an employer for a job interview; contacting an employment agency, friends, or relatives; sending out resumes; answering a job advertisement; placing an advertisement in a newspaper; or checking a union or professional register. By contrast, looking at job advertisements or attending job training programs or courses is defined as a passive search for work, and does not meet the criterion of being unemployed. At the same time, persons on temporary layoff who have been given a date to return to work or who expect to return to work within six months, are classified as unemployed, even if they do not seek other work.

Persons age sixteen years and over who are not employed or unemployed are classified as "not in the labor force." A separate category of marginally attached workers covers discouraged workers plus persons who are neither working nor looking for work, but indicate they want and are available for work and have looked for work sometime in the recent past. "Discouraged workers" are persons sixteen and older who want a job and have looked for work in the last twelve months, but are not currently looking for a job because they believe jobs are unavailable in their area or in their line of work, or because they believe they would not qualify for existing job openings.

The information used in deriving the UR is obtained from a monthly survey of a sample of about 60,000 occupied households, called the Current Population Survey (CPS). The CPS sample is benchmarked to the 2000 population census beginning in 2003.[2] The sample is also updated annually on a limited basis to reflect current changes in residential locations associated with new housing construction data prepared by the Census Bureau. Survey responses are actually obtained from about 55,500 households each month. For the remaining 4,500 households, no responses are obtained because the occupants refuse to participate in the survey, are not at home, or are unavailable for other reasons after repeated efforts by the survey interviewer to contact them. The U.S. Bureau of the Census conducts the survey for the U.S. Bureau of Labor Statistics.

In order to avoid placing too heavy a burden on the households selected for the sample, one-fourth of the households in the sample is changed each month, with each household being interviewed for four months, dropped from the rotation for the next eight months, and again interviewed for the subsequent four months; participation in the survey ends after this sixteen-month period. As indicated by the survey questions summarized below, persons are not directly asked whether they are unemployed. Rather, they are asked a series of questions to determine if they are working (employed) or actively seeking employment (unemployment). Unemployment is determined from the respondent answers to all of the questions; this ensures that the same unemployment definitions are used for all survey participants. Other groups of questions are asked to determine employment and labor force status, full-time and part-time work, earnings, multiple jobholders, discouraged workers, industry and occupation, and other labor market indicators.

A personal interview is conducted for nearly all households in the first and fifth months that they are in the survey. For most of the remaining months in the sample, telephone interviewing is used. If an adult member of the household who answered the questions in one month is unavailable at the time of the interview in a subsequent month, another adult member of the household (such as a spouse) who is familiar with the individual's employment status may answer the questions by proxy.

The survey is conducted during the calendar week, Sunday through Saturday, that includes the twelfth day of the month (called the "reference week"). The survey interviewing is conducted in the following week (called the "survey week").

The following CPS questions are asked of respondents who reported they did not work during the week of the twelfth and had no job or business from which they were absent or on layoff:

Determination of Unemployment

- Have you been doing anything to find work during the last four weeks?
- What are all of the things you have done to find work during the last four weeks?

Follow-up questions to obtain specific job search actions: You said you have been trying to find work.

- How did you go about looking?
- Can you tell me more about what you did to search for work?
- Last week, could you have started a job if one had been offered?

Follow-up if the answer is "No":

- Why is that?
- Before you started looking for work, what were you doing: working, going to school, or something else?

Follow-up if the answer is "Working":

- Did you lose or quit that job, or was it a temporary job that ended?
- When did you last work at that job or business? Month and year.
- As of the end of last week, how long have you been looking for work?

Weeks, if possible. Othewise, months or years.

• Have you been looking for full-time work of thirty-five hours or more per week?

Sampling Error

Estimates derived from a sample of 55,000 households may not be fully representative of the demographic and economic characteristics of America's 109 million households as of 2001. The chances are that in two of three cases, the sampling error in the monthly movement of the UR is plus or minus 0.1 percentage point. For example, if the UR is 5.0 percent, it most likely is in the range of 4.9 to 5.1 percent. Because of this sampling error, a single month-to-month change of plus or minus 0.1 percentage point is not statistically significant, but a change of plus or minus 0.2 percentage point is statistically significant. By the same token, cumulated changes in the UR in the same upward and downward direction of 0.1 percentage point a month for two or more consecutive months are statistically significant. If the reliability range is raised to nineteen of twenty cases, the sampling error for the monthly movement rises to 0.2 percentage point, and the above example is increased accordingly. Thus, a UR of 5.0 percent would have an error range of 4.8 to 5.2 percent, and a monthly movement would have to be at least plus or minus 0.3 percentage point to be statistically significant.

ALTERNATIVE MEASURES OF LABOR UNDERUTILIZATION

Table 9.1 provides six alternative measures of labor underutilization, referred to as U-1 to U-6, for November 2001 (the end of the 2001 recession) and July 2003.[3] The measures reflect different ways of counting unemployment. Alternative monthly estimates U-1 to U-3 are seasonally adjusted, but the monthly estimates for U-4 to U-6 are not. Therefore, not seasonally adjusted data are used in the table for all six measures.

The narrowest alternative measure (U-1) is limited to persons who are unemployed for fifteen weeks or longer. The broadest alternative (U-6) comprises the official designation of unemployment (U-3) that specifies persons sixteen years and older who are available for work and have actively looked for work sometime during the four weeks ending with the survey reference week, plus marginally attached workers, plus persons working part-time who would work full-time if such jobs were available.

The range between the U-1 and U-6 extremes in Table 9.1 is considerable. It was 1.5 and 9.0 percent in November 2001 at the end of the 2001 recession, and 2.3 and 10.5 percent in July 2003. Unemployment under the official definition was 5.3 and 6.5 percent in November 2001 and July 2003, respectively

Table 9.1

Alternative Measures of Labor Underutilization, Not Seasonally Adjusted: November 2001 and July 2003

	November 2001	July 2003
U-1. Persons unemployed 15 weeks or longer, as a percent of the civilian labor force	1.5%	2.3%
U-2. Job losers and persons who completed temporary jobs, as a percent of the civilian labor force	3.0	3.4
U-3. Total unemployed, as a percent of the civilian labor force (official unemployment rate)	**5.3**	**6.3**
U-4. U-3 plus discouraged workers, as a percent of the civilian labor force plus discouraged workers	5.5	6.6
U-5. U-4 plus all other marginally attached workers, as a percent of the civilian labor force plus all marginally attached workers	6.2	7.3
U-6. U-5 plus total employed part time because full-time jobs are not available	9.0	10.5
Addendum:		
U-3. Official unemployment rate, seasonally adjusted	**5.6**	**6.2**

Source: U.S. Bureau of Labor Statistics.

(the comparable seasonally adjusted official measurers were 5.6 and 6.2 percent in November 2001 and July 2003, respectively).

Thus, unemployment in all six categories rose from November 2001 (the end of the 2001 recession) to July 2003, even though this twenty-month period was a cyclical recovery from the 2001 recession, unemployment rose in all categories over the recovery period. Measures that showed a greater deterioration than the official UR were persons unemployed fifteen weeks or longer (U-1) and persons working part-time because full-time jobs were not available (U-6).

This lag in the unemployment movements compared with economic growth in the overall economy results from the tendency of employers during a recovery to first raise the hours worked of existing employees before hiring new workers, because of the uncertainty of the robustness of the recovery. And in the late stages of a cyclical expansion as demand weakens, employers tend to reduce hours of existing workers before laying them off, and reduce new hiring. But because the labor force continues to grow, job growth on the eve of a recession is not strong enough to absorb the growth in the labor force, thus increasing the UR. These differing tendencies around the turning points of the business cycle result in the UR being a leading indicator at the peak of an expansion and a lagging indicator at the trough of a recession (see chapter 14 on the leading indicator system). For the decline in job growth during the 2002–03 recovery, see chapter 8 under Jobless Recoveries of 1991–92 and 2002–03.

Another dimension of the cyclical aspects of the UR is the tendency of workers to be conditioned by the immediately preceding periods of job growth and job decline. Thus, toward the end of an expansion and early in a recession when layoffs begin to spread through the economy, workers who lost their jobs tend to stay in the labor force in search of new jobs with some optimism of becoming employed. This behavior raises the UR. Then, as the recession deepens and finally bottoms out and the recovery begins, some workers have stopped looking for jobs because they are pessimistic about finding new employment. This withdrawal from the labor force keeps the UR from rising as much as it otherwise would, as occurred in July 2003. These changes in the behavioral job-seeking tendencies of workers are too complex to extract the necessary data from the labor force statistics on marginally attached workers in order to estimate their effects on the UR. The problem with quantifying these effects on the UR is the difficulty of determining when the marginally attached workers left the labor force.

Although their movements over time are similar, the alternative unemployment definitions indicate a varying absolute range of slackness in the economy. They therefore tend to be cited selectively by persons characterizing the extent of unemployment, depending on social or political perspectives. For example, those who wish to emphasize the economy's success in generating employment (political conservatives) highlight the U-1 end of the spectrum with the lowest URs, while those who wish to emphasize the economy's failure to provide jobs (political liberals) highlight the U-6 end with the highest URs. This does not necessarily reflect the tendency of the political party in power, which whether liberal or conservative, would seek to show it is providing more jobs.

The official UR, U-3, is the most widely accepted measure. It is the most neutral in terms of value judgments related to demographic components of the labor force. It includes all unemployed workers and gives equal weight to each unemployed person, regardless of age, duration of unemployment, reason for not working at the previous job, and full-time or part-time labor force status. Other subcategories of the official UR are provided, such as those by age, gender, color, Hispanic origin, and family relationship, which highlight differences among various population groups in obtaining work. In addition, there is a measure of unemployment based on unemployment insurance benefit payments, which is based on different data and is not comparable to the six labor force alternative measures, as discussed later.

The analyst should monitor the alternative measures of labor underutilization for changes in differential rates among the various labor force classifications. Significant changes in the differentials could suggest subsequent impacts on persons entering and leaving the labor force, the official unemployment rate, and worker incomes.

ANALYSIS OF TRENDS

Demographic Changes Affecting the Labor Force and Unemployment

Demographic movements over decades reflect both population growth and labor force participation rates. Shorter cyclical movements are linked more closely to economic growth (chapter 3) and employment (chapter 8).

Long-Term Population and Labor Force Movements

Population changes resulting from long-term birthrate cycles have the most pronounced impact on the labor force over five- and ten-year periods, mainly because of the lag in the effect of birthrates in previous decades until the children reach working age in later decades. Changing immigration, emigration, and death rates are less important factors affecting the working-age population. For example, the low birthrates of the depression in the 1930s led to a low annual increase (compounded) of the working-age population in the 1950s of 1.0 percent. But the baby boom of the late 1940s and of the 1950s resulted in faster average annual increases in the working-age population of 1.5 percent in the 1960s and 2.1 percent in the 1970s. The subsequent drop in birthrates during the 1960s and 1970s lowered the annual working-age population increases in the 1980s and from 1990 to 2002 to 1.2 percent. The decline in birthrates was directly related to the growing participation of women in the labor force.

The labor force is the sum of employed and unemployed persons, as noted previously in the Methodology section. The labor force participation rate (LFPR) represents the number of persons in the labor force as a proportion of the civilian noninstitutional population sixteen years and older.

Table 9.2 shows the LFPR from 1950 to 2000 by decade and 2002 separately for men and for women sixteen years and older, and for teens 16–19 years old. Changes in the LFPR over the period reflect changes in lifestyle and perceptions of the availability of jobs. The total participation rate for men and women rose from 59 percent in 1950 to the 66.5 to 67 percent range in 1990–2002. This overall increase is the net effect of the increasing proportion of women pursuing a career that more than offsets the declining proportion of men in the labor force, the result mainly of earlier retirement, though the LFPR has also fallen for younger men. The rate for women rose from 34 percent in 1950 to 60 percent in 2002, while that for men declined from 86 percent to 74 percent over the same period. The direction of the patterns was consistent from the 1950s to the

Table 9.2

Labor Force Participation Rates: 1950–2000 by Decade and 2002

	Total*	All men*	All women*	Teens**
1950	59.2	86.4	33.9	51.8
1960	59.4	83.3	37.7	47.5
1970	60.4	79.7	43.3	49.9
1980	63.8	77.4	51.5	56.7
1990	66.5	76.4	57.5	53.7
2000	67.1	74.8	59.9	52.0
2002	66.6	74.1	59.6	47.4

Source: U.S. Bureau of Labor Statistics.

Note: Represents the labor force as a percentage of the civilian noninstitutional population separately for men, women, and teens.
  *16 years and older.
  **Both genders, 16–19 years old.

early 2000s, though with men having the largest decreases in the 1950s and 1960s, and women having the largest increases in the 1960s, 1970s, and 1980s. The total LFPR changed very little in both the 1950s and the 1990s to the early 2000s.

The factors causing the slowdowns in the LFPR changes for men and women in the 1990s and early 2000s are unclear. Conjectures include the changing preferences of men to retire later and for women to be at home with their children. In fact, the LFPRs for men age 60–64 and 65–69 gradually rose from 1985 to 2001, as Richard Johnson notes.[4] Johnson focused on three possible factors causing this reversal in the LFPRs for older men—Social Security reform, declining use of defined-benefit pensions in private retirement plans, and the overall slower growth in the U.S. labor force. *Except for one aspect of the Social Security reform, Johnson found that the effects of the three factors on the upturn in the LFPRs for older men were inconclusive.*

The LFPR for teens fluctuated from the 1950s to the early 2000s, as teens showed changing proclivities to enter the labor market while in high school and after. The teen rate declined in the 1950s, increased in the 1960s and 1970s, and decreased from the 1980s to the early 2000s. Generally, one-half of all teens has been in the labor force since the end of World War II.

Effect of Changing Demographics on Unemployment

Unemployment would not be affected by changing distributions of men, women, and teens in the labor force if the three groups had similar URs. Table 9.3 shows

Table 9.3

Unemployment Rates, Percent: 1950–2002

	Total	Adult men*	Adult women*	Teens**
1950	5.3	4.7	5.1	12.2
1960	5.5	4.7	5.1	14.7
1970	4.9	3.5	4.8	15.3
1975	8.5	6.8	8.0	19.9
1980	7.1	5.9	6.4	17.8
1982	9.7	8.8	8.3	23.2
1990	5.6	5.0	4.9	15.5
1992	7.5	7.1	6.3	20.1
2000	4.0	3.3	3.6	13.1
2002	5.8	5.3	5.1	16.5

Source: U.S. Bureau of Labor Statistics.

*20 years and older
**16–19 years old

the URs for adult men and women twenty years and older, and for teens 16–19 years old, from 1950 to 2002. These indicate that the URs for men were 0.5 to 1.5 percentage points lower than those for women until the 1980s, but that the differential disappeared and in some years women's URs were lower than men's from the 1980s to the early 2000s. By contrast, teen URs were two to three times higher than adult rates during the five decades. Thus, the total UR is affected by the differential URs for men and women until the 1980s, and for teens over the entire period.

The result is that the increasing proportion of women and the decreasing proportion of men in the labor force increased the total UR from 1950 to 1980, but not from 1980 to 2002. While the direction of the labor force gender trends of the 1980s to the early 2000s continued those of the previous decades, they did not affect the total UR from 1980 to 2002, because the URs for men and women were similar in the later decades. However, the changing proportions of teens in the labor force did affect the overall UR, raising it from the 1960s and 1970s, and lowering it in the 1980s to the early 2000s.

Figure 9.1 shows the shares of total employment accounted for by adult men, adult women, and teens from 1955 to 2002. They indicate a continuous rise for women, a continuous decline for men, and a fluctuating rate for teens. But there also was a marked slowdown in these trends for the adult shares from 1990 to 2002. The men's share declined only slightly, and actually increased from 2000 to 2002. And the women's share rose only slightly. These slowdowns are consistent with the slowdowns in the LFPR in Table 9.2 noted previously.

Figure 9.1 **Employment of Adult Men, Adult Women, and Teens as a Percentage of Total Employment: 1950–2000 by Decade and 2002**

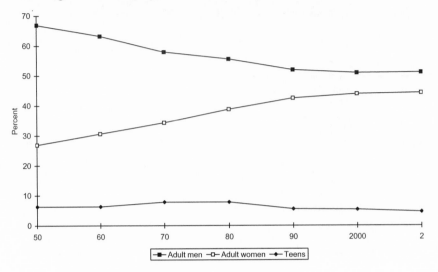

Source: Based on U.S. Bureau of Labor Statistics data.

Note: Adult men and adult women are 20 years and older. Teens are 16 to 19 years old.

In 2002, adult men held 51 percent of all jobs, adult women held 44 percent of all jobs, and teens held 5 percent of all jobs. The teen share was under 10 percent over the entire period. The decline in the teen share from the 1980s to the early 2000s reflected the decline in births in the 1960s and 1970s and only small increases in births in the 1980s.

Paul Flaim estimated that if the labor force composition had remained the same between 1959 and 1979, the civilian UR would have been 1.4 percentage points lower than it was in 1979 (4.4 percent compared with the actual 5.8 percent).[5] The study found that most of the rise in unemployment due to demographic factors over the period resulted from the increased number of teens in the population rather than from the increasing LFPRs of women, because of the much higher teen URs than those for men and women. The study also projected that the lower birthrates of baby-boom parents would contribute to a further UR decline in the 1990s by 0.3 percentage point because of the continued decline in the proportion of teens in the labor force. This was confirmed in the later study cited in the next paragraph.

In an assessment of the effect of the changing teen share of the labor force on the UR, Lawrence Katz and Alan Krueger report that the declining share of teens in the labor force from 1985 to 1998 was due to the maturing of the baby boomers. This resulted in a drop in the UR of 0.4 percentage point over the period.[6]

The analyst should assess long-run shifts in the demographic composition of the labor force and in LFPRs to determine when changes in direction are likely to affect the UR. This includes the maturing of children into the teens and of the teens into the twenties, and shifts in the LFPR for adults and teens.

Effect of Welfare Reform on the UR

The U.S. welfare reform legislation of 1996 caused large numbers of persons who had been on welfare and not in the labor force to become part of the labor force. When they obtained a paid job they were counted as employed, and when they were not hired they were counted as unemployed. In their previous status of not being in the labor force, they were not counted as unemployed if they did not have a paid job.

Some rough calculations have been made of the effect of this transformation in the welfare laws on the measured UR.[7] They are based on assumed percentages of the previous welfare recipients who became part of the labor force. They also include assumed percentages of former welfare recipients who were not in the labor force and who now are employed or unemployed. The calculations suggest that the UR was raised by 0.15 to 0.30 percentage point as a result of the welfare reform.

Matching the Unemployed with Job Openings

One approach for assessing the potential for unemployed workers to obtain jobs is to compare unemployment with available job vacancies. Ideally, this would match the job skills of unemployed workers with the available job openings. But the difference between these two ideal aggregates, whether it shows more jobs than unemployment or more unemployment than jobs gives, at best, a notion that part of the unemployment could be absorbed. It is, of course, the geographic location of the unemployed workers together with the specific available jobs in terms of the skills of the unemployed that is the first level in determining the extent of an efficient match of workers and jobs. The second level of an efficient match is linking the geographic location of where the workers live with the location of the job vacancies. Clearly, not all workers are perfectly mobile in seeking employment, and the worker-job match is most efficient when both are in the same metropolitan area, because it puts the job within commuting distance. Job vacancies that require the worker to move to another area lessen the efficiency of the match.

The new Job Openings and Labor Turnover Survey (JOLTS), which is prepared by the U.S. Bureau of Labor Statistics, is an important advance in assessing the relationship between the number of unemployed workers and job vacancies, as noted by Kelly Clark and Rosemary Hyson.[8] The JOLTS data are provided monthly beginning with May 2001. The JOLTS program is considered experimental.

The data are provided at the national level, and separately for ten broad private industry categories, the federal government, state and local governments, and four census regions. The published data sets are: job openings, job hires, total separations, quits, and layoffs and discharges. They are provided as absolute levels and as rates. The rates represent the percentage that the openings, hires, separations, etc., are of total employment. The data are obtained from a probability sample of 16 thousand business establishments.

Occupational data are not obtained for the JOLTS because the judgment in designing the survey was that including occupational detail in the monthly survey would considerably lower the response rates of the surveyed establishments. Seasonally adjusted data are first planned to be provided around 2006 when sufficient data will be available to calculate the seasonals. There may be a future breakdown between total metropolitan and nonmetropolitan areas. In general, more industry and geographic detail would require a larger sample of surveyed businesses and governments, which in turn would require more funding for the program.

The JOLTS data will be useful for analyzing the ongoing dynamic labor market flows of job creation and job destruction. They will also provide the basis for developing the inverse relationship between job vacancies and unemployment, which is referred to as the Beveridge Curve. The Beveridge Curve can shed light on whether the efficiency of matching workers with jobs is improving or worsening. Shifts in the efficiency are caused by changes in such factors as occupational skills, geography, and hiring discrimination.

The JOLTS data do not provide the occupational and geographical detail that workers need for a practical job search. But at an overall level, the JOLTS data fill a long-standing gap in employment statistics for assessing changes in the macroeconomic dimensions of job markets that affect the potential for job vacancies to absorb some of the existing unemployment. Such analyses may also lead to employment programs to make the worker-job match more efficient.

Impact of Cyclical Movements on the Labor Force and Unemployment

During cyclical expansions and recessions, changes in the LFPR of persons entering and leaving the labor market are dominated by short-term economic conditions. Typically, more people enter the labor force in expansions than in recessions, as the prospects of finding a job are higher in expansions than in recessions. Yet even in recessions, there tends to be a general upward thrust in the size of the labor force because of the long-term underlying upward trend resulting from population growth.

Monthly and quarterly movements of the LFPR are key items affecting the cyclical UR because they indicate how individuals perceive their immediate chances of finding work. Intuitively, one would expect that more persons would enter the labor force during expansions than during recessions because they would be more hopeful of getting a job when the economy is growing. The effect has also been observed in studies related particularly to periods of recession and high unemployment.

The issue during periods of high unemployment may be viewed as follows: If one member of a family loses a job, does this cause another family member to seek work to supplement the family's income (the added-worker effect)? Or, does the declining job market discourage some people from seeking work (the discouraged-worker effect)? Studies have indicated that the discouraged-worker effect is greater than the added-worker effect, as noted by Robert Pindyck and David Rubinfeld.[9] One reason the additional-worker effect is not stronger is that the large increases that have occurred in the women's LFPR (discussed previously) have reduced the pool of potential "additional workers."

Over the post-World War II business cycles, the UR moved as expected—declining in expansions and rising in recessions. The only exception was the expansion from 1945 to 1948, when the exceptionally low UR of 1.9 percent in 1945 was not sustained in the subsequent demobilization of war production and the reduction of the resident armed forces (from 11.4 million in 1945 to 1.5 million in 1948). Thus, the UR averaged 3.9 percent in 1946 and 1947 and 3.8 percent in 1948. In retrospect, these were the lowest "peacetime" URs in the postwar period. The relatively low URs in 1946–48 resulted from the strong civilian economy, and from the return of many veterans to full-time schooling, which removed them from the labor force. In terms of timing at cyclical turning points, the UR is a leading indicator at the peak of expansions and a lagging indicator at the trough of recessions, as noted previously.

Figure 9.2 shows the UR at the peaks of expansions and troughs of recessions from 1968 to January 2003 (the vertical scale is inverted from its usual position).[10] Three long-term features of the UR movements are noteworthy. First, unemployment levels worsened during the 1970s and early 1980s, drifting upward so that typically the low point of the UR at the peak of each expansion was higher than it was at the peak of the previous expansion. But this pattern changed at the peak of the 1980s expansion that ended early in 1990, when the UR low point was below that at the peaks of the two previous expansions. And the new pattern continued at the peak of the 1990s to 2000 expansion, when the UR was below that at the peak of the 1980s expansion. These developments are related to the changing demographic composition of the labor force discussed previously. Second, the UR has not been below 3 percent other than in 1952–

246

Figure 9.2 **Civilian Unemployment Rate, Inverted Scale: 1958–2003**

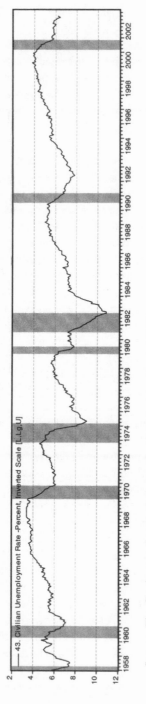

Source: The Conference Board, *Business Cycle Indicators*, August 2003.

Note: Vertical bars are recession periods.

L., Lg., U: L signifies unemployment rate leads at expansion peaks. Lg signifies unemployment rate lags at recession troughs. U signifies unemployment rate is unclassified for the entire business cycle in terms of leads and lags.

53 during the Korean War, and it was below 4 percent for a sustained period only in 1966–69 during the Vietnam War. Third, the UR was below 5 percent from 1997 to 2001, reaching a low of 4.0 percent in 2000.

In contrasting the UR during periods of peace and war, one aspect that stands out is that the UR dipped below 4 percent only during periods of extended conflict, such as the Korean and Vietnam Wars, except for the 1946–48 peacetime period after World War II. The Persian Gulf War of 1991 and the Iraq War of 2003 lasted one to two months. But it is also true that the economy was weak with high unemployment during these wars, in contrast to the robust economies of the early 1950s and the late 1960s, so there was no possibility of the UR declining below 4 percent in 1991 or 2003. This does not mean that the UR cannot drop below 4 percent in peacetime. It indicates only that except for the 1946–48 period, it has not been below 4 percent. In a related perspective associated with the length of cyclical expansions and recessions, expansions that included war periods lasted longer than expansions that occurred only in peacetime, while there was little difference in the length of recessions during peacetime or wartime (see chapter 1 under Changing Characteristics of Business Cycles Since the Nineteenth Century, and the preceding Table 1.1).

The analyst should evaluate fluctuating movements in and out of the labor force for their effect on the UR. The labor force movements lessen the UR declines in expansions and lessen the UR increases in recessions.

Unemployment Goals

Economic analysis has a major policy interest in determining the lowest UR level that can be sustained over long periods without causing inflation. Over the years this concept has been referred to variously as "full," "maximum," or "high" employment, "natural" unemployment, and the "nonaccelerating inflation rate of unemployment." Regardless of the terminology, the intent is to establish a UR toward which the nation should strive.

The goal of achieving a minimum level of unemployment, corresponding to a notion of "full employment," without causing inflation has changed. In the 1960s it was believed the lowest feasible UR was 3 to 4 percent. In the 1970s this number rose to 5 to 7 percent. The Full Employment and Balanced Growth Act of 1978 specified unemployment goals of 4 percent (see chapter 2 under Humphrey-Hawkins Act Unemployment and Inflation Goals).

In estimating a minimum UR, it is assumed there will always be some unemployment, for two reasons. First, there is never a perfect match between persons in the labor force and the skills required by employers, because of residual outmoded skills from declining industries, lack of training, geographic immobility of workers, or age, color, gender, and other discrimination in hiring, all of which are referred to as "structural unemployment." Second, there is an inherent time lag in finding jobs whether persons are newly entering the labor force or whether they have lost their jobs, which is referred to as "frictional unemployment." In practice, determining a minimum UR that would accommodate both structural and frictional unemployment, without causing additional price inflation, has been based on past relationships between unemployment and inflation, rather than on an analysis of what the micro labor markets in the economy would generate. This approach is referred to as the nonaccelerating inflation rate of unemployment, or NAIRU (see chapter 2, "Framework for Macroeconomic Analysis and Policies"). Although a micro analysis is theoretically more appealing than the NAIRU approach, it would require an assessment of the myriad transactions of buyers and sellers in product, labor, and financial markets that could be translated into the overall macro economy. This is a monumental task, and the methodology of economics is not yet capable of doing it.

The analyst should monitor reports in the press that suggest changes in structural and frictional unemployment which could lead to changes in minimum UR levels.

UNEMPLOYMENT INSURANCE

A different measure of unemployment based on persons collecting unemployment insurance (UI) benefit payments is provided weekly by the Employment and Training Administration in the U.S. Department of Labor. State governments run the UI program under general federal standards that give the states complete discretion to determine who is eligible, the dollar amount of benefit payments, and how long they are paid. Legally, the states are not required to pay any UI benefits, but all states pay them since it would be politically impractical not to.

However, the dollar benefit payments vary considerably among the states. In 2002, the national average of weekly UI benefit payments was $257, accounting for 51 percent of nonfarm gross average weekly wages and salaries (before the payment of income and Social Security taxes and all other deductions). But among individual states, the highest and lowest amounts were very different.

Table 9.4 shows the average weekly benefit payments in 2002 for states having average weekly benefit payments above $300 and below $200. Average weekly benefit payments in the three lowest states—Alabama, Missisippi, and Arizona—were $167 to $176. Average weekly benefit payments in the three highest states—Massachusetts, New Jersey, and Washington—were $329 to $360.

The table also shows—for the U.S. average—the percentage that average weekly benefit payments were of nonfarm gross weekly wages and salaries for 1971, 1980, 1990, and 2002. This proportion rose from 42 percent in 1971 and 1980, to 47 percent in 1990, to 51 percent in 2002. As a rough estimate allowing for deductions for income and Social Security taxes, group insurance, bonds, and union dues from average *gross* weekly wages and salaries, in 2002 the

Table 9.4

Unemployment Insurance Average Weekly Benefit Payments: 2002, 1990, 1980, and 1971

States with weekly benefit payments above $300–2002		States with weekly benefit payments below $200–2002	
Massachusetts	$360	Alabama	$167
New Jersey	331	Mississippi	168
Washington	329	Arizona	176
Minnesota	318	Montana	187
Colorado	313	Alaska	193
Virginia	311	Louisiana	197
Rhode Island	304	South Dakota	198

U.S. average weekly benefit payments as a percentage of nonfarm average gross weekly wages and salaries

1971	42%
1980	42
1990	47
2002	51

Sources: Unemployment insurance average weekly benefit payments—U.S. Employment and Training Administration.

Nonfarm average gross weekly wages and salaries—U.S. Bureau of Labor Statistics.

national average UI benefit payments were about 60 percent of *net* wages and salaries.

Employers in each state must pay a federally mandated tax for each employee into the UI state trust fund which is used for benefit payments regardless of the state's benefit program (referred to as the FUTA tax for the Federal Unemployment Tax Act). The employer's tax varies according to the level of UI benefits paid to former employees who were laid off—an employer with a high layoff rate pays a higher tax than an employer with a low layoff rate (referred to as "experience rating"). The administration of the state programs is paid for by the FUTA tax, much of which is offset by a tax credit for employers in states having UI laws that meet federal standards.[11]

UI Data on Unemployment

The data on UI unemployment are obtained from records of the state employment agencies that administer the program. Their main use for macroeconomic analysis is that the data on persons filing initial claims for benefit payments when they first become unemployed are a component of the composite index of leading indicators (chapter 14). In addition, because the UI data are available weekly, they provide an early signal of changes in job markets before the monthly UR data become available. Analysts use the weekly UI data as a rolling four-week average to even out weekly fluctuations.

The UI unemployment data are limited to persons filing claims for unemployment insurance benefits and consequently are a much less comprehensive unemployment measure than those based on the household survey discussed above. In 2002, for example, a weekly average of 3.6 million unemployed workers received benefits under state UI programs, compared with a monthly average of 8.4 million workers counted as unemployed in the household survey. Thus, UI data represented only 43 percent of all unemployment represented in the UR.

In 2002, the UI rate was 2.8 percent (persons receiving unemployment insurance benefits as a percentage of all persons covered under unemployment insurance programs), compared with the labor force UR of 5.8 percent. The differential reflects the fact that UI excludes such groups as young persons looking for their first job after graduation, former workers who are re-entering the labor force, those who have exhausted their unemployment benefits, and those who are otherwise ineligible for unemployment benefits, while all persons in these groups who meet the labor force criterion of actively seeking work are included in the UR measure (the numerator of the calculation). This is moderated by the fact that the number of persons covered in the UI program is smaller than the number of persons in the UR labor force (the denominator of the calculation).

The UI benefit payments vary both in the dollar amounts and the eligibility criteria among the various state governments. In general, only workers who meet the following eligibility criteria can receive unemployment insurance payments:

- Jobs are covered by the UI system.
- Unemployed workers applied for benefit payments.
- Workers lost their job for good reason based on UI criteria. But eligibility criteria vary by state. For example, some states provide UI benefits for some workers who quit their jobs, not just for those who were laid off. Another example: in some states, workers on maternity leave who subsequently lose their jobs do not get UI benefit payments.
- Workers were on the job long enough to be eligible for benefit payments (e.g., six months).
- Workers have not exhausted the number of weeks during which they may collect UI benefit payments (typically, twenty-six weeks).

In assessing future effects of the administration of unemployment insurance programs on unemployment, the analyst should monitor the tendency of the various state governments to become more generous or more stringent in the interpretation of who is eligible to receive unemployment benefits. Increasing generosity would tend to raise the UR, while greater stringency would tend to lower the UR.

Effect of UI in Moderating Recessions

UI benefit payments function as automatic stabilizers for the overall economy. During recessions, the benefit payments bolster incomes of unemployed workers, which in turn contribute to consumer spending (see chapter 2 under Fiscal Policy, Automatic Stabilizers). And when unemployment declines during expansions, benefit payments decline and thus reduce the stimulus to consumer spending.

An econometric analysis of the effects of UI benefit payments during the recessions of 1969–70, 1973–75, 1980–80, 1981–82, and 1990–91 was prepared by Lawrence Chimerine, Theodore Black, and Lester Coffey.[12] The analysis concluded that the UI benefit payments saved an average number of 131,000 jobs annually during the recessions, and lessened the decline in the real gross domestic product by about 15 percent in all quarters of each recession. The study also showed that the UI benefit payments were most effective in the 1970s recessions, were least effective in the 1980s recessions, and improved in effectiveness in the 1990s recession. The UI benefit payments in the study covered the regular program benefits plus the extended benefits and supplemental benefits programs.

REVIEW QUESTIONS

- The household survey of the labor force does not ask the direct question of the respondent, "Are you unemployed?" What are the strengths and weaknesses of this survey technique?
- In some months, the unemployment rate increases when employment increases. How can this happen?
- Characterize how the official unemployment rate differs from other measures of labor underutilization.
- How did the demographic changes in the labor force affect unemployment rates in the 1980s to the early 2000s?
- Welfare reform has raised the unemployment rate. Is that "good"?
- Why is the official unemployment rate higher than the one based on unemployment insurance data?
- Why are unemployment insurance benefit payments considered counter-cyclical?

- What aspects of the labor force would have to change to have zero unemployment?
- How are the new data on job openings useful for economic analysis?

Extra Credit

- Table 9.3 shows that the UR for women typically exceeded the UR for men before 1980, but since then the two rates are very similar, with the UR for men exceeding the UR for women in some years. What explains the closing of the gender UR gap? What are the economic conditions that result in the UR for men and women differing in particular years?
- How would policies designed to combat structural unemployment differ from those designed to combat unemployment related to recession?

NOTES

1. Alberto Alesina and Nouriel Roubini with Gerald D. Cohen, *Political Cycles and the Macroeconomy* (MIT Press, 1997), p. 67.
2. Mary Bowler, Randy E. Ilg, Stephen Miller, Ed Robinson, and Anne Polivka, "Revisions to the Current Population Survey Effective in January 2003," *Employment and Earnings*, February 2003.
3. John E. Bregger and Steven E. Haugen, "BLS introduces new range of alternative unemployment measures," *Monthly Labor Review*, October 1995.
4. Richard Johnson, "The Puzzle of Later Male Retirement," *Economic Review*, Federal Reserve Bank of Kansas City, Third Quarter 2002.
5. Paul O. Flaim, "Population changes, the baby boom, and the unemployment rate," *Monthly Labor Review*, August 1990.
6. Lawrence F. Katz and Alan B. Krueger, "The High-Pressure U.S. Labor Market of the 1990s," *Brookings Papers on Economic Activity* 1, 1999, p. 37.
7. Based on estimates that Harry Holzer of the Urban Institute gave me in a conversation.
8. Kelly A. Clark and Rosemary Hyson, "New tools for labor market analysis: JOLTS," *Monthly Labor Review*, December 2001.
9. Robert S. Pindyck and Daniel L. Rubinfeld, *Microeconomics*, 3d ed. (Prentice-Hall, 1995), p. 7.
10. The vertical scale in Figure 9.2 shows the lowest number at the top and the highest number at the bottom, which is contrary to the typical order. The typical treatment shows a rising graph when the numbers are rising, in line with the general perception that more is better. But in the case of unemployment, less is better. So the scale is inverted to show that less unemployment is better.
11. Thomas E. West and Gerard Hildebrand, "Federal-State Relations," *Unemployment Insurance in the United States: Analysis of Policy Issues*, ed. by Christopher J. O'Leary and Stephen A. Wandner (W.E. Upjohn Institute for Employment Research, 1997), p. 548.
12. Lawrence Chimerine, Theodore S. Black, and Lester Coffey, *Unemployment Insurance as an Automatic Stabilizer: Evidence of Effectiveness over Three Decades*, Unemployment Insurance Occasional Paper 99–8, Employment and Training Administration, U.S. Department of Labor, July 1999, p. 85.

10

Productivity

Productivity represents the efficiency of producing goods and services. Increasing the output of goods and services is a key factor in improving the material well-being of the population and maintaining a secure defense. There are two ways to increase the volume of goods and services available for private and public use: increase the amount of labor and capital equipment used as inputs in production, or increase the efficiency of these factors in producing the output. The latter defines the economy's productivity and is a primary factor determining the growth of the nation's total output (see chapter 3, "Economic Growth," for the contribution of productivity to economic growth). Productivity is increased through improvements in technology and equipment, education and skills of the work force, executive direction, managerial know-how, public sector spending which substitutes for private spending infrastructure such as for roads, airports, and sewers, and many other factors.

In the context of a firm or a worker, increasing productivity is an important element in generating greater profits and wages. In the context of the nation, rising productivity is fundamental to improvements in living conditions throughout the population. Thus, sustained productivity increases over time are the basic means by which the economy generates overall improved living conditions for each generation. Higher productivity is required for children to have a higher level of material well-being than their parents, and concomitantly for the nation to have the resources to protect itself against foreign enemies.

Improved technology can also temporarily lower productivity. Productivity may be reduced in the initial transition period when lack of familiarity with new equipment causes workers to take longer to do a job than they took with the older technology, or when breakdowns and bugs occur in the new equipment and have to be corrected. Problems associated with the introduction of new computer systems and advanced communications systems are examples of this phenomenon.

But productivity is not an unmixed blessing. Not everyone shares equally in productivity advances. Rising productivity can cause employment dislocation because the introduction of new technology changes or eliminates some jobs. Displaced workers with outmoded skills may not be able to find new jobs or may find only lower-paid work. At the economy-wide level, however, rising productivity does not necessarily lead to higher unemployment or lower wages, because other workers find better paying jobs in new fields. Thus, the greater incomes and lower prices attributable to rising productivity cause overall spending and employment to increase. But this does not alleviate the hurt of those workers who cannot obtain new jobs, or only jobs at much below the wages of their previous jobs that were eliminated. It points up the need for cushioning the effect of lost jobs through job retraining and other assistance to displaced workers.

Productivity measures are prepared by the Bureau of Labor Statistics (BLS) in the U.S. Department of Labor. They are published in the monthly BLS journal, the *Monthly Labor Review* (www.bls.gov). There are two basic measures of productivity, labor productivity and multifactor productivity. Labor productivity data are provided quarterly and multifactor productivity data are provided annually.

This chapter covers both labor and multifactor productivity for the business sector of the economy. Other topics include productivity and returns to scale, the productivity rebound that began in the mid-1990s, the effect on productivity of private industry spending to combat terrorism, and productivity and price change.

METHODOLOGY OF MEASURING PRODUCTIVITY

Productivity is the output of items produced in relation to the inputs required for the production of the items.[1] Mathematically, this is expressed as:

$$\text{Productivity} = \frac{\text{Output}}{\text{Input}}$$

Labor-Hour Productivity: Business Sector

The broadest measure of labor productivity is the output of goods and services per hour worked in the business sector of the economy. Mathematically, labor productivity in the business sector is expressed as:

$$\text{Labor-hour productivity} = \frac{\text{Output}}{\text{Input}} = \frac{\text{Real business GDP*}}{\text{Labor hours**}} = \text{Real business GDP per labor hour}$$

*Gross domestic product, excluding households, not-for-profit organizations, rental value of owner-occupied housing, and general government, adjusted for inflation.
**Hours worked by paid employees, the self-employed, and unpaid family workers.

Output is represented by the gross domestic product (GDP) in the business sector, adjusted for price change. Business GDP is smaller than the GDP, as described below. The GDP comprises the goods and services produced in the household, business, government, and international sectors of the economy (chapter 3). The GDP is defined on a value-added basis that covers the labor costs, depreciation costs on equipment and structures, business profits, interest, and sales and property taxes in producing the nation's output. This excludes the purchases of intermediate goods and services from other industries. Otherwise, the intermediate items would result in continuous double-counting, with the production of the same goods and services being re-counted as they become components in successive stages of fabrication until they are incorporated in a final end-use item. For example, steel sheets are used in the manufacture of an automobile. A steel sheet originates with the extraction of iron ore, and the iron ore in turn goes through several stages of fabrication, including the use of other products, until it is finally transformed into a steel sheet.

Because of statistical problems in measuring the output of households, not-for-profit organizations, and government functions, the output of these sectors in the GDP is defined as the inputs of wages and salaries paid to their workers. Since the outputs equal the inputs of these sectors, there is no measured change in their productivity. Therefore, the output measure used in estimating both labor and multifactor productivity excludes the output of households, not-for-profit organizations, and general government, because to include them would bias the productivity growth measures downward.[2] The rental value of owner-occupied housing in the GDP is also excluded because there is no corresponding input for it. The resultant measure of output is the GDP in the business sector.

Input comprises the labor hours used in production. Labor hours are the product of the number of employees and their average weekly hours worked. Labor hours include paid employees, the self-employed, and unpaid family workers. The definition of hours represents hours at work, which is limited to time at the job site, and includes paid time to travel between job sites, coffee breaks, and machine downtime. It excludes paid leave for vacations, sickness, or other reasons, which is associated with data on "hours paid." The data on hours for the self-employed and family workers are less clear. Given the nature of the compensation for these groups, measures of their labor input can be described as "hours worked" or "hours paid."[3]

Returning to the quotient in the mathematical expression above, which is labor productivity, we see that labor productivity is an aggregate of all the factors contributing to productivity change, except for the labor hour inputs that are included as inputs in the denominator of the expression. The elements of this aggregate are not quantified. They include: the skills and effort of workers not captured by the schooling, experience, and compensation surrogates in the labor hour inputs; the quantity and technology of capital equipment and structures; research and development; executive direction; managerial know-how; level of output; utilization of industrial capacity; consumption of energy; quality of materials; roads, airports, sewers, and other public sector infrastructure; and the interaction of these and all other factors not specified. Multifactor productivity is sometimes referred to as "total factor productivity."

Multifactor Productivity: Business Sector

Multifactor productivity is an aggregate of production efficiency and many other factors affecting productivity except labor and capital inputs. The elements of this aggregate are not quantified. They include: changes in the skills and effort of workers not captured by the labor hours inputs; research and development; technology of capital equipment not captured by the capital facilities inputs; production efficiency; executive direction; managerial know-how; level of output; utilization of industrial capacity; energy consumption; quality of materials; roads, airports, sewers, and other public sector infrastructure; and the interaction of these and all other factors.

Because the labor productivity measure contains the effect of capital inputs, it does not provide estimates of the contribution to productivity separately for capital inputs and the aggregate of all other factors. Capital inputs are equipment, structures, land, and business inventories.

The multifactor productivity measure of output is GDP in the business sector, excluding government enterprises, adjusted for inflation. This is the same as the output measure of labor productivity, except for the exclusion of government enterprises (see note 2).

Multifactor productivity refines the estimate of labor inputs that is included in the above measure of labor productivity, and adds a separate component of capital inputs. The labor hours data in multifactor productivity reflect statistical adjustments that give greater weight to workers with more schooling, experience, and higher compensation adjusted for inflation, to reflect differences in the capabilities between workers.[4] The assumption is that as the workforce is composed of an increasing proportion of workers with a greater amount of schooling, experience, and compensation, the workforce itself becomes more productive. By including this changing composition of the workforce in the labor hours inputs in the denominator of the productivity formula, the resultant multifactor productivity labor input measure abstracts from the effects of both the changing number of hours worked and the changing composition of the workforce on the nation's output. These adjustments are a surrogate for estimating the changing efficiency of the workforce, as direct data on overall labor efficiency are not available.

The capital inputs in multifactor productivity represent the services that flow from the stocks of capital.[5] They include the rental value services of capital facilities, adjusted for price change, used in the production of goods and services—equipment, structures, inventories, and land. The capital inputs incorporate the quantity and the composition of equipment and structures facilities. The quantity of capital is based on the value of (a) existing equipment and structures resulting from the cumulated investments in previous years minus the depreciation and removal of the facilities, (b) business inventories used in production, and (c) land. Adjustments for the composition of equipment and structures facilities are made by giving more weight to short-lived than to long-lived equipment items, because short-lived assets provide more services per year than long-lived assets, per dollar of asset. Other adjustments are implicit in the inflation-adjusted equipment and structures facilities, because the price indexes used to estimate the quantity, as distinct from the current-dollar value of these facilities, include some estimates for quality change (for quality change in price indexes, see chapter 11, "Inflation and Deflation"). These adjustments are a surrogate for estimating the changing efficiency of capital facilities, as direct data on the overall efficiency of equipment and structures are not available.

By including both labor hours and capital services as inputs in the denominator, multifactor productivity is the resultant of all the factors contributing to productivity, except work hours and capital facilities inputs. Ideally, multifactor productivity would represent the effects of technology and production efficiency on productivity. But as an aggregate, it includes much more, as noted above.

The research and development (RD) measure is an estimate of the RD share of multifactor productivity growth, and thus is the one item within the multifactor aggregate for which explicit estimates are prepared. But multifactor productivity is not adjusted to exclude the effects of RD, because RD is associated with advances in knowledge, technology, and production efficiency, which fit more into the ideal notion of what multifactor productivity should be. If multifactor productivity were adjusted to exclude RD, the remaining aggregate would be further removed from the ideal notion.

Mathematically, multifactor productivity in the private business sector is expressed as:

$$\frac{\text{Output}}{\text{Input}} = \frac{\text{Real business GDP*}}{\text{Weighted labor hours** and capital services***}}$$
$$= \text{Real business GDP per unit of labor and capital services}$$

*Same as business GDP in labor productivity above, excluding government enterprises.

(*Continued*)

**Hours worked by paid employees, the self-employed, and unpaid family workers, modified for the schooling, experience, and inflation-adjusted compensation of different groups of workers.
***Rental value of equipment, structures, inventories, and land adjusted for inflation. Depreciated value of equipment and structures modified for short-lived and long-lived equipment items.

Note on the Accuracy of Productivity Statistics

The productivity measures are prepared from many different data sources, some of which are inconsistent and also have known data problems, as noted by Edwin Dean.[6] The statistical estimation of productivity is also based on indirect procedures, which are used in the absence of direct measures. The most serious problems appear in the service industries because of the difficulty of calculating the output of some services. The regular quarterly and annual revisions to the productivity measures, based on more complete and refined underlying output and input data, enhance the consistency and the closeness of the data to the productivity definitions over time.

ANALYSIS OF TRENDS

This section covers both long-term shifts in productivity slowdowns and rebounds, the cyclical aspects of productivity during expansions and recessions, and the effect on productivity of private industry spending to combat terrorism.

Long-Term Movements

Table 10.1 shows long-term movements in labor productivity, capital intensity, labor composition, multifactor productivity, and research and development from 1948 to 2001. The components of capital intensity (contribution weighted by capital's share of current dollar inputs), labor composition (contribution weighted by labor's share of current dollar inputs), and multifactor productivity sum to labor productivity. Research and development is a supplementary item that is an estimate of its share of multifactor productivity.

The trends indicate a sharp slowdown in productivity growth during 1973–79, a continuation at this low level during 1979–90 and 1990–95, a rebound during 1995–2000, and a slowdown in 2001. Because data for multifactor productivity for 2002 will first become available in 2004, Table 10.1 does not show the strong increase in labor productivity in 2002 shown in Figure 10.1 below.

Table 10.1

Trends in Labor Productivity and Its Components, Business Sector:
1948–2001 (output per work hour, annual percentage growth rates)

	Labor productivity[a]	Capital intensity[b]	Labor composition[c]	Multifactor productivity[d]	Research and development[e]
1948–73	3.3	0.9	0.2	2.1	0.2
1973–79	1.3	0.7	0.0	0.6	0.1
1979–90	1.6	0.8	0.3	0.5	0.2
1990–95	1.5	0.5	0.4	0.6	0.2
1995–2000	2.7	1.1	0.3	1.4	0.2
2000–01	1.3	1.7	0.6	−1.0	0.3
1948–2001	2.5	0.9	0.2	1.3	0.2

Source: U.S. Bureau of Labor Statistics.

Note: The sum of capital intensity, labor composition, and multifactor productivity does not always equal labor productivity due to rounding.

a. Business gross domestic product (GDP) divided by labor hours.

b. Contribution of capital services of structures, equipment, inventories, and land. Contribution weighted by capital's share of current dollar costs.

c. Contribution of adjustment for worker schooling, experience, and compensation. Contribution weighted by labor's share of current dollar costs.

d. Residual of business GDP growth per work hour after accounting for labor and capital inputs.

e. Estimate of R&D share of multifactor productivity. Calculated only for the nonfarm business sector.

While the 1995–2000 rebound is substantial, productivity growth was still close to one percentage point below the highest rates during 1948–73.

Multifactor productivity growth was the dominant component of labor productivity growth during 1948–73, 1995–2000, and 1948–2000. But it declined sharply in 2001 and was actually negative in that year. Previous years when it was negative were 1969, 1970, 1974, 1979–80, 1982, and 1991, all years of either slow growth or recession, indicating a strong cyclical component to multifactor productivity. There is, in fact, a cyclical component in all productivity measures.

Capital intensity growth was slightly higher than that for multifactor productivity during 1979–90, while multifactor productivity growth and capital intensity growth were similar during 1973–79 and 1990–95. The contributions of labor composition and research and development to productivity growth were relatively small.

In the broader context of economic growth, the contribution of the component shares of labor inputs, capital inputs, and multifactor productivity to economic growth was discussed in chapter 3 under Supply Perspectives of Economic Growth and the accompanying Figure 3.3.

Various partial explanations have been offered for the substantial productivity slowdown in the 1970s. They include decreasing technological advances due to lower research and development spending, less investment in equipment and structures as higher energy prices caused business to use more labor relative to energy-using machinery, and more hours paid for than hours worked because of increases in paid vacations and sick leave. However, actual measures of these and other possible reasons related to multifactor productivity by Jerome Mark and William Waldorf and by Edward Denison provide estimates that account for only about 20 percent of the decline, and the factors causing the slowdown are not well understood.[7]

Charles Morris and Michael Darby have suggested that the measured productivity growth slowdown in the 1970s is a statistical illusion associated with the price controls of the early 1970s.[8] Their analyses assume that the official price measures used to estimate the inflation-adjusted gross national product in 1973 understated price inflation, and consequently overstated output and the productivity level in 1973. The idea is that without this distortion, there was a productivity slowdown from 1968 to 1973, but no further slowdown after 1973. However, empirically substantiating the extent of the price measurement problem is difficult, and this view has not gained general acceptance over the official measure that shows productivity slowing down during most of the 1970s. It is also noteworthy that productivity slowdowns occurred in virtually all industrialized countries in the 1970s, most of which did not have price controls.

It is also hard to identify specific causes for the continuation of low productivity increases from the 1980s through the first half of the 1990s, and then the upturn in the second half of the 1990s to the early 2000s. Explanations associated with the shift from goods to services, company downsizing, outsourcing, and computerization, and overstatement of inflation in the consumer price index (CPI) are either a continuation of long-term trends that are not a break with the past, or in themselves did not cause sharp changes. In the first category of continued long-term trends are the shift from goods to services in which productivity in services is more difficult to measure than in goods; the increasing computerization which is a continuation of the long-term incorporation of technological innovations in office automation and communications, as noted by Daniel Sichel[9]; and the overstatement of inflation in the CPI used to deflate current dollar data to real output has also been a long-term phenomenon. In the second category of changing business practices that do not materially affect productivity are downsizing associated with discontinuing low-profit or unprofitable product lines, which is not in itself an increase in productivity; and outsourcing activities previously done in-house to outside contractors tends to be an offset between manufacturing and service industries, with the outsourcing by manufacturers to service industry contractors raising measured manufacturing industry productivity and lowering measured service industry productivity, as noted by Sharon Kozicki.[10]

Another explanation of the productivity slowdown that extended into the 1990s is related to changes in the age of the capital stock of equipment and structures, as noted by Edward Wolff.[11] The point is that an aging capital stock is less efficient and therefore lowers productivity increases, while a young (newer) capital stock is more efficient and raises productivity. I question whether the data are robust enough to generalize on the relationship between changes in the age of the stock and productivity. Thus, the relatively small changes in the capital stock ages and the indirectness of the methodology in preparing the capital stock estimates diminish the case for linking them to the productivity slowdown (see chapter 5 under The Age of Structures and Equipment).

Returns to Scale

Returns to scale reflect, as part of the production process, the effect on output of changing the quantity of inputs, assuming no change in the technology of production. For example, when a company increases the number of workers and the use of machinery and materials in its operations, and there is a proportionate increase in the output of its products, the result is referred to as constant returns to scale. An increase in inputs that leads to a proportionately greater output is referred to as increasing returns to scale, reflecting greater efficiencies. And an increase in inputs that leads to a proportionately lesser output is referred to as decreasing returns to scale, reflecting greater inefficiencies.

Returns to scale can shift over time. An initial increase in inputs can lead to increasing returns to scale for a time, as the existing fixed costs of production, such as the upkeep of the structure and the employment of minimum maintenance crews, result in lower unit costs of production, because the production costs are spread over a greater volume of items produced. But when the greater volume of production leads to greater unit costs of production because of hiring less productive workers, bringing outmoded and less reliable equipment that had been replaced into operation, instituting excessive specialization or bureaucratic layers, or laxness by management in holding down costs when business is thriving (referred to as "X-efficiency"), decreasing returns to scale set in.[12]

The possible quantification of returns to scale at the industry level that could be aggregated to the overall economy are an area that potentially could shed light on the shifting productivity trends. But the difficulty of developing estimates of returns to scale for industries that can be aggregated to the economy-wide level is formidable. An example of the complexity of doing this is the analysis of Aklilu Zegeye and Larry Rosenblum.[13]

The Productivity Rebound

There are several analyses of the productivity rebound from 1995 to the early 2000s. One assessment was made by the U.S. Council of Economic Advisers (CEA).[14] Multifactor productivity data were available only to 2000 when the CEA's analysis was prepared, so the CEA added its own estimates for 2001 and 2002. The analysis recognized the important role of multifactor productivity in propelling the productivity rebound. But it also recognized that because multifactor productivity is developed indirectly as a residual aggregate of many items, it does not explain the causes of the rebound.

Another assessment of the rebound, by Susanto Basu, John Fernald, and Matthew Shapiro, focused on the importance of investments in computers and telecommunications equipment.[15] The authors concluded that while significant capital investments were made in the first half of the 1990s, the investments were initially subject to adjustment costs that diverted resources from utilizing the new technology. Adjustment costs are associated with a learning curve following the introduction of new capital equipment that results in output being temporarily slowed. During this period, technology improvements do not occur, and with the slower output growth, productivity declines. According to the analysis, the adjustment period ended in the first half of the 1990s, and technology and productivity improvements emerged in the second half of the 1990s. This is an interesting finding, but it is based on complex and indirect techniques that leave the finding far from definitive. It spotlights the opaqueness of the multifactor aggregate for identifying the causes of the rebound.

Cyclical Movements

Figure 10.1 shows that the year-to-year movements of labor productivity in the business sector from 1980 to 2002 fluctuated considerably. The range was from –0.4 percent in 1982 to 5.3 percent in 2002. The highest sustained rates were during 1983–86 (2.0 to 5.3 percent) and during 1996–2002 (2.0 to 5.3 percent). The average increase over the twenty-three-year period was 1.9 percent. The year-to-year volatility was due to the sharper cyclical changes in the GDP output measure (numerator) than the changes in the labor hours input measure (denominator). Although not shown in the figure, the same phenomenon occurred in the quarterly movements.

The greater stability of the labor input measure than of the GDP output measure reflects the fact that because employers are uncertain if shifts in demand for their products are permanent or transitory, they resist hiring and laying off workers in response to initial changes in demand. The substitution of changing the hours worked of existing workers for hiring or laying off workers during uncertain periods probably results in smaller changes in total hours worked than if workers were hired or laid off. Also, some workers whose skills are specific

Figure 10.1 **Labor Productivity in the Business Sector, Annual Percentage Change: 1980–2002**

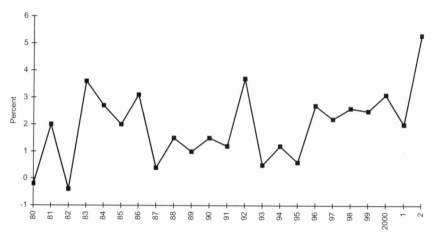

Source: Based on U.S. Bureau of Labor Statistics data.

to the firm are considered too valuable to lay off every time demand slacks off, so employers tend to hoard some workers during recessions. The combination of these two patterns leads to labor input that is less cyclical than output, and therefore productivity appears to have a cyclical component. The cyclical pattern was reflected in the sharp increases in productivity in 2002 and 2003, when companies were able to produce greater levels of output without replacing the laid off workers. Further, capital, which is not part of the labor productivity measure, may also be more heavily utilized when demand increases, which may contribute to the cyclical labor productivity pattern.

Lawrence Fulco points out that because of this practice of only partially changing labor inputs during periods of cyclical uncertainty, productivity rises more in expansions than in recessions, irrespective of changes in labor skills, capital equipment, and other basic factors affecting productivity.[16] And Matthew Shapiro finds that when changes in production and employment in manufacturing industries are accounted for by changes in capacity utilization rates and night shifts, there is no evidence of a cyclical productivity pattern.[17] The underlying factors driving productivity cumulate slowly over time as they become more widely diffused throughout the economy, and thus do not create significant quarterly and annual changes.

Figure 10.2 shows labor and multifactor productivity from 1980 to 2001. Multifactor productivity was available only to 2001 at the time of this writing. The data for labor productivity in Figure 10.2 do not include the revised data shown in Figure 10.1 (which became available in August 2003), in order to maintain their consistency with the multifactor productivity data which did not

Figure 10.2 **Labor and Multifactor Productivity in the Business Sector, Annual Percentage Change: 1980–2001**

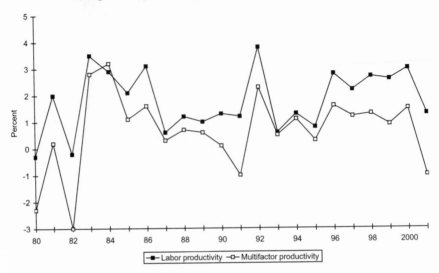

Source: Based on U.S. Bureau of Labor Statistics data.

Note: Multifactor productivity for 2002 not available at time of writing.

incorporate those revised data. The range for labor productivity was from –0.2 percent in 1980 and 1982 to 3.5 percent in 1983. The highest sustained rates were during 1983–86 (2.1 to 3.5 percent) and during 1996–2000 (2.2 to 3.0 percent). The average increase over the twenty-two–year period was 1.8 percent.

The range for multifactor productivity was –3.0 percent in 1982 to 3.2 percent in 1984. The highest sustained rates were during 1983–86 (1.1 to 3.2 percent) and during 1996–2000 (0.9 to 1.6 percent). Multifactor productivity had negative changes in 1980, 1982, and 2001. The average increase over the twenty-two–year period was 0.6 percent.

Both labor and multifactor productivity had volatile and similar directional year-to-year movements. But labor productivity rose noticeably more that multifactor productivity (1.8 percent compared with 0.6 on average from 1980 to 2001). The smaller increases in multifactor productivity are consistent with the patterns in the average long-term rates discussed previously in relation to Table 10.1.

Effect on Productivity of Private Industry Spending to Combat Terrorism

The terrorist attacks of September 11, 2001, have led to increased spending by private businesses, not-for-profit organizations, households, and the federal and state and local governments variously for security guards, scanning equipment, and other protective devices. Because of the difficulty of measuring the output of governments, not-for-profit organizations, households, and the rental value of owner-occupied housing, productivity estimates are confined to private for-profit businesses, as noted in the Methodology section.

In January 2002, as part of its long-term projections of the U.S. economy, the Congressional Budget Office (CBO) estimated that the additional spending for security in the private sector would lower the future level of multifactor productivity growth by 0.3 percentage point.[18] The reduction in multifactor productivity was based on assumed additional spending by companies for security guards and the delays in transportation due to the heightened security. The cost of such spending for the year 2002 was estimated at $20 billion. In addition, the projected future growth in multifactor productivity was lowered by 0.03 percentage point per year to reflect the diversion of some business investment to alarm systems, facility access systems, surveillance cameras, protective fences, etc. None of this increased spending for security personnel and equipment contributes to the measured output of the economy, and therefore the additional labor hour inputs of the security workers reduce measured productivity. This is analogous to the treatment of business spending for antipollution equipment, which also is not included in the measured output of the economy, while any additional workers used in operating the antipollution equipment become labor inputs and reduce measured productivity.

In January 2003, the CBO eliminated the 0.3 percentage point downward change in multifactor productivity growth based mainly on an evaluation of data on the employment of security guards and private detectives for the twelve months following the September 2001 attacks.[19] These data showed no increase in the employment growth of these workers above the long-term trend. But the CBO maintained the diminution of 0.03 percentage point in the projected annual future growth in multifactor productivity associated with the diversion of business investment to security equipment.[20] The impact of terrorism on economic growth is discussed in chapter 3 under Terrorist Attacks.

PRODUCTIVITY AND PRICE CHANGE

Prices are determined by both the markets for goods and services (demand) and production costs (supply). This section focuses on the supply effects. Price movements are discussed more fully in chapter 11, "Inflation and Deflation."

Productivity affects price change through its effect on the costs of producing goods and services. If costs rise, business will be motivated to increase prices in order to maintain profit rates (profits as a percentage of sales). If costs remain the same or decline, they do not exert a pressure for higher prices to maintain profit rates. In fact, if costs decline, prices can decline and profits still be maintained.

A key item affecting production costs is the relation between employee compensation per hour and labor productivity, which is referred to as unit labor costs (ULC).[21] ULC also may be expressed as compensation per unit of output, because "labor hours" is the common term in compensation per hour and productivity that cancels out in the mathematical expression below. Mathematically, ULC are expressed as:

$$\text{Unit labor costs} = \frac{\text{Compensation per hour}}{\text{Productivity}} = \frac{\dfrac{\text{Compensation*}}{\text{Labor hours}}}{\dfrac{\text{Output}}{\text{Labor hours}}} = \frac{\text{Compensation}}{\text{Output}}$$

*Wages and salaries plus fringe benefits

If compensation per hour increases more than productivity, ULC increase and there is upward pressure on prices. If compensation per hour increases less than productivity, ULC decreases and there is downward pressure on prices.

Figure 10.3 shows the annual change in ULC and the GDP implicit price deflator (IPD) for the business sector from 1980 to 2002. Following the high ULC and IPD rates during 1980–82, 7 to 11 percent and 6 to 9 percent, re-

Figure 10.3 **Unit Labor Costs and GDP Implicit Price Deflator in the Business Sector, Annual Percentage Change: 1980–2002**

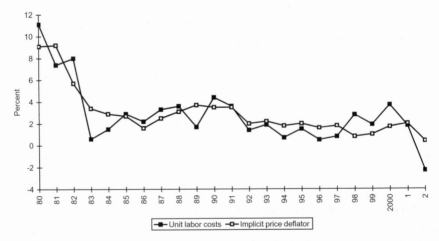

Sources: Based on U.S. Bureau of Labor Statistics and U.S. Bureau of Economic Analysis data.

spectively, there was a sharp drop in the early 1980s and a continued decline into the 1990s and the early 2000s. Generally, the ULC IPD rates during 1983–91 were in the 2.0 to 3.5 range, which during 1992–2002 lessened to the 1 to 2 percent range. The only negative change occurred for ULC in 2002.

The average annual increase from 1980 to 2002 was 2.8 percent for ULC and 3.0 percent for the IPD. Excluding the high rates during 1980–82, the average increase from 1982 to 2002 was 1.9 percent for ULC and 2.2 percent for the IPD.

The figure indicates broadly similar movements in both indicators, though they sometimes moved in opposite directions. The differential movements typically were within one to two percentage points. The yearly ULC movements were more volatile than the price movements. The ULC volatility reflects the inclusion of the volatile productivity component in its formulation (see Figure 10.1 for the volatility of productivity).

The analyst should include the following aspects of productivity in assessing their future effects on the economy:

- *It is essential to distinguish between short-term cyclical and long-term structural changes in productivity. Only structural changes have long-term substantive impacts on the efficiency of producing goods and services.*
- *By abstracting from the quantity and some attributes of the quality of labor and capital inputs, multifactor productivity focuses attention on an aggregate of other features of the economy that affect productivity. Until elements of this aggregate are quantified, which is a challenging methodological problem, changes in the future impact of the multifactor elements on productivity are probably best monitored from anecdotal reports in the press.*
- *Unit labor costs are a broad indicator of inflationary price pressures stemming from production costs.*

REVIEW QUESTIONS

- How does productivity affect living conditions?
- Why are cyclical changes in productivity a problematic indicator of fundamental changes in productivity?
- What analytic interest does multifactor productivity add to the traditional measure of labor productivity?
- What factors would you analyze in explaining productivity slowdowns and accelerations? How would you apply them?
- Assuming that prices are determined solely by unit labor costs, calculate the effect of the changes in productivity and compensation on the price-change rate from the following:

Productivity	Compensation per hour	Price change				
		2%	6%	9%	−1%	−6%
5%	4%	—	—	—	—	—
2	4	—	—	—	—	—
0	6	—	—	—	—	—

Extra Credit

- There is a general consensus that productivity is procyclical, rising in expansions and falling in recessions. How do the movements in Figure 10.1 fit this view?
- Suppose a person who has been keeping house full time joins the labor force, gets a job in the business sector, and is less productive than the average worker. What happens to the official measure of labor productivity? How would your answer differ if housework were counted as part of the business sector?

NOTES

1. For a description of the productivity statistics methodology, see Bureau of Labor Statistics, U.S. Department of Labor, *BLS Handbook of Methods*, April 1997, ch. 10.
2. General government covers government functions which are financed from tax revenues. General government accounts for the preponderance of government functions. Government enterprises are government functions that cover a substantial part of their operating costs by selling goods and services to the public.
3. Mary Jablonski, Kent Kunze, and Phyllis Flohr Otto, "Hours at work: a new base for BLS productivity measures," *Monthly Labor Review*, February 1990.
4. Bureau of Labor Statistics, U.S. Department of Labor, *Labor Composition and U.S. Productivity Growth*, Bulletin 2426, October 1993.
5. For a detailed description of the capital stock estimates, see Bureau of Economic Analysis, U.S. Department of Commerce, *Fixed Reproducible Tangible Wealth in the United States, 1925–94*, 1999.
6. Edwin R. Dean, "The accuracy of the BLS productivity measures," *Monthly Labor Review*, February 1999.
7. Jerome A. Mark, William H. Waldorf, et al., *Trends in Multifactor Productivity*, Bulletin 2178, Bureau of Labor Statistics, U.S. Department of Labor, September 1983, chs. III and IV. See also, Edward F. Denison, *Trends in Economic Growth, 1929–82* (Brookings Institution, 1985).
8. Charles S. Morris, "The Productivity 'Slowdown': A Sectoral Analysis," *Economic Review*, Federal Reserve Bank of Kansas City, April 1984. See also Michael R. Darby, "The U.S. Productivity Slowdown: A Case of Statistical Myopia," *American Economic Review*, June 1984.

9. Daniel E. Sichel, *The Computer Revolution: An Economic Perspective* (Brookings Institution, 1997), ch. 5.
10. Sharon Kozicki, "The Productivity Slowdown: Diverging Trends in the Manufacturing and Service Sectors," *Economic Review*, Federal Reserve Bank of Kansas City, First quarter 1997.
11. Edward N. Wolff, "The Productivity Slowdown: The Culprit at Last? Follow-Up on Hulten and Wolff," *American Economic Review*, December 1996.
12. In prosperous times, managers probably have less pressure or incentive to seek more efficient operations or eliminate marginal activities than in periods of slow growth or recession, when business tends to be more aggressive in cutting costs. These practices over the course of the business cycle are difficult to quantify, but they are intuitively plausible and also are reported anecdotally in the press. They are related in the literature to the idea of "X-efficiency," which typically associates differences in competitive pressures between monopolistic and more competitive industries. See Harvey Leibenstein, "Allocative Efficiency vs. 'X-Efficiency,'" *American Economic Review*, June 1966; and F. M. Scherer, *Industrial Market Structure and Market Performance*, 2d ed. (Rand McNally College Publishing: 1980), pp. 464–66.
13. Aklilu A. Zegeye and Larry Rosenblum, "Measuring Productivity in an Imperfect World," *Applied Economics* 32, 2000.
14. *Economic Report of the President together with The Annual Report of the Council of Economic Advisers*, February 2003, Box 1–5, pp. 67–69.
15. Susanto Basu, John G. Fernald, and Matthew D. Shapiro, *Productivity Growth in the 1990s: Technology, Utilization, or Adjustment?* Working Paper 8359, National Bureau of Economic Research, July 2001.
16. Lawrence J. Fulco, "Strong post-recession gain in productivity contributes to slow growth in labor costs," *Monthly Labor Review*, December 1994.
17. Matthew D. Shapiro, "Macroeconomic Implications of Variation in the Workweek of Capital," *Brookings Papers on Economic Activity* 2, 1996.
18. Congressional Budget Office, Congress of the United States, *The Budget and Economic Outlook: Fiscal Years 2003–2012*, January 2002, Box 2–3, p. 39.
19. Congressional Budget Office, Congress of the United States, *The Budget and Economic Outlook: Fiscal Years 2004–2013*, January 2003, pp. 44–46.
20. *Budget and Economic Outlook: Fiscal Years 2003–2012*, p. 39.
21. Bureau of Labor Statistics, U.S. Department of Labor, *BLS Handbook of Methods*, April 1997, ch. 10.

11

Inflation and Deflation

Prices influence and reflect many aspects of the private and government sectors of the economy. They are both a driving force and a culmination of the various elements of demand and supply in the marketplace. Different geographic, industrial, financial, real estate, and labor markets vary considerably in their competitive and monopolistic features, and prices are the summation of the varying degrees of market imperfections. Prices are also affected by extra-market considerations, such as war or threat of war, the environment, and natural disasters (e.g., drought, floods, earthquakes, tornadoes).

Prices of goods and services vary considerably among individual items bought and sold in the marketplace. There is the intrinsic difference in the absolute price of one item in comparison to another at a point in time, such as the price of a car and of college tuition. There are continuing differences in the movements of prices over time, such as price changes of a car and of college tuition from one year to the next. Some items rise in price more than others, some decline in price more than others, and some are unchanged from one period to the next. These differential price movements reflect actual or perceived shortages or surpluses among buyers and sellers and varying degrees of price competition for particular items. Changes in overall price levels for the total of all goods and services are the net effect of the varying upward, downward, and stable movements of the vast number of items sold in markets around the United States.

There are also varying degrees of inflation (price increases) and deflation (price decreases) that have differential effects on the economy. In general, overall price movements affect the economic well-being of the population in the following way: people are better off if their incomes increase more than prices increase, or if their incomes fall less than prices fall.

There are sometimes sharp differences between the price movements of goods and services produced on a current basis and the price movements in the sales of real property and financial assets that are a measure of wealth. Real property asset values of housing prices and financial asset values of common stock prices became prominent in the late 1990s and early 2000s for their effect on the purchasing power of households in spending on goods, services, and new and existing housing. This is referred to as the "wealth effect."

This chapter focuses on the consumer price index (CPI) as the prime measure of inflation and deflation in the economy. The CPI is the most widely cited measure of price change, and most government programs such as Social Security and business and labor contracts with price escalation formulas are linked to the CPI. Over time, the CPI implicitly incorporates price movements of the producer price indexes that gauge the price movements of all U.S. produced goods, and the price indexes associated with the gross domestic product (GDP) that encompass price movements of the household, business, government, and international sectors of the economy (chapter 3, "Economic Growth," covers the GDP). The CPI measures prices of items bought by households as representative of the price movements over time associated with the *production* of all goods and services. The chapter also includes a discussion of the inflationary and deflationary implications of the price movements of common stock and housing *assets*.

DEFINITIONS

Inflation is the general term given to a rise in overall prices for the total of all goods and services in the economy on an ongoing monthly, quarterly, and annual basis. Deflation represents a decline in overall prices of goods and services. Zero inflation occurs when there is no change in overall prices. It results from offsetting price increases and decreases among the individual items.

There are varying inflationary gradations that both affect and are affected by the economy quite differently. Examples of these gradations are: core inflation, accelerating inflation vs. disinflation, creeping inflation vs. hyperinflation, and tolerable inflation.

Core inflation is an objective measure of price change that excludes changes in energy and food prices. It is sometimes called the "underlying rate of inflation" because it abstracts from temporary price fluctuations in food and energy that may have nothing to do with long-term price pressures in the economy. Food prices fluctuate in large part due to changes in the weather associated with rainfall and frosts, as well as with natural disasters of floods and hurricanes. These physical elements directly affect plantings and harvests of grains, fruits, and vegetables, which in turn affect cattle prices through feed grain prices, with larger harvests tending to lower prices and smaller harvests tending to raise prices. Energy prices fluctuate as the discipline of member nations in maintaining cartel prices among the Organization of Petroleum Exporting Countries (OPEC) strengthens and weakens. When the nations tend to regulate their oil production in line with OPEC guidelines, the effect is to bolster prices, and when they do not follow the production guidelines, the effect is to weaken prices. Daniel Yergin illuminates the political problems of maintaining discipline among the OPEC nations in adhering to agreed-on country output quotas.[1]

Accelerating inflation and *disinflation* represent opposite movements of inflation. Accelerating inflation occurs when the rate of inflation increases, say from 2 percent in period one to 3 percent in period two. Disinflation occurs when the rate of inflation decreases, as from 3 percent in period one to 2 percent in period two.

Creeping inflation, sometimes called *price stability*, and *hyperinflation*, are qualitative terms for sharply differing rates of inflation. Creeping inflation is characterized by annual inflation rates of 1 to 2 percent. Hyperinflation reflects annual inflation rates in double digits, such as the 10 to 14 percent range from 1979 to 1981. The term hyperinflation is typically reserved for much greater price increases, such as 1,000 percent a year or more, that have occurred from time to time in other countries.[2] Use of this term for much lower price increases in the United States reflects the much lower political tolerance for inflation in the United States before strong anti-inflation fiscal and/or monetary policies, and as a last resort, temporary price-wage voluntary guidelines or mandatory controls, are implemented (see chapter 2 under Fiscal Policy, Monetary Policy, and Incomes Policies).

Tolerable inflation is another qualitative term, which typically represents an annual inflation rate of around 3 to 5 percent. It incorporates a value judgment that implies inflation should be lower, because the rate erodes the incomes of large segments of the population whose wages, profits from self-employment, interest and dividends from savings and investments, or retirement annuities do not keep pace with inflation. At the same time, the rate is not thought to cause extreme speculative behavior among households and businesses, nor does it lead to spiraling increases in interest rates.

Price and Wage Expectations

As measured by the average annual change in the CPI, prices of goods and services items typically bought by households have risen in all years from the 1940s to the early 2000s, except for 1949 and 1955. By contrast, consumer prices declined in four years of the 1920s and six years of the 1930s. Thus, inflation, though at varying rates, seems to be built into the economy since the end of the depression of the 1930s. One reason is that some prices and wages are set by multiyear contracts that call for scheduled increases over the life of the contract regardless of changing economic conditions. Another is that while some prices and wages actually decline during recessions or during periods of slow economic growth, the more typical experience during such periods is that the rate of increase only slows. Expectations of price change are an important intangible to monitor because they affect the behavior of businesses, workers, lenders, and borrowers in the determination of prices, wages, and interest rates. Expectations, at least temporarily, tend to be self-fulfilling forecasts. For example, when there is an expectation of high inflation, the various groups try to insulate themselves by raising price, wage, and interest rate demands in order to maintain the purchasing power of their future incomes. Similarly, an expectation of low inflation leads to smaller price, wage, and interest rate demands. Inflationary expectations helped fuel the large price increases in the 1970s, while lower inflationary expectations in the 1980s, 1990s, and early 2000s helped moderate price increases in those periods.

The general resistance by business to lowering prices of the products it sells and raising the wages and fringe benefits of its workers reflects its experience and perceptions from the business vantage point. Resistance to price decreases stems from the belief that gains in sales from the lower prices would not offset the declines in profits from the lower prices. Business also believes that small wage increases or even wage decreases would enable them to lessen or forego price increases for the products it sells in order to remain competitive, and thus limit job layoffs or increase hiring.

In contrast, workers favor large wage and fringe benefit increases from their vantage point. They believe that small wage increases or wage decreases would not result in stable or lower prices sufficient to stimulate enough sales of the products they produce in their workplaces to avoid job layoffs or to lead to increased hiring.

Differences between Goods and Services

Part of the long-term rise in measured inflation results from the continuing shift in the American economy from the consumption of commodities to the consumption of services. For example, from 1990 to 2002, the CPI increased at an annual rate of 2.7 percent, while the commodities component increased at an annual rate of 1.7 percent and the services component increased at an annual rate of 3.5 percent. This pattern of higher price increases for services occurred in all periods from the 1950s to the early 2000s.

The higher rate of increase for services is partly due to the higher labor content in the production of services in contrast to commodities, which use proportionately more machinery in their production. Services do not benefit as much as commodities from cost-saving productivity improvements in machinery (see chapter 10, "Productivity"). Another part of the difference reflects statistical difficulties in quantifying quality changes in services such as housing; transportation; medical care; education; personal, business, and professional services; and entertainment. If quality improvements are understated in services, the price increases are also overstated, but if the quality improvements are overstated in services, the price increases are understated (discussed in the following section on Methodology).

CPI METHODOLOGY

The CPI is prepared monthly by the Bureau of Labor Statistics (BLS) in the U.S. Department of Labor. It is published in the BLS monthly journals, the *Monthly Labor Review* and *CPI Detailed Report* (www.bls.gov).

Price indexes represent the combination of a wide range of goods and services into a single number in order to obtain an overall measure of price change from one period to the next. Two aspects in the preparation of price indexes have a major influence on the measured price change. One is how the various goods and services items are combined into a single number, which is discussed below under the subject of "weights." The other is accounting for improvements or deterioration in the performance, safety, and durability of the items being priced over time, which is discussed below under the subject of "quality." As background to this section, the reader may find it useful to review the section in chapter 1 under Index Numbers.

Structure of the CPI

The CPI combines the prices of the various goods and services purchased by households into an overall measure of the change in prices from one period to the next. The particular goods and services included in the CPI are weighted according to their proportions of spending in household budgets. At broad levels of aggregation, the component items of the CPI are food and beverages, housing, apparel, transportation, medical care, education and communication, and other goods and services. In practice, the computations are made in detail for many items within each major component. Food prices, for example, are calculated for a wide range of bakery, meat, dairy, produce items, beverages, and the like, and distinctions are made between food consumed in homes and in restaurants.

The data on household expenditures for specific goods and services items are obtained from surveys of households in geographic areas around the country conducted for the Bureau of Labor Statistics by the Census Bureau. These expenditure patterns are the distributional share that each item is of total expenditures. They are referred to as "weights," that sum in ratio form to 100. The weights are updated every two years. Each updated period is defined as the "base period" weights. Later weights representing the most recent period are defined as the "current period" weights. In 2002, weights averaging the spending patterns for 1999–2000 were introduced into the index. In 2004, weights for 2001–02 will be adopted, in 2006 the weights will represent 2003–04, and so on. Prior to 2002, the expenditure weights were updated approximately every ten years. A major question in index number construction is how to treat the base period and the current period weights. This is discussed below under Differential Averaging of Weights.

To calculate the CPI every month, monthly prices are obtained in surveys of retail and service business establishments, utilities, and households. The relative price movement from the base period month to the current month for each item is multiplied by its weight, and the sum of the products of all of the items is the index for the month.

Three CPI measures are published: the CPI-U, the C-CPI-U (chain CPI-U), and the CPI-W. They vary in expenditure weights and in the methods of averaging the weights between the base period and the current period of the index. The CPI-U and the C-CPI-U represent urban workers in all occupations, the unemployed, and retired persons, that account for 87 percent of the noninstitutional population. The CPI-W represents urban wage and clerical workers that account for 32 percent of the noninstitutional population.[3] The expenditure weights exclude spending patterns of rural households, military personnel, and persons in institutionalized housing such as prisons, old-age homes, and long-term hospitals.

General Attributes of the CPI

The CPI measures the relative change in prices as the percent movement between two periods. It does not measure the dollar amount of the costs. Thus, while the CPIs are prepared for local areas as well as for the national level, comparisons of the CPIs between local areas indicate only the differential percentage movements of prices between the areas, but not the actual dollar prices in the two areas. For example, the CPIs for the New York and the Cleveland metropolitan areas may indicate that prices have risen faster in Cleveland than in New York, but in dollars it may cost more to live in New York.

The CPI incorporates the actual transaction price of the item. This includes sales taxes, premiums and discounts from list prices, and import duties. In practice, there probably are a minority of cases in which actual prices net of premiums and discounts from list prices are not obtained.

Quality Change in the CPI

An essential concept of a price index is that its movements from one period to the next reflect only those price changes for goods and services items that occur independently of quality changes. Measuring quality change, both improvements and deterioration, is continuously examined in the ongoing work of preparing price indexes. This differs from the use of one weighting structure or the other noted above, which is a routinized computer operation whichever structure is adopted.

The CPI measure of quality change includes adjustments to the market price for the improvement or deterioration in the performance or in the size of an item. By contrast, no adjustments to the market price associated with changes in an item's aesthetic attributes are made in the CPI. For example, if a loaf of bread is increased (decreased) in size or nutrients, the changes are defined as quality improvements (deterioration). Similarly, if an automobile's specifications are changed to increase (decrease) its braking power, maneuverability, impact safety, or comfort, such changes are quality improvements (deterioration). By contrast, a change in styling such as sculptured lines or chrome in an automobile may result in a market price change, but styling is not defined as a quality change. Quality adjustments are discussed further below. The implementation of quality changes in the CPI is governed by the availability of data on the extent of the change. The CPI reflects the changes only if the dollar value of the quality change can be quantified.

Table 11.1 shows how changes in the quality and market price of an item translate into the price used in the CPI. In the monthly pricing of an item in the CPI, the price is compared with the item's specifications to determine if changes in specifications have occurred since the previous month. If there is a change in the specifications, and an estimate of the production cost of the specification changes is obtained, the table indicates how they combine with the market price in the CPI. The various combinations indicate that an increase or decrease in the market price in the store may be an increase, no change, or decrease in the CPI, and that no change in the store price may be a price increase, decrease, or no change in the CPI.

Two methods are used for estimating the effect of quality change on price changes: production costs and hedonic prices.

The *production cost* method is used for pricing most goods and services items. The quality adjustments are based on cost estimates associated with the quality change for producing the item. The adjustments are based on the premise that a quality improvement most likely means more and/or better labor or materials are required to produce the item, while a quality deterioration assumes that fewer or lower-grade resources are used in producing the item. The cost estimates are obtained from the manufacturer or service provider of the item. For example, if the impact safety of an automobile is improved by a better airbag or a better construction of the frame of the car, the increased production cost of the improvement is obtained from the automobile manufacturer.

While the above example is of quality improvements, the same procedure applies for quality deterioration, which is presumed to be associated with a decrease in production costs. If no credible estimate of the production cost of

Table 11.1

Relationship of Quality Change and Market Price in the CPI

Quality change	Market price	CPI price
Improvement	Increase by amount of improvement cost	No change
Improvement	Increase less than improvement cost	Decrease
Improvement	No change	Decrease
Improvement	Increase more than improvement cost	Increase
Deterioration	Decrease by amount of deterioration cost	No change
Deterioration	Decrease less than deterioration cost	Increase
Deterioration	No change	Increase
Deterioration	Decrease more than deterioration cost	Decrease
No change	Increase	Increase
No change	Decrease	Decrease
No change	No change	No change

the quality improvement or deterioration is available, the quality change is not incorporated in calculating the CPI.

A *hedonic price index* traces the effects of a group of attributes of a product that influences the price of an item, both through (a) the utility of the attributes to the buyer (demand), and (b) the cost of making the item to the producer (supply). Use of the word "hedonic" reflects its root meaning of pleasure, as the characteristics of a product in a hedonic price index are assessed for the pleasure, or utility, they give the buyer.

The hedonic method is currently used for pricing men's and women's apparel, computers, television sets, telephones and telephone/answering machine combinations, video cassette recorders (VCRs), digital video disk (DVD) players, camcorders, microwave ovens, refrigerators, clothes washers and driers, audio products, refrigerators, and college textbooks. Hedonic pricing requires far more data than production cost pricing, including continuous updates in the specifications of each product's component items.[4]

Use of hedonic price measurement substantially lessens the problem of accounting for complex issues of quality change for which the production cost method is inadequate. One such issue is the effect of rapid fashion changes in apparel. When new fashions are first introduced at the beginning of each winter, spring, summer, and fall season, their prices are typically higher than the previous year's prices. But the high prices are often short-lived, as they decline considerably toward the end of each season. Another such issue is the counterintuitive situation in which items having improvements in quality decline in price. Computers are an example of this, where quality improvements in capacity, speed, and portability have been accompanied by lower prices.

Table 11.2

Consumer Price Index Weights: Expenditure Patterns for 1999–2000

	CPI-U	CPI-W
Food and beverages	15.719	17.229
Housing	40.873	38.141
Apparel and upkeep	4.399	4.831
Transportation	17.055	19.393
Medical care	5.810	4.620
Recreation	6.019	5.649
Education and communication	5.813	5.637
Other goods and services	4.312	4.499
All items	100.000	100.000

Source: U.S. Bureau of Labor Statistics.

Sampling Error in the CPI

Because the monthly price data are collected from a sample of retail and other businesses selling to households, the CPI is subject to errors associated with sampling rather than surveying an entire group. For 2002, the standard error for the CPI-U was plus or minus 0.06 percentage point for the month-to-month change. Thus, if the CPI increases from one month to the next by 0.2 percent, in two of three cases the true price increase ranges from 0.14 percent to 0.26 percent, and in nineteen of twenty cases, the increase ranges from 0.08 percent to 0.32 percent.

Differential Weights of the CPI-U and the CPI-W

Table 11.2 shows the weights based on the 1999–2000 expenditure patterns for CPI-U and CPI-W (the CPI-U and the C-CPI-U have the same weights). The largest expenditures in both indexes are for housing, transportation, and food. The main differences in the indexes occur in food, housing, transportation, and medical care. The CPI-U contains proportionately more spending for housing and medical care than the CPI-W, while the CPI-W contains proportionately more spending for food and transportation.

Differential Averaging of Weights

The CPI estimating procedures for combining the various goods and services items into one overall number vary in the extent to which the three indexes incorporate geometric averaging. Geometric averaging, in contrast to arithmetic averaging, treats weight changes and price increases and decreases symmetrically, without the distortion of shifting bases between beginning and ending periods.[5] Arithmetic averaging assumes the same proportions of item expenditures in both the beginning and ending periods. Geometric averaging represents the changes in item proportions that actually occur over time. The advantage of geometric averaging is that it accounts for shifts in household expenditures from one product to another because of quality, price, advertising, tastes, or any other reason.

The calculation of the CPI in terms of the weighting structure is done in two steps. In step 1, the C-CPI-U, the CPI-U, and the CPI-W all are based on geometric averaging for items within generic categories, such as for different models of refrigerators and of ranges. In step 2, the C-CPI-U takes geometric averaging to the higher levels of aggregation by averaging between different generic categories, such as between refrigerators and ranges, and in fact between all categories of spending.

As of 2003, the C-CPI-U uses geometric averaging for all items except for rent, utilities, and medical services. This reflects the fact that there is little ongoing substitution shopping for these items: rental housing is often based on a contract period; alternative electric, natural gas, and water utilities under deregulation typically are not available to households; and medical services are often determined by insurance plans. In the future, however, if ongoing substitution of these items becomes more prevalent, they would be incorporated into the C-CPI-U with geometric averaging.

The difference between the CPI-U and the CPI-W on the one hand, and the C-CPI-U on the other, is the inclusion in the C-CPI-U of full geometric averaging across all expenditure categories, not just within generic categories, as in the CPI-U and the CPI-W. The distinction is caused by the delay in obtaining up-to-date expenditure patterns from the household surveys. Because household expenditure data are obtained with a lag of approximately one year, they are incorporated as a revision into the C-CPI-U thirteen months after the initial estimates were published. This contrasts with the CPI-U and the CPI-W, which are final when published, as revisions are made only as exceptions due to a particular problem that appears later, rather than on an ongoing routine basis. The "finality" of the CPI-U and the CPI-W is important in the real-world uses of the CPI for Social Security and other legislated programs and for wage and business contract escalations. Finality allows the escalations to be implemented without the uncertainty of subsequent revisions in the CPI.

The delay in the household survey data has been reduced from the previous lag of two years to one year, and perhaps a further shortening to less than a year will be made in the future, but there will always be some delay in the

C-CPI-U that will probably limit its use in legislative, wage, and contract applications.

The C-CPI-U is new, with the first estimates being published for 2000. The BLS considers the price movements of the CPI-U and the C-CPI-U to be equally valid. Indexes based on geometric averaging are referred to as superlative indexes.

Development of a Cost-of-Living Index

The CPI is sometimes referred to as a cost-of-living index (COLI), though it only partially conforms to a theoretical COLI. A COLI measures price movements associated with the minimum expenditures necessary to maintain a constant standard of living. In contrast, the CPI moves toward this concept in the process of updating expenditure patterns and introducing geometric averaging, but because of delays in obtaining data that represent expenditures on a current basis, the CPI is not a COLI. The CPI also does not include other attributes of a COLI, such as accounting for household preferences between work and leisure, how changes in income tax rates affect the household's after-tax income and thus the household's financial ability to buy the same goods and services as in the base period, and social problems of crime and pollution that cause households to move to other areas or buy protective items, as noted by Patrick Jackman.[6]

The BLS has long used the concept of a COLI for handling practical questions in designing the CPI, as noted in the *BLS Handbook of Methods* and by John Greenlees.[7] The general principle is that prices should represent the actual dollar impacts on household budgets. Examples of such applications in the CPI that were consistent with the COLI concept are: (a) the housing index for owner-occupied single-family houses, which had been based on the change in housing prices of actual purchases of new or existing housing financed with FHA mortgages plus the change in mortgage interest rates associated with the acquired housing, plus the change in property taxes and insurance for all homeowners, was replaced with the implied rent that would be charged for an owner-occupied house based on the contract rent charged for similar houses in the local area; (b) the costs of complying with the requirements of the Clean Air Act to reduce pollution are not deducted from the prices of new cars and gasoline; and (c) the introduction of geometric averaging noted above. There is an ongoing interest in moving the CPI toward a COLI as much as possible, as indicated in the report of the National Research Council, and in the Workshop on the NRC report, and in articles by Charles Schultze and Katharine Abraham.[8] These define a COLI as a measure of change in expenditures that a household would have to make in order to maintain a specified standard of living that is constant over the time period being measured. Thus, it abstracts from changes in income or tastes that would lead to a change in the standard.

There are two versions of the idea of a COLI. One is an unconditional COLI that encompasses such factors as life expectancy, crime, and the environment that are related to issues of public policy. The other is a conditional COLI that is confined to private goods and services in which the public issues are held constant. The preference in the references cited in the above paragraph is for a conditional COLI.

But while the preference is for a conditional COLI, there is no consensus on whether the development of a COLI should be pursued. This reflects the vexing issues of maintaining a constant standard of living measure because rising incomes and changing tastes in fact result in changing standards, as well as the complex statistical methodologies and data collection that would have to be satisfactorily met.

ANALYSIS OF TRENDS

Figure 11.1a shows inflation rates in the CPI-U including and excluding food and energy prices from 1980 to 2002. The sharp disinflation during 1981–86 included a deep recession, accelerated weakness in the bargaining position of labor unions with the rising use of replacement workers by companies and the federal government in the face of strikes, and weakness in oil prices stemming from energy conservation and the development of additional world sources of oil supplies that began in the 1970s. Inflation accelerated during 1987–90, during most of which time economic growth was strong, but growth then declined into the 1990–91 recession (the recession period also bracketed the Gulf War buildup and the war itself).

Inflation was generally stable around 2 to 3 percent during 1992–2002. Economic growth as measured by the real GDP accelerated from an annual average of 3.2 percent from 1991 to 1996 to 4.1 percent from 1996 to 2000 (chapter 3 discusses the real GDP). Economic growth fell to 0.3 percent in the 2001 recession year and rose to 2.4 percent in the 2002 recovery year. The cyclical expansion from the early 1990s to 2000 was extraordinary for maintaining relatively low price inflation during a period of rising demand for goods and services. One explanation for the low inflation was the rise in productivity (see chapter 10 under The Productivity Rebound).

Relative Movements of the C-CPI-U and the CPI-U

The C-CPI-U was first published for the year 2000. The C-CPI-U had smaller price increases than the CPI-U in both 2001 and 2002. Preliminary estimates of the differential in 2001 were 0.7 percentage point (2.8–2.1) in 2001 and 0.4

percentage point (1.6–1.2) in 2002. The differentials reflect the effect of the changing weights in the C-CPI-U that encompass more recent household expenditures for items that decline in price more or increase in price less than the item weighting structure in the CPI-U. Specifically, this reflects the introduction of full geometric averaging across all expenditure categories in the C-CPI-U, not just within generic categories as is done in the CPI-U (see above under Differential Averaging of Weights).

Computers are an example of a growth product in which geometric averaging is important because computer prices have been falling while computer expenditures have been increasing rapidly over time. This reflects the fact that new higher-quality computers have been lower in price than the old lower-quality computers had been when they were introduced. Thus, the weight of computers in geometric averaging is much larger than it is in arithmetic averaging.

Core Price Change

Core price change, which excludes the volatile food and energy prices, was less volatile than the all-items CPI in Figure 11.1a (see Definitions at the beginning of the chapter). The more stable core rate was particularly apparent during 1984–91 and 1996–2002.

Figure 11.1b shows the breakdown of energy and food prices. While food price increases fluctuated within a range of 1 to 9 percent (more typically in the 2 to 4 percent range), energy prices were far more volatile. For example, energy prices increased by 31 percent in 1980, declined by 13 percent in 1986, increased by 8 percent in 1990, decreased by 8 percent in 1998, increased by 17 percent in 2000, and declined by 6 percent in 2002. The energy component represents 6.7 percent of the CPI, of which motor fuel accounts for 46 percent, electricity for 36 percent, natural gas for 15 percent, home heating oil for 2 percent, and other household fuel (coal, propane, wood) for 1 percent.

I am not aware of analytic assessments that specifically address the spillover of sharp changes in energy prices into the nonenergy sectors. Spillover leads to the higher (or lower) energy prices becoming embedded (or diminished) throughout the economy, where they result in a longer-term higher (or lower) level of production costs and prices of consumer goods. In practice, estimates are sometimes based on rules of thumb derived from econometric models that incorporate the effect of price movements as they filter through the economy. The distinction that separates energy prices from other prices in the CPI does not get at the spillover effects.

In the two decades following the energy crisis that erupted in the early 1970s with the Arab oil embargo, and that was intensified by the Iranian revolution in the late 1970s and early 1980s, and then in the early 1990s by the Persian Gulf War, there has been a relative decline in the consumption of oil in the U.S.

economy, and in fact worldwide. The focus on oil in this discussion reflects the dominance of oil in overall energy usage. Based on a United Nations report of the GDP per unit of energy use, which uses the purchasing power parity measure for developing comparative GDP levels in different countries, the U.S. ratio rose from 1.6 in 1980 to 3.9 in 2000. This pattern also occurred in practically all other countries where data for both years are available.[9] This relative decline in oil consumption mitigates the dependence of the world economies on oil and the vulnerability of the world economies to sharp increases in the price of oil. It means that on a relative basis, a disruption of oil supplies in the 2000s would cause less economic distress than it did in the 1970s.

Several factors appear to have contributed to the relative decline in consumption of energy worldwide, including energy conservation, more efficient use of energy in the production of goods and services, and the long-run trend toward services which consume less energy than goods per unit of output in their production. The absolute amounts of energy consumption have of course increased over time due to worldwide population growth and industrialization. In turn, the absolute rise in fossil energy consumption drives the long-run increase in global warming, with its attendant current and future negative economic and noneconomic consequences.

Commodities versus Services

The production of commodities (goods) is typically less labor intensive than the production of services. Thus, commodity production benefits more than services production from the use of increasingly efficient equipment, intermediate materials, and energy consumption, which technologically results in greater productivity increases for commodities than for services. Also, the inflation-adjusted real output of commodities is often easier to quantify than the real output of services. For example, the production of apples, coats, cars, and television sets is easier to measure than the output of teachers, doctors, lawyers, scientists, accountants, stock brokers, athletes, secretaries, computer programers, and hair stylists.

Figure 11.1c shows the CPI movements of commodities, commodities excluding food and energy, and services from 1980 to 2002. These indicate that the prices of services are far more stable than those of commodities. But the prices of commodities excluding food and energy appear no more volatile than those of services. Energy prices account for most of the volatility of the food and energy component, as is apparent in Figure 11.1b, but the BLS does not prepare regular calculations of the commodities component excluding energy.

Table 11.3 shows long-run average annual price movements for the CPI-U for the all-items aggregate and the commodities and services components from 1960 to 2002. For the entire period and in all decades, services prices increased

Table 11.3

**CPI-U All Items, Commodities, and Services, Annual
Percentage Change: 1960–2002**

	All items	Commodities	Services
1960–70	2.7	2.2	3.8
1970–80	7.8	7.5	8.3
1980–90	4.7	3.6	6.0
1990–2000	2.8	2.0	3.4
2000–2002	2.2	0.2	3.6
1960–2002	4.4	3.6	5.3

Source: Based on U.S. Bureau of Labor Statistics data.

more than commodities prices. Over the entire forty-two–year period, the annual increase for the all items aggregate averaged 4.4 percent, commodities increased at an annual rate of 3.6 percent, and services increased at an annual rate of 5.3 percent.

Domestic Price Change and Imports

Imported goods and services provide additional choices for U.S. households, businesses, and governments in the specification, quality, and price of items purchased. Imports are also a surrogate additional industrial capacity when there is a shortage of some items.

The effect of import prices on domestic inflation cannot be determined from the comparisons of price movements of imported goods and the CPI. In exceptional situations where imported items have a significant role in the U.S. economy and the prices of those items change sharply, such as oil, a broad gauge of their short-term effects can be estimated. In the case of oil, economy-wide price changes in the CPI both including and excluding energy are regularly published, so the effect of sudden sharp changes in oil prices on the overall economy is apparent.

Theoretically, imports would be expected to lessen inflation in the United States through the increasing competition they bring to American markets. But there are no systematic analyses of the magnitudes of this.

Moreover, focusing on imported and domestic prices neglects the basic problem that U.S. manufacturing has lost its competitive position for many products in world markets, as discussed in Chapter 3 under Reclaiming American Manufacturing. In this context, relative movements of U.S. and foreign prices for particular goods is in effect a non issue.

Figure 11.1a **Consumer Price Index-U, All Items versus All Items Excluding Food and Energy—Annual Percentage Change: 1980–2002**

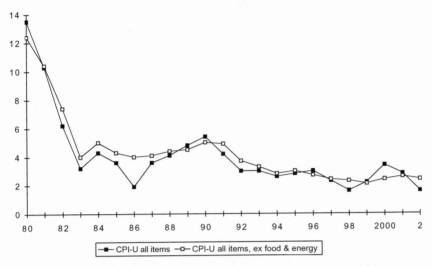

Source: Based on U.S. Bureau of Labor Statistics data.

Figure 11.1b **Consumer Price Index-U, Energy versus Food Prices—Annual Percentage Change: 1980–2002**

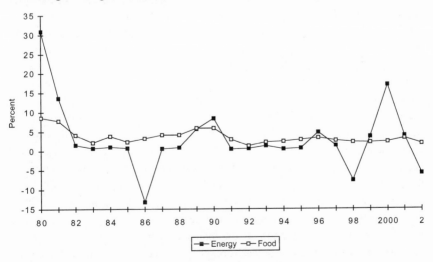

Source: Based on U.S. Bureau of Labor Statistics data.

**Figure 11.1c Consumer Price Index-U, Commodities versus Services—
Annual Percentage Change: 1980–2002**

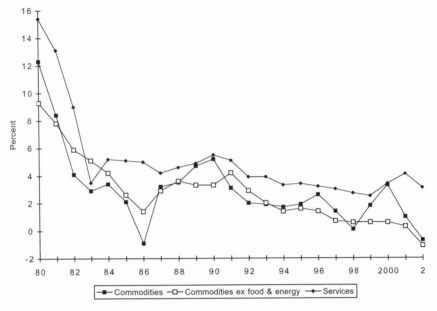

Source: Based on U.S. Bureau of Labor Statistics data.

In terms of the effect of changes in the value of the dollar on the U.S. inflation rate, the issue hinges on the extent to which the change in the value of the dollar is reflected in offsetting prices of imported goods, which is referred to as pass-through rates (chapter 6 discusses the value of the dollar). In an analysis of the relationship of changes in the value of the dollar to the CPI inflation rate over the 1973–95 period, Roberto Chang found that changes in the value of the dollar had a relatively small effect on inflation.[10] For example, a sizable decline in the value of the dollar of 10 percent leads to an increase in the CPI of 0.76 percent (i.e., of what it would otherwise be) in the first year following the shock. Assuming an initial inflation of 3 percent, the first year after the dollar decline would raise the rate to 3.02 percent (3 × 1.0076). Subsequent increases of 0.96 percent in the second year, 0.45 percent in the third year, and 0.21 percent in the fourth year would have similarly small inflationary increases (of course, the percentages are interesting for their low magnitude, not for the specific numbers). The study shows a much smaller effect of a rise in the value of the dollar lowering inflation. Chang explains the relatively small effect of a dollar decline on inflation as due to the fact that foreign firms exporting to the United States price their products in light of the competitive prices in U.S. markets. Thus, following a decline in the dollar, the firms consider making price changes in their products in part to maintain their market share (maintain current prices), and in part to maintain profit margins (raise prices). This limits the extent of price change following a dollar change, and results in part of the dollar decline being absorbed by lower profits. It is referred to as "pricing to market," and is contrary to the "law of one price," which presumes that firms charge the same price for the same item in all countries. In a review of the literature on pricing and exchange rates, Pinelopi Goldberg and Michael Knetter found that pricing-to-market is the worldwide practice.[11]

In an earlier study, Wing Woo came to a similar conclusion regarding the importance to foreign firms exporting to the United States in pricing their products to be competitive in U.S. markets.[12] Thus, a primary factor determining prices of foreign goods was the aim of foreign exporters to maintain their market share in pricing actions following a change in the value of the dollar. Woo also noted that changes in the value of the dollar can affect inflation through their effect on demand, as the markets for items produced by U.S. export and import-competing firms are influenced by fluctuations in the dollar.

In an assessment of various econometric models of the effects of sharp increases or decreases in world oil prices on economic growth and employment in the United States and other countries, Douglas Bohi and Michael Toman found conflicting evidence of substantial impacts.[13] Thus, they are skeptical that the sharp price increases of the 1970s had macroeconomic disruptions of the magnitude that led to cyclical recessions in the 1970s and the 1980s.

In evaluating the effects of imports and the value of the dollar on inflation, the analyst should focus on large changes in prices over sustained periods. With the notable exception of oil prices, the effects of changes in the value of the dollar and import prices tend to have a small effect on inflation for short periods.

Concern about Deflation: Common Stock and Housing Asset Prices and the CPI

This section focuses on concerns about the possible deleterious effects on the economy of a deflation in the asset prices of common stocks and housing and in the prices of goods and services produced on a current basis. Deflation is defined as a decline in overall prices. Asset prices represent wealth of the holders of the assets. By contrast, the CPI represents prices of goods and services bought for household consumption. The CPI implicitly incorporates the price movements of capital investments in equipment and structures that are part of the production costs of the household goods and services.

Common stock and housing assets are a source of income when they are sold, and are a source of collateral for borrowing when they are held. Depending on the difference in the purchase and sale price of the asset, the holder realizes

Figure 11.2 **Common Stocks Price Index and House Price Index (Asset Prices) and the Consumer Price Index, Annual Percentage Change: 1975–2002**

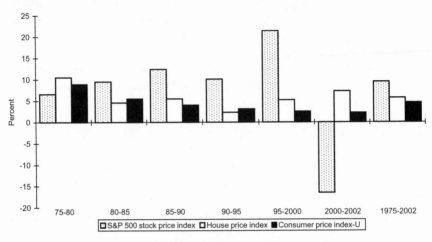

Sources: Based on Standard and Poor's, Office of Federal Housing Enterprise Oversight, and U.S. Bureau of Labor Statistics data.

a profit or loss from the sale. The income derived from the sale of assets can be used for buying goods and services or other assets or for saving. Common stock is also a source of current income from dividend receipts.

Price movements of common stock and housing assets impact the wealth effect for spending on goods and services. The wealth effect represents the income from the sale of assets or from their use as collateral for borrowing as in home equity loans (see chapter 4 under the Wealth Effect). Price movements of stock and housing assets also affect retirement incomes.

Figure 11.2 shows the average annual price movements of the Standard and Poor's 500 common stock price index (S&P), the house price index of single-family houses (HPI), and the consumer price index (CPI-U) during subperiods from 1975 to 2002. The S&P and the CPI-U are calculated from *annual averages* of the beginning and ending years of each time period (e.g., 1975 beginning year and 1980 ending year for the 1975–80 period). The HPI is calculated from the fourth quarter of the beginning year to the fourth quarter of the ending year (e.g., 1975:4 to 1980:4).

The S&P contains common stocks of 500 companies traded on the New York Stock Exchange, the Nasdaq, and the AMEX. (In 2003, the market value of companies on the NYSE accounted for 84.8 percent of the S&P index, Nasdaq companies accounted for 15.0 percent, and AMEX companies for 0.2 percent.) The stocks are averaged in the index according to the market value of each company, which gives price movements of companies with large market values more weight than those with small market values.

The HPI is prepared quarterly by the Office of Federal Housing Enterprise Oversight, an independent agency under the U.S. Department of Housing and Urban Development (www.ofheo.gov).[14] The HPI is based on repeat sales or refinancings on mortgages for single-family houses that have been purchased or securitized through secondary mortgage transactions by the Federal National Mortgage Corporation and the Federal Home Loan Mortgage Corporation. The pricing of repeat sales for the same house helps control for differences in the quality of houses included in the sample of houses in the HPI. This is referred to as a "constant quality" house price index, though the HPI does not adjust for improvements to the house between sales. Repeat sales for the same house that occur years apart are averaged at quarterly rates of change in the intervening period. Greater weight is given in the HPI to repeat sales that occur in a short rather than in a long time frame because of the greater likelihood that improvements were made to houses with long periods between sales. This treatment reflects the fact that improvements diverge from the constant quality definition. The HPI covers conventional mortgages only and is limited to mortgage loans that do not exceed a "conforming loan limit." The conforming loan limit is based on the amount of the mortgage loan, not the value of the house. In 2002, the conforming loan limit was $300,700, which thus included houses of higher values. But the HPI does not cover expensive houses with larger mortgage loans. Condominiums and multi-unit housing are excluded from the HPI.

Figure 11.2 indicates that over the 1975–2002 period, stock prices had the highest average annual price increases (9.5 percent), followed by house prices (5.7 percent) and the CPI (4.6 percent). Within five-year intervals from 1975 to 2000 and the two-year interval from 2000 to 2002, stock prices had the greatest price increases except during 1975–80, and they also had the only price decrease, which occurred during 2000–02. House prices increased more than the CPI except during the 1980–85 and 1990–95 periods.

The volatility of stock prices was highlighted by the average annual increase of 21.4 percent during 1995–2000 followed by the annual decrease of 16.5 percent during 2000–02. The speculative bloating of 1995–2000 fed part of the economic growth during that period, which resulted in wide and long-lasting ramifications for economic growth in the first decade of the 2000s, as discussed in chapter 3 under Assessment of Economic Growth in the First Decade of the twenty-first Century (the stock market is covered further in chapter 12, "Finance").

Deflation and the Economy

Why is there a concern about deflation? It results from three potential snowballing effects. First, price declines in stock market and housing assets can diminish the wealth effects of household spending. Second, declining prices of goods and services lower business profits, which can result in job layoffs and lower worker incomes, and in declines in capital investment in equipment and structures. Third, expectation of future price decreases encourages delays in spending, thus weakening economic growth. All of these are envisioned as interacting in feeding a continuous decline in economic growth that brings much hardship.

I summarize here the historical studies of the depression of the 1930s and the general economic processes of deflation that can lead to economic distress, as articulated by Bradford DeLong.[15] Starting with the depression which had an important antecedent in the stock market speculation of the 1920s as a precursor to the crash in 1929, there are various interpretations of the propagation in the 1930s of collapsing production, employment, and business enterprises, plus losses of homes and life savings. Interpretations of the effects of deflation in the depression, with the authors' last names in parentheses, include: falling prices and the fear of falling prices caused businesses to cut production (Keynes); deflation caused bankruptcy or near bankruptcy for financial and leveraged nonfinancial companies (Fisher); deterioration of banks' balance sheets from the lowered value of collateral and declining interest payments by debtors led to a contracting money supply and production that was intensified by the inadequate response of the Federal Reserve in fostering an expansive monetary policy (Friedman and Schwartz); deflation caused corporate debt to worsen corporate balance sheets, generating the fear that businesses would go into bankruptcy, which lessened the likelihood of lenders to envision extending loans to businesses (Temin); internationally, the fear of some countries that other countries would depreciate their currencies led to deflationary policies that reduced the money supply (Eichengreen); for countries that devalued their currencies, its businesses and banks that borrowed abroad in gold could not pay the interest on their debts, causing destructive consequences for them (Kindleberger); those who were not heavily invested in the stock market still found it advisable to cut back on spending (Romer). In retrospect, given these differing explanations of the causes of the depression, one may reasonably conclude that we still do not understand the depression.

Still, there is a common theme of financial fragility affecting business balance sheets throughout the above accounts of the depression, though the financial fragility is approached from different perspectives. The extrapolation of financial fragility to the economic conditions in the first decade of the twenty-first century is an important issue affecting the possible adverse consequences of deflation currently. The risk involves stock market securities and real estate holdings that were pledged as collateral for loans. If the stock market drops even further than it did during 2001 and 2002, and if housing and other real estate prices decline, the financial vulnerability associated with the loan collaterals will increase.

In terms of monetary policy, the low interest rates pursued by the Federal

Reserve from 2001 to 2003 have not been effective in stimulating economic growth (see chapters 2 and 11 for the Federal Reserve and monetary policies). Price expectations also can be important, as DeLong notes. Thus, when investors and financial markets expect week economic growth and prices, even the interest rates for three-month U.S. Treasury bills of under two percent in 2002 and close to one percent in the first half of 2003 have limited effects on bolstering economic growth. A further deterrent to the effectiveness of low nominal interest rates is that deflation raises real interest rates (nominal interest adjusted for inflation) with the consequent restraining effect on economic growth.

For those who want to follow through on the analysis and implications of deflation, I recommend researching the balance sheets of American businesses for assessing the vulnerability of the economy to deflation. One data source for such analyses is the Quarterly Financial Report *prepared by the Census Bureau.*

INFLATION AND CAPACITY UTILIZATION

The capacity utilization rate (CUR) measures the proportion of industrial structures and equipment that is used in producing industrial output. Structures and equipment are the indicator of capacity. For example, if a factory with the structures and equipment capacity to produce 1,000 cans of paint a month actually produces 800 cans a month, its CUR is 80 percent and its unutilized capacity is 20 percent.

The Federal Reserve Board provides monthly CUR measures for the manufacturing, mining, and electric and gas utilities industries (www.federalreserve .gov). The capacity measures are integrated with the Federal Reserve's industrial production index. The data are available for manufacturing industries beginning with 1948 and for mining and utilities beginning with 1967.

Theoretically, the direction and level of CURs indicate the degree of inflationary pressure in the economy. A rising CUR tends to reduce unit costs of production for a time, as the existing capacity produces a larger volume of goods. The cost advantage of the larger volume (increasing returns to scale) continues until the CUR reaches a level at which further increases in production raise unit costs (decreasing returns to scale). The latter occurs because of machinery breakdowns, increasing use of older and less efficient equipment, hiring of less productive workers as unemployment falls, and laxness by managements in holding down costs, which are referred to as X-efficiency (see chapter 10 under Returns to Scale).

The CUR level at which the turnaround in returns to scale first impacts costs and then inflation varies among industries and is hard to quantify precisely. At this threshold, increasing production and rising production costs foster higher prices, and decreasing production and costs foster stable or declining prices. Analogously, rising production costs spur companies to reduce costs by increasing capacity through new investment in structures and equipment, and relatively low and falling CURs reduce business incentives to expand capacity. Replacements of run-down and outmoded capital facilities account for greater shares of structures and equipment investment during slow growth periods, as discussed in chapter 5.

This outline of changing returns to scale of production costs is complicated for their effects on prices because prices are affected by the demand for a product as well as by the costs of producing it (supply). Thus, a rising CUR implies a rising demand, which leads to a higher price than that simply associated with lower unit production costs. Carol Corrado and Joe Mattey point to different product cost responses to higher CURs depending on the technologies of continuous processing in such industries as aluminum, steel, petroleum refining, paper, cement, and industrial chemicals, and for various types of assembly operations.[16] They also note that increasing returns to scale for several individual manufacturing industries were reported in two studies. But they find it is difficult to extrapolate increasing returns to scale for individual industries to aggregate price levels in the economy because rising wage and other production costs during periods of high economic growth are accompanied by increasing CURs throughout the economy that lead to overall price increases.

Capacity Utilization Methodology

The CUR measure is the percentage that the industrial production index is of industrial structures and equipment capacity in the manufacturing, mining, and electric and gas utilities industries. The industrial production index is the numerator, industrial capacity is the denominator, and the ratio is multiplied by 100.

$$\text{Capacity utilization rate} = \frac{\text{Industrial production index}}{\text{Industrial capacity}} \times 100$$

The industrial production index (IPI) measures the output of the manufacturing, mining, and electric and gas utilities industries. The monthly output data are based on direct data on production volume adjusted for inflation, and indirect data on production worker hours or electric kilowatt-hour consumption in the various component industries, depending on the available information for each industry. The indirect labor and electricity data are converted to production based on projections of historical trends on labor productivity and of technological trends in the usage of electricity in the various industries. Annual revisions to the IPI incorporate a greater proportion of direct production data than the monthly data. The various component industries are combined into the index by weights associated with each industry's value added in the five-year economic censuses.

An industry's capacity is measured by its capital structures and equipment facilities that are operated on a schedule of the typical working day and week. The capacity measures assume an eight-hour day and five-day working week for most industries, though these are higher for some industries such as steel, petroleum refining, and utilities, that maintain production around the clock. The capacity measures for manufacturing are developed mainly through an indirect estimating procedure based on a Census Bureau survey of capacity utilization in manufacturing. For selected other industries such as paper, industrial chemicals, petroleum refining, and motor vehicles, capacity estimates are based on production rates data obtained from trade sources.

Capacity (the denominator of the CUR) rises at a relatively steady rate with no cyclical ups and downs because in any period, capacity is composed mainly of existing facilities, with only marginal net changes made for the addition of new investment and deduction of depreciated facilities. The CUR for all manufacturing industries usually ranges from 75 percent to 85 percent because of cyclical movements of industrial production (the numerator of the CUR).

The CUR for all manufacturing typically does not approach or exceed 100 percent. The major exception is high mobilization during wars, when industry undergoes a widespread conversion to two and three eight-hour shifts a day. Because such multiple shifts are not considered typical capacity levels that can be sustained over long periods in peacetime, they do not result in an upward adjustment in the estimated capacity levels. Thus, the CUR theoretically may reach the 100 percent range. However, industry would probably operate at this level only during a full-scale war, and perhaps not even then. For example, the peak manufacturing CUR in the Korean and Vietnam wars was 92 percent and then only for a few months. There are no estimates for World War II, because CUR measures were not developed until 1948. It remains unclear whether even a full-scale war would raise the CURs to the 100 percent range.

Measurement Problems

Production capacity is an elusive concept to define and measure. Theoretically, a business' ultimate capacity is the output it could produce if it operated seven days a week, twenty-four hours a day, with allowance for maintenance of existing equipment, shortages of materials, and other downtime. This level of operation is referred to as "engineering capacity." Other than in wartime, it is realistic only for industries with continuing process operations in which it is more efficient to operate around the clock. "Practical capacity" refers to the usual operations schedule that is realistically maintained on a continuing basis. These vary among industries from single and multiple eight-hour shifts over a five-day week to continuous operations seven days a week, as noted above. Practical capacity is the implied definition in the CUR measures.

Another continuing problem with any statistical measure of capacity is whether plants that are closed down in recessions are considered permanently removed from production, or if this capacity is considered "found" and available again in expansions. While the Federal Reserve uses consistency checks with alternative data and statistical procedures to modify aberrant movements in the capacity figures, a considerable amount of indirect estimating is associated with the preparation of the capacity figures. Also, the capacity data do not include imports of goods, which are an important source of added supply in some industries, and which when temporary, increase short-term capacity, and when permanent, increase long-term capacity.

In short, the capacity measures have basic limitations both in their definitions and in quantification. Therefore, measures of capacity and of capacity utilization should be considered broad orders of magnitude.

Trends in the Capacity Utilization and Inflation Relationship

The relationship between the CUR and CPI here focuses on the CUR in all manufacturing industries. Manufacturing accounted for 14.7 percent of the GDP in 2001, and the other components of the CU measure totaled 3.6 percent of the GDP (mining was 1.4 percent and electric and gas utilities 2.2 percent). The analysis is confined to manufacturing because the production of manufactured goods incorporates purchases of mineral products and electric and gas energy.

Figure 11.3 shows the CUR (annual percentage level) and the CPI-U (annual percentage change) from 1955 to 2002. It indicates that when the CUR rises above the often-cited threshold level of 82 percent, the CPI increase is often no more than 3 percent. In fact, higher CURs that were accompanied by higher rates of CPI inflation seemed to be more related to periods of sharply rising oil prices as in the early 1970s, the late 1970s and the early 1980s, and the early 1990s. These were all periods of politically related interrupted oil supplies— the Arab oil embargo, the Iranian revolution, and the Persian Gulf War. In the 1960s, before the emergence of OPEC as an aggressive cartel, it was only when the CURs reached the exceptionally high rates in the high 80s, that the CPI inflation rate peaked at 5.5 percent and 5.7 percent in 1969 and 1970, respectively. This period reflected both the expanding civilian economy and the accelerated increase in military spending for the Vietnam War. But these inflation rates were below several of the years from the early 1970s to the early 1980s, which approached and exceeded double digits.

Figure 11.3 **Capacity Utilization Rate versus Consumer Price Index-U: 1955–2002**

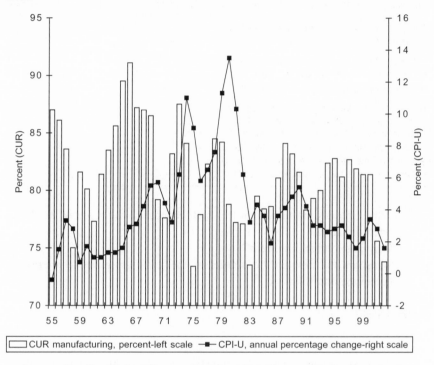

Sources: Based on Federal Reserve Board and U.S. Bureau of Labor Statistics data.

This record suggests features of the relationship between the CUR and the CPI. First, a threshold CUR level above 82 percent does not by itself signify a period of sharply rising inflation. Second, when a period of rapidly rising inflation did occur, it was in the context of rising oil prices.

REVIEW QUESTIONS

- What is the nature of price movements during periods of accelerating inflation, hyperinflation, disinflation, zero inflation, and deflation?
- Why is the weighting structure important for a price index? Use the C-CPI-U as an example.
- How would the CPI have to change to be a cost-of-living index?
- What is the effect of the following quality and market price changes on the CPI?
- How do sharp changes in energy prices affect overall prices?

	CPI Price		
Quality Characteristics and Market Price	No change	Increase	Decrease
A loaf of bread is made smaller and the price is changed.	—	—	—
Airbags are made standard equipment on a new car and the price of the car is increased by the cost of the airbags.	—	—	—
An apartment building is renovated by dividing each four-room apartment renting for $800 a month into two two-room apartments each renting for $600 a month. The renovation cost is $100 a month for each two-room apartment.	—	—	—

- What factors limit the extent to which changes in the value of the dollar affect inflation?
- Why is deflation a concern?
- What are the problematic aspects of the relationship between capacity utilization and inflation?

Extra Credit

- Suppose you were writing a business contract calling for payments over the next several years to be indexed to a major inflation gauge. What measure would you choose (CPI-U, C-CPI-U, CPI-W)? Why?
- How do stock market and housing asset prices differ from the CPI in their impacts on the economy?

NOTES

1. Daniel Yergin, *The Prize: The Epic Quest for Oil, Money, and Power* (Simon and Schuster, 1991), pp. 522–25, 636–38, 718–21, 746–51, 758–64.
2. Robert J. Gordon, *Macroeconomics*, 6th ed. (Harper Collins College Publishers, 1993), pp. 284–85.
3. The CPI-W encompasses wage and clerical workers who work at least twenty-six weeks per year and whose income from work accounts for 50 percent or more of their total annual income. The occupations of workers in the CPI-W whose expenditure patterns are measured are: administrative support including clerical, protective services, forestry, fishing, and groundskeeping; machinist, repairers, and precision production; construction and mining; handler, helper, and laborer; machine operator, assembler and inspector; transportation operator; and sales retail.
4. For examples of the hedonic method, see Paul R. Liegey, "Apparel price indexes: effects of hedonic adjustment," *Monthly Labor Review*, May 1994; and Paul Liegey and Nicole Shepler, "Using hedonic methods to quality adjust VCR prices: plucking a piece of the U.S. CPI's 'low hanging fruit,' " *Monthly Labor Review*, September

1999. Hedonic price adjustment for computers was first developed by the BLS for the producer price index for finished goods, and that methodology is also used for the CPI computer hedonic price index, see James Sinclair and Brian Catron, "An experimental price index for the computer industry," *Monthly Labor Review*, October 1990.

For critiques of the hedonic method, see Jerry Hausman, "Sources of Bias and Solutions to Bias in the Consumer Price Index," *Journal of Economic Perspectives*, Winter 2003; and David E. Lebow and Jeremy B. Rudd, "Measurement Error in the Consumer Price Index: Where Do We Stand?" *Journal of Economic Literature*, March 2003. For a recommendation that the BLS expand experimental research on hedonic methods but be cautious in introducing more items based on the hedonic methodology into the CPI, see Panel on Conceptual, Measurement, and Other Statistical Issues in Developing Cost-of-Living Indexes, *At What Price? Conceptualizing and Measuring Cost-of-Living and Price Indexes*, Charles Schultze and Christopher Mackie, eds., Committee on National Statistics, National Research Council (National Academy Press, 2002), ch 4.

5. For example, a price increase from $4 to $5 in the ratio of 1.25 is plus 25 percent, while a price decrease from $5 to $4 in the ratio of .80 is minus 20 percent. The arithmetic mean shows the price increase as more important than the price decrease, while the geometric mean gives the same weight to both the price increase and the price decrease. Technically, geometric averaging is the *nth* root of the product of *n* numbers, and arithmetic averaging is the sum of *n* numbers divided by *n*. See Brent R. Moulton, "Basic components of the CPI: estimation of price changes," *Monthly Labor Review*, December 1993, p. 14.

6. Patrick C. Jackman, "The CPI as a Cost of Living Index," paper presented at the 65th annual conference of the Western Economic Association, San Diego, June 29–July 3, 1990.

7. Bureau of Labor Statistics, U.S. Department of Labor, "The Consumer Price Index," Bulletin 2490, *BLS Handbook of Methods*, April 1997, ch 9, p. 170; and John S. Greenlees, "The U.S. CPI and the Cost-of-Living Objective," BLS paper prepared for the Joint Economic Commission for Europe/International Labor Organization Meeting on Consumer Price Indexes, Geneva, November 1–2, 2001.

8. *At What Price? Conceptualizing and Measuring Cost-of-Living and Price Indexes*, chs. 2 and 3; Bureau of Labor Statistics and Commission on National Statistics *Workshop on the NRC/CNSTAT Panel's Report: "At What Price? Conceptualizing and Measuring Cost-of-Living and Price Indexes,"* 2003; Charles L. Schultze, "The Consumer Price Index: Conceptual Issues and Practical Suggestions," *Journal of Economic Perspectives*, Winter 2003; and Katharine G. Abraham, "Toward a Cost-of-Living Index: Progress and Prospects," *Journal of Economic Perspectives*, Winter 2003.

9. United Nations Development Programme, *Human Development Report: 2002: Deepening Democracy in a Fragmented World* (Oxford University Press, 2002), Human Development Indicators 19, pp. 212–215. The measure of gross domestic product per unit of energy use is real GDP per kilogram of oil equivalent.

10. Roberto Chang, "Is a Weak Dollar Inflationary?" *Economic Review*, Federal Reserve Bank of Atlanta, September/October 1995.

11. Pinelopi Koujianou Goldberg and Michael M. Knetter, "Goods Prices and Exchange Rates: What Have We Learned?" *Journal of Economic Literature*, September 1997.

12. Wing T. Woo, "Exchange Rates and the Prices of Nonfood, Nonfuel Products," *Brookings Papers on Economic Activity* 2, 1984.

13. Douglas R. Bohi and Michael A. Toman, *The Economics of Energy Security* (Kluwer Academic Publishers: 1996), pp. 48–52.

14. Charles A. Calhoun, "OFHEO House Price Indexes: HPI Technical Description,"

Office of Federal Housing Enterprise Oversight, U.S. Department of Housing and Urban Development, March 1996; and Office of Federal Housing Enterprise Oversight, "House Price Index," quarterly, text on Frequently Asked Questions (www.ofneo.gov).

15. J. Bradford DeLong, "Should We Fear Deflation?" *Brookings Papers on Economic Activity* 1, 1999.

16. Carol Corrado and Joe Mattey, "Capacity Utilization," *Journal of Economic Perspectives*, Winter 1997. This is an analysis of the relationship between inflation and capacity utilization. The article also provides an overview of the preparation of the capacity utilization measures.

12

Finance

Money is a lubricant for the economy. It allows a greater specialization of production and division of labor and thus higher productivity and better living conditions than are possible in a barter economy. Money also has a life of its own in financial markets, which affect the economy. These financial aspects of money are the subject of this chapter.

Monetary and fiscal policies are the two major instruments of macroeconomics that are used to influence economic growth and price movements. Monetary policy refers to Federal Reserve (FR) System actions that affect bank reserves and interest rates. Monetary policies aim at moderating cyclical fluctuations of high price inflation during expansions and high unemployment during recessions, with the goal of achieving steadier economic growth, high employment, and low inflation over the long run. For an overall perspective on the relationship of monetary to fiscal policy, interest rates and economic growth, and how the FR implements monetary policies, see chapter 2 under Monetary Policy.

Fiscal policy consists of the spending and taxation actions taken on the federal government budget by the Congress and the president. For an overall perspective of how fiscal policy impacts the economy through changes in the size and direction of the federal budget, see chapter 2 under Fiscal Policy. An analysis of the spending and tax components of federal, state, and local government budgets is given in chapter 6.

Fiscal policy arises from federal spending programs and tax laws designed to meet the nation's civilian and defense needs. But spending and taxes encompass a broad array of public and private needs, only some of which focus specifically on overall economic growth, employment, and price movements.

By contrast, monetary policy is geared solely to influencing the economy. Monetary policy is also more flexible than fiscal policy because it can be modified quickly and often, while fiscal policy responds more slowly to changing economic conditions because of the lengthy political process involved in changing spending programs and tax laws.

This chapter discusses the tools of monetary policy, the passive role of the money supply as a monetary tool, interest rates, and the stock market. The appendix summarizes the organization and independence of the FR system.

IMPLEMENTING MONETARY POLICIES

When lenders perceive that the FR is pursuing a monetary stimulus that will lead to greater inflation, they attach an "inflation premium" that raises interest rates. The inflation premium results in interest rates rising more than when greater economic growth is not expected to generate greater inflation. Lenders attach an inflation premium to interest rates to keep the purchasing power of their incomes from deteriorating due to inflation when the loan is repaid. A different pattern of expectational factors weighing heavily may occur during recessions and periods of high unemployment when, despite lower interest rates, households and businesses do not increase their borrowing and spending because of slowly growing or declining incomes.

The limited influence of FR policies in the face of expectational and other complex factors affecting the economy is suggested by the use of the colloquial expressions, "pulling the string" and "pushing the string" to describe FR policies. Generally, the FR is considered to be more effective at slowing economic growth by raising interest rates (pulling the string) than at quickening economic growth by lowering interest rates (pushing the string).

The FR uses three tools to influence interest rates: Open market operations, the discount rate, and reserve requirements. All three tools can be used to affect bank reserves, interest rates, and bank loans.

Open market operations are the purchase and sale of U.S. Treasury debt securities by the FR in the secondary market of previously issued securities. Since banks invest in federal securities as a source of income and nonbank investors in federal securities also maintain bank checking accounts, bank reserves are increased when the FR buys and decreased when the FR sells federal securities. These operations, which are typically conducted a few days a week, are the FR's primary means of influencing bank reserves on a current basis. The FR also uses open market operations to influence the federal funds interest rate, as noted below.

Federal funds is the interest rate charged for loans between banks. These typically are for overnight loans that allow banks to meet reserve requirements, although there are "term" federal funds with maturities from a few days to over one year (the average is less than six months). Because banks do not receive interest on their reserve accounts with the FR, banks typically keep their reserves at the minimum required, but they sometimes fall below the minimum which causes the need to borrow, while banks holding reserves above the minimum requirement gain interest by lending the surplus. The name "federal funds" reflects the transfer of these funds at FR banks.[1]

The federal funds interest rate on interbank loans is targeted to reach a specified level, and thus is the clearest indicator of current FR monetary policy. The FR's open market operations either raise or lower bank reserves and consequently the availability of bank credit for loans. Open market operations virtually determine movements in the federal funds rate. In addition, interest rates on commercial short-term securities such as certificates of deposit and commercial paper reflect movements in the federal funds rate. Commercial banks typically obtain such loans to meet short-term liquidity needs when other sources of funds are unavailable. The federal funds rate should not be confused with the FR discount rate noted below.

The *discount rate* is the interest rate that the twelve regional FR banks charge commercial banks in their regions for loans (the Appendix covers the FR organizational structure). Discount rate changes are proposed by the FR regional banks subject to the approval of the Board of Governors of the Federal Reserve System. But the board sometimes encourages the FR regional banks to propose a change in the discount rate (see Appendix, note 20).

The FR introduced a new discount rate program in January 2003 that provides two types of credit to banks.[2] Primary credit, which is available to banks with adequate capital and which obtain high ratings for safety and soundness, may be used for any purpose, not just for short-term liquidity.[3] The primary credit rate was set above the federal funds rate, initially at 100 basis points (1 percentage point) above the target federal funds rate; the 100 basis point policy had prevailed through mid-summer 2003 as of this writing. Secondary credit, which is available to banks that do not qualify for primary credit, may be used only for short-term liquidity. The secondary credit rate is set above the primary credit rate. When necessary, the FR changes the discount rate to bring it in line with other short-term interest rates, or to signal a change in FR policy of monetary stimulus or restraint. The symbolic importance of the discount rate exceeds its importance as a price of money actually borrowed.

Reserve requirements are the legally required reserves that each commercial bank, thrift institution, and credit union must maintain with the FR bank in its region in proportion to its demand (checking) deposits and NOW accounts. Since the Depository Institutions Deregulation and Monetary Control Act of 1980, commercial banks that are members of the FR System, as well as nonmember banks, are subject to the reserve requirements. One purpose of reserve requirements is to ensure that banks maintain sufficient liquidity to conduct daily operations such as clearing checks and meeting the ongoing needs of customers. The existence of reserves also facilitates the implementation of monetary policies in conjunction with open market operations.

Thus, if there were no reserve requirements, the FR would have a less effective fulcrum for inducing banks to expand or contract loans. Because commercial banks, thrift institutions, and credit unions have their own demands for reserves for their business operations, the FR probably would have to model these financial institutions' demands for reserves to its monetary policy open market operations and to its targeted federal funds rates. This would lessen the likelihood of achieving interest rate targets because the bank demands for reserves are more difficult to ascertain than the FR imposed reserve requirements which are known. It also would lead to a greater volatility of interest rates and impair the FR's effectiveness in conducting monetary policies, as noted by Gordon Sellon and Stuart Weiner.[4] Thus, open market operations would be less effective because there would be no regulatory limit on the volume of money and loans that the banking system could create.

The FR may change reserve requirements within certain legally prescribed limits, but because even small changes can significantly affect banks' liquidity, the requirements are changed infrequently, and then typically open market operations are undertaken to ensure no net change in bank reserves.[5] Reserve requirements have been used to counteract developments in particular financial markets, such as varying international interest rates that cause money to flow between the United States and other nations in a way that hinders the implementation of domestic monetary policies, or as a signal that the FR is changing its policies toward stimulus or restraint.

However, reserve requirements are not used to maintain the financial solvency of banks. This is done by the banking regulatory agencies—the FR for state-chartered FR member banks, the Comptroller of the Currency in the U.S. Department of the Treasury for nationally-chartered banks, and the Federal Deposit Insurance Corporation for state-chartered nonmember banks that have FDIC insurance—in their supervision of bank operations.[6] The supervision includes ensuring that banks meet capital requirements, which specify the levels of bank owners' equity investment as a percentage of total bank assets. Proposals have been made to reorganize the banking regulatory system which, if enacted in legislation, would change the supervisory responsibilities of the existing three agencies and/or create a new supervisory agency.

Reserve requirements also put an upper limit on the ultimate increase in bank deposits resulting from bank loans. When a bank gives a customer a loan, it increases the customer's checking deposits by the amount of the loan. The expansion of bank deposits from when the customer first uses the loan to buy a car, pay school tuition, or purchase other goods and services, multiplies several times as the car dealer and the school deposit their receipts in their respective banks, and those banks in turn extend loans with the new deposits, and so on.[7] Since the re-lending and re-spending occur in successive time periods, it may be several years before the cumulative ultimate expansion of bank deposits from a single loan is reached.

Passive Role of the Money Supply

The money supply has received considerable attention over the years as an important factor driving economic growth. The Full Employment and Balanced Growth Act of 1978 (Humphrey-Hawkins Act) required the FR to report to Congress twice a year (in February and July) on its plans for the growth in the money supply during the calendar year. But the FR discontinued setting targets for the money supply when the Act's requirement for setting targets expired in 2000 because the relationship between the money supply on the one hand, and economic growth and price movements on the other, had become progressively weaker.[8]

The money supply measures are prepared weekly by the FR in three alternative definitions—M1, M2, and M3. They range in their coverage of financial assets and in their degree of liquidity, from M1 as the most limited and most liquid to M3 as the broadest and least liquid. Liquidity is the ease with which money can be withdrawn from accounts or obtained from the sale of assets without the risk of losing value.[9] M1 includes only currency, demand (checking) deposits, interest bearing deposits that are used for writing checks (e.g., NOW accounts), and nonbank bank traveler's checks. M2 includes M1 plus small time and savings deposits (including money market deposit accounts) and money market mutual funds. M3 includes M2 plus large time deposits and money market mutual funds, Eurodollars, and repurchase agreements. The money supply measures exclude such financial assets as corporate stocks, commercial and government bonds, and life insurance.

I believe the focus on the money supply as an active factor influencing cyclical fluctuation in economic growth and price movements has been misplaced. The money supply is in fact a passive factor that plays out as a statistic at the end of the deposit creation process resulting from bank loans, as described above.

To illustrate the passive nature of the money supply, in the first decade of the twenty-first century, if the labor force grows at the same annual rate as it did during 1992–2002 of 1.2 percent, and if productivity grows at the same annual rate as it did during 1992–2002 of 2.2 percent, the implied annual money supply growth would be 3.4 percent (1.2 + 2.2). But during 1992–2002, the money supply measures noticeably diverged from the implied 3.4 percent rate—M1, M2, and M3 averaged 1.7 percent, 5.4 percent, and 7.3 percent, respectively. Growth rates for the inflation-adjusted money supply measures (based on the consumer price index) during 1992–2002 also diverged noticeably from the implied 3.4 percent rate—M1, M2, and M3 averaged –0.8 percent, 2.8 percent, and 4.7 percent, respectively. It is obvious that use of the money supply as a gauge of the long-run sufficiency of money growth in the economy is weak.

During 1992–2002, unemployment averaged 5.4 percent, ranging from 4.0

percent in 2000 to 7.5 percent in 1992, and inflation based on the consumer price index averaged 2.3 percent, ranging from 1.6 percent in 1998 and 2002 to 3.4 percent in 2000. This period includes one year of recession (2001), three years of recovery (1992, 1993, and 2002) and seven years of expansion (1994–2000). Thus, the period includes substantially different rates of economic growth, which were accompanied by several years of declining unemployment and relatively low rates of inflation. But in seeking to replicate this record in the first decade of the twenty-first century, the implied required growth in the money supply of 3.4 percent seems reasonable for gauging the long-run sufficiency of money in the economy. However, the money supply growth of 1992–2002 did not conform to the implied growth rate, which further negates the use of the money supply for economic analysis.

INTEREST RATES

Interest is the price of money. Major elements determining the interest rate on a loan include: (a) competing opportunities for lenders' funds in other loans or investments (referred to as "opportunity cost"); (b) risk of default on the loan; (c) expectation of inflation in discounting the future value of interest payments and repayment of the principal of the loan; and (d) availability of alternative sources of funds for loans from banks and investors (i.e., the supply of loanable funds). There is a direct relationship between the first three elements and the level of interest rates—the greater the opportunity cost, the risk of default, or the expectation of price inflation, the higher the interest rate. In contrast, a greater supply of loanable funds tends to lower interest rates, which is an inverse relationship.

Intuitive Theoretical Relationships

Theoretically, the relationship of the federal government budget and debt positions to interest rates, and the relationship of interest rates to economic growth, seem clear. Federal government budget surpluses or declining deficits lessen the federal borrowing needs, and so are associated with low and/or declining interest rates, while rising budget deficits or declining surpluses are associated with higher and/or rising interest rates. The federal debt, which represents the net effect of the cumulative budget surpluses and deficits from previous years, seems to have the same relationship to interest rates as the budget surpluses and deficits, with borrowing needs rising to refinance a growing debt, and borrowing declining as debt refinancing needs decline.

But there is a basic difference in the effects on economic growth between federal budget surpluses and deficits on the one hand, and federal debt on the other. Budget surpluses and deficits impact economic growth directly through spending and taxes as well as their indirect effect on interest rates in financial markets. However, debt affects economic growth only indirectly through interest rates, as the repayment, extension, or turnover of the debt takes place in the financial markets. For more comprehensive discussions of the role of the government in the economy, see chapter 2 under Fiscal Policy and chapter 6, "Government."

Similarly, the theoretical relationship between interest rates and economic growth seems clear. Low or declining interest rates stimulate borrowing and spending and so bolster economic growth, while high or rising interest rates restrain borrowing and spending, and so lessen economic growth.

The economy is, of course, more complex than this one-dimensional outline. More factors than interest rates, as well as feedbacks among the factors, affect economic growth. So too, more factors than the federal budget and debt positions affect interest rates. But as a starting point, it is useful to observe simplified ideas statistically.

Real Interest Rates and Economic Growth

Real interest rates are defined as the market (nominal) rate minus inflation. Real interest rates here are calculated as the yield on Treasury securities with three-year remaining maturities less the current inflation rate represented by the gross domestic product chain price index.

Table 12.1 shows average real interest rates and economic growth (the gross domestic product adjusted for inflation, or real GDP) at approximate five-year intervals from 1960 to 2002. Real interest rates fluctuated considerably over the period, from around 2 percent in the 1960s, to under 1 percent in the 1970s, to 5 to 6 percent in the 1980s, to 3 to 4 percent in the 1990s, to under 3 percent in the early 2000s. Real interest rates were exceptionally low in the 1970s (actually negative in 1974 and 1975), even though both price inflation and nominal interest rates were high and accelerating. One explanation is that lenders assumed that the high inflation was only temporary, and therefore nominal interest rates would be sufficiently high to compensate for any future loss in purchasing power arising from inflation when interest payments and the principal of the loan became due.

The overall relationship between real interest rates and real GDP is weak. Relatively low real interest rates were associated with high economic growth in the 1960s, lower real interest rates in the 1970s were associated with lower economic growth than in the 1960s, higher real interest rates in the 1980s were associated with similar economic growth as in the 1970s, lower real interest rates in the 1990s were associated with similar economic growth as in the 1980s, and lower real interest rates in the early 2000s were associated with lower economic growth than in the 1990s.

Table 12.1

Real Interest Rates and Real Gross Domestic Product: 1960–2002

	Interest rate on three-year constant maturity U.S. Treasury securities, adjusted for inflation (annual percentage)	Real gross domestic product (annual percentage change)
1960–64	2.4	4.2
1965–69	2.0	4.6
1970–74	0.9	2.8
1975–79	0.4	3.7
1980–84	5.8	2.3
1985–89	5.1	3.7
1990–94	3.3	2.2
1995–99	4.1	3.8
2000–2002	2.6	2.1

Sources: Based on U.S. Department of the Treasury and U.S. Bureau of Economic Analysis data.

Note: Constant maturities on securities are an average of bonds that encompass a range of remaining maturities of three years and do not represent a particular bond issue. Interest rates are adjusted for inflation by the annual change in the gross domestic product chain price index.

Establishing a linkage between real interest rates and economic growth requires that both the level as well as the movement of interest rates be taken into account. What is the break-even type threshold of real interest rates that is suggestive of future high or low rates of economic growth? I am not aware of such a threshold that has been developed from economic analysis.

In assessing the relationship between real interest rates and the real GDP, the analyst should keep abreast of research that relates the level of real interest rates to economic growth.

Relationship of the Federal Budget and Federal Debt Positions to Interest Rates

Changing directions and magnitudes of the federal budget surplus/deficit position and the federal debt held by the public can affect interest rates.[10] These movements are summarized in the above section on Intuitive Theoretical Relationships in the context of rising budget deficits raising interest rates, and declining budget deficits or rising surpluses and declining debt lowering interest rates. Such movements run counter to the spending and tax impacts of fiscal policy on economic growth, with lower interest rates stimulating economic

Figure 12.1 **Federal Budget Surplus/Deficit versus Three-Month Treasury Bill Interest Rate: 1978–2002**

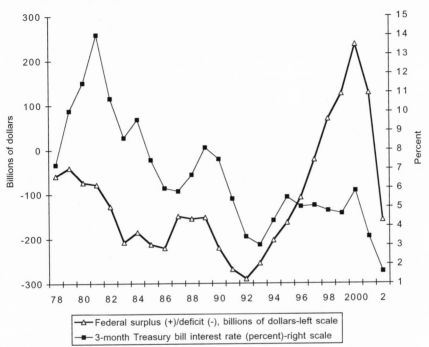

Sources: Based on U.S. Office of Management and Budget and U.S. Department of the Treasury data.

growth and the accompanying lower government deficits or rising surpluses restraining economic growth, while higher interest rates restrain economic growth and the accompanying greater deficits or declining surpluses and rising debt stimulating economic growth. Thus, there are at least some offsetting effects built into the fiscal budget and monetary interest rate connections on economic growth. Fiscal stimulus brings the restraint of higher interest rates, and fiscal restraint brings the stimulus of lower interest rates.

Figures 12.1 and 12.2 show the federal surplus/deficit and the federal debt positions in relation to the three-month Treasury bill interest rate, respectively, from 1978 to 2002. These indicate that neither the budget/surplus movements nor the debt movements correspond to the expected effects on interest rates. For example, the surplus/deficit-interest rate relationship moved as expected only in 1979–81 and 1996–99 (Figure 12.1), while the debt–interest rate relationship moved as expected only in 1979–81, 1987–88, 1992–93, and 1995–99 (Figure 12.2).

Figure 12.2 **Annual Change in Federal Debt Held by the Public versus Three-Month Treasury Bill Interest Rate: 1978–2002**

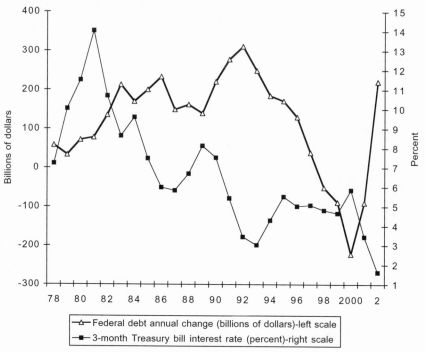

Sources: Based on U.S. Office of Management and Budget and U.S. Department of the Treasury data.

The relatively weak fiscal-monetary relationship appearing in Figures 12.1 and 12.2 suggests that there is no simple connection between the two. For one thing, the rate of economic growth may be more dominant, though to underscore the complexity, economic growth itself is affected by government budgets and interest rates. Economists also disagree on the extent of the fiscal-monetary relationship, as noted by Douglas Elmendorf and David Reifschneider.[11]

Inflation and Interest Rates

One factor affecting interest rates is the prospect of price changes over the duration of the loan. When prices are expected to rise in the future, interest rates include an "inflation premium" to protect the purchasing power when the loan is repaid.

Figure 12.3 shows the annual percentage change in the GDP chain price index in relation to the three-month Treasury bill interest rate from 1978 to 2002. The

Figure 12.3 **Gross Domestic Product Price Change versus Three-Month Treasury Bill Interest Rate: 1978–2002**

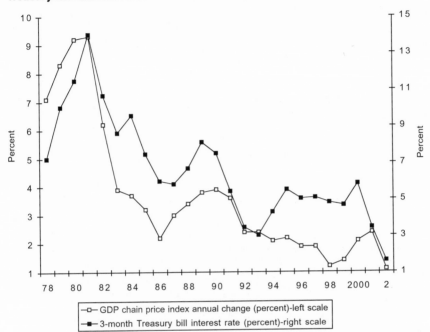

Sources: Based on U.S. Bureau of Economic Analysis and U.S. Department of the Treasury data.

annual movements in both prices and interest rates were generally similar from 1979 to 1993. The movements diverged from 1994 to 1999 and again in 2001.

The divergence from 1994 to 1999 was characterized by price movements trending downward, while interest rates rose in 1994 and 1995 and remained close to the higher plateau from 1996 to 1999. This suggests that the rising economic growth during the period bolstered the demand for loans which was weightier in affecting interest rates than the slowdown in price inflation.

Short-Term Interest Rate and Economic Growth

The intuitive theoretical relationship between interest rates and economic growth is that they move in an inverse relationship, as outlined previously. Thus, a declining interest rate is associated with rising economic growth, as the lower interest rates stimulate borrowing and spending. And a rising interest rate is associated with declining economic growth, as the higher interest rate restrains borrowing and spending.

Figure 12.4 **Three-Month Treasury Bill Interest Rate versus Real Gross Domestic Product: 1978–2002**

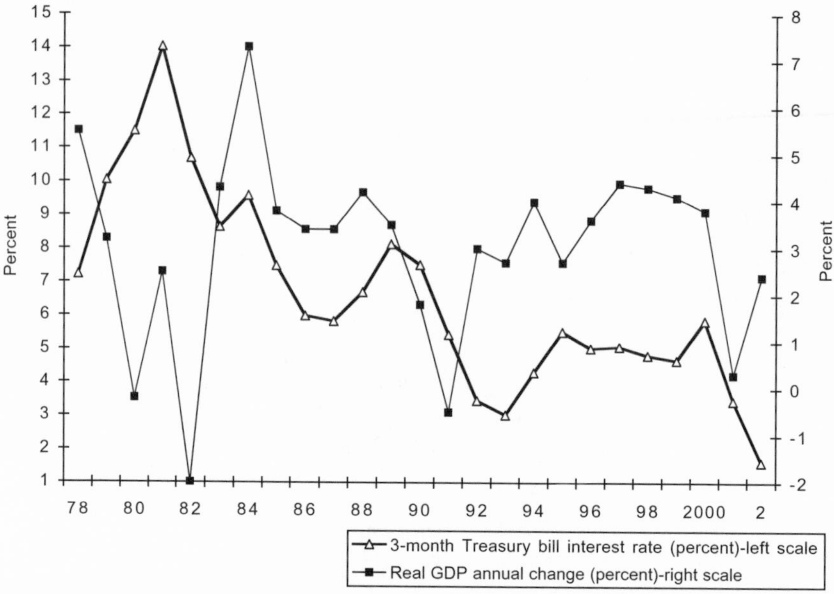

Sources: Based on U.S. Department of the Treasury and U.S. Bureau of Economic Analysis data.

Figure 12.4 shows the three-month Treasury bill interest rate and the annual percentage change in the real GDP (the measure of economic growth) from 1978 to 2002. The inverse relationship appeared in 1979–80, 1983, 1992, 1995–97, 2000, and 2002. Thus, the theoretical inverse relationship occurred as the exception rather than the rule, indicating that the sum of other factors had a greater impact on economic growth.

Yield Curves

The various interest rates charged on different kinds of debt instruments are influenced by several factors. They include the maturity period of the debt (i.e., the length of time before repayment is due), the relative risk of default by borrowers, and the differing tax rates assessed on interest from commercial and government securities.

To visualize the influence of maturity on interest rates, analysts often draw yield curves that depict the differentials between short-term and long-term interest rates for bonds with similar risk and tax characteristics. Typically, yield curves are drawn for U.S. Treasury securities since these securities have no risk of default and are taxed at a uniform rate because they are exempt from state and local taxes.

There are two main reasons that maturity influences interest rates on debt instruments—liquidity and expectations of future interest rates. In terms of liquidity, short-term rates tend to be lower because short-term debt instruments can be sold for cash with less risk of a significant capital loss on the initial amount of the loan than is the case for long-term debt. Thus, other things being equal, the yield curve is typically upward sloping with long-term rates higher than short-term rates.

Expectations about future short-term interest rates is the other main driver of the yield curve. For example, when short-term interest rates are expected to rise in the future, the yield curve will steepen. A steeply rising yield curve typically occurs when a recession is perceived to be bottoming out and the anticipated recovery and subsequent expansion are expected to provoke greater loan demand and concomitantly higher long-term interest rates. By contrast, a flat or downward sloping yield curve typically occurs during an inflationary period when the FR temporarily tightens credit. Tighter monetary policy raises short-term interest rates but can lead to lower long-term rates by lowering expected future inflation and thereby lowering expected future interest rates.

The model of rising and falling yield curves is not unanimously accepted, however, as Henry Kaufman points out.[12] Some analysts say that the focus on the importance of future short-term interest rates in determining the yield curve is misguided. They argue that particular borrowers and lenders tend to specialize in either short- or long-term loans and that short- and long-term interest rates are determined separately by the supply and demand relationships in each of these distinct markets.

Figure 12.5a shows interest rates on securities of three-month bills, three-year constant maturity, ten-year constant maturity, and thirty-year constant maturity for selected years in which the following year is in a cyclical expansion from 1995 to 2002. Constant maturities on securities are an average of bonds that encompass a range of remaining maturities of specified years that do not represent a particular bond issue. The U.S. Department of the Treasury discontinued publication of the thirty-year constant maturity in 2002.

According to the theory of yield curves noted above, when investors' expectations of future economic growth lead to interest rates rising on securities of increasing longer maturities, the years in Figure 12.5a should show progressively higher interest rates from three-month bills to thirty-year constant maturities. Figure 12.5a is consistent with that pattern.

Figure 12.5b shows interest rates on securities of three-month bills, three-year constant maturity, ten-year constant maturity, and thirty-year constant maturity for selected years in which the following year is in a cyclical recession from 1979 to 2000. According to the yield curve theory, the years in Figure

Figure 12.5a **Yields on Treasury Securities with Lengthening Times to Maturity for Selected Years Preceding Expansion Years: 1995–2002**

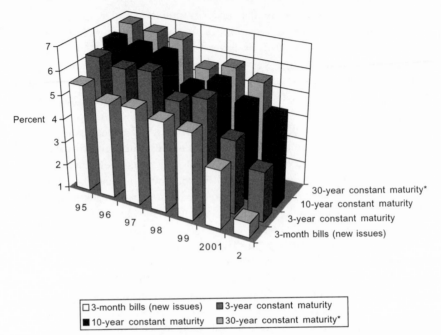

Source: Based on U.S. Department of the Treasury data.

*Publication of 30-year constant maturity discontinued in 2002.

12.5b should show progressively lower interest rates from three-month bills to thirty-year constant maturities. The data are consistent with that pattern, except for the move from the three month bill to the three-year constant maturity. In that case, the interest rate rose from the three-month to the three-year maturity in three of the four selected years.

Interest rate spreads on yield curves are components of the leading index and the experimental recession index covered in chapter 13. Analytic studies using yield curves to predict recessions indicate that they have a modest relevance for economic forecasting. Modest forecasting properties of yield curves for recessions were also found by Arturo Estrella and Frederic S. Mishkin and by Arturo Estrella, Anthony Rodrigues, and Sebastian Schich.[13]

Yield curves do not appear as a dominant factor in forecasting the economy. In assessing the relationship between the yield curve and future movements of economic growth and prices, the analyst should treat the yield curve as confirming or rejecting other analyses of economic growth and inflation.

Figure 12.5b **Yields on Treasury Securities with Lengthening Times to
Maturity for Selected Years Preceding Recession Years: 1979–2000**

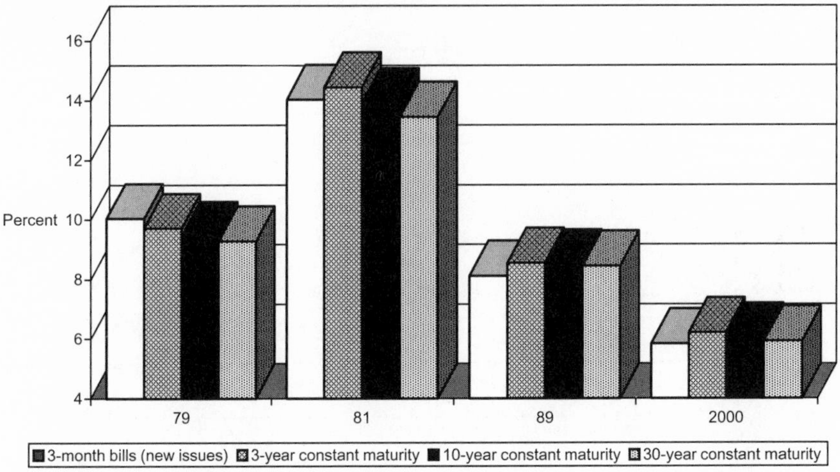

■3-month bills (new issues) ▨3-year constant maturity ■10-year constant maturity ▣30-year constant maturity

Source: Based on U.S. Department of the Treasury data.

Note: Year 1979 preceded 1980 recession, 1981 preceded 1982 recession, 1989 preceded 1990 recession, 2000 preceded 2001 recession.

THE STOCK MARKET

The stock market has both an active and reactive relationship to the overall economy. In the active role, stock market prices affect consumer and investment spending. When the stock market is rising, households that own rising stocks feel more prosperous and are more willing to spend than when the paper value of their stocks is low or declining (see chapter 4 under Wealth Effect). Similarly, when stock prices are rising, it is easier for businesses to finance new investments by issuing new equity stock than when stock prices are low or falling. In general, rising stock prices also inject a feeling of optimism about the future which encourages spending, while falling stock prices lessen confidence in the economy and the incentive to spend.

In the reactive role, stock market price movements reflect the actual and expected movements in economic growth. Thus, stock market prices initially respond to changing economic growth rates. It is only then that stock market price changes become the active instrument noted above.

Stock Market Trends

Figure 12.6 shows the earnings-price ratio and the dividends-price ratio for the Standard & Poor's 500 composite stock price index from 1965 to 2002. Of the

Figure 12.6 **Stock Market Earnings-Price Ratio and Dividend-Price Ratio: 1965–2002**

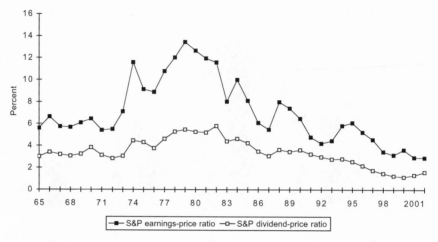

Source: Based on Standard and Poor's 500 composite common stock price index.

total market value of the S&P index at the end of April 2003, companies on the New York Stock Exchange accounted for 84.8 percent, companies on the Nasdaq accounted for 15.0 percent, and companies on the AMEX accounted for 0.2 percent. When stock prices rose more or declined less than earnings and dividends, both the earnings-price and dividends-price ratios declined, while when prices rose less or declined more than earnings and dividends, both ratios rose. The Standard & Poor's 500 composite stock price index is a component of the leading index covered in chapter 13.

Both earnings and dividends had similar long-term patterns of stability from the mid-1960s to the early 1970s (around 6 percent and 3 percent, respectively), after which the earnings ratio rose to a peak of over 13 percent in 1979 and the dividends ratio rose to a peak of close to 6 percent in 1982. From those peaks there was a general decline in both ratios, though with annual interruptions, to lows for the entire period in the late 1990s and early 2000s to around 3 percent in the earnings-price ratio and 1.5 percent in the dividends-price ratio.

The earnings-price ratio was noticeably more volatile than the dividends-price ratio, indicating that dividends and prices had closer movements than earnings and prices. The general decline in both ratios from the 1980s to the late 1990s indicated that prices rose more than earnings and dividends over the period. The stability of the long-term low levels from the late 1990s to the early 2000s indicates that prices, earnings, and dividends moved at similar rates. This stability of 3 percent for the earnings-price ratio and 1.5 percent for the dividends-price ratio (dividend yield) during the late 1990s to the early 2000s was at

Figure 12.7 **Manufacturing Profits after Income Taxes as a Percentage of Stockholders' Equity and Profits after Income Taxes per Dollar of Sales: 1978–2002**

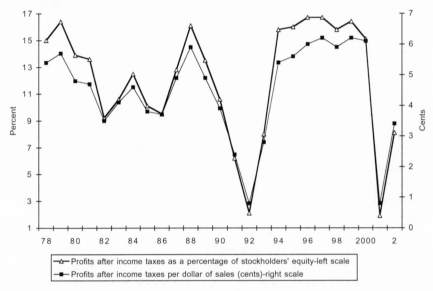

Source: Based on U.S. Bureau of the Census data for all manufacturing industries.

Note: Profits are after the payment of federal, state, and local income taxes.

one-half the level of the previous period of stability of the ratios from the mid-1960s to the early 1970s (see above). Overall, these trends reflected a long-term increase in stock market prices in relation to earnings and dividends.

By contrast, Figure 12.7 shows actual operational profits after the payment of income taxes, sales, and stockholders' equity (based on company balance sheets) of manufacturing companies from 1978 to 2002. Profits appear as a percentage of stockholders' equity, and also as per dollar of sales. Profits as a percentage of equity showed no upward or downward trend, though there was considerable volatility associated with recession years (1982, 1990–91, and 2001) and the recession aftermath years. The year-to-year volatility of the profits-equity ratio typically fluctuated within 9 to 17 percent, though it fell to 2 percent in 1992 and 2001. A similar movement appeared for profits per dollar of sales, which typically fluctuated within 4 to 6 cents, though it fell to 1 cent in 1992 and 2001

Thus, the long-term declines in the stock market earnings-price ratio and the dividends-price ratio contrasted with the absence of a long-term upward or downward trend in manufacturing operating profits in relation to stockholders' equity and company sales from the early 1980s to the late 1990s point up the increasing divergence of the prices of company stocks from the real profitability and growth of companies. The effect of the long-term rise in stock prices was to discount company earnings and dividends growth further and further into the future. This growing speculative behavior of the stock market was magnified in the late 1990s by the rise in stock prices of telecommunications companies, which often were operating at a loss or making minimal profits, and which also paid little or no dividends.

Company Buybacks and Dividend Yields

Company repurchases of some or all of its outstanding shares of stock are referred to as buybacks. By reducing the number of company shares outstanding, buybacks increase the value of each remaining share owned by stockholders. Thus, buybacks can be considered as distributing company cash to stockholders, and as a dividend payment. In this light, dividends are the sum of actual dividend payments plus company buybacks.

The company dividend yield of actual dividend payments represents the dividend payment to stockholders as a percentage of market price of the company's stock. The dividend yield of company buybacks is calculated as the percentage that the value of the repurchased stock is of the company's balance sheet equity value. I believe the buyback yield is appropriately called an implicit dividend yield, because the buyback yield provides no direct payment to stockholders.

In an analysis of company reports to the Securities and Exchange Commission (10–K reports) of a sample of the largest companies in the Standard and Poor's 500 composite common stock price index for 1994 to 1998, Nellie Liang and Steven Sharpe estimated the dividend yield that would be attributable to buybacks of company stock.[14] There were 144 companies in the sample from 1994 to 1997, which was reduced to 138 companies in 1998 in order to maintain sufficient detail necessary to conduct the analysis. The sampled companies accounted for about 75 percent of the share repurchases and the dividend payments of all S&P 500 companies during 1994–98. The analysis of repurchase dividend yields included a downward adjustment for the effect of the exercise of employee stock options.

The surge in buybacks minus the issuance of new stock shares—i.e., net repurchases—began in 1994.[15] Before then, in the early 1990s, companies issued more shares than their repurchases of outstanding stock.

Table 12.2 shows the dividend yield excluding buybacks, the buyback yield, and the dividend yield including buybacks. The yield excluding buybacks declined from 2.8 percent in 1994 to 1.4 percent in 1998. The yield including the buybacks declined from 3.95 percent in 1994 to 2.9 percent in 1998, which was interrupted by an increase in 1997. The buyback yield ranged from 1.2 percent in 1994 to 2 percent in 1997.

Table 12.2

Dividend Yields on Common Stocks, Excluding and Including Company Buybacks: 1994–1998

	Dividend yield, excluding buybacks	Buyback yield[a]	Dividend yield, including buybacks
1994	2.76%	1.19%	3.95%
1995	2.41	1.34	3.75
1996	2.06	1.56	3.62
1997	1.73	1.98	3.71
1998	1.41	1.49	2.90

Source: J. Nellie Liang and Steven A Sharpe, "Share Repurchases and Employee Stock Options and their Implications for S&P 500 Share Retirements and Expected Returns," Finance and Economics Discussion Series, Federal Reserve Board, 1999, 59, Table 1.

a. Company net cash outflow from repurchases (repurchases minus exercise of employee stock options). I refer to the buyback yield in the text as an implicit yield.

Thus, while the dividend yield level was raised by the inclusion of the repurchase yield, the downward trend occurred in both the dividend yields excluding and including the repurchase yield. Also, the raised level of the dividend yield including the repurchase yield to the 3 to 4 percent range was still significantly below the dividend yield excluding the repurchase yield for the entire S&P 500 composite common stock price index of 5.2 to 5.8 percent during the late 1970s and early 1980s.

Implications of the 2000–02 Stock Market Decline

I believe the run-up in the already overpriced stock market in the late 1990s was accompanied by realized and unrealized gains that spawned a growing array of enterprises and employment that directly or indirectly depended on financial support from the capital gains that investors derived from the stock market. With the collapse of the telecommunications companies when they could no longer continue operating without making a profit, and the drop of the S&P stock index from the peak price level of 1461 in April 2000, to 1331 in December 2000, to 1145 in December 2001 to 899 in December 2002, the weak underpinning of the newly created and underperforming companies was exposed.

The stock market decline was exacerbated by the financial scandals of corporate executives exposed in 2001 and 2002. And not surprisingly, it was the previous rigging of stock market values by some executives that in part led to the speculative rise in stock prices. The rigging also is a blatant departure from the proclaimed advocacy of free competitive markets by corporate executives in which buyers (investors) and sellers (issuers of corporate stock) are both assumed to have relevant and accurate information.

The resultant collapse of those companies, and the contraction of others caught in the undertow, brought with it the decline of 1.6 million nonfarm jobs from March 2001 (eve of the 2001 recession) to November 2001 (end of the recession), plus a further loss of 1.0 million nonfarm jobs during the recovery from November 2001 to July 2003. The total nonfarm job loss from March 2001 to July 2003 was 2.7 million (based on unrounded data).

Relationship of the Stock Market to the Economy

This experience points up the direct relationship of the stock market to the overall economy. It also highlights the different nature and aftermath of the 2001 recession from previous recessions. Previous recessions were more cyclical in nature in that declining demand for the products of ongoing businesses bottomed out and began a strong resurgence by the second year of the recovery, but that did not occur during the first half of 2003.

Thus, for substantial and sustained economic and job growth to emerge in the mid- to late 2000s, the development of new products with mass markets will be necessary to replace the lost markets of the telecommunications companies and of the other new enterprises that were dependent on the subsidization from the capital gains generated in the stock market. It will also be necessary to reclaim manufacturing produced in the United States from the production in substandard low-wage countries. Both of these elements are elaborated on in chapter 3 on Economic Growth.

In addition, the stock market is too important to allow the corporate reform legislation of 2002 to be undermined. This refers specifically to the following reform goals: (a) full disclosure of the production and financial operations of companies, (b) independent auditing in which auditors have no direct or indirect consulting or other conflict-of-interest association with the company being audited, and (c) the elimination of research advice given by brokerage firms and investment banks in underwriting new issues or in promoting existing stock and bond securities in which they have a direct or indirect stake in the companies they are either touting or disparaging.

This requires that the Securities and Exchange Commission, the stock exchanges, and the various newly established and existing standards and oversight boards in the securities, accounting, and auditing industries not submit to industry pressure and thus deflect from the vigorous implementation of their functions. It also means that the U.S. Department of Justice will need to actively

enforce the letter and intent of the corporate reforms laws in the courts. If the
implementation of these reforms is watered down, the stock market will continue
to be a vehicle for speculative behavior that diminishes economic growth.

APPENDIX: FEDERAL RESERVE ORGANIZATION AND INDEPENDENCE

The Federal Reserve System is headed by a seven-member Board of Governors in Washington, DC and twelve regional Federal Reserve banks located around the country.[16] The seven governors are appointed by the president, subject to confirmation of the Senate, and are permanent members of the Federal Open Market Committee (FOMC). The FOMC establishes overall monetary policies. The governors' terms are for fourteen years, with one term expiring every two years. This limits a president's ability to "pack" the board, though more than one vacancy can occur during a presidential four-year term. The chairman of the board's term is four years, but it does not coincide with the presidential four-year term.

Each FR bank has a board of nine directors—six are elected by the commercial banks in the region (three represent the member banks and three represent the public) and three public members are appointed by the FR Board. The FR Board designates the chairman and deputy chairman from the three public members it appoints. The FR Bank's board of directors appoints the bank's president subject to FR Board approval. Five presidents of the FR banks are members of the FOMC at all times, four on a one-year rotating basis, and the Federal Reserve Bank of New York's president is a permanent member of the FOMC.[17]

The presidents of the FR banks bring to the FOMC deliberations a special knowledge of the patterns of economic growth in different sections of the country as well as of the economic concerns of each geographic region. Because these regional concerns vary (for example, local areas have different levels of unemployment), they could lead the presidents of the FR banks to vote on the FOMC from a regional rather than from a national vantage point. But in analyzing the Bank presidents' votes, Geoffrey Tootell concluded that the bank presidents voted from a national rather than from a regional perspective.[18] In addition, because the presidents are representatives of commercial banks, there is a concern that this background leads them to concentrate on fighting inflation more than nonbank representatives would, and thus vote for higher interest rates more often than persons who do not represent commercial banks. In an analysis of the voting records of all FOMC members, Geoffrey Tootell concluded there was no significant difference between the voting records of the FR bank presidents and the FR Board governors once the political party affiliations of the bank presidents and the board governors were taken into account.[19] Democrats and Republicans on the banks and the board tended to vote in line with their political affiliations, Democrats tending toward lower interest rates than Republicans. However, others believe the voting records show that the FR bank presidents favor higher interest rates more frequently than the FR Board governors.

The FR Board, the FR banks, and the FOMC have different monetary policy powers. The FR Board determines reserve requirements, each FR bank proposes changes in the discount rate in its region subject to FR Board approval, and the FOMC directs open market operations. In general, there is considerable interplay between the board and the banks (particularly through the FOMC), but the FR Board has greater authority. The board alone changes reserve requirements. The board must approve changes proposed by the FR banks in the discount rate, but sometimes the Board encourages the FR banks to propose a rate change.[20] The discount rate has long been uniform throughout the country. The board's governors represent seven of the twelve members of the FOMC.

Institutionally, the FR Board reports to Congress. It is legally independent of the president. Since the executive branch does not participate in formulating monetary policies and the FR does not participate in formulating fiscal policies, coordination can be a problem. The FR and the president are in fact sometimes at odds, a situation that has been criticized for leading to unbalanced fiscal and monetary policies. Such disagreement usually occurs when unemployment is rising, or when unemployment is high and is not declining or is declining only slowly, and the president wants to stimulate employment growth while the FR emphasizes its traditional inclination to hold price inflation down. This did not occur during 2001–03 when unemployment rose and inflation was low.

This leaves Congress as the only branch with direct links to all parties engaged in developing monetary and fiscal policies: the FR for monetary policy and the president for fiscal policy. While congressional review of the FR's annual and semiannual monetary reports could provide a vehicle for coordination between Congress and the FR, in practice this does not occur. Congress does not have the authority to redirect FR policies if it is dissatisfied with them. Congress can only force the FR to report and testify to it. But because Congress feels uneasy, and perhaps even inadequate, in assessing the economic and financial relationships, it does not change the FR charter to enable it to direct the FR to take specific monetary policy actions. Indeed, while individual members of Congress occasionally express their opinions, Congress as a legislative body does not articulate its own view of FR policies. More members express disagreement with FR policies when unemployment is rising, just as the president does, as noted above. Obviously, Congress and the president are more responsive to election prospects than are appointed FR officials. There is also a conspiratorial-type suggestion that Congress deliberately does not intrude in monetary policymaking in order to be freer to criticize FR performance when unemployment and/or inflation are high.

Despite the general principle of FR independence, the FR has been subject to political pressures from presidents. The most notable ones involved Harry Truman and Richard Nixon, of which there have been several accounts.[21] In both cases, the presidents advocated low interest rates to stimulate economic growth, and in the case of President Truman also to hold down interest costs on the federal debt. The episode with President Truman led to the "Treasury-Federal Reserve Accord" of 1951, which freed the FR to act independently, and thus enacted a major change in the relationship between the FR and the president. Twenty years later, President Nixon tried to undo the 1951 accord by pressuring Arthur Burns, Chairman of the FR at that time, to influence the FOMC to lower interest rates in order to boost the economy and thus help Nixon win re-election in 1972. The effect of presidential pressure on FR actions is disputed, but that it occurs is indisputable. One view of the effect of such pressure is that when the pressure is public, the FR resists in a show of independence, and that the White House effort may be counterproductive.

REVIEW QUESTIONS

- What would happen to the effectiveness of open market operations if reserve requirements were abolished?
- Reserve requirements are used to oversee the financial solvency of banks.
  _____True_____False
- Contrast the monetary policy roles of the discount rate and the federal funds rate.
- How do yield curves suggest future changes in borrowing and economic growth?
- How can the stock market affect the economy?
- How does the independence of the Federal Reserve differ from the independence of the Supreme Court?
- What is the concern about including Federal Reserve bank presidents on the Federal Reserve Open Market Committee?

Extra Credit

- Why is an inverted yield curve—i.e., one showing short-term interest rates higher than long-term rates—a sign of an impending recession?

NOTES

1. For a good discussion of federal funds, see Federal Reserve Bank of Richmond, *Instruments of the Money Market*, 7th ed., 1993, ch. 2. The 8th edition is available only on the Federal Reserve Bank of Richmond's Web site: www.rich.frb.org.

2. For the final rule adopting the new discount rate policy, see Federal Reserve Press Release, October 31, 2002. The new program was implemented in January 2003 (Federal Reserve Press Release, January 6, 2003).
3. For a good discussion of the new discount rate program, see David C. Wheelock, "Replacement Windows: New Credit Program at the Discount Window," *Monetary Trends*, Federal Reserve Bank of St. Louis, May 2003.
4. Gordon H. Sellon, Jr. and Stuart E. Weiner, "Monetary Policy without Reserve Requirements: Analytical Issues," *Economic Review*, Federal Reserve Bank of Kansas City, fourth quarter 1996.
5. Also, frequent changes in a bank's reserve requirements would complicate its financial planning. In addition, reserve requirements that exceed the reserves a bank would voluntarily hold for its business operations impose a cost to banks by the amount of foregone interest, and the FR hesitates to raise reserve requirements because it would increase that cost.
6. Savings banks and savings and loan associations (thrifts) are supervised by the U.S. Office of Thrift Supervision, and credit unions are supervised by the National Credit Union Administration.
7. In this example of how loans create new bank deposits, we use a 10 percent reserve requirement on transaction deposits for banks, thrift institutions, and credit unions. Transactions deposits are checking or similar accounts from which transfers of funds can be made. Ten percent was the rate in 2003 for institutions with transactions deposits above $42.1 million.

   Suppose customer A deposits $10,000 in the Atlantic bank. The Atlantic bank then lends $9000 to customer B by increasing B's checking account by $9,000 ($10,000 minus the 10 percent reserve). Customer B then buys a car for the $9,000 loan, and the car dealer deposits the payment in the Pacific bank, which increases the bank's deposits by $9,000. At this point, deposits in the Atlantic bank are reduced by $9,000, resulting in a net increment of $1,000 from customer A's initial $10,000 deposit. The Pacific bank then lends $8,100 of the new deposits of $9,000 it obtained from the car dealer (again allowing for a 10 percent reserve requirement) to customer C. Customer C then spends the $8,100 for college tuition, and the college deposits the $8,100 in the Continental bank, which reduces the Pacific bank's net increment in deposits to $900 ($9,000 − $8,100). The chain continues with the Continental bank lending $7,290 (10 percent less than $8,100) to customer D, and so on.

   The total amount of new deposit creation through this mechanism is the sum of the net increment of deposits that each bank has after its loan is spent by the borrower. In the example, the increments to the deposits of the Atlantic and Pacific banks of $1,000 and $900, respectively, add $1,900 to all bank deposits.

   This fractional reserve system adds decreasing increments to bank deposits in the successive rounds of lending and spending from the initial $10,000 by customer A until the process diminishes to zero. Mathematically, the limit to this increase in bank deposits is obtained by dividing the initial deposit by the reserve ratio, in this case $10,000/0.10, which amounts to $100,000. Thus, the initial deposit of $10,000 can result in an ultimate increase of $100,000 in bank deposits. This is referred to as the deposit multiplier, which in this case is 10 (100,000/10,000), and in a simple form is obtained by 1/0.10 (i.e., 1/reserve ratio).
8. Federal Reserve Bank of New York, "The Money Supply," *Fedpoints*, September 2000.
9. For example, among the M1, M2, and M3 component financial assets, nonbank travelers' checks function as currency; demand deposits often require minimum balances below which penalties are paid; saving deposits may forfeit some interest payments if withdrawn before certain dates; and money market securities are subject

to current market interest rates, which impose a greater risk regarding the future value of these assets.

10. Federal debt held by the public fluctuates more with government borrowing needs than does debt held by government trust funds, see Congressional Budget Office, *The Budget and Economic Outlook: Fiscal Years 2004–2013*, January 2003, p. 16.

11. Douglas W. Elmendorf and David L. Reifschneider, "Short-Run Effects of Fiscal Policy with Forward-Looking Financial Markets," *National Tax Journal*, September 2002.

12. Henry Kaufman, *Interest Rates, the Markets, and the New Financial World* (Times Books, 1986), ch. 12.

13. Arturo Estrella and Frederic S. Mishkin, "Predicting U.S. Recessions: Financial Variables as Leading Indicators," *Review of Economics and Statistics*, February 1998; Arturo Estrella, Anthony Rodrigues, and Sebastian Schich, "How Stable Is the Predictive Power of the Yield Curve? Evidence from Germany and the United States," *Review of Economics and Statistics*, August 2003.

14. J. Nellie Liang and Steven A. Sharpe, "Share Repurchases and Employee Stock Options and Their Implications for S&P 500 Share Retirements and Expected Returns," *Finance and Economics Discussion Series* no. 59, Federal Reserve Board, 1999.

15. Kevin Cole, Jean Helwege, and David Laster, "Stock Market Valuation Indicators: Is This Time Different?" *Financial Analysts Journal*, May/June 1996. This estimate of net repurchases is referenced by Liang and Sharpe in note 14, footnote 1.

16. Board of Governors of the Federal Reserve System, *Purposes and Functions*, 8th ed., 1994, ch. 1. The 9th edition of *Purposes* is expected at the end of 2004.

17. The FR Bank of New York president is a permanent member of the FOMC monetary policy decisions that involve buying and selling Treasury securities in open-market operations and through buying and selling the U.S. dollar in foreign exchange markets; the foreign exchange interventions are done in cooperation with the U.S. Treasury Department, which has the overall responsibility for U.S. international financial policy. This special role of the New York Bank evolved over time and reflects the bank's geographic location in the center of financial markets and the legacy of the influence of its forceful president, Benjamin Strong, in the 1920s. See William Greider, *Secrets of the Temple: How the Federal Reserve Runs the Country* (Simon and Schuster, 1987), pp. 292–93, note 15.

The rotating sequence of the eleven other FR bank presidents on the FOMC varies slightly. The Chicago and Cleveland FR bank presidents serve alternately every other year. The other FR bank presidents serve alternately every third year from the following three groups: (1) Boston, Philadelphia, Richmond; (2) Atlanta, St. Louis, Dallas; (3) Minneapolis, Kansas City, San Francisco. There is no record of why the Chicago and Cleveland presidents are on the FOMC more frequently than the other nine bank presidents. This may be because, in the early 1930s before the FOMC was established by law in 1935, Chicago and Cleveland were part of an open-market executive committee of five FR banks (the others were New York, Philadelphia, and Boston), and Chicago was the second-largest city and financial center, and Cleveland represented heavy industrial areas.

In passing the Federal Reserve Act of 1913, Congress left the designation of which cities would have regional FR banks to a three-member Reserve Bank Organizing Committee, composed of the Secretary of the Treasury, Secretary of Agriculture, and the Comptroller of the Currency (see Roger T. Johnson, *Historical Beginnings . . . The Federal Reserve*, The Federal Reserve Bank of Boston, revised December 1995, pp. 35–51). This reflected the political pressure from various constituencies to have a Reserve bank in their district, which may not have been possible to resolve legislatively. When the Committee's recommendations were questioned as being politically motivated, the House of Representatives held hearings in 1914, and the recommendations were upheld. In a much later analogy, Congress took a similar tack on the military base closings in the 1990s, when it set up a commission to recommend specific base closings that Congress could only accept or reject as a whole, thus making the closings politically feasible by absolving Congress from the ire of particular constituencies.

Despite the reliance on the Reserve Bank Organizing Committee, there were several allegations that politics had a role in which cities were recommended to have Reserve banks, resulting in the House hearing noted above (see Roger Johnson, *Historical Beginnings*, pp. 49–51). For example, Missouri, a relatively small state, is the only state with two FR banks, St. Louis and Kansas City. But when the Federal Reserve Act was passed in 1913, the Speaker of the House of Representatives, Champ Clark, was from Missouri, and Senator James Reed, an influential senator, was from Kansas City; also, David Houston, the Secretary of Agriculture and a member of the Reserve Bank Organizing Committee, was from St. Louis. Other examples of suspected political influence are that Cleveland won out over Cincinnati and Pittsburgh because Newton Baker, the Secretary of War and a prominent member of President Woodrow Wilson's cabinet, was from Cleveland; and that Richmond won out over Baltimore because of the influence of Representative Carter Glass, who was from Virginia, and because John Williams, the Comptroller of the Currency and a member of the Reserve Bank Organizing Committee, was from Richmond.

18. Geoffrey M. B. Tootell, "Regional Economic Conditions and the FOMC Votes of District Presidents." *New England Economic Review*, March/April 1991.
19. Geoffrey M. B. Tootell, "Appointment Procedures and FOMC Voting Behavior." *Southern Economic Journal*, July 1996.
20. For example, on January 3, 2001, the board indicated that it would approve a reduction of 0.25 percentage point in the discount rate, and on January 4, 2001, the board approved a proposed reduction of 0.25 percentage point in the discount rate by all FR banks. See Federal Reserve Press Releases, January 3, 2001 and January 4, 2001.
21. A. Jerome Clifford, *The Independence of the Federal Reserve System* (University of Pennsylvania Press, 1965), ch 8; William Greider, *Secrets of the Temple*, ch 10; Donald F. Kettl, *Leadership at the Fed* (Yale University Press, 1986), chs. 3 and 5; and William Safire, *Before the Fall: An Inside View of the Pre-Watergate White House* (Doubleday, 1975) pp. 491–496.

13

Leading Indicator System

The leading indicator system is based on the concept that each phase of the business cycle contains the seeds of the following phase. The four phases of the business cycle of rising and falling economic growth are: recovery, expansion, recession, and contraction (discussed in chapter 1). By focusing on the factors operating in each phase, the leading indicator system provides a basis for monitoring the tendency to move from one phase to the next. The system assesses the strengths and weaknesses in the economy as clues to a quickening or slowing of future rates of economic growth, as well as to cyclical turning points in moving from the upward expansion to the downward recession, and from the recession to the upward recovery, but it does not provide specific forecasts. A supplementary experimental model of the system forecasts the probability that the economy will be in a recession six months later.

The Conference Board publishes the leading indicator system in its monthly journal, *Business Cycle Indicators* (www.conference-board.org). James Stock and Mark Watson publish monthly experimental recession indexes.

This chapter covers the historical development and theoretical premises of the leading indicator system, the calculation of the composite indexes, assessment of the performance of the system, and a supplementary system of the probability of future recessions.

OVERVIEW

Development of the leading indicator system evolved over a quarter of a century. In 1937, Secretary of the Treasury Henry Morgenthau, Jr., requested Wesley Mitchell to compile a list of statistical series to observe for clues as to when the recession that began in 1937 would turn up into a recovery, which Mitchell did in collaboration with Arthur Burns. In 1950, Geoffrey Moore revised this list and added a new set of indicators to observe when an expansion is likely to turn down into a recession. And in 1961, Julius Shiskin developed the leading, coincident, and lagging composite indexes that are the framework of the leading indicator system today.[1]

The terms "leading," "coincident," and "lagging" refer to the timing of the turning points of the indexes relative to those of the business cycle. The leading index turns down before a general recession begins and turns up before the recovery from the recession begins. The coincident index moves in tandem with the cyclical movements of the overall economy, tending to coincide with the designations of expansions and recessions discussed in chapter 1 under Determining Business Cycle Phases. The lagging index turns down after the beginning of a recession and turns up after the beginning of a recovery.

The system is based on Wesley Mitchell's theory that expectations of future profits are the motivating force in the economy.[2] When business executives believe their sales and profits will rise, companies expand production of goods and services and investment in new structures and equipment, but when they believe profits will decline, they reduce production and investment. These actions generate the recovery, expansion, recession, and contraction phases of the business cycle. The leading indicator system treats the future course of profits in two alternative perspectives: (1) businesses' expectations of future sales (leading index), and (2) the differential movements between current production (coincident index) and production costs (lagging index).

The system has been criticized for being excessively empirical and lacking a theoretical framework. Reference is often made to a 1947 article by Tjalling Koopmans that criticized the work by Mitchell and Burns in general and particularly attacked their 1946 book, *Measuring Business Cycles*.[3] I disagree with these criticisms and argue below that the system is grounded in economic theory.

THE PROCESS OF CYCLICAL CHANGE

For background, it is useful to summarize the cyclical phenomena considered to be the major elements underlying the leading indicator system. To illustrate, assume as the cyclical starting point the beginning of the recovery from the low point of the previous recession. In this initial stage, an impetus for increasing production starts an upward movement. Sales increase as households begin purchasing durable goods they had deferred buying during the recession. Unit costs of production decline because the increasing volume of sales is spread over the fixed depreciation and maintenance costs of existing structures and equipment, as well as over the lowered work force and other services resulting from the cutbacks of nonessential costs in the preceding recession. Thus, recoveries have greater efficiencies than would otherwise prevail solely due to the rise in output because of the cutbacks of nonessential costs during recessions. The result is that profits, which are the residual of sales minus costs, increase.

As the momentum spreads and employment and household spending increase, business executives become more optimistic about future sales and order more goods for inventories and invest in new structures and equipment to increase and modernize productive capacity. This is heightened by the increased number of new businesses that start up in anticipation of continued growing markets and higher profits, which in turn stimulates more production, hiring, and spending. When production rises above the high point of the previous cyclical expansion, the recovery turns into the expansion phase of the cyclical upturn.

However, at some point the upward momentum slows. Sales of some items are no longer as brisk because households' needs have changed, and higher prices cause households to defer purchases. Unsold inventories of goods accumulate, leading to reduced prices to sell them, and to reduced orders for new goods to replace them, and thus lower future production. But these goods had been produced at high costs, as the high industrial capacity utilization during the expansion led to an increasing use of outmoded and less efficient equipment, hiring of less efficient workers as unemployment rates fell to low levels, and obtaining loans at high interest rates when the overall demand for money was strong. The high production costs lead businesses to try to maintain prices in order to limit reductions in profit margins, but the resistance to lowering prices in turn leads to lower sales. The combination of lower sales and higher production costs reduces profits enough to dampen incentives for investing in new structures and equipment capacity. The slowdown in sales leads to lower production, and the consequent lower employment, incomes, and spending.

The slowdown has a snowballing effect, analogous to the upward spiral in the earlier stages of the expansion, as households and businesses retrench in their spending. The high point of the expansion has been reached. There is less incentive to take out additional loans which would bolster spending, because thanks to lower incomes, existing loans have become a greater burden to repay. Production and employment are further reduced, lowering worker incomes and household spending, bringing on a recession. Increasing numbers of businesses close down during the recession, and existing businesses cut costs by maintaining lower inventories and reducing employment. If production declines during the recession below the low point of the previous cyclical recession, the recession turns into the contraction phase of cyclical downturn. Technically, the 1981–82 recession turned into a contraction, as the coincident index at the low point of the recession in the fall of 1982 was below the low point of the previous recession in the summer of 1980. But this was so minimal that it hardly qualifies as a contraction. In fact, the last occurrence of a contraction was during the depression of the 1930s, when production was clearly below the previous recession low in 1927 (see chapter 1 under Determining Business Cycle Phases).

The depressed level of production ultimately runs its course as households that have deferred spending because of the economic uncertainty begin to replace their older goods and buy new housing at the lower recession-induced interest rates. This turnaround in sales encourages businesses to order more goods for inventories, thus stimulating production, and the stage is set for the recovery phase, which completes the cycle.

While this is a highly simplified version of cyclical economic movements, it depicts the basic rationale of the leading indicator system. But each business cycle has its unique characteristics due to variations in price movements, unemployment, population growth, development of new products, soundness of the banking system, the stock market, competition from abroad, wars and their anticipation and aftermath, terrorism, and other factors. And it is this uniqueness that makes business cycles unpredictable and intrinsically characterized by surprise.

Because each business cycle is unique, the upturn and downturn of any particular cycle are not fully replicated in any other cycle. Therefore, in assessing economic relationships based on past data, the analyst should be alert to similarities and differences between the current and previous economic environments. It is, in fact, the uniqueness and disruptions of recessions that bring the personal and social stress of high unemployment and lower worker incomes and business profits. These stresses make recessions vastly more harmful than seasonal variations throughout the year, which are fairly predictable and which workers and business have experience coping with, as Victor Zarnowitz points out.[4] Zarnowitz also notes that seasonal changes are appropriately handled by private parties, while cyclical disruptions require government involvement. Seasonal variations are discussed in chapter 1 under Seasonality.

Duration of Cyclical Expansions and Recessions

While recessions have been less frequent since the end of World War II than previously, they have not gone away (see chapter 1 under Changing Characteristics of Business Cycles Since the Nineteenth Century). The continuing appearance of recessions has raised the question about whether there is a greater likelihood of a recession occurring the longer an expansion continues. Research on this by Francis Diebold, Glenn Rudenbusch, and Daniel Sichel concludes that before World War II there was a greater chance of a recession occurring the longer an expansion was in progress. However, after World War II, there is no indication of a linkage between the length of an expansion and the onset of a recession.[5] In an assessment of this issue under the designation of "Do Expansions Die of Old Age?" Victor Zarnowitz concludes that it is not the passage of calendar time that is relevant, but rather the events, actions, and perceptions of the economy over time that count.[6]

Endogenous Nature of the Indicator System

The leading indicator system is grounded in interrelationships and sequences among economic phenomena of spending, income, production, employment, investment, prices, wages, and so on that occur *within* the economy, and so are defined as endogenous, as Philip Klein notes.[7] External shocks, such as the sharp rise in oil prices following the Arab oil embargo in the fall of 1973 and again during the Iranian revolution in the late 1970s and early 1980s, and the impacts of the September 11, 2001, attacks, such as the sharp, short decline in overall output, while reflected in the movements of the composite indexes, are not part of the theoretical underpinning of the leading indicator system, as summarized above under The Process of Cyclical Change.

Because such shocks are exogenous, that is, *outside* the premises of the leading indicator system, the system cannot "explain" the economic impact of the shocks in their immediate aftermath. Robert Gordon defines endogenous variables as "variables explained by an economic theory," and "exogenous variables as variables that are relevant but whose behavior a given theory does not attempt to explain; their values are taken as given."[8]

External Shocks

External shocks to the economy are surprise exogenous events that, as noted in the previous section, are not explained by a given economic theory. Victor Zarnowitz and Jacinto Torres assessed the effects of sixteen potential business cycle shocks from the Cuban missile crisis in 1962 and the assassination of President John Kennedy in 1963 (both occurred in the early phase of the 1960s expansion), to the September 11, 2001, attacks and the revelation of corporate accounting and executive malfeasance in October 2001 (both occurred in the late phase of the 2001 recession).[9] The sixteen potential cyclical shocks all occurred in various cyclical upturn periods from early recovery to late expansion, except for the Iraqi invasion of Kuwait in 1990, which coincided with the beginning of the recession of 1990–91, and the September 11 attack and the corporate scandals of 2001, which occurred in the late phase of the 2001 recession, as noted above.

The sixteen potential cyclical shocks typically had short and limited effects on economic growth, including the stock market crash of 1987. The exceptions were the Arab oil embargo in 1973, and the Iranian revolution in the late 1970s and the early 1980s. Both were associated with supply shocks and exploding oil prices that were in part related to rising and high inflation along with lagging productivity and economic growth in the 1970s and early 1980s.

Zarnowitz and Torres concluded that the effects of the terrorist attacks of September 11 were mainly in the drop and slow revival of spending in the airlines, hotels and motels, insurance, recreation, travel, and entertainment industries. Their other findings include the following. Most of the 2001 recession had played out by the time of the attacks, and the drop in overall output after the attacks was deep but brief. The main problem for the recovery in economic growth is the weakness in business investment in equipment and structures, which was a leftover of the excessive investments in the late 1990s and 2000. The corporate scandals affected the depressed stock market in 2002 through a decline in investor confidence.

Imbalances

There are frequent references in the leading indicator system to imbalances. Imbalances refer to economic excesses and deficiencies that divert the economy from less than optimal growth. They include a wide range of economic phenomena, such as investment based on unrealistically optimistic or pessimistic assumptions regarding future economic growth, unused or overused industrial capacity, price inflation resulting from supply shocks, price deflation of assets resulting from a previous speculative binge, high unemployment, shortage of workers with needed skills, and unplanned inventory accumulation or depletion.

While the leading indicator system does not provide forecasts of cyclical turning points or the rate of economic growth, it can suggest, with supporting analysis, if economic growth is headed for a stable course, an accelerating or decelerating rate of growth, or an absolute decline. Such indicated movements in economic growth result from changes in the imbalances that are implicit in the composite leading, coincident, and lagging indexes.

This spotlights the need for the analyst to focus on examining the nature and extent of the current imbalances.

THE PRIMARY ROLE OF PROFITS

The leading indicator system is based on the idea that profits are the driving force in the private enterprise economy. Business decisions on production, prices, employment, and investment are understood in relation to profits—both the trends of past profits and the perception of future profits. Thus, changing expectations of profits affect the direction and pace of economic growth.

Rationale for the Components of the Three Composite Indexes

The system combines several component economic indicators into a composite leading index, a composite coincident index, and a composite lagging index. The following discussion capsulizes the three composite indexes and the rationale for several of the components, as developed by Feliks Tamm.[10]

The *composite leading index* indicates business perceptions of future profits. It represents businesses' anticipation of future economic developments, and the response in actions and plans to those expectations. The ten component economic indicators of the leading index are:

1. *Average weekly hours of production workers, manufacturing.* Because of uncertainty in the economic outlook, employers are more likely to adjust the hours of previously hired workers before hiring new workers at signs the recession is ending, or laying off workers at signs the expansion is weakening.

2. *Initial weekly claims for unemployment insurance.* Increases or decreases in unemployment indicate business expectations of the demand for labor.

3. *Manufacturers' new orders, consumer goods, and materials* (price-adjusted dollars). Business commitments to buy items indicate future levels of production.

4. *Vendor performance, slower deliveries diffusion index.* Delivery time reflects the strength of demand, brisk when the time from the placement of the order to delivery is long because of the large backlog of orders, and weak when the delivery time is short.

5. *Manufacturers' new orders, nondefense capital goods industries* (price-adjusted dollars). Business commitments in the volatile cyclical industries that fluctuate considerably between expansions and recessions.

6. *New private housing units authorized by local building permits.* Permits provide advance indication of housing construction, which is cyclically sensitive to changes in interest rates and expected changes in employment.

7. *Stock prices, 500 common stocks* (Standard & Poor's). Stock prices reflect investor expectations of economic growth and profits, and thus future investment and household spending, and as noted above, expectations can be self-fulfilling. High stock prices make it easier for businesses to raise funds for structures and equipment investment and other ventures by selling new stock to the public (equity financing), which entails no required payback to the buyer of the value of the stock or the payment of dividends. By contrast, low stock prices make it more likely that businesses will obtain funds from the public by selling bonds— that is debt financing, in which the principal is repaid and there are specified interest payments. Stock prices also affect household wealth, and in turn, future household spending. Stockholders perceive they have more to spend when stock prices, and thus their wealth, are rising than when they are falling. However, stock market prices also reflect speculation, insider trading, and program trading, which are not associated with underlying economic factors. *Therefore, I disagree with the inclusion of the stock market prices in the leading index.*

8. *Money supply, M2* (price-adjusted dollars). The amount of financial liquid assets generated by the interplay of investments, savings, borrowing, and lending affects the purchasing power available for business and household transactions, such as buying materials, hiring labor, investing in structures and equipment, and buying consumer goods. *I disagree with the inclusion of the money supply in the leading index because, in my view, the money supply is a passive, rather than an active agent, in the economy—see chapter 12 under Passive Role of the Money Supply.*

9. *Interest rate spread, ten-year Treasury bonds less federal funds.* The interest rate spread is associated with the stance of monetary policy. A wider spread indicates a looser monetary policy tending toward lower interest rates, and a narrower or negative spread indicates a tighter monetary policy tending toward higher interest rates.

10. *Consumer expectations* (University of Michigan). Household attitudes on the outlook for the economy and their own financial well-being give clues to future household spending. In a sense, expectations are self-fulfilling; that is, if people think the economy will do well, they are more likely to spend freely and make the economy do well. However, household opinion surveys only give slight improvements in forecasts of the economy, as noted in chapter 4 under Consumer Optimism and Pessimism Opinion Surveys.

The *composite coincident index* measures various aspects of production that reflect the current pace of economic output. It indicates whether the economy is growing or declining, and thus is the primary gauge of expansion and recession periods. The coincident index corresponds closely to the designation of the cyclical turning points of recession and recovery by the National Bureau of Economic Research Business Cycle Dating Committee, although the two statistics are prepared independently. The four component economic indicators of the coincident index are:

1. *Employees on nonagricultural payrolls.* Represents the labor inputs in producing goods and services.

2. *Personal income less transfer payments* (price-adjusted dollars). Real income earned by workers and investors reflects the resources used in producing the nation's output.

3. *Industrial production index.* Because manufacturing, mining, and gas and electric utilities tend to be the more cyclically volatile industries, current production levels in these industries are a good indicator of the cyclical elements in the economy.

4. *Manufacturing and trade sales* (price-adjusted dollars). Movement of goods within the economy between manufacturing plants, from manufacturers to wholesalers, from wholesalers to retailers, and from retailers to households and businesses traces the flows of goods in production and from production to distribution.

The *composite lagging index* represents production costs and inventory and debt burdens that may encourage or retard economic growth. A slow increase or a decline in the lagging index is conducive to economic growth, while a rapid increase in the lagging index is conducive to a recession. The lagging index also confirms that a cyclical upturn into a recovery and a cyclical downturn into a recession has occurred. The seven component economic indicators of the lagging index are:

1. *Average duration of unemployment* (weeks). This indicator is plotted on an inverted scale, appearing to rise when the average duration of unemployment actually falls. As the labor market strengthens in an expansion, the ranks of the unemployed come to be dominated by people who have just started to look for work. Unlike the long-term unemployed, they may not take the first job offer they receive, and so a low average duration of unemployment is associated with rising wage pressures in the economy.

2. *Inventories to sales ratio—manufacturing and trade* (price-adjusted dollars). Inventories are a major cost factor for businesses. The higher inventories are relative to sales, the more expensive they are to hold, because they entail borrowed money which results in interest costs, or because they tie up company funds.

3. *Labor cost per unit of output, manufacturing* (monthly change). Labor costs in relation to production affect profits, which in turn influence decisions to expand or contract production, employment, and investment.

4. *Average prime rate charged by banks.* Interest rates charged for business loans indicate the cost of borrowing, which affects profits and the willingness to borrow.

5. *Commercial and industrial loans outstanding* (price-adjusted dollars). The interest burden on existing loans is higher, and the availability of money for new loans is lower, the greater the level of outstanding loans.

6. *Consumer installment credit outstanding to personal income ratio.* The debt burden of consumers suggests they are likely to take on more loans when the ratio is low and thus increase spending, and repay existing loans when the ratio is high and thus decrease spending.

7. *Consumer price index for services, annual rate* (monthly change). Prices of services reflect price pressures stemming from production costs in labor-intensive industries.

In assessing monthly changes in the leading, coincident, and lagging composite indexes, the analyst should consider whether the movements represent those of most of the component indicators, or if they result from relatively large movements in a small number of the component indicators. The movements of the composites are more significant when most of the components move in a similar direction than when they are driven by large movements in a small number of components.

LIMITATION FOR FORECASTING

The leading indicator system is a striking example of how revisions to preliminary data affect analyses of the state of the economy (see chapter 1 under Data

Table 13.1

Composite Leading Index—Lead Times Provided by Real Time and Revised Data before Cyclical Turning Points of Recessions and Recoveries: 1969–2001 (in months)

	Real time data[a]	Revised data
Peak expansion month on the eve of recession		
December 1969	3	8
November 1973	0	9
January 1980	10	15
July 1981	3	3
July 1990	0	6
March 2001	0	14
Trough recession month on the eve of recovery		
November 1970	1	7
March 1975	0	1
July 1980	2	3
November 1982	8	8
March 1991	1	2
November 2001		

Sources: Based on U.S. Bureau of Economic Analysis and The Conference Board data.

a. Measures derived by the author. See text.

Accuracy). Based on revised data, the system provides early signals of a cyclical downturn well before the onset of most recessions and of a cyclical upturn that is observable before about half of all recoveries. The problem is that many of the "advance" signals become apparent only years later when the revised data are incorporated into the system. The real-time (contemporaneous) data that are available to analysts during the critical months preceding recessions and recoveries often do not provide such early indications of cyclical turning points, as noted by Evan Koenig and Kenneth Emery and by H.O. Stekler.[11]

Table 13.1 compares the real-time data of the leading index with the historical revised data of the leading index for the months preceding the six recessions and the five recoveries from 1969 to 2001. I derived the real-time monthly data in the table from previously published data for the recessions beginning in 1969, 1973, 1980, 1891, and 1990, when the leading indicator system was conducted by the Bureau of Economic Analysis in the U.S. Department of Commerce, and from previously published data for the recession beginning in 2001 by The Conference Board, which assumed responsibility for the system in December

1995. The real-time data are based on taking the data series as they existed on the eve of the peak of each expansion and the eve of the trough of each recession (the leading index data are first available one month after the reference month).

Of the six recessions, the real time data gave no months' notice of a downturn in three cases, three months' notice in two cases, and ten months' notice in one case. In contrast, the revised data, which became available in subsequent years, showed advance indications of six to fifteen months before a downturn in five of the six recessions. Thus, the real-time data only gave a usable signal of a pending recession in one of the six cases.

For example, data for March 2001, which is the high point of the expansion preceding the recession that began in April 2001, first became available at the end of April. In reviewing these real-time data, which were available at the end of April, I determined that the leading index for the preceding fifteen months had declined from 110.7 in January 2000, to 110.3 in June 2000, to 108.5 in December 2000, and then fluctuated with no upward or downward movement to March 2001, hardly a clear sign of a pending recession. In contrast, the revised data showed fourteen months of advance notice of a recession.

The revised data are superior in establishing lead times of at least six months before the onset of a recession because they incorporate economic indicators and statistical methodologies that better represent the economy of the period than the real-time data, the data available at the time. Major revisions of the composite indexes occurred at ten- to fifteen-year intervals through the 1980s, but became more frequent in the 1990s. Two types of changes are usually made: (a) the composition of the indexes is changed to replace some data components with new or modified ones, and (b) new formulations of the statistical factors such as weights and standardization factors are introduced. In addition to these basic structural changes, monthly data are continuously revised on a current basis as part of the routine preparation of revised economic data series. Revised data are important for developing historical analytic relationships, but they obviously do not ensure that the subsequent real-time data will give observable advance signals of cyclical turning points. Because the economy is continually changing and every business cycle is different, indicators selected based on their performance in past cycles do not always provide the same level of performance in future cycles.

The lack of advance indications of cyclical turning points in the real-time data significantly limits the use of the leading indicator system for economic forecasting. This highlights the need for the analyst to assess rates of change in the composite indexes along with their change in direction for clues of future economic movements. Because the leading index, on a real-time basis, may not turn down several months before the onset of a recession, or may not turn up several months before the onset of a recovery, it is important to be watchful of

*a slowing in the rate of increase during expansions and a slowing in the rate
of decrease during recessions.*

Improving the Real-Time Data

There are two aspects to improving the real-time performance of the composite
leading index. One is a minor one associated with the one-month data lag in
the availability of three components of the composite index: new orders for
consumer goods and materials in price-adjusted dollars, new orders for nondefense capital goods in price-adjusted dollars, and the money supply (M2) in
price-adjusted dollars. To compensate for these one-month lags, the Conference
Board projects the expected values for the one month of missing data in advance
of their availability based on the previous movements of each indicator (referred
to as an auto-regressive statistical procedure).[12] Because the one-month data lags
in the three component indicators are corrected in each subsequent month, they
are not a significant real-time problem.

The major problem with the real-time data stems from the size of the revisions in later years for several component indicators of the composite leading
index. This causes the difference between the real-time and the revised data in
Table 13.1. Thus, the basic needed improvement for the real-time data is to
reduce the size of these later-year revisions.

One approach for making the real-time data relevant for forecasting cyclical
turning points is to develop a methodology for "forecasting" the likely extent
of the later-year revisions. This would be analogous to what is done in projecting
the expected data one month in advance for the three components of the leading
index that are available with a one-month lag, as noted above.

*The reduction of revisions to the component indicators of the composite lead-
ing index should be a priority for research in the leading indicator system.*

CALCULATION OF THE COMPOSITE INDEXES

The leading, coincident, and lagging composite indexes are developed by combining the component economic indicators within each of the three composites
into the single aggregate number.[13] The three indexes for each new month are
calculated based on the monthly movements of the components. The general
concept is described in chapter 1 under Index Numbers.

Many economic indicators are evaluated to determine their appropriateness
for inclusion in the composite indexes.[14] The overall considerations in selecting
them are: (a) their theoretical role in the leading, coincident, and lagging process,
and (b) how they perform empirically in terms of leading and lagging general
business cycles after World War II. The specific criteria used are economic
significance (cyclical timing is economically logical); statistical adequacy (data

collected and processed in a statistically reliable way); consistent timing (data exhibit a consistent timing pattern over time as a leading, coincident, or lagging indicator); conformity (data conform well to the business cycle); smoothness (month-to-month data movements are not too erratic); and currency (data are published on a reasonably prompt monthly schedule).

The component data series selected for use are then combined into the three composite indexes using equal weights for each component economic indicator. Equal weights, in which all component indicators have the same importance, are assigned to all components because research indicated that differential weights used in the past did not materially affect movements of the composite indexes.[15] A modification is made to ensure that components with relatively large upward and downward movements do not dominate the index. This is achieved by using differentiated "standardization factors" for each component indicator of the leading and lagging composite indexes so that the volatility of the monthly movements is the same as the volatility of the coincident composite index. The volatility is the variance of the month-to-month percent changes in the coincident index.

Inversion of Unemployment Indicators

Economic data that are plotted on charts typically are depicted as reflecting a rising economy when the line moves upward and a declining economy when the line moves downward. These upward and downward movements conform to the directional movements of the upward (expansion) and downward (recession) phases of the business cycle.

However, for two indicators of the leading indicator system, initial claims for unemployment insurance (leading index) and average duration of unemployment (lagging index), this movement is reversed. For them, a decline indicates a rise in or stimulus to production, as they conform to the business cycle phases in the reverse direction. Consequently, the scales on the vertical axes of their charts are inverted, so that graphically, an increase is shown as declining and a decrease is shown as rising. This makes their directional movements visually consistent with general business cycle movements. They are also inverted when used to calculate the monthly movements of the leading and lagging composite indexes, so that the unemployment numbers do not distort the indexes' movements. If they were not inverted, they would have invalid movements.

ASSESSMENTS OF THE LEADING INDICATOR SYSTEM

This section discusses the cyclical movements, coincident/lagging ratio, and false signals of the leading indicator system.

Cyclical Movements

Figure 13.1 shows the movements of the three composite indexes covering seven downturns to recession and six upturns to recovery from 1960 to March 2003. The Business Cycle Dating Committee of the National Bureau of Economic Research is the arbiter in designating the turning points of the general business cycle (see chapter 1 under Determining Business Cycle Phases). The vertical bars represent recession periods. The data in Figure 13.1 represent revised data, not the real-time data that were available when the cyclical turning points occurred, as summarized in Table 13.1 above under Limitation for Forecasting.

The behavior of the three composite indexes is consistent with their theoretical role discussed earlier. The leading index turns down before a recession and up before a recovery. The direction and timing of the coincident index are close to those of the general economy, as the turning points of the coincident index are identical or very close to those in the overall economy. The cyclical turns in the lagging index occur after those in the general economy, except for the case noted below. Because the lagging index is last in the sequence of cyclical movements, it also confirms that a cyclical turn has or has not occurred.

For the leading composite index, the lead time in signaling the onset of a recession varied considerably among the seven recessions. In the four recessions from 1960 to 1980, and in the recession beginning in 2001, the lead time ranged from eight to fifteen months. The lead times of three and six months in the recessions beginning in 1981 and 1990, respectively, were noticeably shorter. The leading index led the upturn of the six recoveries by two to eight months.

For the lagging composite index, the cyclical variations were even more stark. The lag time after the onset of a recession also varied considerably among the cycles, ranging from two to thirteen months in the five recessions from 1960s to 1980s. But counter to the theory, the lagging index led the onset of the recessions beginning in 1990 by twelve months and in 2001 by four months. In fact, the lead of the lagging index exceeded the lead of the leading index by six months at the onset of the recession beginning in 1990. The lag in the lagging index in the six recoveries ranged from three to twenty-two months.

The above analysis centers on the likelihood of a prospective turning point in the business cycle. There is no assessment of the relationship between the size of a decline in the leading index preceding a recession and the size of the decline in the coincident index during the recession. Similarly, there is no assessment of the relationship between the size of the rise in the leading index during a recession preceding a recovery and the time it takes for the coincident index during the recovery to reach the peak level of the previous expansion, above which the recovery turns into the expansion phase of the business cycle.

The leading indicator system is most relevant for assessing the strengths and weaknesses of the economy in terms of growth rates, but not for forecasting a cyclical downturn into a recession or an upturn into a recovery. There are wide variations both in respect to the anticipatory onset of a recession and a recovery in the composite leading index, and in the confirmation that a recession and a recovery began in the lagging composite index. This is accentuated by the still weaker advance signals in the real time, as distinct from the revised indexes. The system requires far more development for it to be useful for signaling cyclical turning points.

Coincident/Lagging Ratio

The coincident index divided by the lagging index is an alternative leading index, as developed by Geoffrey Moore.[16] Theoretically, this ratio is significant because it relates production to costs, providing in effect another view of profits, which is the underlying concept of the leading indicator system. This reflects the fact that profits are the difference between production and costs. For example, if the coincident index (production) increases or decreases at the same rate as the lagging index (costs), there is no change in the profit picture, thus signifying continued economic growth at the current rate. However, differential movements in the two indexes suggest other tendencies in the economy. If the coincident index increases at a faster rate or decreases at a slower rate than the lagging index, this indicates an increase in profits (since production is rising faster than costs) and higher economic growth in the future. But if the coincident index increases at a slower rate or decreases at a faster rate, a decline in profits and lower future economic growth are indicated. Algebraically, the relationship of the coincident/lagging ratio to profits appears as follows:

$$\frac{\text{Coincident}}{\text{Lagging}} = \frac{\text{Production}}{\text{Costs}} = \text{Profit rate}$$

Figure 13.1 shows that the coincident/lagging ratio had monthly leads similar to those of the leading composite index before two of the seven recessions from the 1960s to the early 2000s—1960 and 1974. The coincident/lagging ratio lead was several months shorter that those of the leading index preceding the onset of the recessions beginning in 1969, 1980, and 2001. The coincident/lagging ratio lead was several months longer than that in the composite leading index in the recession beginning in 1981.

Before the onset of recoveries, the coincident/lagging ratio had shorter leads than the composite leading index in the recoveries of 1960, 1975, and 1980 (the coincident/lagging ratio actually had no leads in 1960 and 1975). The coincident/lagging ratio had longer leads than the composite leading index in the recoveries

340

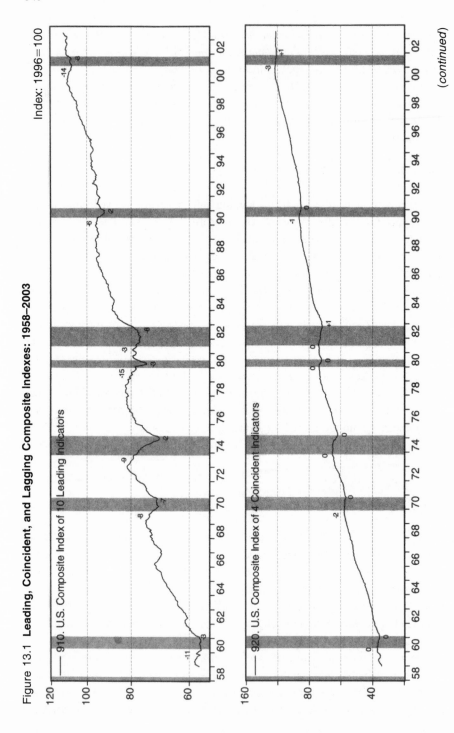

Figure 13.1 **Leading, Coincident, and Lagging Composite Indexes: 1958–2003**

Index: 1996=100

910. U.S. Composite Index of 10 Leading Indicators

920. U.S. Composite Index of 4 Coincident Indicators

(continued)

Figure 13.1 (*continued*)

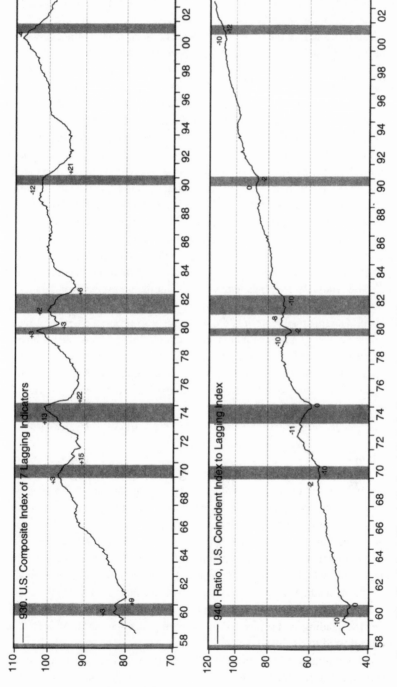

Source: The Conference Board, *Business Cycle Indicators*, August 2003.

Note: Vertical bars are recession periods. Numbers are monthly leads (−) and lags (+) from cyclical turning points.

of 1970 and 1982. The coincident/lagging ratio and the composite leading index had the same leads in the recovery of 1991.

The lead times before the onset of recessions typically were noticeably longer than the lead times before the onset of recoveries in both measures, with the following exceptions. In the 1969–70 and the 1981–82 recessions, the lead times of the recoveries exceeded those of the recessions. And the coincident/lagging ratio showed no lead at the onset of the recession beginning in 1990.

The coincident/lagging ratio showed noticeable variations in the pattern of lead times for individual cycles, similar to the experience of the leading composite index. This uniqueness of each cycle limits the usefulness of applying historical relationships to the current phase in any cycle, as noted previously.

An advantage of using the coincident/lagging ratio to predict economic movements is that it is based on different data and a different concept from those in the leading composite index. This independent measure, internally generated from composite indexes within the leading indicator system, is a check on the leading composite index. In addition, the coincident/lagging ratio suggests a concept of equilibrium between sales and costs in which the economy is considered to be relatively well balanced with no significant excesses or deficiencies in production, incomes, costs, and prices. Yet, this state may never be reached in practice, as adjustments are made continuously to production, prices, wages, and interest rates—all aimed at increasing profits, as noted by Wesley Mitchell.[17]

Cyclical patterns of the coincident/lagging ratio vary noticeably from cycle to cycle and from the timing of the leading composite index. In periods when movements of the coincident/lagging ratio and the leading composite index are similar, the analyst should give greater credence to the signals of the leading indicator system than when the two measures have divergent movements.

False Signals

The economy moves unevenly in both cyclical expansions and recessions, slowing down and speeding up as well as declining for short spells in expansions and rising for short spells in recessions. Because of these variations, it is often difficult in the current period to determine if a changing rate of growth or a reversal of direction signifies a fundamental change or a temporary countermovement from which the previous trend will reappear. Temporary reversals of direction in the leading indicator system—reversals, that is, suggesting a cyclical change that did not follow—are commonly referred to as "false signals." For example, the leading composite index temporary declines in 1966, 1984, and 1995 are referred to as false signals.

Those downturns suggested possible oncoming recessions, but the movements were subsequently reversed. A slowdown in economic growth, as measured by the coincident index, followed these downturns, but the declines were limited and did not turn into a recession.

Thus, reference to these periods as false signals seems misplaced, because false signals reflect an assumed forecast of cyclical turning points by the leading indicator system. However, the forecasting property of the system is nuanced, and does not identify cyclical turning points.

PROBABILITY OF FUTURE RECESSIONS: EXPERIMENTAL INDEXES

The leading indicator system does not forecast when turning points in the business cycle will occur, as noted previously. However, James Stock and Mark Watson developed on an experimental basis two monthly recession indexes that predict the likelihood of a recession six months ahead.[18] Their measures are available through the National Bureau of Economic Research (NBER), though the forecasts do not necessarily represent the views of other researchers or the directors or officers of the NBER, and they are not a publication of the NBER (http://ksghome.harvard.edu/~.JStock.Academic.Ksg/xri).

The Stock and Watson recession indexes are based on establishing a leading index and a coincident index that are rigorously linked to each other in terms of their historical relationship. The goal of their system is for the leading index to predict what the coincident index will be at a future date. Based on the historical experience of the indicators, they construct a leading and a coincident index so that the leading index typically leads the coincident index by six months. Using these indexes, they can make statements such as, "The probability that the economy will be in a recession six months from now is X percent."

The coincident index in the experimental recession indexes has the same four components as the coincident index in the leading indicator system, except that the experimental index uses "employee-hours" in place of "employees" in non-agricultural industries.

The component indicators of the experimental leading indexes differ substantially from those in the leading indicator system. The system's leading composite index has ten domestic components, three of which are financial. One experimental leading index has seven components, three of which are financial, and thus it has a substantially greater representation of financial variables than the system's leading composite index. This experimental leading index also includes an international item and an employment item related to slack work, neither of which is in the leading composite index. The component items of the experimental leading index are:

1. New private housing building permits
2. Unfilled orders for durable goods manufacturers (price-adjusted dollars)

3. International nominal exchange rates between the United States and the United Kingdom, Germany, France, Italy, and Japan, trade weighted
4. Workers employed part-time due to slack work in nonagricultural industries
5. Ten-year Treasury bond interest rate (constant maturity)
6. Interest rate spread between six-month commercial paper and six-month Treasury bills
7. Yield curve difference between ten-year Treasury bonds and one-year Treasury bonds (constant maturity)

An alternative experimental recession index is based on forecasts of seven nonfinancial leading indicators. Three are the same as those in the above experimental leading index with financial indicators: housing building permits, manufacturers' unfilled orders, and foreign exchange rates. The four other indicators are a help-wanted index (which is a substitute for the slack-work indicator), average weekly hours in manufacturing, vendor performance (percentage of companies receiving slow deliveries), and capacity utilization in manufacturing.

The coincident and leading indexes underlie the preparation of the two experimental recession indexes. The weights of the coincident composite index are derived from a statistical model that estimates the co-movement in time series. The weights of the leading composite index are derived from a statistical model in which the weights are chosen so that the resultant composite index is an "optimal" predictor of six-month-ahead movements in the coincident index.

The two experimental recession indexes' estimates of the probability of a future recession are based on forecasts of overall economic activity six months ahead. These six-month forecasts, which are updated every month, reflect the expected movements of each of the seven component indicators of the experimental financial and nonfinancial leading indexes, based on statistical analysis.

The probability that the economy will be in a recession six months ahead is derived from a comparison of the expected future movements of the experimental leading and coincident indexes with their behavior in previous expansions and recessions. This technique is referred to as statistical pattern recognition, in which the data set matches, or is in a class of, prespecified patterns.

The experimental recession indexes did a poor job of predicting the recessions that began in August 1990 and in April 2001. For example, based on revised data, in the months leading up to the August 1990 recession, the recession index that included the financial indicators peaked at a 24 percent probability in April that the economy would be in a recession in October 1990, while the probability for the index excluding financial variables peaked at 38 percent in April that the economy would be in a recession in October 1990. Thus, the recession index excluding financial variables had a superior, though still weak indication of an oncoming recession. Both indexes declined from the peak probabilities in the next few months. Based on the experience of the traditional leading indicator system, it is likely that the probability of recession in 1990 was lower based on the contemporaneous data that were available in 1990.

An even lower probability of a recession appeared in the months leading up to the April 2001 recession, based on revised data. The recession index that included the financial indicators peaked at a 12 percent probability in November 2000 that the economy would be in a recession in May 2001, while the probability for the index excluding financial variables peaked at 13 percent in December 2000 that the economy would be in a recession in June 2001. Both indexes declined from the peak probabilities in the next few months. Thus, there was little difference in the likelihood of a recession in the two indexes, contrary to the experience in the 1990 recession noted above. Also, as noted above, based on the experience of the traditional leading indicator system, it is likely that the probability of recession in 2001 was lower based on the contemporaneous data that were available in 2000 and early 2001.

The higher probability of a recession in the experimental recession index excluding financial variables in 1990 reflects the fact that monetary policy preceding the 1990–91 recession generally was neutral rather than restrictive. For example, the federal funds rate on interbank loans, which is a good indicator of Federal Reserve monetary policies, declined during the last half of 1989 and was level during the first half of 1990 (federal funds are discussed in chapter 12 under Implementing Monetary Policies). Mark Watson notes that financial variables in the recession index were modestly optimistic about future economic growth.[19] This differed from the tight monetary policies of higher interest rates in combating inflation that typically preceded earlier recessions. The statistical analyses of those periods based on revised data indicated that the recession index that included financial variables performed better than the nonfinancial recession index.

By contrast, in the period leading up to the 2001 recession, there was little difference in the probability of a recession in the two recession indexes. This occurred despite the anti-inflationary policy followed by the Federal Reserve. Thus, it raised the federal funds rate from February 1999 through July 2000, and then kept the rate at the high level of 6.5 percent through November 2000, before beginning the long term series of cuts from December 2000 to a historic low of 1 percent in July 2003 (see chapter 3 under Federal Reserve Policies Preceding the 2001 Recession).

While both recession indexes were poor predictors of the 1990 and 2001 recession, the index excluding financial variables had a better record than the index including financial variables. This does not diminish the importance of interest rates in the economy. It means that the statistical model did not adequately account for the effect of interest rates.

The experimental indexes are an interesting development in the field of leading economic indicators, but they need more research to improve their forecasting capability. This research should focus on improving the forecasting power of the experimental indexes using contemporaneous data.

REVIEW QUESTIONS

- The leading indicator system is based on two main ideas: (a) the current phase of the business cycle contains the seeds of the next phase, and (b) profits are the prime mover of the economy. Describe the role of profits as the economy moves from expansion to recession to recovery to expansion.
- How do data revisions affect the usefulness of the leading indicator system?
- What is the conceptual difference between the leading index and the ratio of the coincident index to the lagging index?
- In reporting on the leading index, newspaper articles sometimes state that a decline in the index for three consecutive months signals a coming recession. What is wrong with this interpretation?
- During an expansion, assume that for several months the leading index turns down but the coincident/lagging ratio continues to rise. What does this suggest for future economic growth?
- What do "false signals" sometimes signify?
- What do the experimental recession indexes contribute to the leading indicator system?

Extra Credit

- Why is the lead time of the leading index before a recession typically longer than the lead time before a recovery?
- The gross domestic product adjusted for price change (real GDP) is the most comprehensive measure of the current health of the economy. Why, then, do we need the index of coincident indicators, in addition to GDP data?
- Why are income transfers, such as Social Security and unemployment insurance benefit payments, excluded from the income component of the coincident index?

NOTES

1. Geoffrey H. Moore, *Business Cycles, Inflation and Forecasting*, 2d ed. (Ballinger 1983), ch. 24. The history is recounted in this book. There are three milestone

publications of the development. See also Wesley C. Mitchell and Arthur F. Burns, *Statistical Indicators of Cyclical Revivals*, Bulletin 69 (National Bureau of Economic Research, 1938), reprinted in: National Bureau of Economic Research, *Business Cycle Indicators*, ed. Geoffrey H. Moore, 1961; Geoffrey H. Moore, "Statistical Indicators of Cyclical Revivals and Recessions," Occasional Paper 31, National Bureau of Economic Research, 1950; and Julius Shiskin, "Signals of Recession and Recovery," Occasional Paper 77, National Bureau of Economic Research, 1961.

2. Wesley C. Mitchell, *Business Cycles: The Problem and Its Setting* (National Bureau of Economic Research, 1927), pp. 105–107.

3. Tjalling C. Koopmans, "Measurement without Theory," *Review of Economics and Statistics*, August 1947.

4. Victor Zarnowitz, *Business Cycles: Theory, History, Indicators, and Forecasting* (University of Chicago Press, 1992), p. 262.

5. Francis X. Diebold, Glenn D. Rudenbusch, and Daniel E. Sichel, "Further Evidence on Business-Cycle Duration Dependence," *Business Cycles, Indicators, and Forecasting*, ed. by James H. Stock and Mark W. Watson (University of Chicago Press, 1993).

6. Zarnowitz, *Business Cycles*, pp. 258–62.

7. Philip A. Klein, "Assessing Business Cycle Indicators: An End-of-the Century Perspective," *Business Cycle Indicators Handbook* (The Conference Board, December 2000).

8. Robert J. Gordon, *Macroeconomics* 6th ed. (HarperCollins College Publishers, 1993), Glossary, p. G2.

9. Victor Zarnowitz and Jacinto Torres, Jr., "Economic Context and Consequences of 9/11, a Year Later," *Business Cycle Indicators*, September 2002.

10. Feliks Tamm, "An Introduction to the System of Coincident, Leading and Lagging Indexes," Mimeo, Bureau of Economic Analysis, U.S. Department of Commerce, 1984.

11. Evan F. Koenig and Kenneth M. Emery, "Misleading Indicators? Using the Composite Leading Indicators to Predict Cyclical Turning Points," *Economic Review*, Federal Reserve Bank of Dallas, July 1991; and H. O. Stekler, "Interpreting Movements in the Composite Index of Leading Indicators," *Business Economics*, July 2003.

12. Robert H. McGuckin, Ataman Ozyildirim, and Victor Zarnowitz, "A More Timely and Useful Index of Leading Indicators," *Economics Program Working Paper Series*, The Conference Board, February 2003.

13. The Conference Board, *Business Cycles Indicators Handbook*, December 2000, Section IV.

14. Ibid., pp. 16–19.

15. Jacinto L. Torres, Jr., "2003 Annual Benchmark Revisions to the Composite Indexes," *Business Cycles Indicators*, January 2003, pp. 2–3.

16. Geoffrey H. Moore, "Generating Leading Indicators from Lagging Indicators," *Western Economic Journal*, June 1969.

17. Mitchell, *Business Cycles*, pp. 186–88.

18. James H. Stock and Mark W. Watson, "A Procedure for Predicting Recessions with Leading Indicators: Econometric Issues and Recent Experience," in *Business Cycles, Indicators, and Forecasting*, ed. by James S. Stock and Mark W. Watson (University of Chicago Press, 1993).

19. Mark W. Watson, "Using Econometric Models to Predict Recessions." *Economic Perspectives*, Federal Reserve Bank of Chicago, November/December 1991.

14

Noneconomic Intangibles

The dependence on statistical measurement in an empirical book such as this is obvious. There are considerable macroeconomic data available, many of high statistical quality, for conducting sophisticated economic analyses. But it is also clear that regardless of the quantity and quality of the data and the mathematical and statistical sophistication used in applying the data in economic analyses, there are many imponderables in understanding the economy. Even in an ideal world with complete and perfect data, the economy is too complex to be fully captured in an analytic system.

One need only think of the often-conflicting theories of Keynesian economics, monetarism, and rational expectations, and the varying forecasting methodologies of econometric models and the leading indicator system, to recognize that despite the obvious richness of theories, data, and methodologies, underlying cause and effect relationships are unclear, and economic forecasts are often misleading. For example, the overwhelming number of short-term economic forecasts in 2000 did not foresee the recession of 2001, and subsequent forecasts of the recovery from the recession have fluctuated between optimism and pessimism. Similarly, long-term economic forecasts as late as 2001 typically projected growing surpluses in the federal government's budget a decade ahead, which since have turned into expected long-term budget deficits.

At a still more difficult level, there are a host of data that are thought of as sociological or political rather than economic which nonetheless affect the economy. The problem is that even when statistics on these phenomena are available, it has not been feasible to translate them into concrete factors affecting the economy. More likely, they are included among the unexplained factors in an analysis such as a statistical regression in which the unexplained factors appear as an agggregate number that is referred to as "the residual."

I refer to these noneconomic phenomena as "intangibles." Intangibles thought to impact the economy may have a positive, negative, or indeterminate effect on economic growth. The effects may appear anecdotally or be thought of intuitively. Capsule descriptions of the ones I think are economically relevant are given below. Some items are in a gray area that combines economic and noneconomic attributes and so are not included here, such as defense spending and large inequalities in household income and wealth (defense spending is covered in chapter 6 on governments, and inequalities in income and wealth are covered in chapter 3, "Economic Growth," and in chapter 4, "Household Income and Expenditures").

- *Law-abiding society of adherence to the letter and intent of laws, allowing for nonviolent dissent (democratic culture settles disputes peacefully)*
  Balance of costs of maintaining a democratic judicial system vs. lessened intimidaton and violence that allows more emphasis on business activities and business vitality.
- *Government civilian services (e.g., courts, police, education, health, transportation, housing, income maintenance)*
  Balance of business taxes to pay for services vs. environment provided by services that fosters business enterprise and worker productivity.
- *Government regulation of workplace health and safety*
  Balance to employer of costs of preventing workplace damages vs. costs of remedial compensation.
- *Government regulation of environmental pollution*
  Balance of business pollution abatement costs and of limitations on economic development vs. pollution-generated health costs to workers and society, and more efficient production facilities from investment in new abatement facilities.
- *Government regulation of economic development of public lands and natural resources*
  Balance of loss of investment opportunities vs. use of undeveloped lands for recreation.
- *Social and private insurance lessens panic-driven actions*
  Balance of payroll taxes and private insurance premiums vs. more rational behavior by households and businesses resulting from increased security.
- *Violence in streets, workplaces, schools, households*
  Costs of protection and remediation plus lessened productivity and learning.
- *Stock market fraud and extortion by organized crime of legitimate businesses*
  These criminal activities increase the costs of business and drain executive and entrepreneurial energy away from the real needs of making the enterprise prosper.
- *Prejudice*
  Detracts from the merit system and lessens productivity and creativity.

Table 14.1

Judgment of Effect of Noneconomic Factors on Economic Growth

	Positive	Negative	Indeterminate
Law-abiding society of adherence to the letter and intent of laws, allowing for nonviolent dissent (democratic culture settles disputes peacefully)	X		
Government civilian services (e.g., courts, police, education, health, transportation, housing, income maintenance)	X		
Government regulation of workplace health and safety	X		
Government regulation of environmental pollution			X
Government regulation of economic development of public lands and natural resources			X
Social and private insurance lessens panic-driven actions	X		
Violence in streets, workplaces, schools, households		X	
Stock market fraud and extortion by organized crime of legitimate businesses		X	
Prejudice		X	
Civil rights laws	X		
Immigration	X		
Tension between constitutional freedoms and order			X
Totals	6	3	3

- *Civil rights laws*
  Balance of equal opportunity that promotes merit system vs. effect of reverse discrimination.
- *Immigration*
  Balance of infusion of "new Americans" bringing competition and vitality to the economy vs. antagonism with other demographic groups already in the country.

- *Tension between constitutional freedoms and order*
  Balance of First Amendment rights of individuals not to be oppressed by government vs. need for physical security.

Table 14.1 shows my judgments of which noneconomic elements have a positive, negative, or indeterminate effect on economic growth. These judgments are only a plus, minus, or unstated identification. They do not provide numerical estimates of the relative importance of each element. All told, of the twelve noneconomic elements covered here, my judgments show six having a positive effect on economic growth, three having a negative effect, and three being indeterminate. Thus, a simple count of these noneconomic elements shows more having a positive effect than a negative one. But if the numerical importance of the various elements were known, and if the relative importance of the elements would differ substantially, it is possible that the aggregate impact on economic growth of all the noneconomic elements would shift from a positive effect shown in the table to a negative effect.

This topic is infused with political and social values that complicate its application to economic analysis. Some would disgree with my selection of topics and my judgments on the effects of the noneconomic elements on economic growth. *But because of the importance of noneconomic factors as the underlying climate in which the economy functions, the analyst should be alert to insights on them that may be forthcoming for shedding light on their economic impact.*

REVIEW QUESTION

- Why are noneconomic intangibles of economic interest?

References

Abraham, Katharine. 2003. "Towards a Cost-of-Living Index: Progress and Prospects." *Journal of Economic Perspectives.* Winter.

Adams, Larry T. 1985. "Changing employment patterns of organized workers." *Monthly Labor Review.* February.

Administrative Office of the United States Courts, Statistics Division. Quarterly. *Statistical Tables for the Federal Judiciary.*

Advisory Committee on Gross National Product Data Improvement. 1997. *Gross National Product Data Improvement Project Report.* Office of Federal Statistical Policy and Standards, U.S. Department of Commerce. October.

Aizcorbe, Ana M., Arthur B. Kennickell, and Kevin B. Moore. 2003. "Recent Changes in U.S. Family Finances: Evidence from the 1998 and 2001 Survey of Consumer Finances." *Federal Reserve Bulletin.* January.

Akerlof, George A. 2002. "Behavioral Macroeconomics and Macroeconomic Behavior." *American Economic Review.* June.

———, William T. Dickens, and George L. Perry. 1996. "The Macroeconomics of Low Inflation." *Brookings Papers on Economic Activity* 1.

Alesina, Alberto, and Nouriel Roubini with Gerald D. Cohen. 1997. *Political Cycles and the Macroeconomy.* MIT Press.

Andrews, Edmund L. 2003. "Study Says Tax Cuts Will Make Deficit Soar." *New York Times.* March 26, p. A12.

Baker, Bruce E. 2003. "Receipts and Expenditures of State Governments and of Local Governments, 1959–2001." *Survey of Current Business.* June.

Basu, Susanta, John G. Fernald, and Matthew D. Shapiro. 2001. *Productivity Growth in the 1990s: Technology, Utilization, or Adjustment?* Working Paper 8359. National Bureau of Economic Research. July.

Becker, Elizabeth, and Edmund L. Andrews. 2003. "China's Currency Is Emerging in U.S. as Business Issue," *New York Times,* August 26, p. A1.

Becker, Eugene H. 1984. "Self-employed workers: an update to 1983." *Monthly Labor Review.* July.

Blanchard, Oliver, and Roberto Perotti. 2002. "An Empirical Characterization of the Dynamic Effects of Changes in Government Spending and Taxes on Output." *Quarterly Journal of Economics.* November.

Board of Governors of the Federal Reserve System. 1994. *Purposes and Functions.* 8th ed.

Bohi, Douglas R., and Michael A. Toman. 1996. *The Economics of Energy Security.* Kluwer Academic Publishers.

Bowler, Mary, Randy E. Ilg, Stephen Miller, Ed Robinson, and Anne Polivka. 2003. "Revisions to the Current Population Survey Effective in January 2003." *Employment and Earnings.* February.

Bracey, Gerald W. 2003. "Media and Public Misrepresentation of Public Education." 2003. *Best Practices, Best Thinking, and Practices in Emerging Issues in School Leadership,* ed. by William A. Owings and Leslie S. Kaplan. Corwin Press.

Bregger, John E., and Steven E. Haugen. 1995. "BLS introduces new range of alternative unemployment measures." *Monthly Labor Review.* October.

Browne, Lynn Elaine with Joshua Gleeson. 1996. "The Saving Mystery, or Where Did the Money Go?" *New England Economic Review.* Federal Reserve Bank of Boston. September/October.

Bureau of Economic Analysis, U.S. Department of Commerce. 1996. "Improved Estimates of the National Income and Product Accounts for 1959–95: Results of the Comprehensive Revision." *Survey of Current Business.* January/February.

———. 1999. *Fixed Reproducible Tangible Wealth in the United States, 1925–94.*

———. Annual. *Fixed Asset Tables.*

Bureau of International Labor Affairs, U.S. Department of Labor. 1992. *The Underground Economy in the United States.* September.

———. 2000. *Wages, Benefits, Poverty Line, and Meeting Workers' Needs in the Apparel and Footwear Industries of Selected Countries.* February.

Bureau of Labor Statistics, U.S. Department of Labor. 1993. *Labor Composition and U.S. Productivity Growth.* Bulletin 2426. October.

———. 1997. *BLS Handbook of Methods.* April.

———. 2002. "Multifactor Productivity Trends, 2000." *News Release.* March 12.

———. 2002. *Employment and Earnings.* June.

Bureau of Labor Statistics and Commission on National Statistics. 2003. *Workshop on the NRC/CNSTAT Panel's Report: "At What Price? Conceptualizing and Measuring Cost-of-Living and Price Indexes."*

Business Cycle Dating Committee, National Bureau of Economic Research. 2003. "The NBER's Recession Dating Procedure." August. Available at: www.nber.org/cycles/recessions.html.

Butterfield, Fox. 2002. "Some Experts Fear Political Influence on Crime Data Agencies." *New York Times.* September 22, p. 23.

Calhoun, Charles A. 1996. "OFHEO House Price Indexes: HPI Technical Description." Office of Federal Housing Enterprise Oversight, U.S. Department of Housing and Urban Development. March.

Case, Karl E., John M. Quigley, and Robert J. Shiller. 2001. "Comparing Wealth Effects: The Stock Market versus the Housing Market." Working Paper 8600. National Bureau of Economic Research. November.

Chang, Roberto. 1995. "Is a Weak Dollar Inflationary?" *Economic Review.* Federal Reserve Bank of Atlanta. September/October.

Chimerine, Lawrence, Theodore S. Black, and Lester Coffey. 1999. *Unemployment Insurance as an Automatic Stabilizer: Evidence of Effectiveness over Three Decades.* Unemployment Insurance Occasional Paper 99–8. Employment and Training Administration, U.S. Department of Labor. July.

Clark, Kelly A., and Rosemary Hyson. 2001. "New tools for labor market analysis: JOLTS." *Monthly Labor Review.* December.

Clifford, A. Jerome. 1965. *The Independence of the Federal Reserve System.* University of Pennsylvania Press.

Cole, Kevin, Jean Helwege, and David Laster. 1996. "Stock Market Valuation Indicators: Is This Time Different?" *Financial Analysts Journal.* May/June.

Conference Board, The. 2000. *Business Cycles Indicators Handbook.* December.

Congressional Budget Office. N.d. *The Congressional Budget Office: Who We Are and What We Do.*

———. 2001. *The Budget and Economic Outlook: Fiscal Years 2002–2011.* January.

———. 2001. *CBO's Method for Estimating Potential Output: An Update.* A CBO Paper. August.

———. 2002. *The Budget and Economic Outlook: Fiscal Years 2003–2012.* January.

———. 2002. *The Effect of Changes in Labor Markets on the Natural Rate of Unemployment.* A CBO Paper. April.

———. 2003 *The Budget and Economic Outlook: Fiscal Years 2004–2013.* January.

Corrado, Carol, and Joe Mattey. 1997. "Capacity Utilization." *Journal of Economic Perspectives.* Winter.

Coughlin, Cletus C., and Kees Roedijk. 1990. "What Do We Know about the Long-Run Real Exchange Rate?" *Review.* Federal Reserve Bank of St. Louis. January/February.

Darby, Michael R. 1984. "The U.S. Productivity Slowdown: A Case of Statistical Myopia." *American Economic Review.* June.

Dean, Edwin R. 1999. "The accuracy of the BLS productivity measures." *Monthly Labor Review.* February.

DeLong, J. Bradford. 1999. "Should We Fear Deflation?" *Brookings Papers on Economic Activity* 1.

Denison, Edward F. 1985. *Trends in Economic Growth, 1929–82.* Brookings Institution.

Diebold, Francis X., Glenn D. Rudenbusch, and Daniel E. Sichel. "Further Evidence on Business-Cycle Duration Dependence." 1993. *Business Cycles, Indicators, and Forecasting,* ed. by James H. Stock and Mark W. Watson. University of Chicago Press.

Economic Report of the President Together with the Annual Report of the Council of Economic Advisers. 2003. February.

Elliott, Kimberly Ann, and Richard B. Freeman. 2003. *Can Labor Standards Improve Under Globalization?* Institute for International Economics. June.

Elmendorf, Douglas W., and David L. Reifschneider. 2002. "Short-Run Effects of Fiscal Policy with Forward-Looking Financial Markets." *National Tax Journal.* September.

Emrath, Paul. 2000. "What Else Home Buyers Buy." *Housing Economics.* National Association of Home Builders. April.

Estrella, Arturo, and Frederic S. Mishkin. 1998. "Predicting U.S. Recessions: Financial Variables as Leading Indicators." *Review of Economics and Statistics.* February.

———, Anthony Rodrigues, and Sebastian Schich. 2003. "How Stable Is the Predictive Power of the Yield Curve? Evidence from Germany and the United States." *Review of Economics and Statistics.* August.

Faust, Jon, John H. Rogers, and Jonathan H. Wright. 2000. "News and Noise in G-7 GDP Announcements." *International Finance Discussion Papers* 690. Board of Governors of the Federal Reserve System. December.

Federal Reserve Bank of New York. 2000. "The Money Supply." *Fedpoints.* September.

Federal Reserve Bank of Richmond. 1993. *Instruments of the Money Market.* 7th ed. The 8th edition is available only on the Federal Reserve Bank of Richmond's Web site: www.rich.frb.org.

Federal Reserve Board. 2002. Final rule adopting the new discount rate policy. *Press Release.* October 31. The new program was implemented in January 2003 (Federal Reserve Press Release, January 6, 2003).

Feldstein, Martin. 1986. "Supply Side Economics: Old Truths and New Claims." *AEA Papers and Proceedings.* American Economic Association. May.

Flaim, Paul O. 1990. "Population changes, the baby boom, and the unemployment rate." *Monthly Labor Review*. August.

Friedman, Benjamin M. 2000. "What Have We Learned from the Reagan Deficits and Their Disappearance?" NBER Working Paper 7647. National Bureau of Economic Research. April.

Fuhrer, Jeffrey C. and Scott Schuh, editors. 1998. *Beyond Shocks: What Causes Business Cycles?* Conference Proceedings. Federal Reserve Bank of Boston. June.

Fulco, Lawrence J. 1994. "Strong post-recession gain in productivity contributes to slow growth in labor costs." *Monthly Labor Review*. December.

Gale, William G., and John Sabelhaus. 1999. "Perspectives on the Household Saving Rate." *Brookings Papers on Economic Activity* 1.

———, and Samara R. Potter. 2002. "An Economic Evaluation of the Economic Growth and Tax Relief Reconciliation Act of 2001." *National Tax Journal*. March.

Garner, C. Alan. 2002. "Consumer Confidence after September 11." *Economic Review*. Federal Reserve Bank of Kansas City. Second Quarter.

Goldberg, Joseph P., and William T. Moye. 1985. *The First Hundred Years of the Bureau of Labor Statistics*. Bulletin 2235. Bureau of Labor Statistics, U.S. Department of Labor. September.

Goldberg, Pinelopi Koujianou, and Michael M. Knetter. 1997. "Goods Prices and Exchange Rates: What Have We Learned?" *Journal of Economic Literature*. September.

Goldstein, Lisa Fine. 2002. "Senate Panel Passes Federal Research Bill." *Education Week*. October 2.

Gordon, Robert J. 1993. *Macroeconomics*. 6th ed. HarperCollins College Publishers.

Greenlees, John S. 2001. "The U.S. CPI and the Cost-of-Living Objective." BLS paper prepared for the Joint Economic Commission for Europe/International Labor Organization Meeting on Consumer Price Indexes, Geneva. November 1–2.

Greider, William. 1987. *Secrets of the Temple: How the Federal Reserve Runs the Country*. Simon and Schuster.

Groshen, Erica L., and Simon Potter. 2003. "Has Structural Change Contributed to a Jobless Recovery?" *Current Issues in Economics and Finance*. Federal Reserve Bank of New York. August.

Hausman, Jerry. 2003. "Sources of Bias and Solutions to Bias in the Consumer Price Index." *Journal of Economic Perspectives*. Winter.

He, Ling T. 2003. "The Effects of Real Stock Returns on Sales of New and Existing Homes." *Journal of Housing Research* 13, no. 2.

Hershey, Robert D., Jr. 1992. "U.S. Officials Defend Data on Economy." *New York Times*. November 19, p. C8.

———. 1992. "This Just In: Recession Ended 21 Months Ago." *New York Times*, December 23, p. D1.

Internal Revenue Service, U.S. Department of the Treasury. 1996. *Federal Compliance Research: Individual Income Tax Gap Estimates for 1985, 1988, and 1992*. April.

Jablonski, Mary, Kent Kunze, and Phyllis Flohr Otto. 1990. "Hours at work: a new base for BLS productivity measures." *Monthly Labor Review*. February.

Jackman, Patrick C. 1990. "The CPI as a Cost of Living Index." Paper presented at the 65th annual conference of the Western Economic Association, San Diego. June 29–July 3.

Johnson, Richard. 2002. "The Puzzle of Later Male Retirement." *Economic Review*. Federal Reserve Bank of Kansas City. Third Quarter.

Johnson, Roger. 1995. *Historical Beginnings . . . The Federal Reserve*. Federal Reserve Bank of Boston. December.

Johnston, David Cay. 2002. "Hunting Tax Cheats, IRS Vows to Focus More Effort on the Rich." *New York Times*, September 13, p. A1.

———. 2002. "IRS Closes Loophole That Let Rich Hide Income." *New York Times*, September 26, p. C1.

———. 2002. "U.S. Proposes Regulations to Restrict Some Tax Shelters for High-Income People." *New York Times*, October 18, p. C2.

———. 2002. "New Rules Order Companies to Disclose Offshore Moves." *New York Times*, November 13, p. C2.

———. 2002. "Pension Fund to Press Issue of Corporate Offshore Homes." *New York Times*, November 17, p. 29.

———. 2003. "I.R.S. Seeks Injunction Against Income-Tax Resister." *New York Times*, March 14.

———. 2003. "I.R.S. Tightening Rules for Low-Income Tax Credit." *New York Times*, April 25, p. A1.

———. 2003. "I.R.S. Seeking Buyers' Names in Tax Shelters." *New York Times*, June 20, p. C1.

———. 2003. "U.S. Moves Against Promoter of Tax-Avoidance Maneuver." *New York Times*, June 20, p. C14.

Joint Center for Housing Studies of Harvard University. 2002. *The State of the Nation's Housing 2002*.

Juhn, Chinhui, and Simon Potter. 1999. "Explaining the Recent Divergence in Payroll and Household Employment Growth." *Current Issues in Economics and Finance*. Federal Reserve Bank of New York. December.

Katz, Lawrence F., and Alan B. Krueger. 1999. "The High-Pressure U.S. Labor Market of the 1990s." *Brookings Papers on Economic Activity* 1.

Kaufman, Henry. 1986. *Interest Rates, the Markets, and the New Financial World*. Times Books.

Kettl, Donald F. 1986. *Leadership at the Fed*. Yale University Press.

Klein, Philip A. 2000. "Assessing Business Cycle Indicators: An End-of-the-Century Perspective." *Business Cycle Indicators Handbook*. The Conference Board. December.

Koenig, Evan F., and Kenneth M. Emery. 1991. "Misleading Indicators? Using the Composite Leading Indicators to Predict Cyclical Turning Points." *Economic Review*. Federal Reserve Bank of Dallas. July.

Koopmans, Tjalling C. 1947. "Measurement without Theory." *Review of Economics and Statistics*. August.

Korns, Alexander. 1979. "Cyclical Fluctuations in the Difference Between the Payroll and Household Measures of Employment." *Survey of Current Business*. May.

Kozicki, Sharon. 1997. "The Productivity Slowdown: Diverging Trends in the Manufacturing and Service Sectors." *Economic Review*. Federal Reserve Bank of Kansas City. First quarter.

Leahy, Michael P. 1998. "New Summary Measures of the Foreign Exchange Value of the Dollar." *Federal Reserve Bulletin*. October.

Lebergott, Stanley. 1986. "Discussion." *Journal of Economic History*. June. Refers to revised pre-World War II data. See Romer and Weir.

Lebow, David E., and Jeremy B. Rudd. 2003. "Measurement Error in the Consumer Price Index: Where Do We Stand?" *Journal of Economic Literature*. March.

Leibenstein, Harvey. 1966. "Allocative Efficiency vs. 'X-Efficiency.' " *American Economic Review*. June.

Liang, J. Nellie, and Steven A. Sharpe. 1999. "Share Repurchases and Employee Stock Options and Their Implications for S&P 500 Share Retirements and Expected Returns." *Finance and Economics Discussion Series*, no. 59. Federal Reserve Board.

Liegey, Paul R. 1994. "Apparel price indexes: effects of hedonic adjustment." *Monthly Labor Review*. May.

Liegey, Paul, and Nicole Shepler. 1999. "Using hedonic methods to quality adjust VCR prices: plucking a piece of the U.S. CPI's 'low hanging fruit.' " *Monthly Labor Review*. September.

Lowe, Jeffrey H. 2003. "An Ownership-Based Framework of the U.S. Current Account, 1989–2001." *Survey of Current Business*. January.

Maddison, Angus. 2001. *The World Economy: A Millennial Perspective*. Organization for Economic Cooperation and Development.

Maki, Dean M., and Michael G. Palumbo. 2001. "Disentangling the Wealth Effect: A Cohort Analysis of Household Saving in the 1990s." *Finance and Economics Discussion Series Working Papers* 2001–21. Federal Reserve Board. April.

Mankiw, N. Gregory, and Matthew D. Shapiro. 1986. "News or Noise: An Analysis of GNP Revisions." *Survey of Current Business*. May.

Mann, Catherine L. 2002. "Perspectives on the U.S. Current Account Deficit and Sustainability." *Journal of Economic Perspectives*. Summer.

Mark, Jerome A., William H. Waldorf, et al. 1983. *Trends in Multifactor Productivity*. Bulletin 2178. Bureau of Labor Statistics, U.S. Department of Labor. September.

Marrinan, Jane. 1989. "Exchange Rate Determination: Sorting Out Theory and Evidence." *New England Economic Review*. Federal Reserve Bank of Boston. November/December.

Mataloni, Raymond J., Jr. 2000. "An Examination of the Low Rates of Return of Foreign-Owned U.S. Companies." *Survey of Current Business*. March.

McCahill, Robert J., and Brian C. Moyer. 2002. "Gross Domestic Product by Industry for 1999–2001." *Survey of Current Business*. November.

McCarthy, Jonathan. 1997. "Debt, Delinquencies, and Consumer Spending." *Current Issues in Economics and Finance*. Federal Reserve Bank of New York. February.

McDonald, Richard J. 1984. "The 'underground economy' and BLS statistical data." *Monthly Labor Review*. January.

McGuckin, Robert H., Ataman Ozyildirim, and Victor Zarnowitz. 2003 "A More Timely and Useful Index of Leading Indicators." *Economics Program Working Paper Series*. The Conference Board. February.

Mead, Charles Ian, Clinton P. McCully, and Marshall B. Reinsdorf. 2003. "Income and Outlays of Households and of Nonprofit Institutions Serving Households." *Survey of Current Business*. April.

Miller, John. 2003. "Why Economists Are Wrong about Sweatshops and the Antisweatshop Movement." *Challenge*. January-February.

Mitchell, Wesley C. 1927. *Business Cycles: The Problem and Its Setting*. National Bureau of Economic Research.

———, and Arthur F. Burns. 1938. *Statistical Indicators of Cyclical Revivals*. Bulletin 69. National Bureau of Economic Research. Reprinted in National Bureau of Economic Research. 1961. *Business Cycle Indicators*. ed. by Geoffrey H. Moore.

Moore, Geoffrey H. 1950. *Statistical Indicators of Cyclical Revivals and Recessions*. Paper 31. National Bureau of Economic Research. October.

———. 1969. "Generating Leading Indicators from Lagging Indicators." *Western Economic Journal*. June.

———. 1983. *Business Cycles, Inflation and Forecasting*. 2d ed. Ballinger.

Morris, Charles S. 1984. "The Productivity 'Slowdown': A Sectoral Analysis." *Economic Review*. Federal Reserve Bank of Kansas City. April.

Moulton, Brent R. 1993. "Basic components of the CPI: estimation of price changes." *Monthly Labor Review*. December.

National Association of Realtors. Monthly. "Housing Affordability Index."

Niemira, Michael P., and Philip A. Klein. 1994. *Forecasting Financial and Economic Cycles*. Wiley.

Office of Federal Housing Enterprise Oversight, U.S. Department of Housing and Urban Development. Quarterly. "House Price Index." Available at www.ofheo.gov.

Office of Federal Statistical Policy and Standards, U.S. Department of Commerce. 1977. *Gross National Product Data Improvement Project Report*. October.

Office of Management and Budget, Executive Office of the President. 1985. "Statistical Policy Directive No. 3: Compilation, Release, and Evaluation of Principal Economic Indicators." *Federal Register*. September 25.

———. 1997. "1997 North American Industry Classification System—1987 Standard Industrial Classification Replacement." *Federal Register*. April 9.

———. 2002. *Statistical Programs of the United States Government: Fiscal Year 2003*.

Okun, Arthur M. 1962. "Potential GNP: Its Measurement and Significance." *Proceedings of the Business and Economic Statistics Section*. American Statistical Association. Reprinted, with slight changes, in Arthur M. Okun. 1970. *The Political Economy of Prosperity*. Norton.

Panel on Conceptual, Measurement, and Other Statistical Issues in Developing Cost-of-Living Indexes. 2002. *At What Price? Conceptualizing and Measuring Cost-of-Living and Price Indexes*. ed. by Charles Schultze and Christopher Mackie. National Academy Press.

Peach, Richard, and Charles Steindel. 2000. "A Nation of Spendthrifts? An Analysis of Trends in Personal and Gross Saving." *Current Issues in Economics and Finance*. Federal Reserve Bank of New York. September.

Perozek, Maria G., and Marshall B. Reinsdorf. 2002. "Alternative Measures of Personal Saving." *Survey of Current Business*. April.

Phillips, A. W. 1958. "The Relation between Unemployment and the Rate of Change of Money Wage Rates in the United Kingdom, 1861–1957." *Economica*. November.

Pindyck, Robert S., and Daniel L. Rubinfeld. 1995. *Microeconomics*. 3d ed. Prentice-Hall.

Ravitch, Diane, and Chester E. Finn, Jr. 2002. "Time to Save Federal Education Data." *Education Week*. October 15.

Romer, Christina D. 1986. "Spurious Volatility in Historical Unemployment Data." *Journal of Political Economy*. February.

———. 1986. "Is the Stabilization of the Postwar Economy a Figment of the Data?" *American Economic Review*. June.

———. 1986. "New Estimates of Prewar Gross National Product and Unemployment." *Journal of Economic History*. June.

Rones, Philip R., Randy E. Ilg, and Jennifer M. Gardner. 1997. "Trends in hours of work since the mid-1970s." *Monthly Labor Review*. April.

Rosotti, Charles O., Commissioner of the Internal Revenue Service. 2002. "Report to the IRS Oversight Board: Assessment of the IRS and the Tax System." September.

Safire, William. 1975. *Before the Fall: An Inside View of the Pre-Watergate White House*. Doubleday.

Scherer, F. M. 1980. *Industrial Market Structure and Economic Performance*. 2d ed. Rand McNally.

Schreft, Stacey L., and Aarti Singh. 2003. "A Closer Look at Jobless Recoveries." *Economic Review*. Federal Reserve Bank of Kansas City. Second Quarter.

Schultze, Charles L. 2003. "The Consumer Price Index: Conceptual Issues and Practical Suggestions. *Journal of Economic Perspectives*. Winter.

Sellon, Gordon H., Jr., and Stuart E. Weiner. 1996. "Monetary Policy without Reserve

Requirements: Analytical Issues," *Economic Review*. Federal Reserve Bank of Kansas City. Fourth quarter.

Shapiro, Matthew D. 1996. "Macroeconomic Implications of Variation in the Workweek of Capital." *Brookings Papers on Economic Activity* 2.

———, and Joel Slemrod. 2001. "Consumer Response to Tax Rebates." NBER Working Paper 8672. National Bureau of Economic Research. December.

Shiskin, Julius. 1961. *Signals of Recession and Recovery*. Occasional Paper 77. National Bureau of Economic Research.

Sichel, Daniel E. 1997. *The Computer Revolution: An Economic Perspective*. Brookings Institution.

Sinclair, James, and Brian Catron. 1990. "An experimental price index for the computer industry." *Monthly Labor Review*. October.

Steinberg, Edward. 2003. "Who Says the Recession Is Over?" *New Haven Register*. August 21, p. A4.

Stekler, H. O. 2003. "Interpreting Movements in the Composite Index of Leading Indicators." *Business Economics*. July.

Stinson, John F., Jr. 1983. "Comparison of Nonagricultural Employment Estimates from Two Surveys." *Employment and Earnings*. March.

Stock, James H., and Mark W. Watson. 1993. "A Procedure for Predicting Recessions with Leading Indicators: Econometric Issues and Recent Experience." In *Business Cycles, Indicators, and Forecasting*, ed. by James S. Stock and Mark W. Watson. University of Chicago Press.

Tamm, Feliks. 1984. "An Introduction to the System of Coincident, Leading and Lagging Indexes." Mimeo. Bureau of Economic Analysis, U.S. Department of Commerce.

Tootell, Geoffrey M. B. 1991. "Regional Economic Conditions and the FOMC Votes of District Presidents." *New England Economic Review*. Federal Reserve Bank of Boston. March/April.

———. 1994. "Restructuring, the NAIRU, and the Phillips Curve." *New England Economic Review*. Federal Reserve Bank of Boston. September/October.

———. 1996. "Appointment Procedures and FOMC Voting Behavior." *Southern Economic Journal*. July.

Torres, Jacinto L., Jr. 2003. "2003 Annual Benchmark Revisions to the Composite Indexes." *Business Cycles Indicators*. January.

United Nations Development Programme. 2002. *Human Development Report: 2002: Deepening Democracy in a Fragmented World*. Oxford University Press.

U.S. Chamber of Commerce. N.d. "What Goes into a U.S. Company's Decision on Whether to Invest Overseas?" or "The Twelve Commandments for International Investors."

U.S. Constitution. Article VI, Clause 2.

U.S. House of Representatives, Committee on the Budget. 2003. *Congressional Budget Office's Analysis of the President's Fiscal Year 2004 Budget*. Committee Hearings. March 25.

Walsh, Mary Williams. 2003. "I.R.S. Tightening Rules for Low-Income Tax Credit." *New York Times*. April 25, p. A1.

Watson, Mark W. 1991. "Using Econometric Models to Predict Recessions." *Economic Perspectives*. Federal Reserve Bank of Chicago. November/December.

Weir, David R. 1986. "The Reliability of Historical Macroeconomic Data for Comparing Cyclical Stability." *Journal of Economic History*. June.

West, Thomas E., and Gerard Hildebrand. 1997. "Federal-State Relations." *Unemployment Insurance in the United States: Analysis of Policy Issues*, ed. by Christopher J. O'Leary and Stephen A. Wandner. W.E. Upjohn Institute for Employment Research.

Wheelock, David C. 2003. "Replacement Windows: New Credit Program at the Discount Window." *Monetary Trends*. Federal Reserve Bank of St. Louis. May.

Wolff, Edward N. 1996. "The Productivity Slowdown: The Culprit at Last? Follow-Up on Hulten and Wolff." *American Economic Review*. December.

Woo, Wing T. 1984. "Exchange Rates and the Prices of Nonfood, Nonfuel Products." *Brookings Papers on Economic Activity* 2.

Yergin, Daniel. 1991. *The Prize: The Epic Quest for Oil, Money, and Power*. Simon and Schuster.

Young, Allan H. 1993. "Alternative Measures of Change in Real Output and Prices, Quarterly Estimates for 1959–92." *Survey of Current Business*. March.

Zarnowitz, Victor. 1992. *Business Cycles: Theory, History, Indicators, and Forecasting*. University of Chicago Press.

———. 1999. "Theory and History Behind Business Cycles: Are the 1990s the Onset of a Golden Age?" *Journal of Economic Perspectives*. Spring.

———, and Jacinto Torres, Jr. 2002. "Economic Context and Consequences of 9/11, a Year Later." *Business Cycle Indicators*. September.

Zegeye, Aklilu A., and Larry Rosenblum. 2000. "Measuring Productivity in an Imperfect World." *Applied Economics* 32.

Zeile, William J. 1998. "The Domestic Orientation of Production and Sales by U.S. Manufacturing Affiliates of Foreign Companies." *Survey of Current Business*. April.

———. 2002 "U.S. Affiliates of Foreign Companies: Operations in 2000." *Survey of Current Business*. August.

Index

Page numbers in *italic* indicate tables and figures.

Norman Frumkin, an economics writer in Washington, D.C., has a long-standing interest in macroeconomic analysis and forecasting, including the meaning and quality of economic statistics. He has worked in the U.S. government and industry, and as an independent consultant. He is also the author of *Guide to Economic Indicators* (M.E. Sharpe, 2000).